II Kings
In a Whirlwind

Pardes | פרדס
Institute of Jewish Studies
מגיד
MAGGID
Yeshivat Har Etzion ישיבת הר עציון

Alex Israel

מלכים ב׳

II Kings

In a Whirlwind

Pardes Institute of Jewish Studies
Yeshivat Har Etzion
Maggid Books

II Kings
In a Whirlwind

First Edition, 2019

Maggid Books
An imprint of Koren Publishers Jerusalem Ltd.

POB 8531, New Milford, CT 06776-8531, USA
& POB 4044, Jerusalem 9104001, Israel
www.maggidbooks.com

Cover photo by solarseven

The publication of this book was made possible through the generous support of *Torah Education in Israel.*

ISBN 978-1-59264-494-0, *hardcover*

A CIP catalogue record for this title is available from the British Library

Printed and bound in the United States

In loving memory of Irving and Beatrice Stone,
who dedicated their lives to the
advancement of Jewish education.
We are proud and honored to continue in their legacy.

Their Children, Grandchildren, and Great-Grandchildren
Jerusalem, Israel
Cleveland, Ohio USA

In honor of the scholarship and teaching of
RABBI ALEX ISRAEL

In grateful appreciation of his unwavering dedication and support of Pardes and personal commitment to transforming Jewish life through rigorous and relevant engagement with Jewish texts for learners of all backgrounds worldwide.

This publication is co-sponsored by Pardes supporters:

GERALDINE GOLDSTEIN BAR-EL
In memory of her beloved husband Georges Bar-El z"l
Yigal Yishai ben Eliyahu v'Blanche, ד׳ אדר, תשע״ח

ALAN AND EDWARD LEE
In honor of the Lee and Richman families

DONSHIK, GENAUER AND JACOBS FAMILIES
In honor of Ruth Genauer on the occasion of her 100th birthday

FRANCES AND HENRY ISRAEL
In memory of Frieda & Walter Israel and Sarah & Joe Richman, grandparents of Rabbi Alex Israel who would have derived such great pleasure from his achievements

DELLA WORMS
In memory of Fred Simon Worms z"l, a longtime benefactor of Pardes and a visionary in Jewish education

WEINER, MILLER, SAAR AND SOLOMONT FAMILIES
In memory of Dr. Mark N. Weiner
מרדכי נחמן בן חיים מאיר ושושנה ז״ל

DR. SIMONE GORDON
In memory of my beloved son, Dr. William Gordon z"l who brought love and light to all

CHANA HANELIN
In loving memory of Shimon ben Tzvi Hirsch HaLevi

CHARLES AND AVIVA FREEDMAN & ANONYMOUS
In honor of our inspiring teacher, Rabbi Alex Israel

Dedicated to my dear wife, Aliza,
and to our wonderful children
Avinoam, Maayan, Hillel, and Yehuda

Contents

Preface

Sometimes I am asked why, of all the books of Tanakh, I chose to write on *Sefer Melakhim*, the book of Kings. In truth, my motivation has been primarily pedagogical. For students who are finding their feet in the world of Tanakh, one of the first and primary challenges is to study the books of *Nevi'im Rishonim*, the "Former Prophets." These are Joshua, Judges, Samuel, and Kings – works that offer a continuous prophetic history of the period of the first commonwealth, from Israel's entry to the land until the destruction of the First Temple and the Babylonian exile. These books are fundamental in that they provide a historical context as well as narrate many of the key stories and familiarize the student with the personalities of this period in Jewish history.

Some books, however, are easier to study than others. Joshua, Judges, and Samuel all have sweeping stories and accessible, rich characters, and are, in the main, quite readable. But when one enters into the world of Kings, the student has a tendency to feel overwhelmed by statistics and logistics, at times disoriented by the lengthy lists and the wealth of confusing names of kings and kingdoms, many of which sound the same and which, for the uninitiated reader, obscure the storyline. Many a student of Tanakh has made it to the book of Kings and then simply abandoned the project, frustrated by the imperceptible flow and drama of the narrative and exasperated by the difficulty of bringing the personalities of its heroes and villains into focus.

This is the educational challenge that I sought to address in my first book, *I Kings: Torn in Two*,[1] and again with this second volume on II Kings. I have been deeply gratified by the overwhelmingly positive reception of my first volume from a wide array of students, laypeople, and teachers around the English-speaking Jewish world, who have found that volume an invaluable resource for studying and teaching the book of Kings. It has fulfilled its objective by adding historical background, framing the narrative, giving depth and color to the characters, spanning ancient and modern commentary, focusing and deepening the reader's attention to the key themes and messages of the biblical text, and in many ways, bringing *Sefer Melakhim* to life. I hope and pray that this second volume will similarly succeed in meeting these goals.

This book is not a line-by-line commentary, but more of a reader's companion to II Kings. To optimize the usefulness of this book, I recommend reading the relevant biblical chapter in its entirety before proceeding to the chapter that discusses it in this volume. In this way, the book will serve to amplify and deepen the reader's understanding of the chapter. My presentation is varied in style and scope. In chapters whose storyline is readily accessible, I have offered a deeper presentation, drawing upon literary intricacy and sophisticated rabbinic interpretation. In chapters that are more challenging to a basic understanding, I have sometimes sufficed with merely narrating the story within its historical backdrop. I hope the reader will appreciate that my key objective is enabling the reader to fully engage with the story, character, and messages of Kings.

The subtitle to this book is *In a Whirlwind*. On one level, this reflects one of the early and most magnificent scenes of II Kings – the heavenward ascent of the great prophet Elijah "in a whirlwind." But on a deeper level, it refers to a far wider motif that underlies the entire book of II Kings. I am referring to the sense that the kingdoms of Israel and Judah are caught in a web of tempestuous forces throughout the period described by this book. Whether the adversary is the powerful kingdom of Aram, or the aggressive empires of Assyria and then Babylonia that

1. Jerusalem: Maggid Books, 2013.

threaten the very existence of the Israelite state, the backdrop of II Kings is of a small nation-state entangled in and subjected to forces much larger than itself, caught as if in a whirlwind.

The Land of Israel is a nexus point of the major near-eastern civilizations, and then, just as in our days, in a region which is often unstable, seething, and volatile, current events do not allow the Jewish state to remain inert. Kings relates the significant cultural, religious, and strategic challenges that confront the kingdoms of Judah and Israel, and the successes and failures of its leadership in upholding the divine covenant on the one hand, and in navigating the tortuous regional politics on the other. As we shall see, the margin of error is frequently slim, and the stakes are high – survival or national downfall.

In many ways, Kings might be experienced as a depressing book. It opens with a strong, unified nation and the excitement of the construction of the Temple, and yet it rapidly spirals downward, through national rupture and fragmentation followed by waves of religious and geopolitical upheaval, until the terrible exile, first of Samaria and then of Jerusalem, and the dissolution of the Jewish state. I frequently wonder how Kings was read during the past 1,900 years of diasporic Jewish life, and whether its tale of failure and woe offered much that could be invigorating or inspiring. And yet, today, with the blessing of a flourishing Jewish state and the reestablishment of Jewish sovereignty, this book takes on a different hue. Rather than a lament to fallen grandeur, we can now reconnect with the triumphs and tragedies, with the successes and mistakes of our early history, and allow the timeless words of the prophets to act as an inspiration as well as an admonition, a critique and corrective to contemporary ills and failures that reflect our ancient sins. In a contemporary context there is much food for thought in Kings.

In this context, I feel deeply blessed to live in *Medinat Yisrael* and specifically in Gush Etzion, in this incredible era of Jewish sovereignty and peoplehood. We have experienced the national return to our historic and holy land, the ingathering of Jews from around the globe, the privilege of self-governance, an army to defend our people, and in a broad sense, the restoration of a deep sense of Jewish pride and dignity. The fact that I can get up in the morning to teach Torah in Jerusalem, the heart of the Jewish people, is nothing less than a direct fulfillment of the consolatory words of Isaiah, Jeremiah, and Zechariah. We have much work to do and farther to go to realize our prophetic visions in the realms of social justice and regarding our moral and religious aspirations, but for me our current reality is a daily source of inspiration and contentment. For these, and for all the other manifold gifts of life, it is to the Almighty that I offer my thanks, "for Your miracles that are with us every day, and for Your wonders and Your goodness that are constant" (from the *Modim* prayer).

In the sphere of Torah study, I feel humbled by the wonderful privilege of publishing my second volume on Tanakh, thereby adding a new Torah work to the bookshelf of Jewish scholarship. I am fortunate "that God has placed my lot among those who sit in the beit midrash" (the prayer recited upon leaving the Torah study hall, Berakhot 28b), spending my hours and days teaching Torah and thinking about Jewish education. For this too I am deeply thankful and pray that I, my family, and my students will always find Torah to be a "tree of life."

Acknowledgments

My special thanks to the people at Koren-Maggid Publishers: to Matthew Miller for his enthusiastic support of my work; to the editorial director, Rabbi Reuven Ziegler; and to Tomi Mager, Shira Finson, and Ita Olesker, for faithfully chaperoning this book from manuscript to finished product.

The material that went into this book is a product of two decades of teaching. In particular, I would like to thank the administrations and students of Midreshet Lindenbaum, the Pardes Institute of Jewish Studies, and Yeshivat Eretz Hatzvi, under whose auspices I have had the honor to teach various segments of II Kings. The classroom is the great laboratory in which we get to observe which ideas are well received and which fall flat. Our students' questions alert us to the weaknesses or strengths of our theories, arguments, and formulations. As a result, all the aforementioned *batei midrash* have made precious contributions to this work.

The first draft of this book was an online series for Yeshivat Har Etzion's Virtual Beit Midrash. I am honored to be part of the VBM team, a website that provides some of the highest caliber Torah content on the web. Thanks to Rav Ezra Bick and Debra Berkowitz for allowing me to write despite regularly breaking my weekly deadlines, and to my editors, Noam Shapiro and Daniel Landman, for their keen reading.

The last word of thanks is to my wonderful family to whom I have dedicated this book. You are my strength and my joy. Mere words cannot express my love and appreciation. Perhaps Solomon's prayer can appropriately articulate my hopes and prayers:

> יְהִי ה׳ אֱלֹקֵינוּ עִמָּנוּ, כַּאֲשֶׁר הָיָה עִם-אֲבֹתֵינוּ: אַל-יַעַזְבֵנוּ, וְאַל-יִטְּשֵׁנוּ.
> לְהַטּוֹת לְבָבֵנוּ, אֵלָיו לָלֶכֶת בְּכָל-דְּרָכָיו, וְלִשְׁמֹר מִצְוֹתָיו וְחֻקָּיו וּמִשְׁפָּטָיו,
> אֲשֶׁר צִוָּה אֶת-אֲבֹתֵינוּ.
>
> May the Lord our God be with us, as He was with our ancestors. May He never abandon or forsake us. May He incline our hearts to Him, that we may walk in all His ways and keep the commandments, the laws, and the rules, which He enjoined upon our ancestors. (I Kings 8:57–8)

Alex Israel
Alon Shevut
Rosh Ḥodesh Tammuz 5778 / June 2018
In the seventieth year of our beloved State of Israel

Introduction

Background to II Kings

Sefer Melakhim, the book of Kings, is a prophetic chronicle that narrates the history of Israel, from the inception of King Solomon's rule, through the period of the divided kingdom, and to the destruction of the Temple and Babylonian exile of 586 BCE. Whereas the style of the book is an alternating history between the kingdoms of Israel and Judah, Kings is not a history book in the contemporary sense of the word, a factual rendition of past events. Rather, archival material about each king and his era is didactically selected to explain the past to the reader of its time, who was probably a refugee grappling with the tumult of national disintegration and the painful loss of its religious center, looking to make sense of the devastation that had been wrought on individual and nation. The central message is this: The religious and moral failure of the monarchs led to the destruction of the Temple and Jerusalem.

Illicit worship is the primary sin in Kings – there was idolatry as well as divine worship outside the Temple, at the northern shrines and illicit altars, called *bamot.* The book charts how all the northern and many of the southern kings failed to meet their covenantal and moral obligations. As a consequence of these actions, it depicts the kingdoms' gradual demise, first through minor disasters, and finally with the exile of Israel, and some 150 years later, Judah. The book records the prophetic warnings presaging the disastrous effects of sin. As such, the catastrophic outcome is a product of fully informed, if errant, choices. Written from the historical vantage point of the national downfall,[1] the purpose of Kings is to educate and teach the nation, to explain the divine perception of the national calamity, justifying God's actions, and to describe the causes of national ruin to ensure that future events do not repeat past misdeeds.

STYLE

The timeline of Kings is constructed by discreet regnal summaries which each list, in a formulaic manner, the duration of the king's reign and key events of his rule. However, this style is maintained only for some segments of the book. Kings is characterized by unexpected changes in the type of material presented, with sudden shifts from dry annalistic writing, heavy with statistical data, to sophisticated narrative, rich with elaborate plot and character development.

During the period of the divided kingdom, Kings synchronizes the chronology of a king to his counterpart in the opposite kingdom, alternating between the history of Judah in the south and Israel in the north so that both stories are told in tandem. While the alternation between north and south reminds the reader that both kingdoms are equally bound by God's covenant, the constant switching also directs attention to the contrast between the kingdoms, which may manifest

1. There is widespread agreement that Kings was composed in the aftermath of the destruction of the First Temple. The Talmud (Bava Batra 15a) names the prophet Jeremiah as the author of Kings, but fails to specify how much of the book drew on earlier material and how much was penned by Jeremiah himself. Academic opinion agrees placing the book's final composition in the same basic timeframe as Jeremiah, although many earlier layers are suggested and Jeremiah's specific authorship is disputed. For an excellent survey of the issues raised in academic study of Kings and the major schools in each debate, see M. Avioz, "The Book of Kings in Recent Research, Part I," *Currents in Biblical Research* 4 (2005): 11–55, which addresses fundamental questions of scholarship, and M. Avioz, "The Book of Kings in Recent Research, Part II ," *Currents in Biblical Research* 5 (2006): 11–57, which addresses questions related to specific stories and segments of the book of Kings.

itself in one kingdom's instability in contrast to the other's stability, or idolatry in one kingdom as opposed to strict loyalty to God's law in the other.

ONE BOOK OR TWO?

In its original form, the entire book of Kings was a single unit. Its division into two segments – I Kings and II Kings – is arbitrary and crude in that it awkwardly interrupts the account of Ahaziah's reign and mystifyingly perforates the smooth flow of the Elijah stories. The division is first found in the Septuagint and the Vulgate, and appears in Jewish sources only from the Venetian printing of the Tanakh in 1525; it has ever since been the standard in Jewish sources. It is apparent that the split was motivated by the need to divide the large and unwieldy scroll of Kings into two more manageable segments. Due to this ungainly rupture, the reader who picks up the thread at the start of II Kings lacks significant background information and perspective. We shall attempt to bridge some of this knowledge by providing requisite introductions and explanations where necessary.

SOURCES

Kings cites its primary sources as the "Chronicles of the Kings of Judah"[2] and "Chronicles of the Kings of Israel,"[3] but these works did not survive the vicissitudes of history. We presume that many other texts formed the historical archive from which Kings was written. In the past 150 years of biblical archaeology, a remarkable array of artifacts has been discovered that corroborate, supplement, and occasionally challenge, the narratives of Kings.

THE STRUCTURE OF II KINGS

The structure of Kings would be best perceived by viewing the book as a single unit. As such, Kings has a chiastic structure, as depicted in the chart on the following page.

---

2. II Kings 8:23; 12:20; 14:18; 15:6, 36; 16:19; 20:20; 21:25; 23:28; 24:5.
3. Ibid., 1:18; 10:34; 13:8, 12; 14:15, 28; 15:11, 15, 21.

The Structure of the Book of Kings

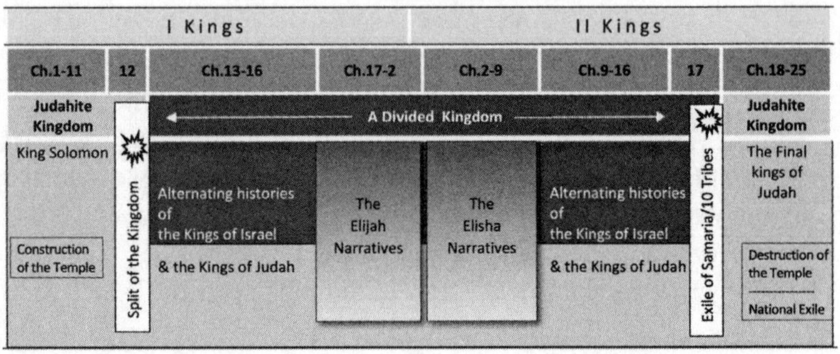

The period of Solomon, during which the kingdom is united with its Temple in Jerusalem, finds its parallel at the close of II Kings, under the rules of Hezekiah and Josiah, who mirror Solomon's greatness, his penchant for national unity, and his adherence to God. The description of the split of the kingdom (I Kings 12–13) and the advent of the northern kingdom of Israel finds its parallel in II Kings in the fall of the northern kingdom and the exile of Samaria. In the center space of Kings are the two great prophets, Elijah and his protégé Elisha, who battle the kings of the Omride dynasty and their religious affiliation to Baal.

The above structure, which spans I and II Kings, divides II Kings into large units. For the reader who is looking for a more specified breakdown of II Kings, we may delineate the broad subunits as follows:

Chs. 1–2	Completion of the Elijah stories from I Kings
Chs. 2–8	The Stories of Elisha
Chs. 8–12	Coups in Aram, Israel, and Judah; the demise of the house of Omri
Chs. 13–17	Synchronic history of Israel and Judah
Ch. 17	Fall and exile of the northern kingdom
Chs. 18–20	The southern kingdom; Hezekiah and the Assyrian invasion
Ch. 21	Manasseh
Chs. 22–23	Josiah

Chs. 24–25 Rise of Babylonia; the fall and exile of the southern kingdom

We have offered these short comments of introduction to orient the reader. Further introductions may be found in this volume's predecessor, *I Kings: Torn in Two*.

II Kings 1

All the King's Men

What should a prophet do when the king of Israel finds his life in peril and turns to an idolatrous deity rather than God? How might God act? This dramatic chapter tells the story of a powerful and violent clash between the prophet Elijah and King Ahaziah, who favors the foreign deity of Baal. This confrontation bears all the pent-up pathos of the extended national struggle between monotheism and the forces of idolatry.

BACKGROUND

Before we encounter Elijah and Ahaziah, let us offer some historical background to explain the context of this altercation, an episode which transpires in the royal court of the northern kingdom.

After the magnificent reign of King Solomon, the kingdom ruptures. Spurred by Jeroboam's revolt, the nation splits into two: Judah in the south with Jerusalem as its capital, and Israel in the north. Samaria eventually becomes its capital.

During the fifty years that follow the split, the northern kingdom flounders, plagued by intermittent mutiny, foreign invasion, and an ongoing state of hostility with its sister kingdom in the south.[1]

1. Split of kingdom, I Kings 12; mutiny, I Kings 15:28; 16:9–10, 16–18; foreign invasion, I Kings 15:20 and archaeological records describing Shishak's rampage through the

It was King Omri and his son Ahab who gave the north a new stability, strength, affluence, and regional hegemony. His dynasty was the most powerful succession of kings that ruled the north. Omri designed and built its splendid capital, Samaria, and his son Ahab forged economic ties with Phoenicia. Ahab's military vanquished his powerful neighbor, Aram. But alongside these raised economic and military fortunes, Ahab and his Phoenician wife, Jezebel, led the kingdom to abandon the God of Israel as they adopted the cult of Baal. They built a Temple to Baal in Samaria, murdered and persecuted God's prophets, and replaced them with a retinue of four hundred prophets of Baal. The kingdom's material success combined with the adverse spiritual state only encouraged national religious waywardness. This set the stage for the clash between King Ahab and his powerful antagonist, the great prophet Elijah, who challenged Ahab's religious deviance. After Ahab is killed in battle, his son Ahaziah continues his religious orientation. Consequently, Elijah will oppose the new king just as he fought his father.

II Kings opens with the sole chapter dedicated to King Ahaziah.

AHAZIAH, SON OF AHAB

> Ahaziah the son of Ahab began to reign over Israel in Samaria in the seventeenth year of Jehoshaphat king of Judah, and he reigned two years over Israel. And he did that which was evil in the sight of the Lord, and walked in the way of his father, and in the way of his mother, and in the way of Jeroboam son of Nebat, wherein he made Israel to sin. And he served Baal, and worshipped him, and provoked the Lord, the God of Israel, according to all that his father had done. And Moab rebelled against Israel after the death of Ahab. (I Kings 22:52–II Kings 1:1)

---

northern province; hostility with the south, I Kings 14:30; 15:6, 16–22; migration southward, II Chr. 11:13–16; 15:9; 16:1.

Ahaziah is the third king of the Omride Dynasty. He is a notably unsuccessful king[2] and rules for only a single year.[3] His early demise is due to an unfortunate domestic accident in which he is mortally injured.[4] He dies without leaving an heir (II Kings 1:17).

Ahaziah "walked in the way of his father, and in the way of his mother (Jezebel)," continuing the idolatrous regime of his parents and their disdain for God's prophets. In the book of Kings there could be little worse than a royal house devoted to a foreign deity. And yet, as we shall see, our chapter demonstrates how Ahaziah manages to take idolatry a step further than even his father.

THE MISSION TO EKRON

Our story begins as the ailing Ahaziah dispatches a delegation to Baal-Zebub, god of Ekron, in search of a medical prognosis or, more likely, seeking a supernatural power to cure him of his injuries.

> He sent messengers, and said to them, "Go, inquire of Baal-Zebub[5] the god of Ekron whether I shall recover from this sickness." An

2. He rises to power at a time of national weakness following Israel's defeat by Aram (I Kings 22), a battle in which his father, Ahab, is killed. The kingdom's hegemony declines yet further after Ahab's death as Ahaziah loses control of Moab (II Kings 1:1). In a similar vein, his seafaring collaboration with the southern kingdom, presumably to further economic interests, ends in ruin (I Kings 22:49–50).
3. Ahaziah ascends the throne in Jehoshaphat's seventeenth year (I Kings 22:52), and his brother Jehoram assumes the throne in Jehoshaphat's eighteenth year (see II Kings 3:1). Since the king reigned in two calendrical years he is considered to have reigned for "two years," but in fact his reign extended only for the duration of a single year.
4. Abarbanel and R. Joseph ibn Kaspi both suggest that this was a divine punishment for his idolatry.
5. Baal-Zebub is called "the god of Ekron," Ekron being one of the prominent Philistine cities. See U. Cassuto, *Encyclopedia Mikrait* (The Biblical Encyclopedia), vol. 2 (Jerusalem: Mossad Bialik), cols. 287–8 [Hebrew], who suggests that Baal-Zebub (Lord of the Flies) may be a pejorative term for a Phoenician Baal god whose real name was Baal-Zebul, meaning "lord of glory/dominion/majesty." Solomon's Temple is referred to as *Beit-zevul*, a stately house (I Kings 8:13). Similarly, it is possible that the name Jezebel – Izevel in Hebrew – was a mockery of her true name, *Bat-Zevul* or *Avi-Zevul*, and that the Bible disparages her by warping her name and giving it an association with manure – *zevel*.

> angel of the Lord said to Elijah the Tishbite, "Arise, go up to meet the messengers of the king of Samaria, and say unto them, 'Is there no God in Israel that you go to inquire of Baal-Zebub, the god of Ekron? Therefore, thus says the Lord: You shall not descend from the bed you ascended, but you shall surely die.'" (II Kings 1:2–4)

Ahaziah's appeal to Baal-Zebub arouses God's ire, and Elijah is dispatched to inform the king of his certain death. Why does this modest appeal to a foreign deity illicit such a swift and exacting divine response? In the past, God did not hasten to condemn idolatrous kings such as Ahab; what is the severity of Ahaziah's infraction?

We suggest that the act of petitioning a foreign god is a step beyond standard Israelite idolatry. The petition to Baal-Zebub would have certainly necessitated a request for access from Philistine royalty, and thus Ahaziah is publicizing Israel's reliance upon foreign powers on an international scale, thereby desecrating the name of God. God's indignation is articulated in Elijah's opening and closing lines:

> Is there no God in Israel that you go to inquire of Baal-Zebub, the god of Ekron? (1:3)

> Since you sent messages to inquire of Baal-Zebub, the god of Ekron, as if there were no god in Israel whose word you could seek, assuredly...you shall surely die. (1:16)

With this gesture Ahaziah essentially broadcasts that Israel's God is inept and irrelevant. Even the most sinful kings of the north such as Jeroboam[6] and Ahab[7] consulted with prophets of God in moments of distress. Ahaziah hereby violates God's reputation. In response, God rules out any option of a royal recovery.

This might be supported by II Kings 9:37: "The carcass of Jezebel shall be like dung on the ground." The notion of Baal-Zebub as the prince of demons is absent from the Hebrew Bible, and originates in the New Testament (Matthew 12:24–25).

6. I Kings 14:1–2.
7. Ibid., 20:13–14, 22, 28.

It is the nations of the world who are to seek God's assurance and assistance, not Israel who should seek the counsel of other gods. A perfect example, the inverse of Ahaziah's appeal to Baal-Zebub, using identical language, features in II Kings 8, where Israel's great nemesis, Ben-Hadad, is on his deathbed in Damascus. He is informed that Elisha, "the man of God," is in the vicinity, and he dispatches his aide, Hazael:

> Take a gift with you and go meet the man of God, and through him inquire of the Lord: Will I recover from this illness? (8:8)

Ahaziah's foreign appeal is not merely a humiliation to God, but it fundamentally inverts the idyllic eschatological image whereby Jerusalem is designated to become an international magnet for those who seek divine wisdom:

> Many peoples shall go and say: Come – Let us go to the mount of the Lord, to the house of the God of Jacob, that He may instruct us in His ways, and that we may walk in His paths.... He will judge many nations, and arbitrate for many peoples. (Is. 2:3–4)

MESSENGERS

A key literary feature of the chapter is that the entire dramatic clash between God and king is enacted by a series of emissaries and intermediaries. Ahaziah sends delegates to Baal-Zebub; in a mirror image, God dispatches his emissary Elijah by means of an angel.

Why does God send Elijah to intercept Ahaziah's delegates? Why not dispatch Elijah directly to the king? This question seems especially pertinent given that the chapter ends with Elijah personally appearing before Ahaziah.

One answer is that Elijah is banned from the royal city, Samaria. Jezebel had issued a death warrant against him, and this could still be in force (Radak). Rather than facing the king, Elijah is forced to engage him remotely, by means of his delegates. Secondly, if Elijah had personally approached Ahaziah, the royal delegates would have continued to Ekron! Elijah must intercept the delegation to forestall the religious embarrassment of an Israelite royal appeal to the Philistine god.

But the issue of emissaries in this chapter goes beyond mere practical concerns. Each emissary – human delegate and angel – is denoted by the noun *malakh*.[8] The text thereby establishes a fundamental symmetry; Elijah is the counterforce to Ahaziah's messengers. Who controls the intermediaries? Is it God and his emissary, Elijah, or the king? This will be the pivotal question of the chapter. In the chapter's initial scene (II Kings 1:3–8), Elijah, instead of engaging directly with the king, manipulates the royal delegation, turning it against its sender. In the second scene (1:9–15), Elijah will contend with a series of military commanders dispatched by Ahaziah and again demonstrate his superior power to control Ahaziah's emissaries.

WHOSE MESSENGERS?

But Elijah goes one step further. If we closely compare Elijah's instruction with the message that the delegates relay to Ahaziah, we discern a subtle but highly significant shift:[9]

> Elijah's instruction:
>
> Arise, go up to meet the messengers of the king of Samaria, and say unto them, "Is there no God in Israel *that you* [plural, *attem*] *go* to inquire of Baal-Zebub, the god of Ekron? Therefore, *thus says the Lord:* You shall not descend... but you shall surely die." (1:3–4)

---

8. Mentioned six times in this passage (II Kings 1:2, 3 twice, 5, 15, 16). The question of delegates and who controls them is the pivotal feature of this story as expressed by the sevenfold usage of the verb SH-L-H, "send" (1:2, 6 twice, 9, 11, 13, 16).
9. Note that a stage is skipped over here. First (1:3–4), the angel instructs Elijah to talk to the messengers. This is followed by "And Elijah went" (1:4). But immediately afterward (1:5–6), we read of the messengers addressing Ahaziah. Where is the middle segment, where Elijah is talking to the messengers? This is a familiar literary feature in Tanakh, whereby a middle, linking stage is omitted. Other examples from Kings include I Kings 21:17–20 and II Kings 4:26. The passage may be skipped merely to speed up the narrative – presuming that Elijah would transmit the communication faithfully. Alternatively, it could be skipped as a stylistic device to ensure a pattern of threefold repetition within the story.

The messengers' words to Ahaziah:

> Go, return to the king who sent you, and say to him, *"Thus says the Lord:* Is there is no God in Israel *that you* [singular, *atta*] *send* to inquire of Baal-Zebub, the god of Ekron? Therefore, you shall not descend... but you shall surely die." (1:6)

Elijah's instruction consists of two separate statements. The first is a challenge and rebuke to the messengers. It is phrased in the plural (*attem*) and chastises the officials themselves for complying with the king's appeal to Baal-Zebub. The second statement is a divine pronouncement of punishment – "Thus says the Lord" – worded in the singular and therefore addressed particularly to Ahaziah, announcing the king's death.

Observe how the delegates adjust and reorient the original message. One might have anticipated that they would solely repeat verse 4, the second statement, and ignore the first. Instead we observe two differences:

1. "Thus says the Lord" is moved to the beginning of the double pronouncement.
2. The rebuke, "Is there no God in Israel..." is now addressed to the king personally (*atta*), blaming the king for "sending" rather than accusing the messengers of "going."

In other words, the messengers reorient the accusation originally leveled at them and turn it, with full divine force, at Ahaziah. It is not merely the punishment but rather the entire guilt that is to be visited upon Ahaziah personally for the mission to Baal-Zebub. As such, the delegates introduce the entire message with the words, "Thus says the Lord."

In essence, these messengers undergo a dramatic metamorphosis. They turn from Ahaziah's representatives into God's mouthpiece. The loyal envoys who initially sought the king's health now condemn their king to death. Those who were sent out (*lekhu*) in search of the foreign deity Baal-Zebub return (*lekhu shuvu*)[10] bearing the message of God.

10. Rabbi Elchanan Samet, *Pirkei Eliyahu* (Jerusalem: Maaliyot Press, 2003), 423–24 [Hebrew], discusses the twin verbs, *lekh* and *shuv*, and their function.

Earlier we contended that Elijah was instructed to intercept the delegation in order to obstruct and forestall the encounter with Baal-Zebub, averting the profanity of a royal Israelite appeal to an idolatrous deity. But the interaction with these officials goes far beyond that pragmatic objective. In this scene, God, through Elijah, exerts His control of the king's men as they transform into God's emissaries rather than those of Ahaziah and Baal.

In the past, Elijah has challenged the dual loyalty that plagued his generation: "How long will you waver between two opinions? If the Lord is God, follow Him; but if Baal is God, follow him" (I Kings 18:21). In this drama, the tug-of-war between those two options is evident, and God enforces His supremacy.

THREE MILITARY CAPTAINS

When the delegation returns with the dreadful prophecy and the king identifies the source as none other than Elijah, he dispatches the first of three military units, "a captain of fifty with his fifty men," to seize the prophet. The story is narrated in a recursive style, with Elijah "sitting on the top of the hill" (II Kings 1:9), expressive of his unassailable position.[11] In the first of the three encounters, he is confronted by the military commander, who addresses the prophet in an aggressive and authoritative tone, ordering Elijah "by order of the king, come down!" (1:9). This is a direct collision between the king and God: On one side, Ahaziah's sovereign power is invested in the hands of his army captain; on the other, God is represented by His surrogate, Elijah – hence Elijah's response: "*If I am a man of God,* let fire come down from heaven and consume you and your fifty men!" (1:10).

Three military units are dispatched to seize Elijah. Three army captains address him. A textual comparison between the scenes illustrates the storyline.

11. The drama of the chapter is illustrated beautifully by its use of the vertical axis. The motif of "up" and "down" as found in the Hebrew roots A-L-H and Y-R-D features twenty-one times in the chapter, most significantly in this scene, as the army officers must "ascend" to Elijah and command him to "descend." Of course, the key line in the chapter also displays this motif: "You shall not descend (Y-R-D) from the bed which you ascended (A-L-H), but you shall surely die."

1. "He climbed up to him... and said to him, 'Man of God, by order of the king, come down!'" (1:9).
2. "He said to him, 'Man of God, by order of the king, come down *at once*!'" (1:11).
3. "The third captain of fifty climbed and *approached and knelt before Elijah and implored him*, saying, 'Man of God, please have regard for my life and the lives of these fifty men, your servants! See, fire has fallen from heaven and consumed the first two captains and all their men. But now have respect for my life!'" (1:13).

The first captain ascends the mountain and delivers the king's decree with full and uncompromising royal authority, as would be expected of a military officer. But he and his men are consumed by fire. The second officer acts more boldly without even approaching Elijah.[12] Instead he issues his command from the foot of the hill, insisting that the prophet respond "at once!" to the king's command. This dauntless exhibition of power leaves Elijah unfazed; his response remains identical to his response to the first officer: "If I am a man of God, let fire come down from heaven and consume you and your fifty men!" The second group is similarly obliterated.

With the approach of the third captain we witness a capitulation, an absolute surrender of royal power to God's power. The officer abandons the confident stride and belligerent tone of the first two. He approaches the prophet deferentially, even timidly, kneeling before him, and pleading for his life and the life of his subordinates. He even "forgets" to mention his royal commission. It is at this point that God's angel assures Elijah that he is safe and allows him to accompany the troops.

This three-stage process illustrates the crumbling of the king's authority. His troops disregard his orders as they cower before the prophet. The balance of power has shifted dramatically. Now Elijah has absolute control of the situation. Elijah, who embodies God's power, has demonstrated God's supremacy, which is now affirmed by Ahaziah's mighty military.

12. His forceful tone could be a sign of boldness, or it may be a cover for his fear after he saw the fate of the first officer and his brigade.

AHAZIAH'S MOTIVES

What is Ahaziah's motivation in ordering Elijah's arrest? Ralbag assumes that he intended to honor Elijah, as fifty soldiers sometimes constitute an honor guard.[13] Alternatively, Abarbanel indicates that the bedridden king might have sought to hear the prophecy personally from Elijah; hence the order to summon the prophet to Samaria.[14] These approaches are problematic, as no appeal is made to Elijah to accompany the troops peaceably. Furthermore, from the very outset, the combative and disdainful tone of the captain would seem to preclude these positive explanations. Rather, it seems that the king sought to harm or even to kill Elijah. Rabbi Elchanan Samet adopts this approach:

> By causing the prophet bodily harm, they are also harming his prophecy and causing it to be annulled. This explains the attempts of several kings in Tanakh to harm or even kill prophets who had uttered prophecies of punishment against them. It is not merely an attempt to silence the opposition, as the modern reader may interpret the move. Rather, it is a "metaphysical" intention to revoke the prophet's undesirable message.
>
> It seems that for Ahaziah, lying in his sickbed and surely terrified that the prophecy conveyed to him from Elijah would be realized, an assault on Elijah represents an act negating the validity of his prophecy. He sends his soldiers to harm Elijah *in order to bring about his own recovery*. The opposition to the "man of God" is therefore, in essence, opposition to the "word of God." The battle against the prophet is an attempt to thwart the realization of his prophecy.[15]

---

13. For example, the honor guard of Adoniah (I Kings 1:5) and that of Absalom (II Sam. 15:1). The imperious tone of the captain here makes the option of an honor guard unlikely. However, we should recall the use of groups of fifty with regard to the prophets of God, both in I Kings 18:4 and in II Kings 2:16. The inverse symmetry is striking.
14. Ralbag and Abarbanel are forced to explain that despite the king's intent to respect or summon the prophet, Elijah objected to the dominant tone of the army officers and insisted that he be granted a higher status than the king. This insistence, obviously unthinkable for the king's courtiers, led to the violent confrontation. Alternatively, there was some misunderstanding, and despite the king's innocent intent, Elijah felt that his life was threatened (Abarbanel).
15. Samet, *Pirkei Eliyahu*, 434 (italics added).

The royal threat to Elijah's life would certainly explain Elijah's aggressive response to the military officer. It also clarifies the angel's reassuring message after the third officer deferentially approaches Elijah: "Go down with him; *do not be afraid*" (1:15).

***

The essence of this story is God's power struggle against the king as played out by Elijah and Ahaziah's delegates. Elijah first dominates Ahaziah's diplomatic messengers as he transforms them into God's mouthpiece. Second, Elijah, invested with God's power, overwhelms Ahaziah's bellicose officers, incinerates his brigades of fifty troops, and crushes their imperious orders. In response to Elijah's sheer force, Ahaziah's men cower before Elijah and again shift their allegiance from king to Elijah, unequivocally establishing God's supremacy over both the king and his foreign gods.

After this high drama in which Elijah has demonstrated God's control, the prophet is granted unhindered access to Samaria and personally delivers God's pronouncement to Ahaziah. This completes the threefold structure:[16]

Introductory exposition (king's sickness) 1:2

1. Prophecy (spoken by the *malakh*) 1:4
2. Prophecy (spoken by the *malakhim*) 1:6
   - *i.* Mission of the fifty
   - *ii.* Mission of the fifty
   - *iii.* Mission of the fifty
3. Prophecy (spoken by Elijah) 1:16

Conclusion (king's death) 1:17

Leaders do not function in a vacuum; they execute their policies through the mechanisms of government. The Talmud states: "There is no agency for an evil deed" (Kiddushin 42b); in other words, a person

16. As presented by Jacob Licht, *Storytelling in the Bible* (Jerusalem: Magnes Press, 1978), 56–57.

may not disavow their personal ethical responsibility and cast it upon the leadership. Each individual must be fully accountable for the morality of his or her actions. In a book that highlights the crimes of the leadership, this chapter draws attention to agency, to the role played by the intermediary in society – those who collaborate, and those who resist – and teaches a lesson which underscores their considerable influence and responsibility.

ELIJAH'S CLOTHING

In I Kings, Elijah's ability to enact miracles, withhold the rain, revive the dead, and elicit heavenly fire has already been established. It also depicts his fearless challenge to the deviant king Ahab. This chapter further compounds our impression of the formidable prophet as a man who can summon divine force at will.

Our chapter furnishes us with an intriguing visual description of Elijah, namely: "A hairy man (*ish baal se'ar*) wearing a leather belt around his waist" (1:8). Evidently this was Elijah's standard comportment, as these sparse specifications allow Ahaziah to instantly identify him: "That is Elijah the Tishbite!" (1:8).

Elijah is not the only prophet with a distinctive manner of dress. We read how Samuel's mother would make him clothing each year:

> His mother would make a little robe (*me'il*) for him and bring it up every year when she made the pilgrimage with her husband. (I Sam. 2:19)

Samuel's mother dressed him in the robe (*me'il*) when he was a young child. And yet, posthumously, when the "medium" raises Samuel from the dead, we read the following account:

> The king answered … "What do you see?"
> And the woman said to Saul, "I see a divine being coming up from the earth."
> "What does he look like?" he asked her.
> "It is an old man coming up," she said, "and he is wrapped in a robe (*me'il*)."

> Then Saul knew that it was Samuel. (I Sam. 28:13–14)

So we see that Samuel has a trademark *me'il* which he wore from infancy to death and by which he could be clearly identified! It would seem that Elijah also dressed in a unique style, and his appearance was unusual and immediately identifiable.

ELIJAH'S HAIR

We have translated the phrase "*ish baal se'ar*" as referring to Elijah's abundance of hair. Possibly his hair or his beard was particularly long and unkempt:

> "A hairy man": with wild hair. "And a leather belt around his waist": and he cannot appear this way before the king. (Malbim)

Beyond personal proclivity, might Elijah have been a nazirite?[17] The classic *nazir* withdraws from society to live in a sacred zone. His long hair marks him as separate from the community, away from the common people. This certainly matches Elijah's reclusive persona.

Others, however, advocate that the phrase refers to a hairy coat worn by prophets rather than to body hair. This is supported by the depiction of prophets as wearing an "*aderet se'ar*" (Zech. 13:4). Elijah too is repeatedly depicted as wearing an "*aderet*," a piece of apparel that will feature prominently in the forthcoming chapter.[18] Does the hairy appearance refer to his coat or cloak?

Whatever the precise explanation, II Kings 2:23 will cite a depiction of Elisha, Elijah's successor, as bald. This stark difference between the hairy man and the bald one will allow us to ponder the differences between the prophet and his student.

---

17. See Rav Nehorai's assertion that Samuel was a *nazir*, in Mishna Nazir 9:5. Likewise, see Amos 2:11–12, which talks in a single breath about nazirites and prophets.
18. I Kings 19:13; II Kings 2:8, 13, 14.

II Kings 2

In a Whirlwind

> A chariot of fire with horses of fire suddenly appeared... and Elijah went up to heaven in a whirlwind. (II Kings 2:11)

This awesome image, the dominant centerpiece of this chapter, is as breathtaking as it is enigmatic. Elijah has been surrounded by miracles in virtually every instance that we have encountered him. His dazzling departure from this world is no exception.

ANTICIPATION AND CONCEALEMENT

The narrative builds the anticipation to its climax in a delicate weave of transparency and concealment, as glimpses of information are exposed but for a brief moment and then hidden. The opening verse announces Elijah's impending demise: "And it came to pass when the Lord took Elijah up to heaven in a whirlwind" (2:1). At first glance this information would seem to steal the sense of drama; however, this foreknowledge only intensifies our suspense as we anxiously accompany Elijah on his meandering journey through Gilgal, Bethel, and Jericho, delaying the designated moment. Repeatedly, the same exchange ensues:

> The disciples of the prophets at Bethel came out to Elisha and asked, "Do you know that the Lord is going to take your

> master from you today?" "Yes, I know," Elisha replied, "but do not speak of it." (2:3)

The disciples of the prophet know that Elijah is to be "taken," yet they dare not speak of it to Elijah. Elisha knows it too, and as we shall see so does Elijah. Everyone is anxiously expecting the auspicious moment, yet to articulate the imminent death of Elijah is unthinkable.

Later, as Elijah and Elisha advance toward the Jordan River and cross it by means of a miracle, they are observed by fifty of their followers "from a distance" (2:7). A momentous act is about to transpire; the anticipation is palpable, but it can be observed only from afar. They dare not approach the two great prophets walking together.

At this point Elijah turns to Elisha and asks, "What can I do before I am taken from you?" (2:9). We hear for the first time that Elijah is fully aware of and acknowledges what is about to transpire, but even then, it is an oblique, almost secondary reference. When the "whirlwind" arrives, it also appears unannounced, unexpectedly, in mid-conversation: "And as they continued walking and talking, a chariot of fire with horses of fire separated one from the other" (2:11).

The key event is cryptic. Did Elijah ascend in a "storm" or in fire? The fifty prophets see, but they don't see everything, as they persist in a three-day search for Elijah. They don't comprehend that he is gone, permanently.

Indeed, this scene is invested with a mysterious, impenetrable aura, the sense of things known and anticipated on the one hand, but unacknowledged and ultimately incomprehensible on the other.

STUDENTS

Elijah's travels on his way to the Jordan River will provide a good starting point for our analysis. His trek begins at Gilgal[1] together with Elisha.

---

1. This is probably Elisha's hometown; see II Kings 4:38, where in Gilgal the "*Benei HaNevi'im* sit before him." The phrase "return to Gilgal" is reminiscent of the prophet Samuel, about whom we read: "And when he would return to Ramah, *for his home was there*" (I Sam. 7:17). See Samet, *Pirkei Eliyahu*, 495–97.

   In the context of this chapter, the identity of this town, Gilgal, presents certain challenges. The Gilgal featured in the book of Joshua is located near Jericho in the

His route is divinely prescribed: "God has sent me to Bethel... God has sent me to Jericho... God has sent me to the Jordan" (2:2, 4, 6). In each location he is welcomed by a revering group of *Benei HaNevi'im*, students of the prophet[2] or possibly young men training in the art of prophecy.[3] What is the purpose of these periodic stopovers in the towns or villages on the way? Rabbi Elchanan Samet suggests:

> Elijah's passage through these cities, at God's command, is meant as a gesture of farewell to the apprentice prophets. As we know from the narratives about Samuel (I Sam. 19) and Elisha (II Kings 4), the prophet of the generation is regarded as the teacher of the apprentice prophets of his generation. While Elijah does not seem to have served as the head of a group of apprentice prophets, as

---

Jordan Valley; this would not work with Elijah's route, which begins in Gilgal: "And they descended to Bethel," indicating that this Gilgal is topographically higher than Bethel. Yehuda Kiel suggests that this Gilgal is situated near Shechem, as evidenced in Deuteronomy 11:30. See Yehuda Kiel, ed., *Daat Mikra*, II Kings (Jerusalem: Mossad HaRav Kook, 1989). Prof. H. Gevaryahu suggests that it is a town near the Arab village known today as Jaljuliya, located a short distance from the modern-day town of Beit El. This is a phonetic match – the hard Hebrew *gimmel* sound is frequently a soft *j* sound in Arabic, and it also fits the geography nicely. See *Encyclopedia Mikrait* (The Biblical Encyclopedia), vol. 2, cols. 487–90, "Gilgal."

2. Rashi's translation. We are unaware of any teachings that Elijah may have imparted to this group. Elisha is viewed as the leader of this group and offers practical assistance (see II Kings 4:1–7, 38–43; 6:1–7) but we have no evidence of formal teachings. The *Sifrei* uses the notion of the *Benei HaNevi'im* as a paradigm of the teacher-student relationship:

   > And thus do you find in every place, that "students" are referred to as "children." As it states: "And the sons of the prophets that were at Bethel came forth to Elisha" (II Kings 2:3). Were these really the sons of prophets? Were they not really their disciples? Rather, [this shows] that students are referred to as children (*Sifrei*, Deut. 6:7).

3. Abarbanel ad loc.; Maimonides, *Mishneh Torah*, Laws of the Foundations of the Torah 7:5: "Those who seek prophecy are called the sons of prophets. Even though they attune their thoughts, the Divine Presence may or may not inspire them." However, in Kings we never witness this group receiving prophecy or engaged in ecstatic activity, as in I Sam. 19:19–24. The only instance of anything close to prophecy is their premonition, in this scene, of Elijah's imminent death. Abarbanel perceives this as a prophetic spillover from Elijah: "With Elijah, his prophecy was so overflowing that many of the *Benei HaNevi'im* prophesied by his power."

> Samuel and Elisha did (perhaps because he was not based in one place), all the "sons of the prophets" of the generation are considered his disciples, and he must therefore take leave of them before he is taken from them.[4]

This whole situation is discordant with the solitary manner in which we have become accustomed to seeing Elijah.[5] Elijah is aware of other prophets but has insisted on depicting himself as "alone,"[6] and is never portrayed in the company of a prophetic community. Suddenly, our chapter depicts him surrounded by followers who are deeply troubled at the thought of his imminent passing, and who desperately search for him for three days. Why is this encounter critical for Elijah's final day on earth? Why do we need to hear about his supporters here and now? Why is this a central feature of the story?

DISTANCING ELISHA

The relationship between Elijah and Elisha is similarly perplexing. Since the day Elijah met Elisha, initiating him into the world of prophecy,[7] we have little information regarding the nature of Elisha's apprenticeship. Elisha was Elijah's attendant for some time: "[Elisha] arose and went after Elijah and became his attendant" (I Kings 19:21), and he is later identified as "Elisha ben Shaphat, who poured water on the hands of Elijah" (II Kings 3:11), indicative of a protracted tutelage.[8] Our narrative presupposes Elisha's

---

4. Samet, *Pirkei Eliyahu*, 497.
5. Even though he is described as having an assistant (see I Kings 18:43; 19:3), the latter plays a negligible role.
6. In I Kings 18:13 he is informed about the one hundred prophets, but later, in 19:10, 14, he talks about his status as the sole prophet.
7. See I Kings 19:16, 19–21. God had instructed Elijah to anoint Elisha ben Shaphat as "a prophet instead of you." That meeting also features Elijah's cloak, which is thrown over Elisha with transformative effect as he immediately responds enthusiastically and "ran after Elijah."
8. Yael Shemesh suggests that the editorial ordering of the chapters, allowing for the wars of Ahab with Aram, Naboth's vineyard, and the Ahaziah encounter (I Kings 20–II Kings 1) to interrupt the flow of the Elijah-Elisha story, are intended to generate the impression of an extended apprenticeship of Elisha at the feet of Elijah. See Yael Shemesh, "The Stories of Elisha: A Literary Analysis " (PhD diss., Bar-Ilan University, 1997), 15 [Hebrew].

status as Elijah's leading student – the disciples describe Elijah's impending death as "The Lord is going to take *your* master from above *your* head"; this is a close master-protégé relationship. But we have no information as to how many months or years they spent together, how Elisha's reputation was built, and whether Elijah publicly or privately named Elisha as his successor. And yet our narrative seems to undermine this impression of closeness with the awkward exchange in which Elijah repeatedly tries to distance Elisha:

> Elijah said to Elisha, "Please stay here, for God has sent me to Bethel." And Elisha said, "As the Lord lives, and your soul lives, I will not leave you." So they went down to Bethel. (2:2)
>
> Elijah said to him, "Elisha! Please stay here, for God has sent me to Jericho." And he said, "As the Lord lives, and your soul lives, I will not leave you." So they came to Jericho. (2:4)
>
> Elijah said, "Please, stay here, for God has sent me to the Jordan." And he said, "As the Lord lives, and your soul lives, I will not leave you." So they went together. (2:6)

What is the nature of this threefold interaction?[9] Does Elijah want Elisha to accompany him? If so, why does he try to discharge him? And if he genuinely seeks his own solitude, why does he so readily capitulate time after time?

A DOUBLE PORTION

Let us look at one additional, difficult scene. It is the final conversation between Elijah and Elisha as they cross the Jordan:

---

9. This threefold structure is but one manifestation of the literary link between chapters 1 and 2. Connections include the multiple usage of the root SH-L-H (see the sevenfold repetition in 2:2, 4, 6, 16, 17) and the centrality of the Hebrew roots A-L-H and Y-R-D in both chapters; the group of fifty "strong men" who search for Elijah in chapter 2, matching the troops of chapter 1; and of course, the stylistic feature of threefold repetition germane to all the Elijah stories.

> It came to pass, when they crossed, that Elijah said to Elisha, "Ask what I may do for you, before I am taken from you." And Elisha said, "Let a double portion (*pi shenayim*) of your spirit be upon me." And he said, "You have asked a hard thing; nevertheless, if you see me when I am taken from you, it shall be so; but if not, it shall not be so." (II Kings 2:9–10)

This is a puzzling dialogue. What is Elisha's request, and what is the response? Is Elisha asking to be twice as powerful as his master? *Metzudat David* comments: "Let the spirit of prophecy rest upon me at twice the level that it rested upon you." Rashi explains Elijah's question: "You have asked a hard thing; how can I grant you more than I have myself?" Read this way, we wonder at Elisha's audacity. How could he, the student, possibly exceed his master?[10] Is Elijah's formidable miracle-making insufficient? Why does Elisha seek a double portion of Elijah's spirit?

Radak and Ralbag offer an alternative perspective:

> It means to say… I should be bestowed a double portion of that which you have bestowed upon each of the other prophets. This is the same word usage as: "He must acknowledge the [status of his] son… as the firstborn by giving him a double share (*pi shenayim*) of all he has." (Deut. 21:17)

Ralbag reads the phrase "*pi shenayim*" to establish a link between Elisha's request and the Torah's inheritance law vis-à-vis the firstborn. The firstborn receives a double sum in his father's inheritance, twice that inherited by his brothers, but he obviously cannot inherit twice his father's wealth! Similarly, what Elisha is requesting here is an elevated status, an unmistakable superiority over his fellow prophets.

The issue concerning Elisha is that of leadership. Who will be the "firstborn" among the community of prophets? Who will succeed Elijah?

10. Radak's first interpretation quotes the Talmud (Sanhedrin 47a), which notes that Elijah performed eight miracles whereas Elisha performed sixteen, so his miracle-making was in fact twice that of his master.

Elisha requests that his prophecy be of sufficient quality and intensity, his miracles powerful enough, to secure his status as the leading prophet.

How does Elijah respond? Obviously Elijah cannot grant the gift of prophecy;[11] that is God's jurisdiction. Instead, he identifies an indicator. He says: If you are capable of observing my heavenward journey, then it will be evidence that you are indeed an exceptional prophet. If you are of the prophetic sophistication to witness God's *Merkava* – His chariot and horses – then certainly your prophecy is of the finest grade.

In the next lines, the text demonstrates that the fifty *Benei HaNevi'im* were unable to discern the images that Elisha saw. Elisha beheld the horses and chariots and in reaction, he declares: "My father, my father! Israel's chariot and horsemen!" (II Kings 2:12).

And even though the chariots and horsemen in Elisha's exclamation seem to refer to Elijah, it is apparent that the choice of metaphor is inspired by the vision he saw.[12] By contrast, the fifty apprentice prophets see only Elijah's ascent. They suggest that "the spirit [literally, wind] of God has carried him off and cast him upon some mountain or into some valley" (2:16), implying that they might have seen Elijah soaring upward but indicating that they saw no divine, fiery chariot.[13] They think that Elijah is still alive somewhere; Elisha, who saw it all, knows that his departure is a permanent one.

This central scene most certainly illustrates the fulfillment of Elisha's request for preeminent status among his fellow prophets.[14]

---

11. Elijah cannot dictate the degree of Elisha's prophecy, but does he assist Elisha in any way? Abarbanel suggests that Elijah deliberately left Elisha his *aderet*, his cloak or mantle: "There is no doubt that the cloak did not fall accidentally but was deliberately thrown at Elisha, for it was a tool to bestow the prophetic abundance upon Elisha, and [Elijah meant for him] to wear it. This is already prefigured by the scene in which Elijah threw his cloak over the young Elisha, thereby designating him as his successor (I Kings 19:19)."
12. Elisha's outburst contains two clauses. The first indicates Elijah as "my father, my father!" The second phrase, "Israel's chariot and horsemen," is read by most commentaries in some variation of the translation offered by the Talmud (Moed Katan 26a): "He was better for the protection of the Jewish people with his prayers than an army with chariots and horsemen."
13. See II Kings 6:17, which indicates that one's eyes need to be specially opened in order to see chariots and horses of fire. It is not an image that is naturally visible.
14. Elisha's initial status bears significant ambivalence. The prophets say to Elisha: "Do you know that the Lord will remove your master from above your head today?" (2:3).

STRUCTURE AND MEANING

If we observe the structure of the chapter as a whole, organizing the narrative on a geographical basis, a striking symmetry comes into focus, with Elijah's fiery ascent at its epicenter:

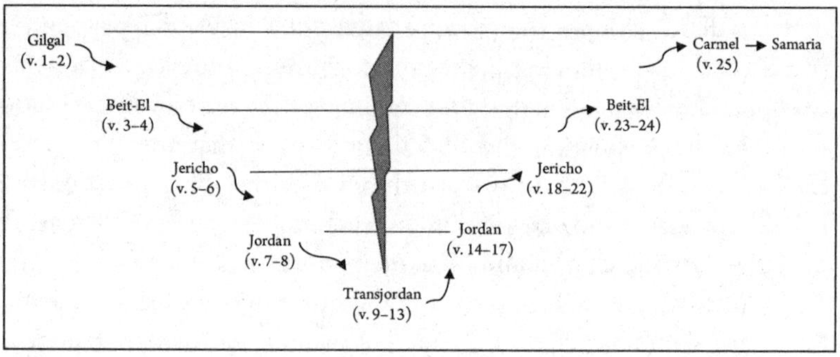

What message does this chiastic structure convey? It creates a symmetry of sorts. Let us take note of the switch in the key personality: the first half tells of Elijah's descent and demise, the second half Elisha's ascent to preeminence. Elisha is veritably retracing Elijah's steps. If we focus on Elisha's final destination, Mount Carmel, we recall that location as the site of Elijah's *pièce de résistance*, his contest against the Baal prophets. Elisha is not merely retracing his master's steps, he is in fact ascending in Elijah's footsteps, an ascent in which Elisha adopts Elijah's preeminent status. When he reaches Mount Carmel, the site which represents the zenith of Elijah's career, he then turns to Samaria, the northern city of royalty, to assume Elijah's position as the national prophet.

The narrative's chiasm vividly illustrates Elisha's newfound status as he acts in Elijah's footsteps, in his image. This is noted by the *Benei HaNevi'im*, who observe Elisha's splitting of the Jordan River as he wields Elijah's mysterious *aderet*. Elisha's ability to replicate Elijah's

---

On the one hand, the phrase "from above your head" indicates that Elijah is high above Elisha, but on the other hand, Elijah is referred to as "*your* master," indicating Elisha's preeminent place as a student of Elijah, who is above Elisha's head and not theirs!

miracles[15] leads to the conclusion: "'The spirit of Elijah rests upon Elisha!' And they came to meet him, and bowed down to the ground before him" (2:15).

REJECTION AND PERSISTENCE

As we progress through the chapter, Elijah repeatedly seeks to deflect Elisha, encouraging him to leave. Why did Elijah want to distance Elisha from him? Rashi suggests that Elijah wished to depart this world alone, "out of humility." However, *Daat Mikra* suggests:

> He sought to test whether he would remain steadfast to him until the very last moment. Elijah tested him twice and three times, and Elisha passed the test.[16]

Elisha's stubborn dedication to his master, his repeated refusal to abandon Elijah articulated in an oath – for God's sake, and for Elijah's sake (2:6) – convinces Elijah to acquiesce. Elijah rejects Elisha three times, but after Elisha's third insistence, master and student walk together. This is articulated by the word *sheneihem,* "the two of them," which features three times in as many verses (2:7, 8, 9), and which indicates unity of purpose and identity. Reflecting Naomi and Ruth's exchange,[17] a dialogue enacted on these same roads connecting Israel and Transjordan, Elisha's unbending persistence is a sign of devotion and commitment. At this point Elijah gives in to Elisha's insistence, allowing his protégé to join him across the Jordan. The master has accepted the student's place alongside him.

---

15. In a rather concrete expression of Elisha's assumption of Elijah's status, Abarbanel suggests that Elisha wore Elijah's clothing: "Elisha tore his original clothes and enrobed himself in other clothing – Elijah's cloak – for he had been detached from his previous level and now remained at the level of Elijah."
16. Kiel, Daat Mikra.
17. Ruth 1:8–19. There too the story ends with the phrase *vatelakhna sheteihem,* "and they walked together."

"MY FATHER!"

Elisha's perseverance can be seen in two ways. The Talmud views Elisha as a paradigm of *shimush talmidei chachamim,* a relationship based less in study and more in lending practical assistance to Elijah:

> R. Yoḥanan further said in the name of R. Shimon b. Yoḥai: The service of the Torah is greater than the study thereof. As it is stated, "Here is Elisha, the son of Shaphat, who poured water on the hands of Elijah" (II Kings 3:11). It is not stated, "who learned," but "who poured water." This teaches that the service of the [teachers of] Torah is greater than its study. (Berakhot 7a)

In this teaching, the student imbibes the wisdom of his master more by loyal devotion and service than by direct instruction. It is the personal example, the small moments, the everyday conversations, the incidental observations, that shape the student, rather than rousing speeches and public lectures. This dedication is the chief factor in Elisha's apprenticeship at the feet of Elijah.

However, their relationship is expressed in higher terms than as teacher and student. As Elijah ascends heavenward, Elisha exclaims, "My father, my father!" (II Kings 2:12). Elisha perceives Elijah as a parent. This brings to mind Elisha's original encounter with Elijah, when Elisha said, "Let me kiss my mother and father and I will [then] follow you" (I Kings 19:20). As he began his association with Elijah, he bade an emotional farewell to his parents. But now after his formative apprenticeship, possibly years afterward, Elijah has become a spiritual parent to Elisha.

Rabbinic literature is familiar with the notion of a rabbi adopting a parental role: "For his father brought him into this world, but his rabbi who taught him wisdom brings him into the World to Come" (Mishna Bava Metzia 2:11). Furthermore, when the Talmud looks for a proof text that a student must tear his clothes on the death of his rabbi just like a child for a parent, it turns specifically to Elisha.[18]

18. Moed Katan 26a.

DIFFERENT CHARACTERISTICS

An alternative way to consider the dialogue between Elijah and Elisha is to view it as reflective of each one's personality. Elijah, as we have said, is a solitary figure. We could almost predict that he would prefer to ascend to heaven in a state of sublime solitude, in spiritual isolation. Elisha is very different. In the scene that we cited above, when Elisha takes leave of his parents, he doesn't merely bid them farewell, as he had expressed to Elijah:

> He turned back from him and took a yoke of oxen and slaughtered [them]... and gave it to the people, and they ate; [only] then he arose and followed Elijah and became his assistant. (1 Kings 19:20–22)

At the moment in which Elisha becomes the great prophet's apprentice, he makes a feast for his entire village.[19] He perceives no contradiction between engagement with God and involvement with society. Reflective of this attitude and temperament, Elisha is always surrounded by people and is deeply sensitive to the needs of others. By contrast, Elijah is the lone spiritual figure.

Why did Elijah want to reject Elisha as his successor? We might suggest that Elijah, the lone, isolated figure, is highly uncomfortable with the thought of Elisha, who is so different from his mentor, as the lead prophet. However, ultimately, by accepting Elisha's company, Elijah likewise accepts that despite his difference in temperament, his successor will succeed in his role as a prophet.

* * *

Our chapter opens: "And it came to pass *when* the Lord took Elijah up to heaven in a whirlwind" (2:1). Elijah's death is not the subject of this chapter. While Elijah is ascending heavenward, Elisha is ascending from the status of student to that of teacher, becoming the master prophet, undertaking the task of prophet to the nation. What manner of a man is Elisha? How does he differ from his master Elijah? The upcoming chapters will depict this unique prophet in detail.

---

19. See Alex Israel, *1 Kings: Torn in Two*, 270–71.

Places in the Elisha Narratives

II Kings 2:15–25

A Remedy and a Curse

Elisha splits the Jordan River using Elijah's cloak, evoking the "God of Elijah" (II Kings 2:14). The assembly of fifty disciples witness this impressive spectacle and immediately salute Elisha as Elijah's successor:[1] "'The spirit of Elijah rests upon Elisha!' And they came to meet him, and bowed down to the ground before him" (2:15).

With this statement, Elisha's status has been firmly established among the *Benei HaNevi'im*. As Elisha takes his first steps beyond the prophetic community, he will again need to prove himself.

At this juncture, we read of two encounters, two starkly contrasting miracles. As we shall see, each is connected to the new role Elisha is undertaking. The first is a scene of assistance and sustenance, as Elisha heals the polluted water spring at Jericho. The second is a disturbing tale of mockery and prophetic anger resulting in the violent death of forty-two children.

1. Just like Moses, Elijah dies in Transjordan. Elisha is Elijah's disciple and incumbent, similar to the Moses-Joshua relationship. Elisha makes his way into Israel by splitting the Jordan, just like Joshua, and proceeds to Jericho like Joshua. What is this parallelism intended to portray? We might suggest that in the same manner that Joshua's role is to bring Moses' legacy to fruition, similarly, Elisha will continue the legacy of Elijah.

HEALING THE WATERS OF JERICHO

> The men of the city said to Elisha, "Look, the situation of the town is pleasant, as my lord can see, but the water is bad and the land causes bereavement." He said, "Bring me a new flask, and put salt in it." So they brought it to him. Then he went out to the spring and cast the salt into it, saying, "Thus says the Lord: 'I have healed this water; death and bereavement shall issue from there no longer.'" And the water has remained healed to this day, according to the word Elisha had spoken. (II Kings 2:19–22)

The spring in the beautiful city of Jericho has become contaminated and is the cause of premature mortality among the local population.[2] Jericho's residents turn to Elisha for help. They do not request assistance directly; possibly they feel it arrogant to make demands of the prophet or they doubt his ability to resolve the problem. Instead they simply share their problem with him, specifying the pollution of the municipal water source.

Without hesitation, Elisha gets to work. He requests "a new flask" filled with salt, and pours the salt into the deadly spring, proclaiming, in God's name, "I have healed this water; death and bereavement shall issue from there no longer" (2:21).

Why must the villagers rather than Elisha procure the salt? One approach is to view Elisha as activating the beneficiaries of his miracle, inviting them to participate, essentially integrating the group into the miraculous procedure. As is evident from subsequent stories, this is a hallmark of Elisha's miracles.[3] Why does he seek this cooperation? For Elisha, God's supernatural kindness may not merely be received passively; the fortunate recipient must take an active role.

2. The spring has been identified as Ein El-Sultan near Jericho, otherwise known as the Elisha Spring. In what manner did it cause "death and bereavement"? Rashi, Radak, and the *Metzudot* commentaries suggest that the spring killed those who drank its waters. A second opinion, based on Gen. 27:45; Exodus 23:26; and Job 21:10 is that it caused the women of the region to miscarry.
3. II Kings 4:2–4, 21, 42; 5:10; 6:7; 13:15–16.

This goes some way to explain the provision of the flask and the salt by the townsfolk, but why did Elisha need a new flask? Abarbanel and Ralbag suggest that the newness of the flask along with the use of salt provided by the villagers authenticated the miracle. As Abarbanel expresses it: "So that none may suggest that something had been boiled or placed in the flask that might have enabled [the curing of the waters]."[4]

Magic uses sleight of hand and subterfuge, but here, when the audience can testify that the raw materials and tools have not been tampered with, the healing of the spring is authenticated as a divine act.

The Rabbis go further, viewing the use of salt as what Rashi calls "a miracle within a miracle," a curious paradox, so incongruous that it would have to be Godly:

> Rabban Shimon b. Gamliel says, Come and see how different are the ways of God from the ways of flesh and blood. Flesh and blood uses the sweet to cure the bitter; not so He who spoke and the world was. He uses bitter to cure the bitter.... "And he went out to the water source and threw in salt" (II Kings 2:21). But is it not so that if you put salt into sweet water, it goes bad immediately? How so, then? He puts something that spoils [water] into something spoiled, in order to perform therewith a miracle. (*Mekhilta, Vayassa 1*)

THE MIRACLE IN CONTEXT

The placement of this story after the splitting of the Jordan reminds us of a similar sequence of stories in the book of Exodus. The story of Marah, in which Moses heals "bitter," undrinkable water, follows the episode of the splitting of the Reed Sea. There we read:

> Moses made Israel set out from the Reed Sea.... They went three days in the wilderness and found no water. They came to Marah. They could not drink the water of Marah because it was bitter; therefore

4. For more on this topic, see Yair Zakovitch, "Control Mechanisms in Biblical Miracle-Narratives," *Shnaton: An Annual for Biblical and Ancient Near Eastern Studies*, vols. 7–8 (Jerusalem: Mandel Institute of Jewish Studies, pub. Magnes Press, 1983–4): 61–73 [Hebrew].

> it was named Marah. The people grumbled against Moses, saying, "What shall we drink?" He cried to God and God showed him a tree. He threw it into the water and the water became sweet. (Ex. 15:22–25)

There are several points of similarity between the stories:

- Marah follows the splitting of the Reed Sea. Our Jericho story follows the miraculous parting of the Jordan River.
- Three Days: Marah followed the crossing of the Reed Sea by three days. Similarly, the events at Jericho transpire three days after the splitting of the Jordan (II Kings 2:17–18).
- In both instances, the water is undrinkable. The people voice the problem to the prophet.
- The water is made drinkable by casting into it (*vayashleḥ*) a substance that would seem unrelated to the treatment of water (tree/salt).
- The proclamation made in God's name that identifies God as their "healer": At Marah, "I am the Lord, your *healer*" (Ex. 15:26). At Jericho, "Thus says the Lord: 'I have *healed* this water'" (II Kings 2:21).

How might we digest the parallelism here? On one level, it aims to integrate Elisha into a historic line of prophets. Elisha, at the very moment of his initiation to the leadership, finds his status boosted with a direct connection to Moses. On another level, the centrality of healing, prominently cited both at Marah and at Jericho, presents God Himself as a provider, a God of kindness and sustenance.

In the context of Exodus, this operates as something of a paradigm shift. The crossing of the Reed Sea signifies the closing of a period in which God functions through retribution and plagues, exacting punishment and ruin upon the Egyptians. From Marah onward, God begins to guide His nation on their route to Sinai, miraculously nurturing the people and attending to their basic needs by providing water at Marah, providing the manna and the quail, and bringing forth water from the rock.[5]

5. Water at Marah, Ex. 15; the manna and quail, Ex. 16; water from the rock, Ex. 17. See also Alex Israel, *Beshalach: From Sea to Sinai – The Path of Faith*, http://www.alexisrael.org/beshalach---from-sea-to-sinai.

With regard to the story of Elisha, the healing of the waters of Jericho represents a similar transition: from Elijah's prophetic style to Elisha's, from God's harsh power to His kindness. Elijah is characterized as a harsh, confrontational prophet, who brings fire from heaven and death in its wake. By contrast, Elisha's leadership is colored by altruism and relief; the focus of his miracle-making is the healing and the procurement of food and water for those around him.[6]

The location – Jericho – throws the Elijah-Elisha comparison into even greater focus. Elijah's opening act also transpires in Jericho.[7] There the great prophet makes a declaration to withhold the rain, committing Israel to a crippling three-year drought. And now, in the same vicinity, Elisha assumes the leadership and perceives his own mandate as the inverse of Elijah's. His inaugural undertaking is the provision of water, healing a poisonous spring, thereby transforming it into a source of life.[8]

Furthermore, the contrast between the two prophets, as manifest in this chapter, extends to the social sphere. It is Elisha's "dwelling" (2:18) in the town of Jericho that enables the town's inhabitants to approach Elisha and share their local problem. Ironically, in the opening segment of this chapter (2:5–6) Elijah visits Jericho. However, the townsfolk never share their problem with him; even the disciples of the prophet dare converse only

---

6. Water, II Kings 3:9–17; food, II Kings 4:7, 43; 7:1; 8:1; healing, II Kings 4:34–35; 5:14; healing with food, II Kings 4:40–41; assistance, II Kings 6:5–6, 8–9.
7. I Kings 17:1. See the connection with 16:34 and Radak there, who suggests that Elijah's statement was made at Jericho.
8. Radak and Abarbanel suggest that the spring had become contaminated in fulfillment of Joshua's curse: "Cursed is the man, before God, who will arise and rebuild this city, Jericho" (Josh. 6:26). When did Joshua's ancient curse become activated? "In his days Hiel of Bethel built Jericho. He laid its foundation at the cost of Abiram his firstborn, and set up its gates at the cost of his youngest son Segub, according to the word of God which He spoke by Joshua the son of Nun" (I Kings 16:34). This verse immediately precedes the inaugural Elijah story, which then creates an interesting chiasm. Elijah's first appearance follows the activation of the curse at Jericho, and at that same juncture Elijah withholds the rainwaters. Now, in the first scene after Elijah's passing, we return to Jericho as Elisha removes its curse and provides life-giving water. In this perspective Elijah represents drought and poisoned waters; Elisha is his antithesis.

with Elisha. Elijah is a daunting figure; Elisha is approachable and amenable. Elijah is generally portrayed alone, elusive and itinerant, and is never the address for personal or communal distress. Elisha lives among the people. Our concise story shines a spotlight on a new style of accessible leadership.[9]

FORTY-TWO CHILDREN

With this next episode, everything we have just said will be thrown into question, even disarray:

> From there [Jericho] he went up to Bethel. As he was going up the road, some boys came out of the town and jeered at him. "Go on up, you baldhead!" they said. "Go on up, you baldhead!" He turned around, looked at them and cursed them in the name of the Lord. Then two bears came out of the woods and mauled forty-two of the children. And he went on to Mount Carmel and from there returned to Samaria. (II Kings 2:23–25)

This is a shocking, and morally challenging, story. At first glance, it sounds as if a group of children teased Elisha about his strange appearance and he cursed them, bringing about the death of forty-two children. Should young children (*ne'arim ketanim*) be to blame for a prank, a tease? And even if these were adults, forty-two casualties is an exceedingly heavy death toll. Was Elisha not aware of the devastating effects of a curse uttered in God's name?

The Talmud, sensitive to the moral difficulty, attempts to exonerate Elisha. In its first approach, it suggests that these "little children" were sinners, somehow unworthy of life:

> R. Eliezer said: *Ne'arim* [children] means they were bare [*menu'arim*] of precepts; "little" means they were little of faith.

9. Others who have dwelt upon this scene as a contrasting parallel between Elisha and Elijah are Y. Shemesh, "The Stories of Elisha: A Literary Analysis"; A. HaKohen, "Elisha and the Waters of Jericho: A Story's Significance in Light of Its Context," *Mishlav* 21 (1992): 84–97 [Hebrew]; and Rabbi Elchanan Samet, *Pirkei Elisha* (Jerusalem: Maaliyot Press, 2007), 35–38 [Hebrew].

> "And he looked behind him and saw them." What did he see? ... Shmuel said: He saw that their mothers had conceived them on the Day of Atonement.[10]
>
> R. Yitzḥak Napḥa said: He saw that their hair was plaited like the Amorites [gentiles].
>
> R. Yoḥanan said: He saw that there was no sap of the commandments in them.
>
> But perhaps there would have been such in their descendants?
>
> R. Eliezer said: Neither in them nor in their descendants unto the end of all generations. (Sota 46b)

This approach resounds with problems. Are children fully culpable for their actions, let alone for their parents' misdemeanors? And if they had sinned in the past, could their sins possibly be beyond repair or repentance?

In a second approach, the Talmud seems to blame the carnage on a lack of parental supervision, suggesting that were the villagers to have accompanied Elisha out of the town, they would have been able to control their youth. The Talmud continues:

> R. Yoḥanan said in the name of R. Meir: Whoever does not escort others or allow himself to be escorted is as though he sheds blood, for had the men of Jericho escorted Elisha he would not have stirred up bears against the children.

However, as the antagonists are children,[11] these answers hardly exonerate Elisha, or alleviate our moral discomfort. The Talmud says as much,

---

10. A day in which sexual relations are prohibited by Jewish law.
11. The phrase *ne'arim ketanim* is imprecise. The word *naar* can refer to a seventeen-year-old (as in Joseph; Gen. 37:2) or even an older person – Joshua was referred to as a *naar* (Ex. 33:11) even after he had served as a national military leader (Ex. 17:8; see also a reference to *ne'arim* in combat – II Sam. 2:18). However, a *naar* can also connote an infant! Exodus 2:6 uses the word *naar* as a reference to baby Moses, and in Is. 7:16 it also refers to a newborn.

and closes the discussion with a condemnation of Elisha: "Our Rabbis taught: Elisha was afflicted with three illnesses: the first, because he stirred up the bears against the children" (Sota 47a).[12]

"GO ON UP, YOU BALDHEAD!"

A close reading of the text, imagining the event as it played out, may bring the episode into a slightly different focus. Let us begin with the identity of these boys, what they were shouting at Elisha, and why. Was this merely innocent banter?

We understand that Elisha left Jericho and "from there he went up to Bethel." Then, "boys came out of the town." Which town, Jericho or Bethel? It first glance, the boys appear to be his reception party at Bethel. However, on a second reading, we notice that they are situated behind him: "*He turned around,* looked at them and cursed them." His tormentors appear from the rear; in other words, from Jericho.[13]

Why are the children of Jericho maligning the prophet? This is the city that he has just saved, removing its "death and bereavement"! Is this the reward for Elisha's assistance to the town? And the children's gibe, "Go on up, you baldhead!" is a fairly uncomplicated reference[14] to Elijah, who is most strikingly identified as a "hairy man" (II Kings 1:7).[15] The barb of baldness, then, is a biting insult, a blatant insinuation that

---

The adjective, "*ketanim,*" certainly points to the younger end of the age scale. Moreover, in II Kings 2:24 the text speaks of forty-two "children" (*yeladim*). Even if this is a literary device to engender sympathy for the victims, it is unlikely that we are dealing with anyone older than a preteen.

12. Another possible support for a critique of this large number of deaths is the number forty-two, which is found elsewhere in connection with mass execution. See Judges 12:6; II Kings 10:14.

13. Rashi, Sota 46b, s.v. "*shehikraḥta,*" quotes a fascinating talmudic theory that the rowdy mob had previously earned their living by transporting water to Jericho. After Elisha fixed the local water source, they are suddenly unemployed! They take out their anger by insulting the prophet.

14. Abarbanel; Malbim. See also Yair Zakovitch, "*Go up, Baldhead! Go up, Baldhead!*: Rings of Commentary in a Biblical Story," *Jerusalem Researches in Hebrew Literature* 7 (1985): 7–22 [Hebrew].

15. It refers either to long and unkempt hair or his prophetic garb, the *aderet se'ar*; see Zech. 13:4; Yehuda Kiel, ed., *Daat Mikra,* I Kings (Jerusalem: Mossad HaRav Kook, 1989), 1:7.

Elisha is unsuitable for the task of a prophecy, that he fails to match his master, his predecessor. He is "bald" in comparison to the "hairy man." This is not mere child's play; it is a provocation, a mockery, a protest, a sabotage of Elisha's newfound status.

Why do these youths mock Elisha? What is their motivation? We can only speculate. Could it be that there was a group of residents in Jericho that vilified the presence of prophets in their midst? Alternatively, might these children have emerged from the prophetic circles in Jericho as an opposition to Elisha's newfound role, possibly supporting an alternative candidate for the leadership? Did the townsfolk of Jericho perhaps resent Elisha for abandoning the town? If these were indeed young children, might they have been expressing attitudes and sentiments heard in their homes?

Precise motivation aside, as we examine their words, we understand that this is a direct affront, even a challenge to Elisha's new status:

> "Go on up, you baldhead!" Because Elijah, his master, had hair, and he was bald, they said in derision and ridicule, "Go up to the heavens like your master, Elijah!" as if to say, "You are not of his pedigree." (*Metzudat David*)

Now let us imagine the scene. Elisha, the new leader of the prophetic community, leaves the town whose waters he has cured, heading out to Bethel. Anyone familiar with the topography of the region understands that he is negotiating an arduously steep ascent. One can picture him climbing the rocky path, panting and sweating, when a large group arrives to heckle him, to hound him out of town. If forty-two "*of* the youths" were killed, then the crowd was larger. Was it fifty, eighty, one hundred youths? More? And as he struggles with the climb they shout out, "Go on up, you baldhead!" Or possibly it is a rhetorical taunt: "Can you go up (*aleh*), baldhead?" Can you "ascend" as your master Elijah "ascended" (to heaven)? No – you are bald and he was hairy! You are of substandard quality! You can't even climb this hill!

TWO BEARS

Elisha curses the youths in the name of God, and two bears emerge and maul some of the youths. The language used – that the two bears "came out" (*vatetzena*), corresponding to the language of the youths who "came out" (*vayetzeh*) of the town – is indicative of a divine measure-for-measure (*midda kenegged midda*) type punishment.

Here the weight shifts from Elisha to God. In Kings, vicious attacks by animals, especially lions,[16] function as the instrument of heavenly retribution, particularly in response to disregard for the prophetic word. If this is a divine response, we wonder why our episode features not lions but bears.[17]

To be precise, the animals in question are female bears, and such creatures feature elsewhere in Tanakh in the specific context of bereavement: "a bear robbed of her young" – *dov shakul.*[18] Generally a bear won't attack humans, but after a mother bear has lost her young she is highly dangerous. This detail is resonant for our story, as Elisha is newly bereaved, experiencing the painful loss of Elijah, his master; he is metaphorically the bereaved female. For Abarbanel, the two bears, "one for Elijah's honor and the other for Elisha's honor," correspond to the mockery made of the two prophets.

The text here offers no direct critique of the carnage unleashed by the prophet. Did Elisha intend to cause the death of forty-two children, or did he merely invoke God's curse and God chose the severity of the punishment? Accordingly, is God the aggressor, independently upholding and fiercely protecting the reputation of His prophet? The early days of a leader's tenure[19] are highly sensitive and set the tone for his future leadership. Accordingly, we would suggest that in their attack of the "holy

---

16. I Kings 13:24; 20:36; II Kings 17:25.
17. See Amos 5:19, where the lion and bear are mentioned in tandem; similarly, I Sam. 17:36. The Torah talks generically about wild animals (*ḥaya raa, ḥayat hasadeh*) as a menace; see Ex. 23:29; Lev. 26:6, 22; Deut. 7:22. Yochanan Aharoni notes that the last bear inhabiting Mount Hermon was shot in Majdal Shams in 1917.
18. II Sam. 17:8; Hos. 13:8; Prov. 17:12. A further linguistic connection tying the bereavement theme to our story is in the previous episode, which phrases the death and bereavement in Jericho as "*meshakalet*" – from the same Hebrew root as *shakul.*
19. Intriguingly, *Ḥazal* (Exodus Rabba 1:30) suggest that Moses killed the Egyptian (Ex. 2:14) by articulating God's name. Whereas the primary connection between God's name and the Egyptian man rests upon an intertextual parallel with Lev. 24, one feels that this midrash is additionally associating the initiation of Elisha and that of Moses whereby they each take human life at the inception of their leadership.

man of God"[20] these children have committed sacrilege. In response they are struck down, irrespective of their nonculpability.[21]

* * *

The previous chapter charted the chiastic nature of II Kings 2, which depicts Elijah's descent from Gilgal to Transjordan and Elisha's corresponding ascent from Transjordan to Mount Carmel and then to Samaria, where he will be in a position to influence the government. This route reflects Elisha's rise to prophetic status. The jeering of Elisha threatens to deflate and attenuate his leadership position more than his person. It is God's honor that is being eroded. Possibly this goes some way to explaining the fierce violence meted out to the youths.

We have presented two stories that seem contradictory. One portrays a kindhearted, benevolent Elisha. The next describes him in the vein of Elijah – zealous and deadly! One is a miracle of deliverance; the second a miracle of punishment. It is difficult to assess the character of Elisha at this point. Is he the opposite of his master, or a reflection of him? Possibly Elisha himself is trying to decide that question. Does he imitate Elijah's style or does he follow his own inner instinct?

As we shall see in the upcoming chapters, for the most part Elisha generously administers assistance, yet in several instances he responds acerbically.[22] As he assumes the mantle of leadership, he demonstrates that he intends to be a healer. But when his legitimacy is challenged he lashes out, calling upon God to verify his mission and to crush those who challenge his authority.

---

20. II Kings 4:9.
21. Prof. Alexander Rofé, *The Prophetic Stories* (Jerusalem: Magnes Press, 2014), 5 [Hebrew], phrases it succinctly: "Not the ethical categories of good and evil are relevant in this and other stories, but those of sacred and profane." Shemesh cites other biblical precedents in which contact with the sacred realm may be life threatening, for example Mount Sinai (Ex. 19:12–13), the Tabernacle (Num. 1:51; 3:10, 38), the Holy Ark (II Sam. 6:6–7), or the beholding of an angel (Judges 13:22). Similarly, the children here are guilty of sacrilege. She concludes: "I believe the story presents the boys who tease the prophet as deserving of their punishment." See Yael Shemesh, "The Elisha Stories as Saints' Legends," *Journal of Hebrew Scriptures* 8 (2008): 10–12.
22. See II Kings 3:14; 5:26–27; 7:2, 19–20.

> The truth, though, is that the stories are complementary. Only the combination of the two opposed stories provides a full picture of the two facets of the man of God and highlights his full powers.[23]

> Together, the two images suggest the ambiguity of sacred power.[24]

23. Shemesh, "The Elisha Stories as Saints' Legends," 14.
24. Burke O. Long, *II Kings* (*FOTL* 10; Grand Rapids, MI: Wm. B. Erdman, 1991), 33.

II Kings 2 excursus

Is Elijah Immortal?

We cannot leave the dramatic spectacle of Elijah's fiery heavenward ascent without touching upon what became of him.

Jewish tradition and literature is replete with the notion that Elijah can and does revisit this world: A chair is set aside for him at a ritual circumcision,[1] he is said to visit our Seder table,[2] the Talmud describes numerous encounters between Elijah and rabbinic figures, and at the End of Days, Elijah is reputed to return to the world and herald the Messiah's arrival. How did these traditions develop, and is there any biblical basis to them?

HOW DID ELIJAH DIE?

On a straightforward reading of the verses, the "chariot of fire and horses of fire" associated with Elisha's death scene leave little doubt that we are reading of his final moments. And of course, he is never seen again in the Bible. Elijah is most certainly dead! Yet the depiction, "Elijah rose heavenward in a whirlwind" (II Kings 2:11), reads as if he remained alive

1. *Shulḥan Arukh, Yoreh De'ah* 265:11.
2. *Mishna Berura, Oraḥ Ḥayim* 460:10.

on his heavenly journey. Elijah himself talks about being "taken" (2:9) from Elisha, avoiding the standard terminology for death.[3]

The traditional commentators debate the question. Radak contends that Elijah died:

> The storm raised Elijah from earth into the air… above the "ball of fire." There his clothes burned, except his cloak; ***his flesh and his physical form were consumed, and his spirit returned to God.***

Ralbag suggests something very different:

> One cannot understand that [Elijah] was taken to heaven, for a human body cannot be taken there. But rather [when it refers to Elijah's ascent "in a whirlwind" to heaven] it means high in the air as "cities, large and fortified, to the heavens" (Deut. 9:1), or [concerning the Tower of Babel,] "a tower with its peak in the heavens" (Gen. 11:4). ***An angelic force of God raised Elijah to an unknown location and he lives there.***

---

3. See similar language in Gen. 5:24 regarding the death of Enoch. The Midrash there directly compares the "taking" of Enoch with the "taking" of Elijah and asserts that Enoch died. Moreover, midrashic opinions asserting Enoch's eternity are ascribed illegitimacy as gentile or sectarian views:

> Some sectarians asked R. Abbahu: "We do not find that Enoch died." "How so?" he inquired. "[The term] taking is employed here, and also in connection with Elijah," they said. "If you stress the word taking," he answered, "then taking is employed here, while in Ezekiel it is said, 'Behold, I take away from you the desire of your eyes' (Ezek. 24:15)." R. Tanhuma observed, "He answered them well."
>
> A matron asked R. Jose: "We do not find death stated of Enoch?" He replied to her: "If it said, 'And Enoch walked with God,' and no more, I would agree with you. Since, however, it says, 'And he was not, for God took him,' it means that he was no more in the world, [having died,] for God took him." (Genesis Rabba 25:1)

Note that in R. Abbahu's thinking, the term "taking" is applied to Ezekiel's wife, who died. If we apply this to Enoch and Elijah, then this word is indicative of death. *Targum Yonatan* takes a different approach, seeing Enoch as retaining some (angelic) life form.

Indeed, the Talmud brings Resh Lakish's view that "Elijah is not dead" (Moed Katan 26a).

BIBLICAL CUES

The notion that Elijah still lives (in some manner of existence) has deeper roots than is evident from this solitary scene. We shall relate to three further biblical sources:

1. A supernatural aura was associated with Elijah in his own lifetime; people thought he possessed abilities to disappear or even fly away at will, vanishing into the unknown, carried by an undefined "wind" or "spirit of God." This is what Obadiah, Ahab's courtier, says to Elijah: "When I leave you, ***the spirit of God will carry you off*** I don't know where; and... he will not find you" (I Kings 18:12). The fifty disciples suggest an almost identical phenomenon: "Perhaps ***the spirit of God has carried him off*** and cast him upon some mountain or into some valley" (II Kings 2:16).

   A legend existed alongside Elijah of a man who could mysteriously soar through the air by the "spirit of God" and remain alive.

2. During the reign of King Jehoram of Judah, "A letter came to him from Elijah the Prophet" (see II Chr. 21:12–15). This episode most definitely postdates Elijah's heavenly ascent, seeing that Elisha was already the national prophet during the reign of Jehoshaphat, Jehoram's father.[4] How would a letter arrive years after Elijah's demise if he were indeed dead?[5] The easiest solution is that Elijah had written the letter before his death and instructed that it be delivered posthumously. Radak suggests, "Elijah appeared in a prophecy to one of the prophets,

---

4. As is evident from the interaction between King Jehoshaphat and Elisha in II Kings 3.
5. Prof. Sara Japhet suggests: "It seems... probable that the Chronicler had a different view of the chronological pattern... which implies a difference of a few years." See Sara Japhet, *I and II Chronicles* (OTL; Louisville: Westminster / John Knox, 1993), 812.

dictated the letter to him, and told him to write it and deliver it to King Jehoram."

However, Ralbag, Malbim, and even Ibn Ezra[6] suggest that Elijah retained some life form after death:

> This was after he [Elijah] had been "taken" and this explains that ***he is still alive*** and extant, and appears periodically, as in the rabbinic tradition. (Malbim)

3. The third and most explicit source anticipating Elijah's reappearance is found in the closing verses of the book of Malachi, a prophetic text attributed to the era of Ezra[7] (circa 450 BCE) during the Second Temple period, some four centuries after Elijah's demise. Malachi prophesies the sending of Elijah before "the great and terrible day of the Lord," a phrase indicative of an eschatological judgment day:

> Behold, I shall send you the prophet Elijah before the coming of the great and awesome Day of the Lord. He shall restore the heart of fathers to their children, and the heart of children to their fathers – lest I strike the land with destruction. (Mal. 3:23–24)

But from where should Elijah be arriving? And why Elijah? He has not been seen for centuries! What is Elijah's role? Why is he the prophet who should "restore the heart of fathers to their children, and the heart of children to their fathers"?

The issue becomes more entangled as the book of Malachi associates the judgment day with the advent of an angel, the "angel of the covenant":

> "Behold, I shall send My angel (*malakhi*), and he shall clear a path before Me, and suddenly God Whom you seek will come to His Temple. And the angel of the covenant

6. Commentaries on Mal. 3:24.
7. Megilla 15b.

> (*malakh habrit*) in whom you delight – behold, he shall come," says the Lord of Hosts. But who can bear the day of his coming, and who shall be standing when he appears? For he is like a smelter's fire and like the washers' soap....
>
> "Behold, I shall send you the prophet Elijah before the coming of the great and awesome Day of the Lord." (Mal. 3:1–2, 23)

Upon observing this interesting parallelism, one might conclude that Elijah is indeed that angel – the "angel of the covenant"; after all, Elijah had always protested Israel's abrogation of God's covenant (I Kings 19:10, 14)! It is on the basis of what is written in the book of Malachi that Elijah is viewed as the herald of the Messiah, preparing the groundwork for the Messianic age and bolstering Israel before God's judgment day.

POST-BIBLICAL SOURCES

Some post-biblical thinkers view Elijah precisely in the role suggested by Malachi. *Ben Sira,*[8] a popular Jewish text from the second century BCE, recounts Elijah's passing, transitioning directly and effortlessly from II Kings to Malachi:

> You were taken aloft in a whirlwind,
> in a chariot with fiery horses.
> You are destined, it is written, in time to come
> to put an end to wrath before the day of the Lord,
> To turn back the hearts of parents toward their children,
> and to reestablish the tribes of Israel.[9]

A first glance *Ben Sira* is essentially restating what was written in the book of Malachi, but in fact, his formulation extends further than Malachi

8. *Ben Sira*, or *The Wisdom of Sirach*, or *Ecclesiasticus*, was a second-century BCE Jewish work. It was popular in ancient Jewish circles and is quoted several times by the Talmud, but was not canonized in the Tanakh. It was included in the Septuagint and the Catholic bible, and preserved in Greek and Latin. More recently, with the discovery of the Dead Sea Scrolls and the Cairo Geniza, Hebrew segments of the book have been rediscovered.
9. *Ben Sira* 48:9–11.

in two significant spheres: First, it presents Elijah's mission as allaying divine wrath. How is Elijah to allay God's wrath? Second, Elijah restores the tribes of Israel. *Ben Sira* is reading Malachi's "He shall restore the heart of fathers to their children, and the heart of children to their fathers" as the restoration of the twelve tribes – the return of the ten lost tribes[10] and the reunification of Judah with Ephraim.[11]

TO MAKE PEACE IN THE WORLD

In a celebrated mishna, this verse from Malachi stimulates a fascinating rabbinic debate. The second-century R. Yehoshua reports a teaching that he attributes to the earliest of sources:

> R. Yehoshua said: I learned from Rabban Yoḥanan b. Zakkai, who in turn heard it from his teacher, and his teacher from the teacher before him, all the way back to Moses at Sinai, that Elijah does not come to declare people impure or pure, nor to distance people or bring them close, but rather to distance those who have come close by force, and to draw near those who have been distanced by force.
> R. Yehuda said: To bring close, but not to distance.
> R. Shimon says: To solve (halakhic) disputes.
> The sages said: Neither to distance nor to bring close, but rather to make peace in the world. (Eduyot 8:7)

This discussion takes Elijah's role as herald of the messianic era for granted, but it probes what his precise function would be. Based in the aforementioned phrase of "restoring the heart of children to their fathers," R. Yehoshua and R. Yehuda suggest that Elijah will use his prophetic insight to clarify questions of genealogy, identifying the legal status of who is Jewish and who is not. Perhaps this is an extension of *Ben Sira*'s portrayal of Elijah restoring the lost tribes. R. Shimon sees Elijah serving a halakhic function – clarifying legal disputes on a wider scale, throughout the gamut of unresolved halakhic discussion.

10. See his symbolic act relating to all twelve tribes in I Kings 18:31 – although he serves exclusively in the northern kingdom of the ten tribes.
11. See Ezek. 37:16–22; Jer. 3:18; 31:1–8.

The final word, however, goes to the sages, who propose an even wider mission of resolution – not the integrity of the nation nor the clarity of halakha, but rather a comprehensive legacy of world peace![12]

A CONGENIAL ELIJAH

These early sources give us a window into the beginnings of the legend of Elijah, who somehow lives on after his passing, whose role is to rehabilitate the nation. The continuation of this legend is found in numerous aggadic stories in the Talmud and Midrash as well as in mysticism and folklore.[13]

But we should note a remarkable and dramatic shift that has transpired in these Second Temple and Mishnaic texts. In Kings, Elijah is an uncompromising, self-professed zealot, an ardent enemy of the king, impassioned by his dedication to God and his abhorrence of Baal. Moreover, Elijah does not merely blame the king; he accuses Israel of forsaking God's covenant. Elijah uses drought and heavenly fire to convince Israel of God's supremacy. His method and style are intimidating, intolerant, and harsh. It is this characterization of Elijah that leads Abarbanel to explain Elijah's death by fire:

> Elijah … hated [the land] and its people, and prayed for its misfortune. His whole essence was fire. It was this [fire] that he brought down upon Mount Carmel, and which appeared to him at Horeb, and which he cast down upon the officers of fifty. Thus, he did not merit to be buried in the land, not to be enshrouded by its soil, but instead by the fire that came out to receive him.[14]

By the time of the composition of the Mishna, however, Elijah has made a sensational transfiguration to a personality of peace, a man who restores the integrity of the nation and resolves halakhic disputes.

---

12. See *Tiferet Yisrael* (R. Israel Lipschitz) and H. Albek commentaries, who propose that the variant views of the Mishna each emphasize a different phrase in the verses from Malachi.
13. For a comprehensive list of Elijah's role as depicted in the Talmud and Midrash, mysticism and folklore, see *Encylopedia Judaica*, vol. 6 (Jerusalem: Keter, 1972), s.v. "Elijah," cols. 632–42.
14. Commentary on II Kings 2.

How might we explain this dramatic turnabout? What happened to Elijah? One approach suggests that God Himself opposed Elijah's harshness, and it was God who compelled Elijah to see the nation from a different, more positive perspective:

> The Holy One Blessed be He appeared to Elijah and said, "What are you doing here, Elijah?"
>
> He answered, "I have been exceedingly zealous" (I Kings 19:9–10).
>
> The Holy One Blessed be He said, "Will you be zealous forever?... By your life, the people of Israel will [henceforth] perform no circumcision without you seeing it with your own eyes."
>
> On this basis, the sages ruled that a place of honor should be set aside for the "angel of the covenant (*malakh habrit*)," as it is written (Mal. 3:1), "And the angel of the covenant, in whom you delight – behold, he shall come." (*Pirkei DeRabbi Eliezer* 29)

This Midrash depicts God Himself as forcing Elijah to temper his zealous criticism of the Jewish people. Instead of wrongly accusing Israel of abrogating the covenant, God forces Elijah to attend every circumcision, the sign of the covenant, to witness Israel's dedication to the covenant. It is God who educates and transforms Elijah; it is God who compels him to revisit the world and appreciate the virtues of Israel.

Rabbi Elchanan Samet understands this approach as explaining Elijah's non-death and his messianic role:

> Elijah does not die, in order that he will continue to be active amidst the reality of Jewish history in the generations to come, and to amend the zealous prophetic approach that characterizes the period of his activity described in Kings. This amendment will become possible when Elijah returns to his people and becomes aware of the great change that has taken place. This is no longer a nation "straddling the two options" (I Kings 18:21), alternating between worshipping Baal and worshipping God; Ahab and Jezebel (and their like) are no longer the leaders. Instead of a strong nation dwelling securely in its land and exposing itself to

pagan influences, Elijah encounters an abused people, suffering persecution and fighting to survive – precisely because of their stubborn loyalty to God. Then Elijah gathers his supernatural strength to help this persecuted nation and its individual members to withstand their struggle for survival. Instead of being zealous for God, as has been his way throughout Kings, Elijah will now be zealous for the welfare of Israel, and he will act to that end. His arguments in heaven will also be reversed, and he will become Israel's defender before God. Thus he corrects and heals his path. His zealousness will now be whole and perfect, insofar as it will be directed to the welfare of Israel.[15]

15. Samet, *Pirkei Eliyahu*, 562–563.

The Military Campaign against Moab

Places underlined are mentioned in the Mesha Stele

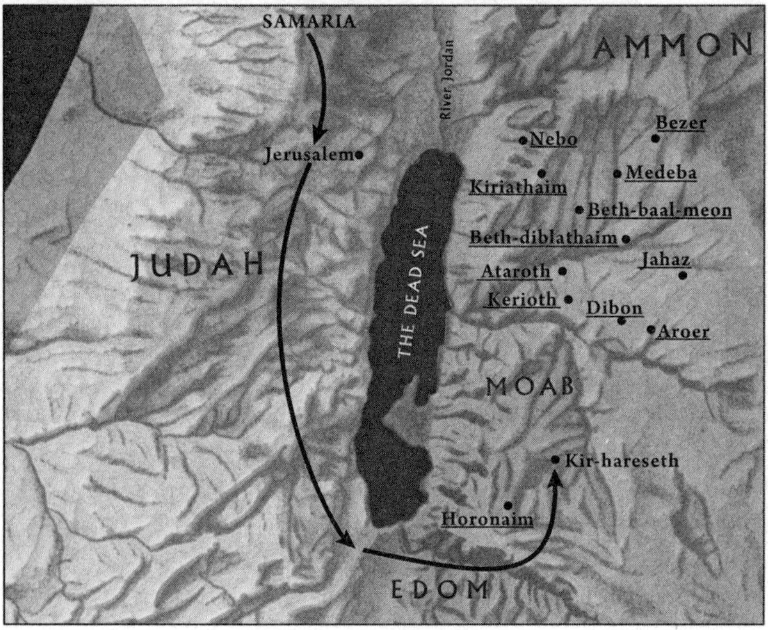

II Kings 3

War with Moab

This chapter chronicles Israel's formidable military campaign against Moab. Under Ahab the kingdom of Israel had dominated Moab. However, following Ahab's death, and afterward during Ahaziah's hapless reign, Mesha, king of Moab, rebels and refuses to pay its annual tribute.[1] Now King Jehoram wages war to restore his former colony.

***

Jehoram joins with King Jehoshaphat of Judah and a third ally, the king of Edom, leading their armies to attack Moab. They take a long, tortuous route through Edomite territory, skirting the southern tip of the Dead Sea toward Moab's southern border.

1. II Kings 1:1; 3:4–5. The incredibly high numbers of livestock that make up the annual tribute may be a way of illustrating Moab's complete vassalage to Israel, and the obvious desire to break free of that arrangement. See M. Cogan and H. Tadmor, *II Kings: A New Translation with Introduction and Commentary* (The Anchor Bible, vol. 11; New York: Doubleday & Co., 1988), 43.

INTRODUCING JEHORAM

The opening formulaic lines of our chapter (II Kings 3:1–3) offer a mixed assessment in their religious depiction of Jehoram. On the one hand, "[Jehoram] did what was evil to the Lord." But surprisingly, his removal of the sacred pillars to Baal is indicative of his rejection of his parents' idolatry:[2]

> He [Jehoram] did what was evil to the Lord, yet not like his father and mother, for he removed the pillars of Baal that his father had made. However, he clung to the sins which Jeroboam ben Nebat caused Israel to commit. (3:2–3)

Indicative of Jehoram's positive affinity to God is that when the allied forces hit a snag, finding themselves stranded in the desert without water, Jehoram repeatedly references God, not Baal:

> Alas! God (YHVH) has summoned these three kings to hand them over to the Moabites. (3:10)

But in contrast to this, Elisha disparages the king, refusing to assist him on account of his idolatry:

> Elisha said to the king of Israel, "What have you to do with me? Go to your father's prophets, or your mother's prophets."
> But the king of Israel said, "Don't! For God (YHVH) has brought these three kings together only to deliver them into the hands of Moab."
> Elisha answered, "As the Lord of Hosts lives, whom I serve, were it not that I respect the King Jehoshaphat of Judah,[3] I wouldn't look at you." (3:13–14)

2. Radak (ad loc.) comments that he removed the Baal pillars dedicated by his father but he could not remove the Ashera of his mother, since she was still alive and she worshipped at it. This comment expresses the complicated reality of idolatry in the northern kingdom and ably illustrates how Jehoram's efforts to eliminate pagan symbols would have been met with steadfast opposition and a thorny political struggle.
3. Elisha's disdain for the idolatrous Jehoram contrasts with his open respect for King Jehoshaphat, whose religious fealty is beyond question. Jehoshaphat campaigned

Elisha's biting words give us the impression that Jehoram affiliates absolutely with Baal, merely continuing his parents' religious regime. After all, in the thick of crisis, it is Jehoshaphat who invites Elisha to prophesy (3:11);[4] Jehoram never entertained the notion of an appeal to God by means of a prophet. And yet again, Jehoram's response to Elisha talks of God. *Targum Yonatan* beautifully amplifies Jehoram's rebuttal – "Don't!" – as a dramatic appeal for Elisha to pray to God:

> "Please! Do not mention our sins at this moment. Appeal for mercy on our behalf."[5]

How shall we assess Jehoram? Is he an exponent of God or Baal? Is Elisha's negative evaluation unwarranted? It is difficult to gain an accurate picture.

WATER

Let us return to the war march to Moab. The advancing armies suffer a crippling setback – they run out of water. One wonders how they could have committed such a basic logistical error. A seven-day march (II Kings 3:9)

---

vigorously against the cult of Baal and actively fostered religious advancement in his kingdom (II Chr. 17:3–9; ch.19). At the same time, Jehoshaphat believed in national unity, having a long-standing policy of partnership with the northern royal house. He collaborated in military coalition with Ahab (I Kings 22:4), on a naval project with Ahaziah (II Chr. 20:35–37), and now with Jehoram. Jehoshaphat also forged family ties with the line of Ahab; his son married Ahab's daughter (II Kings 8:18). He overlooks the religious dissonance between the two kingdoms despite prophetic censure for this union (II Chr. 19:2; 20:37).

4. There are several parallels between this story and the final war between Ahab and Aram in I Kings 22. In both instances Jehoshaphat joins enthusiastically with the king of Israel. See Jehoshaphat's response here: "I will do what you do, my troops shall be your troops, my horses shall be your horses" (II Kings 3:7), which is identical to I Kings 22:4. In both cases, the king of Judah asks, "Isn't there a prophet of God (YHVH) here?" (I Kings 22:7; II Kings 3:11). In both stories the prophet shows antagonism toward the king of Israel. We may be surprised then at the dissonance between the two outcomes. Whereas I Kings 22 results only in negativism toward Ahab, our chapter shows Elisha in support of the armies of Israel. Despite Elisha's sentiments, it seems that God views Jehoram in greater favor than Ahab.
5. Commentary on II Kings 3:13.

through the desert is impossible without access to water.[6] They are certainly aware of the hostile and arid desert conditions! We must presume that the itinerary was planned to pass through a wadi or spring known for its reliable and constant water supply, but it was found to be dry unexpectedly. Alternatively, the route was surprisingly inaccessible; sometimes after a flash flood, a mountain passage becomes impassable due to fallen debris.

The kings consult Elisha, who predicts a swift resolution to the crisis: "You shall see no wind, you shall see no rain, and yet the wadi shall be filled with water" (3:17). Most likely he is referring to a flash flood that would bring rainwater from the Jordanian hills down toward the Jordan Rift Valley.[7]

The nighttime rain that fell far away in the hills, undetected by Moab, flows down to the camp by morning. When the Moabite sentries detect the pools in the morning light, they interpret their reddish hue as blood. Why did the water appear as red? It could be that the floodwaters drew red mud in their wake, coloring the water stream; alternatively, the reflection of the color of the picturesque mountains of Moab gave the water a reddish tint in the morning light. The Moabites draw a radical conclusion. They assume that infighting among the attacking Israel-Judah-Edom coalition resulted in a bloodbath and that they are witnessing a huge pool of blood! In response they advance to plunder the Israelite camp.

Things are not as they seem, however. When Mesha's troops arrive they are met by the Israelite counterforce, which decimates Moab, pushing the Moabite army back into its last stronghold.

> Israel rose up and fought them until they fled, and they invaded the land and slaughtered Moab. They destroyed the towns ... only

---

6. See Ex. 15:22, where "they walked for three days in the wilderness and found no water."
7. This phenomenon is familiar to us from the western "Israel" side of the Dead Sea. When it rains in Hebron and Jerusalem, the drainage through the wadis of the Judean Desert generate fierce flash floods in the valleys near the Dead Sea. A flash flood can happen near the Dead Sea while the sky is absolutely clear, with no sign of rain, so it is entirely feasible that "water suddenly came from the direction of Edom, and the land was covered by the water" (3:20), and the Moabite army was totally unaware of the presence of a body of water in that vicinity.

> the wall of Kir-Haresheth[8] was left, and the catapults surrounded it to destroy it. (3:24–25)

SCORCHED-EARTH POLICY

Elisha's prophecy – part-prediction, part-instruction – is that Israel will utterly ravage the Moabite landscape:

> You will overthrow every fortified city and every major town. You will cut down every good tree, stop up all the springs, and ruin every good field with stones. (3:19)

These words are fulfilled to the letter:

> They destroyed the towns, and each man threw a stone on every good field until it was covered. They stopped up all the springs and cut down every good tree. (3:25)

This prophetic injunction is problematic, however, in that it seems to contravene an explicit ordinance that guides the Torah's ethics of war:

> When you lay siege to a city for a long time, fighting against it to capture it, do not destroy its trees by putting an ax to them, because you can eat their fruit. Do not cut them down. Are the trees of the field people, that you should besiege them? (Deut. 20:19)

The mitzva of *bal tashḥit* (Do not destroy) mandates a besieging army to respect the countryside, and specifically to preserve the fruit trees. Why would Elisha issue a policy of total devastation, making the Moabite landscape absolutely uninhabitable, in contravention of a Torah law?

---

8. This city is also identified as Kir-Moab (Is. 15:1) or Kir-Heres (Is. 16:11; Jer. 48:31). It was the capital of Moab, now known as Kerak, situated on the King's Highway (Num. 20:17, 21:22) in the south of the country. The steep natural inclines of this mountaintop fortress would have made it particularly difficult to capture.

> Even though the Torah says, "Do not destroy its trees," this was a direct divine instruction of a provisional nature. (Ralbag)
>
> This is a law only for an army in a siege situation. (Radak)
>
> In this situation [God] permitted [destroying trees] because they were contending with a disgraceful and lowly nation, as it states, "Do not seek their welfare or goodness" (Deut. 23:7); this refers to their trees. (Rashi)

All the classic commentaries assert that the war against Moab was anomalous in its aggression, demanding nonstandard rules of engagement. But why? Radak proposes that *bal tashḥit* applies in a protracted siege, not in a short and focused military assault. But Rashi suggests that there was something "disgraceful," unusually degenerate, about Moab. What could it be?

THE MESHA STELE

The answer may be found in a stunning archaeological discovery, the Mesha Stele. In 1868, a Prussian missionary named Fredrik Klein identified a remarkable historical artifact some twenty miles east of the Dead Sea, at Dibhan, Jordan. It was a smashed basalt monument, four feet in height, inscribed with thirty-three lines of text. When it was reassembled and deciphered, archaeologists determined that this was a victory tablet in which King Mesha records the Moabite revolt against the dynasty of Ahab, king of Israel. He attributes his triumph to his god, Chemosh. It is a remarkable piece of textual evidence, if only because it corroborates the Tanakh so strongly – mentioning Mesha and Ahab, and also the Tetragrammaton. The stele narrates Moab's vicious revolution against Israel in which Moab attacks Israelite towns and villages throughout the Transjordan, killing the Israelite inhabitants and humiliating Israel's God:

> I fought against the city [Atarot] and captured it. And I killed all the people of the city as a sacrifice for Chemosh and for Moab.... And Chemosh said to me, Go take Nebo against Israel, and I went

> in the night and I fought against it from the break of day till noon, and I took it. And I killed in all seven thousand men, but I did not kill the women and maidens, for I devoted them to Ashtar-Chemosh; and I took from it the vessels of YHVH, and offered them before Chemosh.

We may propose the following reconstruction of the events.[9] After Ahab's death and during Ahaziah's reign, Mesha stages his bloody rebellion against Israel as recorded in the Mesha Stele. This revolution is characterized by widespread slaughter of the Israelites living in Transjordan as well as the abasement of the God of Israel.

Jehoram launches a war to regain control. If Moab's strength is concentrated in the northern territories, as recorded by the Mesha Stele, this goes some way to explain why the Israelite force attacks specifically from the south. However, whereas for the king, the campaign is about regaining prestige, recovering lost territory, and recouping tax monies, the motivation for the prophet and for God is most certainly about avenging the religious insult wielded by Moab.

And so, as prophesied by Elisha, God issues a writ of devastation to Moab to avenge Moab's blasphemy and disgrace of God.[10] This war is indeed extraordinary, and only on this basis can we better comprehend the inconsonant divine directive to destroy fields, trees, and water sources.

FAILURE

However, as the Israelite forces are poised to conquer the final stronghold, King Mesha makes a desperate move which unexpectedly generates a military upheaval. The armies withdraw, and Israel's imminent victory disintegrates:

9. See also Cogan and Tadmor, *II Kings*, 50–51.
10. This episode has much in common with I Kings 20. There too, Israel seemed stuck against a bitter adversary, Aram. God assured Israel of victory: "And you shall know that I am the Lord" (I Kings 20:28). Israel defeats Aram, but at the critical moment Ahab releases their king. This obscures the divine victory, as it leaves the victory elusive in the public eye. In contrast, the scorched-earth policy would be a means of asserting a very public and uncontestable victory in God's name.

> When the king of Moab saw that the battle had gone against him, he took with him seven hundred swordsmen to break through to the king of Edom, but they failed. Then he took his firstborn son, who was to succeed him as king, and offered him as a sacrifice upon the city wall. There was great wrath against Israel; they broke camp and returned to their own land. (II Kings 3:26–27)

Mesha's sacrifice of his son turns the tables of the war, and Israel fails in its effort to overwhelm Moab. However, why did this pagan act lead to Israel's retreat? What was it that frustrated the Israelite assault? And how might we identify the "great wrath against Israel"? Was it God's wrath? The wrath of Moab? And how was it manifest?

"GREAT WRATH"

The first option is to understand the "great wrath" as invoked and ordained by God.[11] This is, of course, difficult; why would Mesha's appeal to his god Chemosh incur divine wrath on the part of the God of Israel? The Talmud (Sanhedrin 39b) raises two options. The first is that Mesha sacrifices to Chemosh.[12] In this reading, Mesha's idolatrous sacrifice recalls Israel's persistent idolatry and stimulates God's disinterest in assisting Israel, as if He was reminded that Israel is no better than Moab. Alternatively, and more unlikely, Mesha sacrifices to the Israelite God directly.[13]

---

11. The noun *ketzef* is predominantly an expression of divine wrath, especially in this grammatical form of *ketzef al*; see Num. 17:11; 18:5; Deut. 29:27; Zech. 1:2, 15; 7:12; I Chr. 27:24; II Chr. 24:18; 29:8; 32:26. On the other hand, the root K-TZ-F used as a verb may indicate human anger, as seen in Gen. 40:2; 41:10; Ex. 16:20; Lev. 10:16; Num. 31:14; II Kings 5:11; 13:19; Jer. 37:15; Est. 1:12.
12. Some academic scholars have suggested that the original Hebrew read: "And there was a great wrath *of Chemosh* against Israel," indicating that this text originally assumed that Chemosh had power even over Israel; this is reflective of pagan theology (J. Gra, *I and II Kings*, 3rd ed. [Philadelphia: Old Testament Library, 1979]). Prof. Yehezkel Kaufmann has strongly rejected this opinion because the attribution of any power to a foreign deity is a total anathema to the Bible: "The wrath of Chemosh is a totally non-biblical image" ("From the Crucible of Biblical Creativity," in *Mi-Kivshonah shel ha-Yeẓirah ha-Mikra'it* [Tel Aviv: Dvir, 1966], 206 [Hebrew]).
13. The midrashic work *Pesikta DeRav Kahana, Ki Tissa 5,* suggests that Mesha drew the concept of sacrificing a child from the traditions of Israel:

In this scenario, his sacrifice of his son, a painful loss for him, highlights Israel's lack of commitment to God: "The king of Moab spared no mercy on his son in order to perform God's will, but Israel angers Him every day" (Radak, Sanhedrin 39b).

In truth, both of these explanations are difficult to accept. Why would Mesha's pagan child-sacrifice stimulate a divine plague against Israel? Had the text listed the crime of Israel's idolatry at this juncture there might be room to support this reading, but without that information, the notion that Mesha's sacrifice would trigger God's wrath against Israel, whether the offering had been directed to Chemosh or to God, seems misplaced.

In a second approach, the "great wrath" is a human "wrath," a renewed morale and determination of the Moabite forces as they make a final onslaught against their attackers. The sight of their king slaughtering and sacrificing his own son spurs and intensifies their resolve to triumph, as they sense both the desperation of their situation and the possibility of their gods coming to their aid. The ferocity of the Moabite resurgence is described as "great wrath," and it rebuffs the Israelite assault, ending the war.

EDOM'S FURY

Radak[14] offers a third approach, linking Mesha's sacrifice (3:27) to the previous verse in which he sought to attack the king of Edom. Radak explains that the King of Moab did not sacrifice his own son; rather, it was the king of Edom's son whom he killed.

> [Mesha] asked his advisors, "What is the secret of this nation that they are subject to these miracles?" They answered, "Their father Abraham offered his son as a sacrifice." He [Mesha] said: "I will do the same."

This midrash is based on the parallelism of sacrificing of a child both in the *Akeda* (the Binding of Isaac; Gen. 22) and in our chapter. However, the attribution of such motivation to Mesha has absolutely no grounding in the text. Moreover, the Talmud (Taanit 4a) conjoins the three biblical instances of child sacrifice – Abraham, Jephthah (Judges 11), and Mesha – and emphatically asserts that human sacrifice totally negates divine intent.

14. In a touching personal comment, Radak attributes his approach to both his father and "my teacher, my brother R. Moshe." His approach is shared by the Malbim.

We can recount the events in Radak's approach in the following way: Mesha frantically seeks a way to break the allied assault. With an attack force of seven hundred swordsmen, he launches an offensive against the Edomite camp. The attack itself fails; however, in the military engagement, Moab succeeds in abducting the son of the king of Edom. Mesha takes the youth and burns him upon the wall in full public view and not upon the city altar; it isn't a religious act but rather a publicity stunt, a piece of psychological warfare designed to shock and intimidate his attackers.

As Edom look on and watch their crown prince being burned, they sense humiliation. The "great fury" is a metaphor for Edom's bitter accusation of Israel. Edom blame Israel and Judah for insufficiently coming to their ally's defense, allowing their crown prince to be killed. With this infighting, the military coalition dissolves, collapsing in a state of mutual recrimination. It is then that Mesha's brilliant, if nefarious, tactic – not God's fury – dismantles the allied coalition, bringing the entire campaign to a dismal close.

The Radak's reading nicely echoes Moab's earlier premonition: "The kings are utterly destroyed; they have killed one another" (II Kings 3:23). It seems that Moab were aware that the coalition was prone to discord. With this public execution, Mesha finds a way to unravel the unity of his attackers.

AN AMBIVALENT CHAPTER

As we stand back and look at this chapter as a whole, we sense a pervading ambiguity to its storyline. First, is the king of Israel idolatrous or God-fearing? Second, is God with the armies of Israel or not? On the one hand, the Israelite forces find themselves stranded without water, an error interpreted by Jehoram as a signal of divine disfavor (3:10, 13). On the other hand, water is provided miraculously; surely a sign that God is with Israel. Third, Elisha prophesies a crushing blow to Moab, but ultimately the allied force abandons the attack with an inconclusive victory. We sense conflicting strands here. Was God in support of this campaign or not? The storyline seems to present incongruent messages.

Rabbi Elchanan Samet addresses this issue:

> The termination of Israel's dominance of Moab was a process that God had no interest in bringing to a halt; it was one of the primary manifestations of the crumbling of the Omride dynasty, something which had been foretold by Elijah[15] and Michaiah.[16] Thus, not only was the purpose of the war undesirable but its objective would not be met. The divine rage against Jehoram and his aspirations to restore the grandeur of his father's kingdom by reassuming sovereignty over Moab found expression in the thirst that attacked the military force and in Elisha's irate response....
>
> The scorched-earth policy on southern Moab suggests that the Israelite forces were to have no intent of remaining in the captured territory. [Elisha's] prophecy directs the kings and their armies toward battle, emphasizing the true religious motive behind the war – to avenge God's vengeance of Moab.[17]

Samet suggests a dual motive for the war with Moab. The religious incentive for the campaign, to punish Moab for their murder and blasphemy, met with divine approval, and this is what Elisha prophesied. But the political objective to restore Israelite control over its former colony, thereby boosting the Omride kingdom, was opposed by God and as such, Israel fail to achieve a conclusive military victory. This ambivalence goes a long way to explain the strange, antithetical outcome of this military campaign.

PROPHECY AND MUSIC

When Elisha is invited by the kings to prophesy, he requests some musical accompaniment:[18] "Now, get me a musician" (II Kings 15). The employment of music in the pursuit of prophecy is a well-documented phenomenon. Saul meets a band of prophets prior to his coronation:

---

15. I Kings 21:19–22.
16. Ibid., 22:19–25.
17. *Pirkei Elisha,* 114–17.
18. The commentaries explain that Elisha had gotten angry in his encounter with Jehoram, and "a person who gets angry... if he is a prophet, his prophecy will elude him" (Pesaḥim 66b).

> A band of prophets coming down ... and before them will be lyres, timbrels, flutes, and harps, and they will be prophesying. (I Sam. 10:5)[19]

We may surmise that music generates happiness, which is one of the conditions for prophecy. But why? What is the relationship between the two? Maimonides explains that music arouses feelings of calm, joy, and an elevated spirit:

> Prophecy does not come to those who are miserable or lethargic, but only to those who are happy.[20] Therefore, the sons of prophets would have before them harps, drums, and flutes, and would seek prophecy. (*Mishneh Torah*, Laws of the Foundations of the Torah 7:4)

The relationship of music to mood and temperament is well known. King Saul resorted to musical relief when he was plagued by bouts of "evil spirit."[21] But music is more than a palliative; it can take a person into a higher, spiritual state of being. In the book of Chronicles we read of King David's preparations for the Temple, and the musicians he employs:

> David ... set apart the sons of Asaph, and of Heman, and of Jeduthun for the service [of the Temple], who *prophesied* with lyres, with harps, and with cymbals ... the sons of Asaph ... who *prophesied* under the direction of the king. Of Jeduthun ... who *prophesied* with the lyre in thanksgiving and praise to the Lord. (I Chr. 25:1–5)

19. See also I Sam. 6:16; 18:10, in which David's playing of the harp alleviates Saul's "evil spirit." We also see the ecstatic bringing of the Ark to Jerusalem accompanied by music in II Sam. 6.
20. See Pesaḥim 117a.
21. I Sam. 16:16–17; 18:10; 19:9.

These three Levites are musicians and composers of religious song. Their names are familiar to us as authors of selected chapters of Psalms. But in a fascinating twist of vocabulary, the verb for their musical work is from the Hebrew root N-B-A, usually indicative of prophecy. It almost sounds there as if music and prophecy are synonymous.

Music is intrinsic to the book of Psalms, and of course, the word "psalm" is derived from the Latin term for a stringed instrument. Numerous chapters in Psalms speak of song and musical instruments.[22] Similarly, music was a key component of the Temple service, for example the singing of Hallel during the paschal sacrifice (Mishna Pesaḥim 5:7), the musical procession of the First Fruits (Mishna Bikkurim 3:4), the daily song (Mishna Tamid 6:6–7), and the joyous water-drawing ceremony on the holiday of Sukkot (Mishna Sukka 5:1, 4). In more recent centuries, music has been elevated to a sacred status by the *niggunim* of hasidic courts. However, it is here that the Tanakh emphasizes the specific relationship between prophecy and music, a connection which has wider reverberations in our connection to God.

22. Including Ps. 6:1; 33:2; 43:4; 57:9; 81:3; 92:4; 108:3; 144:9; 147:7; 149:3; 150:3–5.

II Kings 4

Elisha: Prophet of Miracles

Our chapter narrates four separate episodes, each of which depict Elisha assisting individuals or groups by miraculous means:

1. 4:1–8 The Widow and the Oil
2. 4:9–37 The Shunammite Woman and Her Son
3. 4:38–41 Poison in the Pot
4. 4:42–3 Providing Bread

These four stories are carefully structured in two groups. The first pair concern women and their children[1] and both vividly mirror Elijah's miracles.[2]

1. Other points of connection between the first two stories: In both episodes, the woman refers to herself as "your maidservant" (II Kings 4:2, 16), and Elisha responds, "What can I/we do for you?" (ibid., 4:2, 13). In both, life is extended to a child: In the first, the widow's children are saved from slavery, and in the second, the Shunammite woman is provided with a son, who later dies and is miraculously revived. In both stories, the miracle is preconditioned by the closing of the door (ibid., 4:4–5, 21).
2. The multiplication of flour and oil (I Kings 17:11–16) and the revival of the son of the widow in Tzarefat (ibid., 17:17–24). See below for a detailed comparison.

The second group narrates two short food miracles among the community of the prophets, the *Benei HaNevi'im*, led by Elisha.[3]

THE WIDOW AND THE OIL (4:1–8)

> A certain woman, the wife of one of the disciples of the prophets, cried out to Elisha: "Your servant my husband is dead, and you know how your servant feared the Lord.[4] And now a creditor is coming to seize my two children as slaves."[5] Elisha said to

3. In an alternative ordering of the chapter, the four stories form a chiasm A-B-B-A. The first and final stories are linked thematically and linguistically: In both, food multiplies in a miraculous manner to provide for the needy. In the story of the widow, a small amount of oil continues to pour out and Elisha says (II Kings 4:7), "You and your children shall live from the remainder (*notar*)." Similarly, in the final, fourth episode, bread that should not feed one hundred men multiples miraculously, as Elisha says (ibid., 4:43–44), "They shall eat and shall leave over (*vehoter*)... and they did leave over (*vehotiru*)." Likewise, the second and third stories are linked by themes of life and death: The death and resurrection of the Shunammite's son (ibid., 4:9–37) would match the "poison [lit., death] in the pot" (ibid., 4:4), which threatens the "sons of the prophets." The prophet then removes the threat of death. Additionally, in both episodes, the trouble starts when one "goes out" (ibid., 4:18, 39), and both explicate the theme of the prophet's lack of knowledge (ibid., 4:27, 39).
4. Midrashic sources identify the deceased husband as Obadiah, Ahab's minister (I Kings 18:4), who endangered his life to save and feed one hundred prophets of God (*Targum Yonatan* 4:1; *Pesikta DeRav Kahana* 2:5; Exodus Rabba 31:4, as cited in Rashi, Radak, Ralbag, and others. Our earliest source for this tradition is in *Antiquities of the Jews* IX, 4:2). Accordingly, the dead husband's debt was incurred as a result of loans taken to finance the food for the prophets. One textual link is that the husband was "God-fearing" just as Obadiah is "exceedingly God-fearing" (I Kings 18:3). Possibly, though, *Ḥazal* conflated the clandestine nature of both stories: Elisha's oil produced behind closed doors mirrors Obadiah's secret provisions for the prophets. Following this connection, God recompenses Obadiah's loyalty by miraculously sustaining his family. The connection with I Kings 18 may be bolstered by the reference in II Kings 4:42–43 of Elisha feeding one hundred men of the prophetic community.

   In the final analysis, however, there is no hard textual or contextual need to identify the husband as Obadiah, Ahab's minister; he is never explicitly identified as a member of the clan of prophets. To include the anonymous woman's deceased husband with the known Obadiah would fit in well to the genre of midrash whereby unnamed biblical characters are commonly identified with named ones (Yitzchak Heineman, *Darkhei Aggada* [Jerusalem: Magnes Press, 1974], 27–35 [Hebrew]).
5. Just as in Jericho, the widow does not state her request directly, but merely presents her harsh situation to the prophet. Rofé, *The Prophetic Stories*, 6, notes: "The attitude

> her, "What can I do for you? Tell me, what do you have in the house?" She replied, "Your maidservant has nothing at all in the house, except a jug of oil." "Go," he said, "and borrow vessels outside, from all your neighbors, empty vessels, and not too few. Then go in and shut the door behind you and your children, and pour [oil] into all those vessels, removing each one as it is filled." She went away and shut the door behind her and her children. They kept bringing [vessels] to her and she kept pouring. When the vessels were full, she said to her son, "Bring me another vessel." He answered her, "There are no more vessels"; and the oil stopped. She came and told the man of God, and he said, "Go sell the oil and pay your debt, and you and your children can live on the rest." (II Kings 4:1–7)[6]

The story begins with a disturbing glimpse of the cruel socioeconomic reality of ancient Israel. One of Elisha's disciples has died, leaving a widow and children; the family has accrued debts and his widow cannot repay the loan. Now, without assets and with no easy means of income, the lender threatens to seize her children and sell them as slaves. Our story emphasizes how this widow "cries out" to Elisha; her cry connects us to the book of Exodus in which God, speaking in the grammatical first person, threatens direct retribution if the outcry of a widow is ignored:

> You shall not ill-treat any widow or orphan. If you do mistreat them, I will heed their outcry as soon as they cry out to Me, and My anger shall blaze forth and I will put you to the sword, and your own wives shall become widows and your children orphans. (Ex. 22:21–23)

---

of fear and admiration toward the Man of God is also evident in the way in which he is addressed. Instead of a direct request for his assistance, his petitioners merely state their troubles. This indirect appeal expresses the intense faith of the common people in the ability of the Man of God to render aid and succor, but at the same time allows him the possibility of not intervening and still preserving his self-respect."

6. For a wonderful literary analysis of this story, see Yael Shemesh, "Elisha and the Miraculous Jug of Oil (II Kings 4:1–7)," *Journal of Hebrew Scriptures* 8 (2008).

But the linkage between Exodus and our story intensifies when we observe that our story concerns a moneylender, termed a *nosheh*. In the subsequent verses in Exodus, the text addresses and significantly regulates the business conduct of the *nosheh*:

> If you lend money to My people, to the poor among you, do not act toward them as a creditor (*nosheh*); exact no interest from them. If you take your neighbor's garment in pledge, you must return it to him before the sun sets; it is his only clothing, the sole covering for his skin. In what else shall he sleep? Therefore, if he cries out to Me, I will pay heed, for I am compassionate. (Ex. 22:24–26)

Acting as a standard "creditor" means charging interest[7] and taking a pledge to secure the investment.[8] When the loan is taken by the poor and destitute, the Torah outlaws these practices. In our story, the widow has "nothing at all in the house, except a jug of oil." She precisely fulfills a situation in which her robe would conceivably be the "sole covering for her skin." If the Torah restricts the lender from withholding her garment as a pledge, he is hardly within his rights in seizing her children![9]

---

7. The Torah bans lending with interest to a kinsman, calling it *neshekh* because it bites – *noshekh* – leaving the poor absolutely destitute. See Lev. 25:36–37; Deut. 23:20.
8. In a remarkable discovery which gives living evidence of this Jewish law, Prof. Joseph Naveh uncovered the "Mesad HaShavayu Ostracon," an ancient letter written on a pottery shard in excellent biblical Hebrew, dated to the seventh century BCE. It documents an appeal by a farmer to a local governor requesting that a confiscated pledge be returned. See J. Naveh, "A Hebrew Letter from the Seventh Century BC," in *Israel Exploration Journal* 10:3 (1960): 129–39.
9. Does the Torah ban the sale of children into slavery? Ex. 21:7 seems to permit a parent selling a child into slavery. However, a careful reading of the passage reveals that this is in fact a type of marriage arrangement. Lev. 25:39–45 makes it clear that Jewish children cannot be sold even in situations of debt. The only case of someone forcibly being sold is a thief; see Ex. 22:2.

   And yet, there is evidence that Jewish slavery was a social reality in ancient Israel, a phenomenon that was condemned at times by religious leaders. Jeremiah urges the people of Jerusalem to release their Jewish slaves (Jer. 34). Nehemiah too, when he takes up the governance of Judea, discovers that children and wives are being enslaved

Elisha certainly "hears" the woman's plight, but he is not God and he cannot punish the creditor. Instead, he turns to alleviate the widow's crisis by providing for her financially, via miraculous means.

EMPTY VESSELS, AND NOT TOO FEW!

Elisha instructs the desperate widow to collect vessels from her neighbors. How did she respond to Elisha's directive and his prediction of a miracle? Did she believe the prophet? The text reflects the challenge she faced in fully trusting him.

Elisha's Instruction	**The Widow's Actions**
Go	She went away
borrow vessels outside, from all your neighbors, empty vessels, and not too few.	—
Then go in and shut the door behind you and your children,	and shut the door behind her and her children.
and pour [oil] into *all those vessels*, removing each one as it is filled.	... she kept pouring. When the vessels were full ...

Elisha instructs her to "Go, borrow vessels outside, from *all* your neighbors, empty vessels, *and not too few*. Then go in and shut the door behind you and your children" (II Kings 4:3). The impression is that she should procure as many containers as possible. Her response is this: "She went away and shut the door behind her and her children" (4:5). What is missing from the verse? Did she indeed borrow extensively from the neighbors? Malbim points out:

---

to repay loans, and he sets his efforts to end this human enslavement: "We [Persian Jewry] have done our best to buy back our Jewish brothers who were sold to the nations; will you now sell your brothers so that they must be sold [back] to us?" (Neh. 5:8). In response, he sets a personal example and forgoes loans that he had issued (ibid., 5:10–11).

For the dissonance between prophetic sources that eschew slavery absolutely, and the Torah which seems to accept a regulated slavery, see Rabbi Yuval Cherlow, *Looketh on the Heart* (Tel Aviv: Yedioth Ahronoth / Chemed, 2007), 154–57 [Hebrew]; and Rabbi Jonathan Sacks, http://www.rabbisacks.org/covenant-conversation-behar-bechukotei-the-chronological-imagination.

> She borrowed only a few vessels, as she says, "Bring me another vessel." He answered her, "There are no more vessels."[10]

Indeed, Elisha instructs the widow to pour oil into all those vessels – "*kol hakeilim*" (4:4); but she fills only *the* vessels – "*hakeilim*" (4:6). It is easy to imagine and appreciate her reluctance in borrowing a maximal number of vessels from the neighbors. She might be skeptical of the probability of the miracle's effectiveness, or embarrassed to explain it to her neighbors.[11] Alternatively, she may have simply been hurrying, feeling an urgent need to know whether Elisha's extraordinary promise would indeed be fulfilled and her children rescued. Had she collected more vessels, the miracle would have been greater in scope. This scene impresses upon us that a miracle's effect is proportionate to the faith invested in it. The beneficiary must do his or her part in procuring the vessels and pouring the oil, so that God may enact the miracle.[12]

SHUTTING THE DOOR

Elisha commands the woman to "shut the door," and she is to continue to pour without stopping; that is why her son is passing her vessels the entire time. One wonders why she had to close the door and why she must pour continuously. Moreover, Elisha begins by saying "What do you have in the house?" to which she replies, "Nothing at all in the house, except a jug of oil." Elisha utilizes her meager possessions as the core of the miracle. Why is this method chosen? If she had no oil whatsoever, could Elisha have not have generated a miracle?

> The honor of a miracle is that it happens in a hidden manner. (Rashi, II Kings 4:4)

---

10. Commentary on II Kings 4:6.
11. Could Elisha's insistence on borrowing empty vessels from the neighbors be symbolic of their empty-handed treatment of the widow and a wake-up call to extend her some assistance? Had they supported her she may not have needed to resort to a miracle.
12. Some have noted a connection between this miracle of the oil and the cruse of oil in the Hannukah story (Shabbat 21b). There too, the divine miracle was predicated upon human effort.

> Because it is the practice of prophets to enact a miracle based on an existent thing, so that there should not be a miracle *ex nihilo*. (Abarbanel ad loc.)

> And this is the manner of all miracles in Torah and Prophets, that man does that which he can perform, and the rest is left to God. (Nahmanides, Gen. 6:19)

This presents an intriguing dichotomy. On the one hand, a supernatural act is being enacted; a diminutive volume of oil cannot multiply by natural means. On the other hand, it must happen out of sight, in private, "in a hidden manner." As the oil multiplies, the jug continues to pour in a steady flow, so that even observers of the miracle fail to identify a blatant act of creation. For the casual observer, all seems normal. Undoubtedly, God performs the miracle, but it is partially obscured. Moreover, the instruction to borrow containers from the neighbors communicates the fact that "this miracle will happen only once!" (Ralbag, II Kings 4:2).[13] Similarly, in the next episode, Elisha employs the selfsame gesture of closing the door, as he performs the revival of the boy in private (4:33).

ELISHA'S MIRACLES

As our study of the Elisha stories progresses, we cannot but observe that he is constantly performing miracles. The four stories of this chapter compound the events of previous chapters: Elisha's splitting of the Jordan River, his healing of the spring of Jericho, the bears that burst out of the woods, and the miraculous waters that save the Israelite army. This miracle-making is a technique unlike anything we have witnessed previously in Tanakh, and it becomes Elisha's hallmark. Although Elijah and other prophets such as Moses and Joshua before him performed miracles and wonders, these wonders were employed sporadically, choreographed to maximal impact as spectacles of exceptional divine power. Moreover, the supernatural

13. As opposed to the story with Elijah where the flour jar and oil jug continue to refill, here the miracle is limited to a single act of pouring. There the widow needs to support Elijah for a protracted period; here the widow needs only a one-time miracle to pay off her debts.

acts always served a national agenda, furthering belief in God, saving the nation in battle, or fighting idolatry. Typically, these miracles functioned as "signs," accompanied by a pronouncement in God's name. They were certainly not a routine modus operandi, and they were not taken for granted.

In contrast, Elisha utilizes miracles in an almost nonchalant, disimpassioned manner as a means of resolving human challenges and everyday foibles. Whether he is healing a polluted spring or rendering a poisonous soup edible, assisting in a search for a lost ax-head or even striking an Aramean battalion with blindness, his miracles, even the most impressive of them, are not intended to make a dramatic impression upon their audience. More often than not, Elisha fails even to invoke God's name as he alters the natural order.

Beyond the casual way in which Elisha dispenses miracles, one fails to identify any national message or mission that drives him. Elisha is not fighting the worship of Baal or directing the nation to repent. In his national engagement, he assists the king more than he rebukes him, and whereas he appears to have the power to paralyze a division of the Aramean army, he fails to harness these supernatural powers to destroy foreign aggression or alleviate a crippling siege. What is Elisha's mission?

The absence of a national agenda in the Elisha stories combined with the chronicle of serial miracle-making has led some to categorize these chapters as "Saints' Legends," a genre of literature that would have emerged from a devoted group of disciples about the wonders of their master, much like hasidic legends.[14] Is that what we have here?

---

14. Rofé, *The Prophetic Stories*, 3–15; Shemesh, "The Elisha Stories as Saints' Legends." Attempts have been made to subdivide or categorize the Elisha episodes. Some have divided the narratives by length: some stories are longer, allowing for rich character development and a textured, sophisticated message (the Shunammite woman [II Kings 4:8–37], Naaman [ibid., ch. 5], the siege on Samaria [ibid., 6:24–7:20]); others are concise episodes offering almost hagiographic miracle tales. An alternative classification sees one genre of stories as depicting practical assistance to individuals or small groups, whereas a second group portrays Elisha as operating at the national level, alongside kings and armies, whether in conflict with Moab or Aram (ibid., ch. 3; 6:8–23), Naaman (ibid., ch. 5), Hazael (ibid., 8:7–15), or the king of Israel (ibid., 5:8; 7:32–33; 9:1–3; 13:14–19). And yet the common thread throughout is Elisha's miracle-making.

THE *BENEI HANEVI'IM*

One contextual point regarding all four stories in this chapter relates to their social backdrop. These episodes all depict Elisha interacting with his students and supporters. In one instance, it is the pious Shunammite woman who attends prophetic gatherings on Rosh Ḥodesh (the New Moon) and Shabbat (II Kings 4:23).[15] The other miracles transpire within the circle identified as the *Benei HaNevi'im*. Elisha has already interacted with this group in chapter 2, but in these stories he resides among them and serves as the address for their daily problems: he resolves the financial distress of a desperate widow affiliated with this group (4:1–8), he assists when they lack food (4:38–43), and the *Benei HaNevi'im* even pressure him to accompany them when they go to chop timber (6:1–6). The group's poverty and scant resources are evident in virtually every scene;[16] presumably they are occupied with matters of the spirit rather than material concerns. Seemingly, Elisha functions more as a social worker than a spiritual leader; we never hear his teachings or witness him training the group in prophecy.[17] And yet under his leadership and influence, this group grows in popularity and expands such that they have to seek out new living quarters: "See the place where we live *under your direction* is too cramped for us. Let us ... build quarters for ourselves to live in" (6:1–2).

Elisha's role toward the nation at large is evidenced by his regular travel from town to town, always surrounded by followers and supporters at Shunem (4:8), Carmel (4:22–25), Gilgal (4:38), Samaria (5:3; 6:32), and the Jordan River (6:2).[18] Elisha appears to be spreading God's

15. The New Moon ranks alongside Shabbat and the festivals as a public holiday, a family sacrificial feast. See Num. 10:10; I Sam. 20:18, 27–29; Is. 1:13; 66:23; Amos 8:4.
16. II Kings: poverty, 4:1; lack of food, 4:38–40, 42–43; an ax on loan, 6:2.
17. One exception is where Elisha dispatches one of the *Benei HaNevi'im* to anoint Jehu as king (II Kings 9:1).
18. One further location is Dothan (II Kings 6:13), but there he is accompanied by his assistant. However, the very fact that his location was known, even by the Arameans, is indicative of a public performance or appearance.

word nationally,[19] but his engagement is at the grassroots level[20] rather than with royalty.

CONTRAST BETWEEN ELIJAH AND ELISHA

If we wish to examine Elisha's role further it may be instructive to contrast him with his predecessor, Elijah. Elisha's miracle of the oil jug is highly reminiscent of Elijah's miracle with the widow of Tzarafat: "The jar of flour shall not end nor will the jug of oil be diminished until the day the Lord gives rain upon the land" (I Kings 17:11). In both stories, the prophet's miracle sustains a widow and her progeny, taking a basic foodstuff and having it multiply itself. And yet the contrast between the two episodes starkly highlights the differences between Elijah and Elisha.

Elijah was sent by God to confront a destitute widow as she was foraging for some wood to cook her last meal. She responds to Elijah:

> "I don't have any bread, only a handful of flour in a jar and a little oil in a jug. I am gathering a few sticks to take home and make a meal for myself and my son, that we may eat it, and die."
>
> Elijah said to her, "Don't be afraid. Go home and do as you have said. But first make a small cake of bread for me from what you have and bring it to me, and then make something for yourself and your son." (I Kings 17:12–13)

The differences are significant:

1. Elisha's miracle is stimulated by the widow's plight. It is the widow who approaches Elisha, understanding that he is an address for people in need. By contrast, Elijah's food-related miracle begins with the prophet approaching the destitute widow and requesting food from her. Whereas Elisha's sole motive is to provide for the widow's welfare – He asks: "What can I do for

19. In this manner, he follows the successful prophet Samuel, who regularly tours the country. See I Sam. 7:15–17; 9:9, 15–25.

20. In the war against Moab (II Kings 3) he goes into battle as one of the rank and file troops and is introduced to the king only when his presence is surprisingly identified.

you?" (II Kings 4:2) – in Elijah's story, the widow is there to assist him, to sustain him as he hides from King Ahab.

2. Elisha does not test the widow. By contrast, Elijah challenges the widow from Tzarafat. He demands that she provide him with food before she herself eats or feeds her son, although her food is sufficient for only one final meal.
3. Elisha does not benefit from the miracle he performs; his is a thoroughly altruistic gesture. Elijah benefits from his miracle: "She *and he* [Elijah] and her household had food for a long time" (I Kings 17:15).
4. In Elisha's miracle God is not explicitly mentioned; there is merely a directive by God or a statement of "So says the Lord." In Elijah's miracle God is highly evident, commanding him to take protection with the widow (I Kings 17:9), and the miracle is explicitly attributed to God (17:6).

Precisely because of its parallelism with Elijah,[21] our story leads to a study of contrasts between the two prophets. Elijah's role is infused with religious zeal. He acts in God's name and is unfazed by the suffering that he inflicts upon the nation in order to fight the worship of Baal and to generate a national commitment to God:

> Elijah was the extreme expression of the demand for an unequivocal breakaway from this domain of corruption [the Baal]. In his refusal to arbitrate either with kings or with the people... he doomed them to starvation and death, because he saw things only in terms of black and white. In his own words: "If the Lord be God, follow Him, but if Baal, then follow him" (I Kings 18:21). Between these two extremes, there was no tolerance, no compromise.[22]

21. Another noticeable contrast between Elijah and Elisha which touches our chapter is the divergence between Elijah's *nahal*, Wadi Cherith, in which "the brook dried up" (I Kings 17:7), and Elisha's prophecy in which a *nahal* fills with water: "That brook shall be filled with water" (II Kings 3:16, 17). The language of fullness as predicted by Elisha spills over into our chapter as the widow's empty and dry jars become "full" with oil (ibid., 4:4, 6).
22. Rabbi Adin Steinsaltz, *Biblical Images* (NY: Basic Books, 1984), 161–67.

> The prophet Elisha lived among his people, and unlike his master, he was a magnet for all aggrieved people. They approach him as individuals or groups to pour out their troubles, expecting his aid. He sees the essence of his role in Israel as a prophet of salvation with equal attention to individuals, entire communities and for the nation as a whole.[23]

Elisha is a stark contrast to Elijah. Here is a prophet who offers support rather than criticism, whose demeanor is that of kindness and assistance (*middat haḥesed*) rather than confrontation, criticism, accusation, and zeal (*middat hadin*).

WHY SO DIFFERENT?

What are the sources of the differences between the two prophets? What lies at the core of Elisha's unusual and unconventional methods? We can suggest a few possibilities.

One aspect begins with Elisha's personality. We have already mentioned Elisha's congeniality as opposed to Elijah's harsh, confrontational, non-worldly personality.[24] A starting point would be to suggest that prophetic leadership style reflects personal demeanor and character. Elisha's personable style leads him to assist and offer relief. But this is surely not enough. Does Elisha not have a divine message to deliver?

Elisha may represent an alternative tactical approach. If one wishes to draw the nation to Judaism, what is the more effective educational method: The stick or the carrot? Confrontation or encouragement? Elijah's strategy sought to pressure the people into affirming their unequivocal religious commitment openly, and to forcefully demonstrate God's supremacy. By contrast, Elisha functions in a generous, supportive manner, practicing kindness and generating miracles which allow the average Israelite to realize that "there is a prophet in Israel" (II Kings 5:8). Elisha intuits that an approach of

---

23. Samet, *Pirkei Elisha*, 198.
24. See our discussion earlier in this volume, in the chapter entitled "In a Whirlwind," in the section "Different Characteristics"; Israel, *I Kings: Torn in Two*, 270–71.

love rather than fear will not merely be more constructive, it will also effect a more successful outcome.

Lastly, the difference between Elijah and Elisha may be a function of the times in which they live and serve. Elijah operates during the reign of King Ahab, when the kingdom enjoys economic prosperity and wields international influence and power. Elisha's era is plagued by Aram's domination of the northern kingdom[25] as well as bouts of famine.[26] Whereas Elijah may feel it necessary to rebuke Israel for its waywardness, presenting a dour and sobering counterbalance in heady times and challenging the leadership in a fortunate era, Elisha senses that during difficult times, such an approach is deeply unjustified. When the nation is under siege, relief, inspiration, and encouragement are needed. There will be times in which Elisha too will play his part in the divine punishment of the house of Omri,[27] but to the largest extent possible Elisha dedicates his róle as prophet to offering hope and healing, highlighting God's special connection with His people, through the miracles he performs and the assistance he offers.

25. II Kings chronicles the attacks of Aram (5:2; 6:8–10, 14, 24; 8:12). Aram eventually decimates the Israelite military (12:18; 13:7). Elisha's final prophecy announces the decline of Aramean dominance and the return of Israelite independence (13:17–19), so his tenure coalesces with Aramean ascendancy over Israel. See a more comprehensive discussion in the chapter entitled "Elisha's Tears."

26. See II Kings 4:38; seven-year famine, 8:1; famine due to siege, 6:24–27:2, 16–18.

27. The story of Hazael, 8:7–15; the anointing of Jehu, chs. 9–10.

II Kings 4:9–37

The Shunammite: Life and Death

This is a tale of miraculous birth, sudden death, and resurrection. Let us begin with a brief summary of the storyline. We encounter the "great woman" of Shunem (II Kings 4:8), a follower of Elisha whom she describes as a "holy man of God" (4:9). When he is in the region, she invites him to eat at her home, and later, she and her husband generously build Elisha an apartment so that he has a place to stay. Elisha, looking to thank his hostess for all her trouble, promises her that "at this season, next year, you will be embracing a son" (4:17). And the prophecy is fulfilled – a son is born at the designated time. However, years later, when the child is with his father in the fields in the heat, he takes ill and dies some hours later. The mother lays her dead child on Elisha's bed and hurries to find the prophet. Locating him at Mount Carmel, she insists that he accompany her without delay to Shunem. He returns to the woman's home and revives her lifeless child.

Our tradition assigns this chapter as the *haftara* for *Parashat Vayera*. What is the connection between the two stories? *Parashat Vayera* is the Torah portion that narrates Abraham's hospitality to three wayfarers, later identified as angels, and their promise to Sarah that "this time next year" she will be blessed with a son. At the close of the *parasha*, we read of Isaac's birth, his near encounter with death at the *Akeda* (Binding of Isaac), and God's sparing of his life.

The two stories[1] share several similarities:

- An older childless couple is blessed with a child in response to their enthusiastic and extraordinary hospitality.
- "And her husband is old" (II Kings 4:14); "and my husband is old" (Gen. 18:12).
- The announcement is formulated as "at this season, next year… a son" (II Kings 4:16; Gen. 18:10).
- The promise is made as the woman is positioned at the doorway (II Kings 4:15; Gen. 18:10).
- The woman expresses skepticism at the prediction.
- A child is born one year later.
- The son dies/is on the verge of death and is saved at the last moment/resurrected.

The episode with the Shunammite woman comprises two miracles that are parallel to those experienced by Abraham and Sarah. The first is the gift of childbirth, with regard to which our story is another example in a biblical genre of barren women – Sarah, Rebecca, Rachel, Leah, Manoah's wife, Hannah – who miraculously conceive. Like Abraham and Sarah, the unexpected announcement of a child for the Shunammite woman and her husband is a reward for extraordinary hospitality. The second parallel is the child on the verge of death who is saved. We can conclude, then, that both are stories of promise and fulfillment, tragedy and relief.

TRANSFORMATIONS AND QUESTIONS

As we examine the two chief protagonists of the story, Elisha and the Shunammite woman, we cannot but observe the way in which each of them undergoes a transformation, even a reversal, as the chapter progresses.

1. See also Rabbi Yehuda Shaviv, http://etzion.org.il/en/parshat-vayera-beloved-son-melakhim-ii-41-37, who draws connections between the first story of II Kings 4 and *Parashat Vayera*.

Initially, the Shunammite is depicted as comfortable and content with life. This "great woman," a term indicative of aristocratic lineage or wealth, venerates Elisha and is uninterested in any special privilege she might merit from her close association with him. When Elisha offers her the opportunity to "talk to the king or to the head of the army" (4:13), the Shunammite woman modestly declines: "I live among my own people" (4:13). When he promises her a child, she is self-effacing: "Please, my lord, man of God, do not delude your maidservant" (4:16), as if to say that she is unworthy of this tremendous gift.[2]

And yet, in the latter segment of the story, her assertiveness and confidence commands our attention as she bursts into frenzied activity, rushing to the prophet, seizing his feet,[3] and berating him: "Did I ask my lord for a son?" (4:28). When Elisha suggests that Gehazi proceed to Shunem to revive her son, she becomes insistent, demanding that Elisha accompany her personally: "As the Lord lives and as you live, I will not leave you!" (4:30).

A dramatic shift has occurred in the Shunammite woman's behavior toward Elisha. Could this be the critical focus of the narrative?

Elisha too finds himself in an unexpected role reversal. At first, we meet him as "a holy man of God" who issues the miracle of childbearing for the Shunammite woman with the same ease with which he talks to the king or the army chief, declaring the supernatural birth without a second thought; and indeed, God fulfills his decree: "The woman conceived and bore a son *at the set time of which Elisha had spoken*" (4:7).

But in the latter part of the story, Elisha falters. When the child dies and he is confronted by the desperate mother, Elisha remarks, "She is in bitter distress *and the Lord has hidden it from me and has not told me*" (4:27). This double phraseology expresses Elisha's dismay that something is deeply amiss. Elisha is in crisis. Why did God not inform Elisha of the death of the child? In the next scene, Elisha dispatches Gehazi with the prophet's staff,

---

2. Prof. Uriel Simon, *Reading Prophetic Narratives* (Bloomington, IN: Indiana University Press, 1997), 243.
3. This is an act of desperation. Worded as "*vataḥazek beraglav*" (4:27), it is in direct contrast to the similar phrase used earlier to express her generous hospitality: "*vataḥazek bo*" (ibid., 4:8).

expecting him to use it to revive the dead child. Yet the attempt is ineffective: "The boy has not awakened!" (4:31). Elisha's intuition has failed him again. The prophet who was so strident, who had dispensed miracles so freely, suddenly discovers that his divine powers have eluded him. Why does Elisha experience this failure? What does this chapter tell us about him?

These questions, however, pale in the face of the most significant one: Why did the child die? Elisha responds to the abundant hospitality from an earnest and childless woman by pronouncing the greatest of all gifts – the birth of a son. God honors Elisha's declaration by granting the gift of life. If God approved of Elisha's statement and the child was born, why did He later allow the miracle-child to die?

We shall present several approaches found in both classical and contemporary scholarship which have all addressed these problems extensively.

AN UNAPPRECIATED MIRACLE

We begin with Rabbi Elchanan Samet, who identifies the personality of the Shunammite woman as the key to the story.[4] He boldly proposes that she was primarily "responsible" for her son's untimely death.

The exposition of the story that introduces the "great woman of Shunem" indicates her wealth, her hospitality, and her interest in her home becoming a regular lodging point for the prophet. However, unlike Sarah, Rachel, and Hannah, nothing is mentioned about her childlessness.[5] Moreover, one of the striking aspects of her interaction with Elisha is that the prophet has no idea she is childless; it takes his assistant, Gehazi, to alert him to the fact (4:14). Samet therefore suggests that she had accommodated her life to a childless family structure,

---

4. Rabbi Elchanan Samet, "The Double Embrace," Herzog College: *Megadim* 13 (Adar 5751 [1991]): 73–97. Samet retains this approach in his book, *Pirkei Elisha* (2007). Interestingly, Samet rests his theological approach heavily upon Rabbi Joseph B. Soloveitchik's *Kol Dodi Dofek: Listen, My Beloved Knocks* (New York: Yeshiva University, and Hoboken, NJ: Ktav, 2006).
5. Simon, *Prophetic Narratives*, 241, makes the same observation but interprets it differently. For him the aspect of barrenness is delayed to underscore the woman's sincerity and pure motives, so that the reader not suppose that the woman's persistence and effort to host Elisha is some ploy to have him cure her infertility.

directing her energies instead to hospitality and spiritual pursuits; she is indifferent to her childlessness.[6]

In the Bible, God's endowment of a child to a previously childless woman – Sarah, Rachel, Manoah's wife, Hannah – generally results in a song of joy, as well as her decision to raise the child to become a leader who will make a significant national contribution – such as Samson or Samuel. Accordingly, the Shunammite woman should have celebrated the miraculous birth of a son, as promised by the prophet, with thanksgiving to God and a commitment to raise the child to an auspicious future. And yet, as Samet observes, the Shunammite woman fundamentally disregards the gift that has been granted her: "Please, my lord... do not delude your maidservant" (4:16). She fails to celebrate his birth and neither comprehends nor appreciates the special responsibility of raising her miracle child. Instead of having the boy study Torah or engage in spiritual endeavors, we witness the youth accompanying his father to the fields. It was this lack of concern for the child's religious upbringing, this spurning of the great gift bestowed by God, that precipitated his untimely death.

However, for Samet, this is merely the turning point. It is this tragedy that spurs the mother to acknowledge the enormous gift that she had received, and she begins to fight for her son, at which point she repairs her flawed attitude and desperately searches for the prophet to restore his life. As she bows to the floor in the final verse, she acknowledges not only the prophet but also the God in whose name he acts. As she carries her resurrected son from Elisha's room, she experiences the rebirth of her son as she now appreciates the great gift of life.

---

6. Rabbi Mosheh Lichtenstein, http://www.hatanakh.com/en/articles/he-holy-man-god, fiercely rejects the critique of the Shunammite woman's seeming nonchalance to the news of her prospective birth. He defends her as someone who has experienced years, possibly decades, of torment and pain due to her childlessness. Her reticence is a result of the deep scars wrought by her infertility, as she dreads the torment of anticipating a child only to have her dreams dashed and her yearnings disappointed. If anything, Elisha was guilty here for playing with a childless woman's sensitive and frayed emotions. Moreover, the intimate scene of mother and child as the Shunammite rocks her boy on her lap until his death (4:20) should dispel Samet's impression that the woman spurns her motherly side.

Samet doesn't withhold his critique from Elisha. His prophetic failures – his sense that God has withheld the woman's distress from him (4:27) and his initial failure to resurrect the boy by means of his staff – are divine indicators of the prophet's dereliction of duty toward the child. The prophet should have chaperoned the family, mentoring the child to greatness. Instead he neglected this mission. Elisha too is granted a second chance as his divine powers are restored and the boy is granted a new lease on life.[7]

ELISHA DISCOVERS HIS LIMITS

Rabbi Mordechai Sabato[8] rejects Samet's approach:

> A comparison with other stories in *Tanakh* of barren women who miraculously conceive shows that there is no mention of any of them having taken extra care in childraising. Yet, none of them were punished.
>
> Although in midrashic conceptions, the place of children is studying Torah, and not going into the fields, this is rarely evidenced explicitly in the text. In fact, the reason the Tanakh focuses so little attention on the Shunammite woman's son results from the nature and purpose of the story. The focus is on the stature and power of the prophet, not on the birth of the child.

Instead, Sabato unveils his own theory, which points an accusatory finger at Elisha. He begins with a midrash:

> Three keys are in the hands of God, and no being has control over them: the key of resurrection, the key of childbirth, and the key of rainfall. (Deuteronomy Rabba 7:6)

7. Samet opens his study with a passage from the Zohar (*Beshallaḥ* 44a–45b), which identifies the resurrected boy as the prophet Habakkuk. I do not know whether Samet sees this as a definitive identification or merely a midrashic pointer to the fact that the miracle child should be destined for spiritual eminence.
8. Rabbi Mordechai Sabato, "The Story of the Shunammite Woman," Herzog College: *Megadim* 15 (Marcheshvan 5752 [1991]): 45. The article, translated into English by Zev Jacobson, may be accessed online at http://www.gush.net/alei/7-4sabato.rtf.

Sabato extrapolates from here:

> Surprisingly, Elisha neglects to engage God with his request of the power to confer a life. In fact, he manipulates the "key" by force, without the consent of its owner… Elisha overstepped the boundaries of his authority when he decreed: "This time next year you will embrace a son." He was a messenger of God, yet behaved as though he could grant life on his own. This stands in contrast to any other episode in Tanakh, where it is exclusively God's prerogative.[9]

Elisha starts the chapter having independently bestowed the gift of life. The entire story narrates the manner in which God educates Elisha, teaching him his prophetic limitations. Elisha's presumptuous largesse – the birth of a child to a childless woman – overstepped the mandate of the prophet; even the Shunammite woman was taken aback by Elisha's offer to grant a son. She senses something inappropriate.

One compelling support for this theory emerges from a textual parallel with the promise of Isaac's birth. When Isaac is born, we read:

> Sarah conceived and bore Abraham a son… at the set time *of which God had spoken.* (Gen. 21:2)

But with the birth of the Shunammite woman's son, the verse states:

> The woman conceived and bore a son at the set time *of which Elisha had spoken.* (II Kings 4:17)[10]

---

9. Ibid., 46.
10. Yael Shemesh, who perceives the Elisha stories as "Saints' Legends," suggests that in several of his stories Elisha plays the role of God Himself regarding, inter alia, the granting of a child, the healing of leprosy, and the provision of food. See Shemesh, "The Stories of Elisha: A Literary Analysis," 272–74. This observation recurs in her other writings on Elisha. Whereas Sabato sees Elisha's presumption of a Godly role as a flaw, an aberration of his prophetic calling, Shemesh views it as a systemic feature of Elisha's prophetic tenure.

This comparison demonstrates quite convincingly that Elisha has usurped God's role.

Nevertheless, God allows the child to be born – and then destines the boy to death – in order to teach Elisha the limits of his role. When Elisha confesses that he is ignorant of the child's death, he is acknowledging that "his divinely inspired ability to discern hidden events has been withdrawn from him."[11] However, he still presumes that his staff, in the hand of Gehazi, can revive the child; initially he doesn't even consider traveling to Shunem!

> However, with lightning speed, Elisha's illusions are smashed. Upon arrival, Elisha sees the full extent of his error: the boy, stiff and cold, lying on his bed. Face-to-face with the lifeless form of the boy, Elisha, reeling from the impact of his discovery, finally turns to God and, in recognition of his own utter insignificance, prays.
>
> Viewed in this context, the child's unexpected death was destined from birth. He entered the world with the sole purpose of dying when he grew up, in order to teach the lesson that life created by Man is non-existent and has no validity. The theme of the narrative is not the miracle of the birth, but rather the power of the prophet, or more accurately, his limitations. As mentioned previously, the focus of the story is not the Shunammite woman and her son, but the transformation and maturation of Elisha the prophet.[12]

According to Sabato, Elisha's mistake is the presumption that he can independently generate life. We may add that he acknowledges this obliquely when he confesses: "The Lord has hidden it from me" (II Kings 4:27). Earlier he had presumed an ability to foresee and determine future events: "At this season next year, you will be embracing a son" (4:16). But now he must admit his ignorance of the future, as a potent divine signal.

---

11. Sabato, "The Story of the Shunammite Woman," 48.
12. Ibid., 48–49.

In the chapter's final scene, Elisha is forced to turn to God directly, praying to Him, acknowledging His exclusive role as the giver of life. Only once Elisha has humbly appealed to God will the boy be revived. In contrast to Samet, who views the transformation of the Shunammite woman as the main drama, Sabato sees Elisha as the chapter's key figure.[13] The story here is the process by which God guides Elisha to a realization of the constraints of his prophetic station.

GEHAZI: THE MEDIATOR

Sabato, however, fails to adequately answer all the questions, for if God sought to inform Elisha that he violated his prophetic mandate, why did He then allow the child to be born at all? If Elisha's original pronouncement had been denied, he would have certainly intuited that he lacked the sanction to grant life. Did the Shunammite woman and her family have to suffer for a lesson that could have been learned by other means?

There are two secondary characters in the story. The Shunammite woman's husband plays a passive role and serves as a stereotypical master of the house; he is consulted regarding the construction of Elisha's residence probably because he manages the family expenses. When his son is sick, he sends the child back to his wife, and she dutifully notifies him when she leaves the homestead.[14] However, he seems personally unengaged with the holy man who visits his home frequently; they never interact, and in this narrative, it is his wife who is active and dominant.

---

13. A similar approach is adopted by Simon using his method of close reading. See *Prophetic Narratives*, 279–316.
14. The two instances where he is mentioned feature as a passive contrast to his wife's impressive alacrity; see Sabato, "The Story of the Shunammite Woman," 51. Simon writes: "The Shunammite is married (not a widow able to come and go as she pleases, like the heroine of the previous legenda), she does not have freedom of action and must either involve her husband in her deeds or neutralize him. Thus, in normal times, she asks his consent to build the upper chamber on the roof of their house; in time of crisis, she conceals the death of their son from him. The narrator tells us these things not only so that her behavior will strike us as socially plausible, but also so that her husband's normal and correct behavior can serve as a contrasting background for her own individuality, both as the leading hostess in Shunem and as a desperate fighter for her son's miraculous resurrection" (*Prophetic Narratives*, 231).

The second character is far more critical to the storyline: Gehazi, Elisha's assistant, features in every key scene. Elisha repeatedly employs him as a loyal intermediary, as his messenger.[15] And yet, in each circumstance, Gehazi's actions meet with failure – a failure that may be viewed, ultimately, as a shortcoming of Elisha.

In the first scene, Elisha seeks a way in which to thank the Shunammite woman for her hospitality. Initially he sends Gehazi to the woman and offers to "talk to the king or to the head of the army" (4:13), but she declines. Elisha communicates with the woman indirectly, through the mediation of Gehazi. Only after the woman rejects Elisha's offer does he express his frustration to his assistant: "What can we do for her?" Gehazi responds: "She has no son, and her husband is old." Elisha then personally relays the portended miracle. It is Gehazi, not Elisha, who first raises the notion of blessing the woman with a son. And the son dies.

After the child dies,[16] the Shunammite woman hurries to Elisha at Mount Carmel. This time as well, it is Gehazi who is initially sent to interact with her: "How are you? How is your husband? How is the child?" (4:26). She curtly dismisses Gehazi and engages Elisha directly, flinging herself on his feet. Gehazi blunders yet again as he "stepped forward to push her away." Elisha corrects him: "Leave her alone, for she is in bitter distress." In this scene too, Gehazi is an unsuccessful mediator, first when his greeting is dismissed and again when he fails to recognize the woman's deep pain.

In the third scene, the revival, Elisha again entrusts Gehazi with the critical mission, anticipating that his staff will resuscitate the child. Gehazi's actions are proven inadequate: "The boy has not awakened"

15. There is a symmetry to the story. Just as in the first scene Elisha addresses the Shunammite initially and unsuccessfully by means of Gehazi (II Kings 4:13) and then proclaims the birth of the child personally (ibid., 4:16), in the second scene the first two approaches through Gehazi are unsuccessful (ibid., 4:26, 29, 31). Only once the prophet gets personally involved (ibid., 4:32–34) will the child be revived.

16. Interestingly, the Shunammite woman never states that the child is dead. Possibly this is a case of language creating the facts. She is frightened that if she says he is dead, that will indeed be the case. On the other hand, if she vaguely alludes to his condition, there is always room for hope. See Shemesh, "The Elisha Stories as Saints' Legends," 22n83.

(4:31). Only once Elisha personally involves himself in the effort to revive the child – praying, placing himself over the child, breathing into him, and warming him – does the child return to life. Here as well, Gehazi's involvement generates a setback which only Elisha can redress.

What is the importance of Gehazi's persona in this story? The promise of a child, his death, and his subsequent resurrection could have been ably communicated without reference to Gehazi, yet his involvement is at the center of every segment of the narrative. His failures seem to reflect poorly upon Elisha. What does his presence add to the chapter?

GEHAZI'S SINS

In the broader context of II Kings, Gehazi is portrayed as a highly negative character, and in the next chapter we will follow his deception of Elisha, resulting in Elisha's rejection of Gehazi. The Mishna further impugns Gehazi by condemning him as one of "four commoners who have no place in the World to Come" (Sanhedrin 10:1). That being said, we shall not jump ahead; we will assess Gehazi solely as he appears in this narrative.

Is Gehazi the problem here? Sabato portrays Gehazi as an aide intoxicated with his master's miraculous powers:

> He ... believes that his master is all-powerful. In the eyes of Gehazi, nothing is beyond Elisha's prowess – not even the ability to bring life into the world. In fact, Gehazi suggested that Elisha grant the Shunammite woman a son. Elisha never imagined that granting a child was within his power, yet Gehazi's suggestion triggers a thought-process within the prophet that leads to his unauthorized decree – "This time next year you will embrace a son."[17]

The following midrash colorfully depicts the scene as Gehazi journeys to Shunem, bearing Elisha's staff, to revive the boy:

> They said to him, "Where are you going, Gehazi?"
> He said to them, "To resurrect the dead."

17. Sabato, "The Story of the Shunammite Woman," 49.

> They said to him, "And can you resurrect the dead? And is it not the Holy One Blessed be He who resurrects the dead? 'The Lord kills and brings to life' (I Sam. 2:6)."
> He said to them, "So too my lord can kill and bring back to life." (*Mekhilta, Amalek* 1)

The very portrayal by the Midrash of a conversation involving Gehazi immediately casts aspersions on him; after all, Elisha had specifically instructed Gehazi: "Take my staff in your hand and go. If you meet anyone, do not greet him; *and if anyone greets you do not answer him*" (4:29).[18] Gehazi's behavior demonstrates a certain brashness. His veneration of Elisha leads him to perceive his master's powers as invulnerable such that any associated restrictions and instructions are immaterial. In Gehazi's mind, the reawakening of the child would be easy for Elisha.

Now as we access the image in which the distraught mother fell at Elisha's feet, we recall how Gehazi tried to distance her.[19] Gehazi's sole

---

18. This midrashic approach is adopted by Rashi, Radak, and Ralbag, and explains why Elisha's plan to have Gehazi revive the boy failed. Had Gehazi followed his instructions perfectly, the placing of the staff would have been successful. Simon, however (p. 20), suggests that "Gehazi had followed Elisha's instructions to the letter." In his reading the emphasis shifts not to instructions ignored but to the need for Elisha's personal appeal to God.
19. This is seen as yet another of Gehazi's flaws. See Berakhot 10b: "'He is a holy man.' R. Jose b. Chanina said: He is holy but his assistant is not holy, for it says, 'And Gehazi came near to thrust her away.' R. Jose b. Chanina said, He seized her by her breast." See Y. Sanhedrin 10:2 for a similar exchange.

    This comment is interesting because it touches upon a latent sexuality in this scene as the Shunammite woman seizes Elisha's legs, and in the story as a whole. And yet, any suggestion of impropriety between the prophet and the Shunammite woman may be rejected when we note the care Elisha takes to speak to the Shunammite woman through an intermediary, and her caution not to enter his chamber; see Ralbag, II Kings 4:13, and Abarbanel ad loc. who understand these details as deliberate, so as to keep an appropriate distance. The Alshich too, in his commentary on Kings, *Marot HaTzov'ot*, sees Elisha as an exemplar of the dictum: "Do not speak excessively with a woman" (Avot 1:5).

    Some years ago, the pages of the Israeli newspaper *Haaretz* became a fascinating arena for a vibrant polemic between MK Shulamit Aloni and Prof. Alexander Rofé on the sexual overtones of this story. See Admiel Kosman, "The Modesty Squad in the Prophet's Court," *Haaretz*, Nov. 28, 1997, and Yairah Amit, "The Shunammite,

focus was the protection of the prophet's prestige, making him oblivious to her extreme anguish. Elisha himself understood that "she is in bitter distress," that her desperate behavior reflected a severe crisis. But Gehazi doesn't see it.

What image emerges of Gehazi? Here is a man enamored of his exceptional master; he idolizes him. His respect for the prophet leads him to suggest inappropriate miracles; his protection of the prophet causes him to guard and ennoble the holy man rather than observe the emotions of the people. He is merely an attendant, and admiration and protection are hardly a crime. Yet these features may point to a deeper problem in the prophet's court.

THE PROPHET'S COURT[20]

Here we need to return to Elisha and appreciate what has come undone in his world. The entire chapter relays the message that for Elisha, miracles are to be performed directly; the people need contact with the "holy man of God."

This theme is expressed by the character of the Shunammite woman, who sees Elisha as a spiritual guide. The text says the she "urged him" to eat with her family, but the phrase is "*vataḥazek bo*" (4:8) – literally, "she seized him" – the emphasis being her desire for direct contact with the prophet.[21]

Yet each time Elisha "converses" with the woman, Gehazi is the mediator in the discussion. Presumably the prophet acts this way out of modesty. But perhaps, as the prophet becomes busier with more demands on his time, he needs to delegate, to assign various responsibilities to assistants and students. An organizational bureaucracy will inevitably mean the distancing of the prophet from the common people, but this distance has the potential to destroy the prophet and his work. The people want to engage directly with the man of God! After

the Shulamite and the Professor: Between Midrash and Midrash," *Journal for the Study of the Old Testament* 93 (June 2001): 77–91, which documents the debate and the question of "modern midrash."

20. I heard this idea from Rav Yaakov Medan.

21. Nonphysical contact; see footnote 19 above.

the death of her son when the woman approaches Elisha in a panicked state, she is first greeted courteously by Gehazi the assistant. But she doesn't seek the prophet's secretary; she needs Elisha! To get that attention she falls on his feet: "*vataḥazek beraglav*" (4:27). She needs to see the prophet in person!

This theme continues at that climactic moment when Elisha assumes that he can send his staff with Gehazi to revive the boy. There, the Shunammite woman understands that the miracle cannot be performed remotely and she says: "As the Lord lives and as you live, I will not leave you!" (4:30). This is a direct parallel to Elisha's own words, his threefold statement, as he devotedly refuses to abandon his master, Elijah: "As the Lord lives and as you live, I will not leave you" (2:2, 4, 6).

From this perspective, the Shunammite woman is the hero of the story in that she reminds Elisha of who he is.[22] The charismatic prophet must interact with his followers, not through assistants and aides. It is the unmediated association with the prophet that people crave.

Here our point differs from that of Sabato. It is not Elisha's presumption to play the role of God. Rather, the issue is Elisha's direct and personal engagement with his followers. He cannot be the master prophet surrounded by advisors and acolytes. The people need access to the prophet himself. That is why God hid the information about the dead child from Elisha. Were he to have discovered it by prophecy, he would have passed on the job to a subordinate. But there is no replacement for a genuine "holy man of God." The people want "*vataḥazek bo*" – direct contact, no courts or hierarchical offices. The prophet must be able to engage with people: looking them in the eyes, sharing their pain.

Our story highlights the danger of religious leaders becoming religious institutions. This episode makes Elisha reassess his mode of leadership. The figure of Gehazi repeatedly falters and fails, but it is not because Gehazi is personally flawed; the problem lies with Elisha.

22. Immediately, "Elisha rose and followed her" (II Kings 4:30), a sign of her dominant persona. Simon comments: "In stories of miraculous births and survivals of a child, there is frequently an element of superior wisdom of the wife and mother, who is not only wiser than the male protagonist but even…gets him to follow her" (*Prophetic Narratives*, 250).

Gehazi cannot succeed because he is not the prophet! If Elisha's role is to inspire and to support, only he must deliver the word of God, in person.

* * *

We have presented several approaches to this chapter, and we invite the reader to discover which reading appeals most. Yet while each of these perspectives as well as our detailed analyses have highlighted various flaws or sins of the major figures in this dramatic episode, we run the danger of losing perspective on the larger picture. While this story may offer a critique of Elisha or his court, the overarching thrust is the miraculous power of Elisha as God's messenger, a man who travels the length of the country preaching, offering assistance, and utilizing his miraculous, life-giving powers to spread God's name. This story suggests that God guided Elisha to correct errant aspects of his mode of operation, and yet the chapter's popularity is testimony to the depiction of Elisha as one of the supreme prophets of Israel.

II Kings 5

The Transformation of Naaman

In this chapter, Elisha's fame extends beyond the borders of Israel, as he heals Naaman, the leprous general of the Aramean army. At face value, this would appear to be just another miraculous episode in the series of tales of Elisha. However, the luxurious length of this story and its carefully structured narrative offer a delicate deliberation upon themes of social hierarchy, personal humility, faith, and faithfulness, furnishing messages beyond the contours of a simple miracle story.

We shall begin with a short summary of the storyline and then progress to a close reading of the text. Naaman, chief of staff of the Aramean military, is a leper. His maidservant, a young Israelite girl captured on one of his raiding missions, suggests that he visit the Israelite prophet Elisha to be cured. Acting upon her advice, he gains royal permission to travel to Israel to visit Elisha. The prophet instructs Naaman to immerse seven times in the Jordan River. Initially Naaman is enraged, perceiving the ablution in the inglorious waters of the Jordan as beneath his personal dignity and that of his kingdom, but he eventually acquiesces and is completely healed. He returns to Elisha, filled with reverence for the prophet and for God. Prior to his return to Aram he proclaims exclusive loyalty to the God of

Israel. Elisha refuses any compensation or largesse; however, after Naaman has taken his leave of Elisha, Gehazi approaches Naaman and deceitfully requests, in Elisha's name, several gifts. In response to this opportunistic betrayal, Elisha afflicts Gehazi with Naaman's leprosy.

THE OPENING VERSES (II KINGS 5:1–4)

Our analysis of this story begins with the opening verse, the exposition, which introduces the key character, Naaman. Note how this verse consists of four clauses:

1. Naaman, the captain of the army of the king of Aram,
2. was a great man before his master,
3. and held in esteem, because the Lord had given victory unto Aram;
4. he was also a mighty man of valor, a leper. (5:1)

Prof. Yair Zakovitch[1] has noted the skillful composition here. Each of the four clauses is comprised of two segments. The first phrase of each clause presents a positive depiction of Naaman, whereas the second phrase modifies, and even minimizes, the first one. This pattern appears in each clause as follows:

1. Naaman is introduced as "the captain of the army," but it isn't his army, it is that of the "king of Aram."
2. He "was a great man (*ish gadol*)," a man of fame and influence. However, this initial sense of power is qualified by his subservience. He stands "before his master," the king. In other words, his acclaim and social standing draw their prestige from the monarch. Moreover, his skills and achievements will not serve his personal interests; they serve his royal sovereign.
3. He is "held in esteem." Why? Is it a result of his personal accomplishments? No – his great military victories are attributed to divine intervention.

---

1. Zakovitch wrote a book-length study of this chapter. Our presentation is based on many of his observations there. See *Every High Official Has a Higher One Set over Him: A Literary Analysis of II Kings 5* (Tel Aviv: Am Oved, 1985) [Hebrew].

4. "He was a mighty man," but his leprosy is obviously a mitigating factor with regard to his health, his ability to appear in public, and his future prospects in the military.

Thus, each glowing accolade is immediately qualified and tempered. With this analysis, Zakovitch showcases the manner in which this introductory verse essentially displays the central themes of the chapter: power and subservience, pride and humility, authority and submission. These themes are further supported by the chapter's two *leitworts*.[2] The first is the sevenfold repetition of the word *lifnei*,[3] which may be translated as "before" or "in front of." The term is indicative of a subordinate status, a recognition of superior authority. The second is the word *adon*, "master" or "lord,"[4] also featured seven times. It underscores the motif of rank and dominance. The *leitworts* subtly but powerfully express the themes of social hierarchy that underpin the narrative.

The next verses eloquently exemplify this hierarchical layering:

> The Arameans had gone out in raiding parties and took captive a young girl from the Land of Israel, and she became an attendant to (*lifnei*) Naaman's wife. She said to her mistress, "If only my master (*adoni*) would come before (*lifnei*) the prophet who is in Shomron!

2. The notion of a leading word, or *leitwort* in German, was identified by Martin Buber. He defined it in the following manner: "By *leitwort* we mean a word or a word root that repeats meaningfully within a text, a sequence of texts, or a set of texts: to the one who pursues these repetitions, a meaning of the text is opened up or clarified, or at any rate will be revealed more insistently. As we have said, it need not be the same word, but rather may be the same word root that recurs in such a way; actually, it is often through the very differences that the dynamic cumulative effect is conveyed. I call it 'dynamic' because within the sounds that are related to each other thus, a movement occurs: the one to whom the whole is present feels the waves batter against one another all around. The measured repetition that corresponds to the inner rhythm of the text, or, better yet, pours out from it, is by all counts the most powerful of means for proclaiming meaning without stating it." Martin Buber, "*Leitwort* Style in Pentateuch Narrative," in *Scripture and Translation*, ed. Lawrence Rosenwald and Everett Fox (Bloomington, IN: Indiana University Press, 1994).
3. II Kings 5:1, 2, 3, 15, 16, 23, 27.
4. Ibid., 5:1, 3, 4, 18, 20, 22, 25.

> He would cure him of his leprosy." Naaman went to his master (*adonav*) and told him what the girl from Israel had said. (5:2–4)

This "young girl" occupies the lowest rank of society; she is a foreigner and a slave. She serves (*lifnei*) her mistress (*gevirta*). "Naaman's wife" is superior to the "young girl" on the one hand, but her lack of name and her designation as referenced to her husband – her "master" (*adon*) – emphasize her subordination to him. Yet even Naaman needs to request permission to approach the prophet in Samaria from *his* "master" (*adon*), the king. The hierarchy, the chain of command, is demarcated.

In a deliberate expression of subversive irony, Naaman's salvation shall emerge from the character of the lowest standing, the Israelite maidservant. At the outset we are struck by the enormous chasm between the "young girl" (*naara ketana*) and the "great man" (*ish gadol*). The inversion of the power structure undercuts the aforementioned hierarchy as the simple, powerless slave child will save the powerful general. This is reinforced by the indication that after Naaman is healed, his skin reverts to that of a "young boy" – *naar katan* (5:14), a clear allusion to the "young girl" who was so instrumental in his recovery. His healing is due to her, and he shall end the story by sharing in her veneration of Elisha.

A ROYAL LETTER (II KINGS 5:5–8)

If the king of Aram is to send his chief of staff to the prophet in Shomron, he must authorize the visit through the appropriate diplomatic channels. The king dispatches a message to the king of Israel:

> The king of Aram said, "Go to the king of Israel, and I will send along a letter." He set out, taking with him ten talents of silver, six thousand shekels of gold, and ten sets of clothing. The letter was brought to the king of Israel: "Now, when this letter reaches you, know that I have sent my servant Naaman to you so that you may cure him of his leprosy."
>
> When the king of Israel read the letter, he tore his clothes and said, "Am I God to deal death and give life, that this fellow writes to me to cure a man of his leprosy? See how he is seeking a pretext against me!"

> When Elisha, the man of God, heard that the king of Israel had torn his clothes, he sent him this message: "Why have you torn your clothes? Let him come to me and he will know that there is a prophet in Israel." (5:5–8)

Surprisingly, the language of the letter strikes us as overly terse and concise; absent are the polite introductions and reverent overtures that one would expect in a communiqué from one head of state to another. Radak suggests that the ceremonial flattery, although part of the original document, was eliminated, leaving only the king's central request: "The letter contained other things (praises, etc.) but the biblical text narrates only that which is essential."

This may not be the case, however. The phrase: "Now, when this letter reaches you" (5:6), returns a few chapters later, when King Jehu issues instructions to his subordinates (10:2). This language and the format of a letter without the honorific preamble are typical of a directive from an authority figure to a subordinate.[5] This phraseology then indicates that the king of Aram perceives the king of Israel as subservient to him. Now we better understand the panicked response of the king of Israel. His stronger neighbor is sending his army captain with a letter ordering the king to heal him of his leprosy. This directive is impossible for the king to fulfill: "Am I God to deal death and give life?" It leaves the king with the obvious conclusion that this is a call to war. In response, he tears his clothes. This scene, too, is a product of the power hierarchy.

CLASHING PERSPECTIVES

In considering this scene, further questions need to be addressed: Why does the king of Aram address his letter to the king of Israel; should he not have dispatched Naaman directly to the prophet? And why does

5. See Zakovitch, *Every High Official*, 38–39, where he demonstrates from ancient letters discovered in Lachish and Arad that whereas a letter will frequently start with *Ve'atta* ("And you"), when a subordinate addresses a senior figure he introduces the letter with phrases of flattery and honor. However, these are absent where a superior addresses a subordinate.

Elisha need to direct the king to "let him come to me"? Why would the king not have thought of that?

> The king of Aram sent the letter to the king of Israel ... for he thought that it was contingent upon him and that the prophet would not function unless under [the king's] instructions. (Malbim)

The king of Aram presumes that prophets function in Israel as they would in Syria and in any royal court in the ancient Near East, whereby they are underlings of the king and under his command.[6] Israel, however, is an environment in which the prophet operates independently, answerable to none but God, frequently critiquing royalty and certainly unwilling to bend to its authority. The king of Aram was incapable of imagining a scenario in which the prophet would not be fundamentally subordinate to the king, and so he sought the prophet by means of the latter. By contrast, the king of Israel couldn't conceive of a situation in which the prophet would be responsive to his control, and so he failed even to entertain the prospect of appealing to Elisha!

Elisha hears that the king has torn his clothes. Is this something he heard via prophecy, or did the king's despair become public knowledge? Whichever is true, Elisha acts in his characteristically supportive role as he offers to assist Naaman, thereby relieving the king of his misery. The king had asked: "Am I God to deal death and give life, that this fellow writes to me to cure a man of his leprosy?" And indeed, as God's envoy, Elisha's role is precisely to mediate life and death.[7] The leper is equivalent to the dead (as implied by Num. 12:12),[8] and in the selfsame

6. For scenes in which prophets are clearly in the service of, and a mouthpiece for, the king, see I Kings 22:11–25; Amos 7:12–14.
7. Elisha refers to life and death repeatedly: II Kings 2:21 – "This is what the Lord says: 'I have *healed* this water. Never again will it cause *death*'"; ibid., 2:23–24 – the bears kill the young children; ibid., 4:7 – "You and your sons can *live* on what is left over." The story of the Shunammite woman and her son clearly concerns the gift of life and its restoration: "O man of God, there is *death* in the pot!" (ibid., 4:40), at which point Elisha heals the food. In II Kings 8 we shall see Elisha proclaiming the death of Ben-Hadad.
8. Nedarim 64a.

manner that our previous chapter narrates Elisha's resuscitating a dead boy, here he will restore life to Naaman.

NAAMAN'S TRANSFORMATION (II KINGS 5:9–14)

> So Naaman came with his horses and chariots and halted at the door of Elisha's house. Elisha sent a messenger to say to him, "Go and bathe seven times in the Jordan, and your flesh shall be restored and you shall be clean."[9] But Naaman was angered and walked away. "I thought," he said, "to me he would surely come out (*yetzeh yatzo*), and would stand and invoke the Lord his God by name, and would wave his hand toward the spot, and cure the affected part. Are not the Amanah and the Pharpar, the rivers of Damascus, better than all the waters of Israel? I could bathe in them and be clean!" And he stalked off in a rage. But his servants came forward and spoke to him. "My father," they said, "if the prophet had told you to do a great thing, would you not do it? How much more so, then, when he has only said to you, 'Bathe and be clean.'" So he went down and immersed himself in the Jordan seven times, as the man of God had bidden; and his flesh became like a little boy's, and he was clean. (5:9–14)

Naaman's anger[10] highlights his personal arrogance. But his disdainful response focuses our attention upon the difference between a pagan religious conception and a Jewish way of thinking. Naaman anticipated that the prophet's act of healing would be dignified, glorious, and

9. The sevenfold bathing in the Jordan is a mode of purification unique to this story. In the Torah, the leper is purified only after the leprosy has disappeared. A complicated process is then undergone, which includes sacrifices and immersion in water on the first day, a wait of seven days, and then more sacrifices and a second immersion in water on the eighth day; see Lev. 14. With regard to instances of sevenfold ritual repetition, blood is sprinkled seven times on the first day of purification and oil is sprinkled seven times on the eighth day of purification, but the Torah offers no sevenfold immersion in water.

10. The speech is enclosed by expressions of Naaman's anger. It is preceded by: "But Naaman was angered and walked away (*vayelakh*)," and closes with: "And he stalked off (*vayelekh*) in a rage" (II Kings 5:11, 12).

impressive, and that it would be undemanding of him. He articulates this point eloquently:

- "I thought to me he would surely come out." The phrase "to me" at the beginning of the sentence highlights how Naaman considers himself to be the focus of this interaction; *he* is the center.
- "*Yetzeh yatzo*" (he would surely come out). This indicates a dignified procession by the prophet to welcome his important guest.
- Naaman didn't anticipate that he would be required to take an active role in the healing process – certainly not to go through the indignity of bathing in the Jordan River! He remains seated in his chariot, stationary, expecting the prophet to perform his magical ritual. Naaman expected to be acted upon, a passive recipient of the wondrous healing; he is surprised and indignant when Elisha instructs him to take initiative.
- Naaman is incensed by the suggestion that he bathe in the paltry Jordan River rather than the great rivers of Syria. Possibly, the idea of bathing, an act that he associated with personal hygiene rather than religious or magical ritual, and certainly something that he had tried, would have struck him as discordant with the magical rite that he expected from the prophet.
- Naaman's entire approach assumes that he controls the prophet. Even his flamboyant entourage expresses this attitude: "'Naaman came with his horses and chariots' – He brought with him a great entourage so that he would be seen as more important in the prophet's eyes and he would work harder to heal him" (Abarbanel).

As we see subsequently (5:15), Naaman expects to pay for the prophet's services. Payment generally indicates that the purveyor is a service provider of one who can make demands and exert control. Naaman seeks to hire the prophet's skill of accessing the higher worlds that control life and death. When Elisha refuses payment, he is not merely ensuring his independence, but he is emphatically stating that he adheres exclusively to God's instructions, and that he places himself in God's service and at the service of no other. This is Judaism's unique perspective:

> Judaism and paganism go in diametrically opposite directions. The pagan brings his offering in an attempt to make the god subservient to his wishes. The Jew, with his offering, wishes to place himself in the service of God; by his offering, he wishes to make himself subservient to the wishes of his God.[11]

As in our chapter's opening scene, an unexpected intermediary intervenes to break the impasse and calm Naaman's indignation. Naaman's servants gently pose a question that succinctly expresses the point:

> My father, if the prophet had told you to do a great thing [*davar gadol*] would you not do it? How much more so, then, when he has only said to you, "Bathe and be clean." (II Kings 5:13)

Once again, it is the small and insignificant action of "bathe and be clean" that will make the difference and not the "*davar gadol*"; no grandiose and pompous behavior is needed. It is only the lowly servants who can convince the "*ish gadol*," the great man, to adopt a humble, submissive stance. And when he does immerse himself, lowering himself by going "down" into the waters, his skin emerges as the flesh of a "*naar katan*" – a young boy.

The following midrash highlights Naaman's sinful pride:

> Leprosy comes for eleven sins.... Excessive pride: This refers to Naaman, as it states, "Naaman, the captain of the army of the king of Aram, was a great man" (II Kings 5:1). What is "great"? He was filled with pride due to his military prowess, and this is the reason he was struck with leprosy. (Numbers Rabba 7:5)

---

11. Rabbi Samson Raphael Hirsch, *Commentary on the Pentateuch*, Lev. 10:2.

NAAMAN'S RETURN (II KINGS 5:15–19)

Following his immersion in the Jordan River, Naaman returns to Elisha with a meek, self-effacing composure:

> And he returned to the man of God – he and all his entourage. He came and stood before him (*lefanav*). He said, "Now I know that there is no God in the world except in Israel." (5:15)

When Naaman first sought out Elisha (5:9), Naaman remained in his chariot at the entrance to the prophet's house; it was beneath his dignity to descend to Elisha's door. That is why Elisha sent a messenger to him. Now Naaman himself approaches Elisha and stands before him (*lefanav*) "as a servant before his master" (*Metzudat David*). Indeed, Naaman refers to himself as Elisha's servant four times in the subsequent verses, and he professes his allegiance to God.

Naaman offers Elisha a gift. The offering of a gift often expresses subservience. (See the similar phrase employed in the story of Jacob and Esau in Gen. 33:11.) Why does Elisha reject the gift so adamantly? He refuses the gift for one simple reason: "As the Lord lives, before whom (*lefanav*) I have stood, I will take nothing" (5:16). Elisha stands before God. His miracle is God's miracle. He refuses to accept anything, because the honor belongs to God alone. There can be no confusion regarding this point.

> He [Naaman] pressed him to accept, but he refused. And Naaman said, "Then at least let your servant be given two mule-loads of earth; for your servant will never again offer up burnt offering or sacrifice to any god, except the Lord. But may the Lord pardon your servant for this: When my master enters the temple of Rimmon to bow low in worship there, and he is leaning on my arm so that I must bow low in the temple of Rimmon – when I bow low in the temple of Rimmon, may the Lord pardon your servant in this." And [Elisha] said to him, "Go in peace." (5:16–19)

Elisha's principled refusal even under pressure and the voicing of his own subservience to God shifts Naaman further toward God. Naaman's subsequent request for soil goes beyond passive acknowledgment of God's greatness, and now he expresses his intent to worship God. However, his is a geographic conception of the divine. For him, the Israelite God is inextricable from the Land of Israel.[12] In a reversal of Naaman's earlier attitude, which denigrated the "waters of Israel" (5:12), Naaman now seeks the very soil of the land. To what purpose? Most commentaries explain that this soil was meant to be the foundation for a ritual altar.[13] It is interesting that Naaman retains his pagan conception that God is connected to a land, and yet affirms that the God of Israel is the supreme deity.

Despite these theological misconceptions, Naaman is committed. He announces that his bowing in Beit Rimmon – a pagan temple – is a sign of his dedication to the king, not to that deity. His ultimate allegiance is to God. Naaman has been transformed; not just physically, but spiritually as well. He leaves the prophet with the word "*Shalom*!"

GEHAZI'S BETRAYAL (II KINGS 5:20–27)

> Gehazi, the attendant of Elisha, man of God, said, "Behold, my master has spared Naaman that Aramean, by not receiving from his hands what he brought. As the Lord lives, I will run after him and take something[14] from him." (5:20)

The final segment of our story opens with Gehazi musing aloud to himself, or possibly to his two assistants (5:22), regarding the squandered opportunity to benefit from the generous gift that Naaman transported from Syria (5:5).

Gehazi is sardonically introduced by the bombastic title of "attendant of Elisha, man of God," and he twice refers to Elisha as "my master" (5:20, 22). But Gehazi is a fraudulent representative of his "master." These

12. This is a familiar Aramean perspective in which God is identified as the "God of the hills." See I Kings 20:23, 28.
13. Rashi; Radak. See Ex. 20:20: "Make for Me an altar of earth."
14. The Hebrew actually reads, "I will take *nothing* from him." Here the text reveals a cognitive dissonance on Gehazi's part as he justifies his indiscretion by insisting that the gifts he will receive are "nothing" compared to Naaman's six thousand shekels of gold (II Kings 5:5).

references, at first glance indicative of Gehazi's subservience to Elisha, are used with a sense of irony and sarcasm, demonstrating the façade used by Gehazi to deceitfully contravene and undermine Elisha's work.

> Gehazi pursued Naaman; when Naaman saw someone running after him, he alighted from his chariot to meet him. "Is everything all right (*Hashalom*)?" he asked. "Everything is all right (*Shalom*)!" Gehazi answered. (5:21)

Gehazi's pursuit of Naaman uses the root R-D-F, which has strongly negative connotations of a chase or hunt. The dissonance between the newly penitent Naaman and the cynical Gehazi is striking; Gehazi is stalking his quarry, yet Naaman, oblivious and innocent, merely sees a man running (*ratz*) from Elisha's vicinity to catch up with him. Naaman is unsuspecting prey, still inspired by the man of God. As such, he eagerly alights from his chariot. The use of the term *shalom*, the very one with which Elisha had sent Naaman on his way, is now employed deceitfully by Gehazi as he prepares to mislead and thieve from Naaman:

> "My master sent me to say, 'Two young men from the company of the prophets have just come to me from the hill country of Ephraim. Please give them a talent of silver[15] and two sets of clothing.'" "By all means, take two talents," said Naaman. He urged Gehazi to accept them, and then tied up the two talents of silver in two bags, with two sets of clothing. He gave them to two of his servants, and they carried them ahead of Gehazi. When Gehazi came to the hill, he took the things from the servants and put them away in the house. He sent the men away and they left. When he went in and stood next to his master, Elisha asked him, "Where have you been, Gehazi?" "Your servant didn't go

15. Note that the text indicates that Gehazi's words demonstrate an element of bashfulness and qualms of conscience. Gehazi requests gifts for two young men, but asks for "a (single) talent of silver and two sets of clothing." It seems that he should be asking for two talents of silver, yet evidently he is embarrassed to request the full amount. Nonetheless, Naaman gets the hint and he volunteers, "By all means, take two talents" – one for each.

> anywhere," Gehazi answered. But Elisha said to him, "Was not my spirit with you when the man got down from his chariot to meet you? Is this the time to take money or to accept clothes – or olive groves and vineyards, or flocks and herds, or male and female slaves? Naaman's leprosy will cling to you and to your descendants forever." Then Gehazi went from Elisha's presence and his skin was leprous; it had become as white as snow. (5:22–27)

Gehazi's standing as Elisha's assistant coupled with Naaman's newfound trust in God and His prophet only deepen the severity of Gehazi's duplicitous crime. Not only does Gehazi fabricate the tale of the sudden arrival of two young men, he attributes his mission to Elisha himself. Furthermore, Gehazi swears in God's name that he will take from Naaman, but this is the inverse of Elisha's explicit statement: "As the Lord lives… I will not accept anything" (5:16).[16] In a further inversion, whereas Naaman had urged Elisha to take gifts (*vayiftzar bo*), only to be met by a principled refusal, now Naaman now urges Gehazi to take gifts (*vayifratz bo*) and, of course, where his master had refused a largesse, Gehazi accepts the gifts (5:23). Gehazi is disdainful toward Naaman, "that Aramean" (5:20), in contrast to Elisha, who refers to him respectfully as "the man" (5:26).[17]

Gehazi, despite his closeness to his master Elisha, totally misses the point, evidently perceiving Elisha's miracles – God's wonders – as a source of personal gain. The power has gone to his head. For Gehazi, man does not stand before God; God stands at the service of man. The former arrogance of Naaman is now visible in Gehazi. Unsurprisingly then, he is afflicted with the illness of which Naaman had just been cured.

When Elisha questions and accuses Gehazi, the latter "stands next to his master," *vayaamod el adonav* (5:25). The language is quite deliberate, pedantically avoiding stating that Gehazi stands "before him" – *lefanav*; Gehazi has ably demonstrated his disdain for Elisha's authority.

16. Numbers Rabba 7:5.
17. The nomenclature is instrumental throughout the chapter. The king of Aram refers to Naaman as "my servant" (II Kings 5:6), the king of Israel talks about Naaman as "the man" (5:7), and Naaman refers to himself as "the leper" (5:11).

He certainly does not stand *lefanav*! Thus, as Gehazi leaves Elisha, leprous as snow, the verse states "He [Gehazi] left his [Elisha's] presence" – *vayetzeh **milefanav*** (5:27). Gehazi has misappropriated God's powers for his personal greed; he has abandoned his subservience both to Elisha and to God. He no longer stands "before Elisha."[18]

* * *

This riveting story is a poignant but simple meditation upon the values of society and religion. It is not the grand ceremonies and gestures but the contrite heart that God sees; not opportunistic manipulation but pure, straightforward honesty and humility that stand before God. Our societies are built such that everyone is entangled in a web of authority and social standing. We imagine that our career, our appointments, and our financial situation grant us authority or rights and privilege. But the truth may come from the mouth of the "little girl." Our titles and positions can become a mask that we hide behind. The recognition of God and self comes when we stand humbly before Him.

---

18. *Ḥazal* critique Elisha's total rejection of Gehazi: "Our Rabbis taught: Let the left hand repulse but the right hand always invite back: not as Elisha, who thrust Gehazi away with both hands, and not like R. Yehoshua b. Perachya, who repulsed Jesus (of Nazareth) with both hands" (Sanhedrin 97a). The message here is that a teacher not absolutely reject a student (both hands), but rather push them away with the weaker, left hand, and invite the errant student back with the right hand.

    Of course, this talmudic teaching raises interesting educational questions as to whether rejection or expulsion can be a prudent tool in dealing with a wayward student. The Rabbis were not averse to using the measure of excommunication in extreme circumstances. Why did they criticize Elisha's rejection of Gehazi? Possibly, they see Gehazi as a person who erred but would, with correct guidance, return to the proper path.

    I would argue that a critical distinction can be made between the *peshat* of this chapter and its application by the Talmud in Sanhedrin. In the Talmud, Gehazi is treated as Elisha's student; if that were the case, then indeed there would be place for a more nuanced approach and the possibility of a return to the beit midrash. However, in the book of Kings, Gehazi is not merely a student; the issue here is one of public service! Gehazi is the "director general" of the prophet's office; he is his public face. A man whose unethical inclinations have led him to misrepresent and misappropriate should absolutely be distanced from a public position.

II Kings 6:1–7

A Floating Ax-head

> The sons of the prophets said to Elisha, "See, the place where we live under your direction is too cramped for us. Let us go to the Jordan, and let us each get a log there and let us make us a place there, where we may dwell." And he said, "Go." And one of them said, "Will you please come along with your servants?" And he said, "I will go." He went with them. (II Kings 6:1–3)

We rejoin Elisha and his followers, the *Benei HaNevi'im,* as they voice their discomfort with their cramped housing conditions and make plans to create a new living space. Evidently the community ranks have burgeoned so considerably that they need to build more spacious and expansive premises.[1]

This could simply be a logistical problem: their original accommodations are unable to house the number of students,[2] and the high cost of city living makes it prohibitive for poorer students to join Elisha's group: "Elisha dwelt in Samaria, and city dwelling is harsh, for it is difficult to

1. In II Kings 2:16 we encountered this group numbering fifty men (although there would seem to groups in other locations); in 4:43 they number one hundred men, and now it would seem that their ranks have continued to expand.
2. Y. Sanhedrin 10:2.

afford lodgings and food" (Malbim). The Malbim, who points to financial distress, is drawing his cue from the scene of the ax-head: borrowed due to the high cost of buying one, its loss throws the student who borrowed it into sudden panic. Previous stories in II Kings about this group of prophets focus on scarcity of food and money;[3] we may surmise that they were an exceedingly impoverished community. The spacious rural environment of the Jordan Valley would certainly resolve these issues.

THE GEHAZI EFFECT

Up until this point in time, Elisha and his disciples live in Samaria[4] and Gilgal.[5] What drives them to relocate so far away, to the Jordan? There is room to suggest that the prophets' discomfort with Samaria, and their motivation to abandon the big city for the countryside, is not practical but ideological. Our starting point is the widely quoted midrash on the chapter's opening verse:

> What did Gehazi do [that caused the masses to sin]? He pushed away the sages from coming before Elisha, as it is written, "And the sons of the prophets said to Elisha, 'Behold, this place where we are staying before you is too cramped for us'" (II Kings 6:1). By inference, until that time [of Gehazi's banishment] it was not cramped.[6]

Radak explains:

> After Gehazi was banished by Elisha there was a surge in the number of students, because Gehazi was bad to them, and many feared to associate with Elisha due to the evil of Gehazi.

Gehazi's negative personality deterred hordes of students who would have otherwise sought Elisha's prophecy, wisdom, and leadership. In

3. The penniless widow, 4:1; foraging for food to cook, 4:39.
4. II Kings 5:3; chs. 6–7.
5. Ibid., 4:38; see also 2:1. Elijah's disciples are found also in Jericho; see ibid., 2:6.
6. Sota 47a; Sanhedrin 107a. See also Y. Sanhedrin 10:2, quoted by Rashi, Radak, and Ralbag ad loc.

the wake of Gehazi's departure, students could engage the prophet directly without Gehazi's off-putting personality. Our previous chapter depicted Gehazi's temptation to leverage the prophet's power for personal gain. A later scene vividly portrays Gehazi as Elisha's media publicist:

> Now the king was talking to Gehazi, the servant of the man of God, and he said: "Tell me all the wonders that Elisha has done." While he was telling the king how [Elisha] had revived a dead person..." (II Kings 8:4–5)

Gehazi has access to royalty; he is well connected, and here we witness the king summoning him to relate the miraculous stories of his master. If we were to transpose this scene to the world of contemporary media, Gehazi would be the type of person to have published the bestseller, the insider "tell-all" exposé of Elisha, appearing on all the talk shows, basking in the limelight as he discusses his career alongside Elisha.

The Talmud offers the following portrayal of Gehazi:

> When Elisha would sit and teach, [Gehazi] would sit outside the door. The students would see him there and say: "If Gehazi doesn't enter, how can we enter?" (Y. Sanhedrin 10:2)

Gehazi controls access to the prophet. He is indifferent to the Torah being taught inside. He is the impresario, the bureau chief, but his commercial intent and non-spiritual persona deter the genuine students. As such, Gehazi's dismissal may have effected change in two dimensions. First, in the absence of the gatekeeper, a huge influx of new students joined Elisha's prophetic circle. Second, this upheaval sparked a desire on the part of certain students to abandon Samaria with its high society and circles of influence, and to head for the more rustic Jordan, an environment that was most likely more conducive to spiritual contemplation.

Interestingly, Elisha doesn't join them. He says *lekhu*, "you go," and until he is explicitly requested to join the group, he is prepared to let the disciples found their new center independently. Elisha, as opposed to these followers, views residence in Samaria as integral to his work. True to his congenial personality, he is averse to spiritual seclusion. Beyond his personal proclivities, he seeks engagement with and to have influence upon the king of Israel, pursuing involvement in national affairs rather than withdrawal from them.

HOW TO FLOAT AN AX-HEAD

> And when they came to the Jordan, they cut timber. As one was cutting down a tree, the ax-head fell into the water; and he cried, and said, "Alas, master! For it was borrowed." And the man of God said, "Where did it fall?" And he showed him the place. And he cut off a stick and threw it there; and made the ax-head float [*vayatzef*]. He said, "Pick it up." And he reached out his hand and took it. (II Kings 6:4–7)

A mishap occurred to one of the *Benei HaNevi'im*, the very student who requested that Elisha accompany the group. While chopping timber, his ax-head became detached from the wooden handle, and the iron fell into the depths of the river. His cry reveals a deep moral sensitivity: "It was borrowed." More than the financial loss, he is concerned that he will not be able to return a borrowed object. Elisha "cut off a stick and threw it there; and made the ax-head float." Why does Elisha need to specially cut a stick? After all, he could just throw the handle of the ax into the water. The commentaries debate the mechanics of the miracle:

> He took wood already cut, and shaped it such that it would fit into the aperture of the ax-head and would act as its handle. This is the miracle – that when he hurled it in, it fit directly into the slot and remained there firmly, as we have already established in the matter of "wonders" ... that they do not change the course of nature.... The wood was of a size that its buoyancy could counter the weight of the ax-head and carry it to the surface. To this end, the piece of wood needed to be large and the [original] handle was inadequate. (Ralbag)

> He took wood and cut it so it had a flat surface such that the ax-head could float upon it.... "And it made the ax-head float": The word *vayatzef* is in the causative form... the wood brought the ax-head to the surface, such that this was a double miracle; the wood, which naturally floats on water, sank, and the ax-head was carried on top of the wood, such that they rose to the surface together. (*Daat Mikra*)

Both of these commentaries explain Elisha's action in a manner that does not contravene the physics of natural materials. These attempts to understand the miracle in a "natural" way feel somewhat forced, however, offering fanciful if creative scenarios. Abarbanel fundamentally rejects this approach:

> The prophet, when shown the precise location that the ax-head had fallen, took a small piece of wood in his hand and threw it to that place... as if the piece of wood was "calling" the ax-head to join it, and immediately the iron rose to the surface... and so it was that the wood, which is light, sank into the water contrary to its nature, and iron, which is heavy, floated! This demonstrates that [worldly] events are determined by God's power, and nature reflects the order instilled by God, and when He so desires He can alter [the natural] course. (Abarbanel)[7]

Whereas Ralbag looks for a natural explanation for the miracle, Abarbanel views supernatural acts as a miracle precisely because they contravene the laws of nature.[8] These are two fundamentally different ways

---

7. Abarbanel sees this as a critical feature of miracles. In his summary to the Elisha stories in his commentary on II Kings 8, he makes some general comments about Elisha's miracles. There he mentions: "He removed leprosy from Naaman and inflicted it on Gehazi; he opened the eyes of his assistant so that he could view that which he was unable to see, and he afflicted the eyes of the enemy soldiers so that they could not see; he stopped the heavens [from producing rain; Abarbanel sees 8:1 as Elisha himself declaring a seven-year drought] and filled the wadi and the pools with water [ibid., ch. 3]; and [effected] many other miracles that are opposites in their varied actions, a feature that points to the hand of God."
8. See also Zakovitch, "Control Mechanisms in Biblical Miracle-Narratives," 61–73, who shows instances in which the specifically unnatural quality of the action is what

of perceiving God's power. Does God seek to work through nature or behind nature? Or is God's way to overpower nature?

HUMAN PARTICIPATION

While we perceive this as supernatural act – it can be performed only by the prophet, who is designated as the "man of God" (II Kings 6:6) – we should note that Elisha never works as a thespian magician, staging a rousing display of his miraculous powers to an enthralled audience. He does not permit himself to become an incarnation of heavenly power; in fact, in several instances, he performs the miracle and then leaves its recipient to complete the process that he has begun.

> **The ax-head:**
> He said, "Pick it up." And he reached out his hand, and took it. (6:7)
>
> **The miracle of the oil:**
> "Go sell the oil and pay your debt, and you and your children can live on the rest." (4:7)
>
> **The revival of the child:**
> He said, "Pick up your son." ... She picked up her son and left. (4:36–37)

Elisha doesn't perform to admiring crowds. The miracle is executed functionally, without pomp, and then is passed along for further action by the beneficiary.

MOSES AND ELISHA: A MIDRASHIC ANALOGY

The miracle wrought by Elisha in this chapter finds a fascinating echo in a midrashic source concerning Moses:

> But how did Moses know where Joseph was buried? It is told that Serah, the daughter of Asher, survived from that

reveals its miraculous essence.

> generation,[9] and she showed Moses the grave of Joseph. She said to him. "The Egyptians put him in a metal coffin which they sunk into the Nile." So Moses went and stood by the Nile. He took a tablet of gold on which he engraved the Tetragrammaton, and throwing it into the Nile, he cried out and said, "Joseph, son of Jacob! The oath to redeem His children which God swore to our father Abraham has reached its fulfillment. If you come up, well and good. But if not, we shall be guiltless of your oath." Immediately, Joseph's coffin came to the surface and Moses took it.
>
> And you need not be surprised at this. Behold it says, "As one was cutting down a tree…. And the man of God said, 'Where did it fall?'" (II Kings 6:5–6). Now, if Elisha, the disciple of Elijah, could make iron come to the surface, how much more so could Moses, the master of Elijah, do it! (*Mekhilta DeRabbi Yishmael, Beshalaḥ*; Tosefta Sota 4:3)

On the one hand the midrash is suggesting that Elisha bears Moses' prophetic powers. Moses and Elisha employ the selfsame technique. For Elisha to be seen as invested with the powerful prophetic spirit of Moses is a high accolade indeed. Moreover, it is possible that this midrashic analogy develops a wider connection between the two stories.

Moses extracts Joseph's casket from Egypt at the moment of the Exodus.[10] The story that follows that scene is the crossing of the Reed Sea. There we witness the pursuit by the Egyptian army, and Israel's terror at the sight of their military forces: "All the *chariot horses* of Pharaoh, his horsemen, and his warriors…. As Pharaoh drew near, the Israelites *caught sight* of the Egyptians advancing upon them. Greatly frightened, the Israelites cried out to the Lord" (Ex. 13:9–10). Moses responds, "*Have no fear*! Stand by, and witness the deliverance which the Lord will work

9. Serah, the daughter of Asher, is mentioned in Gen. 46:17 as one of the seventy children of Jacob to descend to Egypt. However, she is also counted in those who left Egypt with the Exodus; see Num. 26:46. As such, legend sees her as a person with extraordinary longevity. See Rabbi Joseph B. Soloveitchik's piece in *Divrei Hagut VeHaaracha* (Jerusalem: World Zionist Organization-Eliner Library, 1982), 146 [Hebrew].
10. Ex. 13:19.

for you today" (Ex. 13:12). Of course, the sea splits and the Egyptians are drowned.

The same pattern and language is manifest in the very next story of our chapter. The king of Aram sends a force of "*horses and chariots*... and encircled the town."[11] Elisha's assistant *sees* the horses and chariots and cries out. Elisha responds, "*Have no fear*! Those who are with us are more than those who are with them" (II Kings 6:14–16).

In both stories we see an attack of horses and chariots, a cry of fright, a reassurance by the prophet, and miraculous salvation which eliminates the military threat.

The intertextual connection is not merely the miraculous raising of metallic objects from a riverbed. For Elisha, as for Moses, the force of horses and chariots need not be intimidating – because after all, it is not the laws of nature, but rather the power of God, that controls nature.[12]

---

11. That town is Dothan, the very area from which Joseph is sold (Gen. 37:17). The only two biblical stories that transpire at Dothan are Joseph's sale and the events of our chapter (II Kings 6:13). Consequently, the Dothan connection might account for the Joseph linkage in the midrash.
12. For this connection between the two stories in II Kings 6 by way of the midrash, see Daniel Sharshevsy, http://www.929.org.il/page/315/post/8483 [Hebrew].

II Kings 6:8–23

If Your Enemy Is Hungry...

Aram's military aggression against Israel escalates with a campaign of regular incursions into Israelite territory.[1] However, this hostility is continually frustrated by Elisha's extraordinary powers. Elisha consistently informs the king of Israel[2] of the whereabouts of the enemy forces, using his prophecy to effectively function as the national military intelligence and thwart the Aramean attacks. The precision of Elisha's alerts, experienced by Aram as a series of military failures, leads the king of Aram to suspect that a spy has penetrated his inner circle, until a courtier reveals that Elisha, "the prophet of Israel, tells the king the very words you speak in your bedroom" (II Kings 6:12).[3] The king of Aram

1. The notion of war is expressed by the verb L-H-M in II Kings 6:8. The repetitive pattern of Aram's attack is not illustrated merely by the phrase "not once or twice" in 6:10 but also by the use of the term *peloni-almoni* as a reference to place, indicating that the attacks recurred in any number of locations. See A. Berlin, "Poetics and Interpretation," in *Bible and Literature*, series 9 (Sheffield: Almond, 1983), 99–101.
2. See the chapter in this book entitled "Chronology and Structure in the Elisha Stories" for an explanation of why the king of Israel is not named.
3. This is similar to the story of Naaman, in which a servant finds a solution for a senior figure. The storylines of Naaman and this episode follow a similar pattern: The border attacks by Aram, the suggestion by a servant that Elisha is the answer to the problem, the king of Aram dispatching a military delegation to Israel in search of

promptly deploys a heavily armed division to besiege the town of Dothan, where the prophet is located, so that they may "seize"[4] Elisha and silence the intelligence "leak" that compromises Aramean strategic supremacy.

VISION AND BLINDNESS

Elisha's attendant awakens early, probably before dawn, and sees the military force encamped around the city. He is gripped by fear. Elisha, however, remains absolutely calm. He tells his panicked assistant, "Those who are with us are more than those who are with them" (6:16). What does Elisha mean? Elisha prays to God to "open the eyes" of his attendant, and suddenly he discerns Elisha's supernatural protection.[5] In stunning symmetry, "horses and chariots of fire" (6:17) surround Elisha, corresponding to the physical army that "surrounds the city, horses, and chariots" (6:15). When the troops begin to advance in the direction of the town, Elisha blinds the armed force,[6] paralyzing their military might.

Elisha, Elisha's miraculous resolution, and the return of the military force "in peace" back to Aram. Both stories close with an Aramean commitment to avoid further belligerence against Israel. We should note that also in the court of Israel, courtiers offer proposals that are adopted by the king; see II Kings 7:13.

4. It is unclear what the king of Aram wishes to do with Elisha. Malbim suggests: "[The king of Aram] has been informed that the prophet knows everything, including that which relates to him. Consequently, [Elisha] will certainly be fully aware that [Aram] is coming to arrest him and will protect himself. Thus it would seem that he didn't wish to capture him to have him harmed but rather he thought that he could shower him with wealth and prestige so that he would reside with him [in Aram], and he thought that the prophet would acquiesce.... The armed guard was for [Elisha's] protection in case the king of Israel would prevent his leaving the kingdom." This is a theoretical possibility; we recall the Moabite king, Balak, showering the prophet Balaam with wealth and honor to persuade him to employ his prophetic powers against Israel (Num. 22). However, it is more likely that the king of Aram wished to kill Elisha, much like II Kings 1, in which King Ahaziah dispatched military forces to arrest Elijah with the probable intent to execute him.
5. Opening of eyes in Tanakh is found in the narrative of the Garden of Eden (Gen. 3:5, 7), Hagar (ibid., 21:19), and Balaam (Num. 22:31). In the two latter cases, the opening of eyes leads to the perception of an angelic being.
6. The Hebrew term *sanverim* used to describe the blindness is found only in this episode and in the story of the destruction of Sedom (Gen. 19:11). There too, in the thick of night, the righteous man is surrounded by a large, aggressive force threatening his life. In order to save him, his angelic guests strike his foes with blindness.

We might ask, if Elisha anyway blinded the enemy force, what was the role of the "horses and chariots of fire"? The simplest resolution[7] is that the army was blinded by the light of the fiery chariots and horses. Their brilliance, the sudden burst of light, especially in the absolute darkness of the night, confused the enemy's vision and "blinded" them.

The story sets up a tension of opposites:[8] natural against supernatural forces, natural against supernatural sight and perception, vision[9] against blindness, and the all-knowing prophet against the feckless and bungling kings of Aram and Israel. These contrasts are accentuated by the chiastic structure of the narrative:

A Background – Aram's attacks against Israel
B King of Aram's proposal, the servant's correction, the deployment of troops to Dothan
C God opens the eyes of Elisha's attendant
D God blinds the Aramean army; Elisha leads them to Samaria
C2 God opens the eyes of the Aramean army
B2 King of Israel's proposal, Elisha's correction, the dispatching of troops back to Aram
A2 Conclusion/Consequence – Aram's attacks stop (6:23)

7. The modern Hebrew root S-N-V-R indicates "blindness" by excess light rather than nonvision. The NJPS translates it as "a blinding light." See Samet, *Pirkei Elisha*, 449.
8. Several wordplays illustrate the reversals endemic to this chapter. The word *vehinneh* (II Kings 6:15, 17, 20) reflects, first, the initial shock of the prophet's attendant when he sees the Aramean army, and second, his surprise as he witnesses the fiery force that surrounds Elisha. Later, *vehinneh* proclaims the surprise of the confused Aramean army as their eyes are opened and they realize that they are in Samaria.

   Though not a comprehensive list, other examples of wordplays in this episode include forms of the following verbs: H-L-KH (6:13, 19), in which the king of Aram's instruction to "go" is usurped by Elisha; and P-K-H, which expresses the "opening" of the eyes of the prophet's attendant (6:17) and which then finds similar expression in the corollary – the "opening" of the eyes of the Aramean soldiers (6:20). Lastly, the king of Aram says: "Where is he?" – *Eikho hu* (6:13), which is reflected by the attendant's comment, "What shall we do?" – *Eikha naaseh* (6:15).
9. The root R-A-H is found six times in the story (6:13; 6:17 twice; 6:20 twice; 6:21); possibly a seventh is implied in the phonetic wordplay of *al tira* in 6:16.

At the center of this structure (C-D-C2) is the miraculous opening and closing of eyes, the awareness that true perception is beyond that which meets the eye. As we have noted, Elisha rarely prays before enacting his miracles. And yet in this episode, each of his supernatural interventions – opening or blinding the eyes of those around him – are prefaced, three times, by a direct appeal to God. The special petition underscores that true vision belongs to God and must therefore be especially requested. By extension, Elisha's remarkable knowledge of the intimate discussions that transpire in the Aramean court is God's gift, an ability that is granted to ensure God's protection of His nation.

WAR ETHICS

Elisha leads the blinded troops to the capital, Samaria, and there he asks God to restore their sight. The text fails to give us a window into the soldiers' emotions: Confusion, perhaps? Shock? Surprise? Fear? Raising our expectations, we, along with the king of Israel, anticipate that these confused troops will be summarily executed, otherwise why lead the enemy to the capital city? The king consults with the prophet: "Shall I slay them, my father?" (II Kings 6:21),[10] to which Elisha responds:

> You may not slay them. Would you slay those whom you have taken captive with your sword and bow? Set bread and water before them that they may eat and drink and go to their master. (6:22)

What is Elisha's opposition to killing the Aramean troops? After all, this is the enemy! The commentaries offer two schools of thought:[11]

> By what right do you slay them? Did you take them captive with your sword and bow? (Radak)

10. This term of endearment indicates a close relationship between king and prophet as evidenced throughout this story. The appellation "father," along with a reference to chariots and horses, is echoed by Joash, king of Israel, on his visit to Elisha's deathbed. See II Kings 13:14. This is a repetition of Elisha's statement in 2:12.
11. Based on an analysis by Samet, *Pirkei Elisha*, 457–60.

> They were brought to you by a miracle! What rights do you have over them? (*Metzudat David*)

In war, the victor, the conqueror, wields power over his captives. In this case, however, God's miracle and not the king's forces entrapped the enemy soldiers. As a consequence, the king has no right to slaughter them. The decision is God's.[12]

But the verse might be making a different point when it stresses the notion of captive soldiers. From this perspective it raises a different moral question – whether prisoners of war may be legitimately executed:

> Is it your way to kill prisoners after you have taken them captive? (Rashi)

> Would you kill prisoners whom you have captured with your sword and bow? It is inappropriate! And it is all the more objectionable when God has taken them captive. (Ralbag)

Both Rashi and Ralbag identify Elisha as objecting to the execution of prisoners of war irrespective of who captured them. Killing the enemy has legitimacy in combat – to repel the mortal threat posed by one's adversary: "He who comes to kill you, precede him and kill him first" (Sanhedrin 72a). However, once the enemy is imprisoned and the threat neutralized, what would justify taking their lives?

For Radak and *Metzudat David*, the issue is a religious one: one may not benefit from God's victory. By contrast, Rashi and Ralbag frame this as a universal ethical issue, displaying a deep humane sensitivity well ahead of its time.[13]

12. Rofé, *The Prophetic Stories*, 47n11, sees the use of the words "sword and bow" as a quintessential expression of human as opposed to divine power. See Ps. 44:4–7; Josh. 24:12.
13. In a contemporary reflection on this story, Prof. Joseph Fleishman connects this episode to the IDF Ethical Code, which states: "The IDF servicemen and -women will use their weapons and force only for the purpose of their mission, only to the necessary extent, and will maintain their humanity even during combat. **IDF soldiers will not use their weapons and force to harm human beings who are not combatants or against prisoners of war**, and will do all in their power to avoid causing harm to their

GREATER IS THE BANQUET

> If your enemy is hungry, give him bread to eat; if he is thirsty, give him water to drink. (Prov. 25:21)

The king of Israel doesn't just grant the attacking soldiers their lives; he hosts a huge feast before allowing them to return to Aram. This act of generosity makes a deep impression upon the Arameans. The result: "The raiding parties of Aram came no more into the Land of Israel" (II Kings 6:23). Regarding this magnanimous treatment, a midrash states:

> Greater is the banquet that Elisha prepared together with the king of Israel than all the battles of Jehoram, son of Ahab, as it says (Eccl. 9:18): "Wisdom is better than weapons of war." (*Eliyahu Rabba* 8)

Rabbi Elchanan Samet examines this strategy in a careful and insightful manner:

> Elisha is not satisfied with a mere victory over the Aramean forces. His mind is incessantly occupied by the question, "What will the troops report to their king, and what conclusions will the king of Aram reach from their story?" Elisha's objective...is to bring the king of Aram to a point at which the military border incursions cease.... Only when the king of Aram will recognize the esteem in which the prophet is held as a "holy man of God" will he change his belligerent intent.
>
> Let us suppose that the Aramean soldiers had been kept as prisoners of war and never returned.... It would likely have stimulated the king of Aram to retaliate in a more aggressive and sophisticated manner....

---

lives, bodies, dignity, and property." He comments, "The ethical code of the IDF follows a similar line to the ethical code of Elisha"! See http://www.929.org.il/page/315/post/8478.

Let us suppose that the Aramean soldiers had been expelled and returned to the king of Aram in a state of humiliation, not only to tell their king of the failure of their mission but also the manner in which the prophet intimidated and fooled them by leading them to Samaria, then deporting them in a state of disgrace...this would merely have raised the enmity of the Aramean king.

Instead the Aramean soldiers returned to their king with a very different story. Even though they had failed in their mission, they did not return home in a state of disgrace, but instead, in joy and exhilaration. They described how that had been blinded, and how the prophet had led them to Samaria. They certainly relayed how the king asked the prophet for permission to execute them, and how the prophet berated the king, saving their lives. But the climax of the story would have been... the great feast which the prophet made for them, and the friendly manner in which he sent them back to their land and king....

Elisha's behavior demonstrates absolute military superiority over Aram, a superiority that would have allowed him... to treat the enemy, without qualms, as he wished. However, his conduct expressed something even higher: a moral superiority. Elisha's actions express a mode of operation high above that of Aram; he harbors no antagonism, and feels no need to take vengeance for the harm they intended to inflict upon him.... In this way, Elisha dismantled walls of antipathy and suspicion that separated them from him. He sends the military force back to their master as admirers of the prophet, ambassadors of peace and good will."[14]

Wars are characterized by aggression and domination. The king of Aram sought to use his firepower to bludgeon Elisha into submission. However, Elisha's way is not the path of confrontation but rather the provision of food and drink, hospitality, kindness, and humanity. Had the king executed the army division another would have been drafted

---

14. Samet, *Pirkei Elisha*, 462–64.

in their place, but now, similar to the situation of Naaman, the troops return with tales of Israel's humanity and generosity. This reaps a greater strategic dividend, and the attacks cease. The story ends with the conclusion: "And the Aramean raiding parties came no more into the Land of Israel" (II Kings 6:23).

* * *

We have told the tale of this chapter as one of victory for Elisha, a morality of compassion, and an exhibition of God's power. Yet as we read further on we wonder whether this impression is correct. The text continues: "After this, Ben-Hadad, king of Aram, mustered his entire army and marched upon Samaria and besieged it" (6:24).

How can verses 23 and 24 be reconciled? Perhaps the king of Aram had been spurred to avenge the humiliation of his troops, blinded and cornered in Samaria. Some commentators propose that there was a significant time lapse between the stories.[15] Others suggest that the king of Aram, now comprehending Elisha's power but still determined to attack Israel, changed his strategy, replacing the vulnerable "raiding parties" and "[mustering] his entire army" instead.[16] As we shall see, this is merely the beginning of a long and bitter campaign by Aram to dominate Israel, a military advance that even Elisha will be unable to defeat.

15. Radak.
16. Ralbag.

II Kings 6:24–7:20

Siege and Salvation

THE SIEGE IN SAMARIA

> And so it was, after this, Ben-Hadad, king of Aram, mustered his entire army and marched upon Samaria and besieged it. There was a great famine in Samaria, and the siege continued until a donkey's head sold for eighty [shekels] of silver, and a quarter of a *kav* of pigeons' dung for five shekels. Once, when the king of Israel was walking on the city wall, a woman cried out to him, "Help me, Your Majesty!" "Don't [ask me]," he replied. "Let the Lord help you! Where could I get help for you; from the threshing floor or from the winepress? But what troubles you?" the king asked her. The woman answered, "That woman said to me, 'Give me your son and we shall eat him today; and tomorrow we'll eat my son.' So we cooked my son and we ate him. The next day I said to her, 'Give up your son and let's eat him'; but she hid her son." When the king heard what the woman had said, he tore his clothes; and as he walked along the wall, the people could see that he was wearing sackcloth underneath. He said, "Thus and more may God do to me if the head of Elisha ben Shaphat remains on his shoulders today." (II Kings 6:24–31)

The Aramean aggression intensifies as the "entire army" besieges the capital city, Samaria, subjecting it to grievous starvation. A variety of images depict the severity of the devastation inflicted by the siege. First, the miserable choice of the available food: a donkey's head and pigeons' droppings sold at exorbitant prices, illustrates the dire situation. The donkey meat is for food, but what of the bird droppings? Radak suggests that it was used for heating and fuel, but Ralbag proposes a more creative option:

> Due to the enemy attack, the countryside was filled with grain (the people couldn't leave the city to harvest it). The doves would feast upon the grains, eating so much that they could not digest it all; hence much of the grain remained in their droppings.

The thought of eating the head of a donkey or picking through bird droppings for undigested grains gives ample insight into the plight of the people of Samaria.

ON THE WALL

A second perspective of the dire hunger is the macabre solicitation of the king by an unnamed "woman" as he tours the city walls, most likely supervising the fortifications and military positions of Samaria's perimeter. The woman's appeal reflects a classic court scene; her initial cry, "Help me, Your Majesty!" is used elsewhere as the initiation of a royal judicial hearing.[1] The case she presents is a squabble between herself and another woman. In the name of justice, the woman claims that she bears rights to the other's child.

The unmediated audience with the king, the two women, the lack of evidence, and the wrangling over a dead child evoke the judgment of Solomon in I Kings 3, yet the obvious comparison merely underscores the vast chasm that separates the two cases: the justice this woman seeks is grotesquely perverted, as she demands that her associate honor her word and give over her son so that they may devour him. This horrific

1. II Sam. 14:4.

scene echoes the worst predictions of the *tokhaḥa*, the "rebuke":[2] "You shall eat the fruit of your own body, the flesh of your sons and of your daughters ... in the siege."[3] This scene resurfaces once more in the vivid ordeals of the destruction of the First Temple.[4]

The depiction of women, who naturally bear, nurse, and nurture their children, as cannibalizing their sons – a most fundamental violation of human nature – is a direct sign that the people have been forced to compromise the most basic aspects of their humanity. In this case, the woman seems oblivious to her self-incrimination as she professes to the king that she consumed her own son. The siege has indeed brought the nation to its knees.

THE KING

The extreme situation, so desperate and hopeless, possibly furnishes an explanation for the vacillating response of the king. At first he reacts with frustrated despair, supposing that the woman is asking him to procure food: "'Don't [ask me],' he replied. 'Let the Lord help you! Where could I get help for you; from the threshing floor or from the winepress?'" But he quickly regains his composure when he understands that she is merely asking him to resolve a dispute. "But what troubles you?" he responds. After listening carefully to the woman's twisted predicament he immediately rips his royal robes; a sign of mourning, shock, and horror. His torn robes reveal that he is wearing sackcloth underneath, evidence that the king is engaged in penitence and prayer.[5]

In his desperation, the king lashes out at Elisha, blaming the prophet for the national ruin and threatening the prophet's life.[6] The

---

2. The curses of Lev. 26 and Deut. 28 are colloquially known as the "rebuke." They warn of the national ruin that will ensue if Israel abandons the observance of God's covenant and laws.
3. Deut. 28:53.
4. "Should women eat the fruit of their womb, the children of their tender care?" (Lam. 2:20); "The hands of compassionate women have boiled their own children" (ibid., 4:10).
5. I Kings 21:27; II Kings 19:1–2; Jonah 3:5.
6. Why does the king blame Elisha? Possibly he felt that Elisha had not exercised his ability to pray (Rashi; Radak), or alternatively, because he had explicitly decreed a seven-year famine in the land; see II Kings 8:1 (Abarbanel). Perhaps the king blamed

king's condemnation[7] seems to reflect a moment of heated panic, which is swiftly rescinded, for in the very next scene a messenger of the king arrives for Elisha, and far from slaying the prophet, appeals to the religious leader in a spirit of reverence and humility: "This calamity is from the Lord; what more can I implore from the Lord?" (II Kings 6:33).[8]

How might we assess this king, who concurrently demonstrates earnest penitence and yet threatens the life of the prophet?[9] The *Midrash HaGadol* articulates the king's ambivalence in a fascinating way:

---

the prophet for freeing the forces of Aram (II Kings 6:22–23), allowing them to regroup and attack a second time. See Oded Bustenai and Michael Kochman, eds., *Olam HaTanakh* (Tel Aviv: Yedioth Ahronoth / Chemed, 2002 [Hebrew]).

7. The king threatens to remove Elisha's "head." Note the interplay with the "head of the donkey" (II Kings 6:25).
8. The scene is textually difficult. Initially the king threatens Elisha's life, with Elisha responding by instructing his men to "shut the door and hold the door fast against him" (ibid., 6:32). However, when the messenger arrives, rather than assaulting Elisha he voices his despair, evoking God's name twice. Moreover, Elisha announces that the king will follow the messenger (see ibid.; this is verified in 7:17), and although the king's arrival is never recorded, his "aide upon whose arm the king was leaning" responds to Elisha's statement, indicating that the king himself was present in the prophet's chamber. Was the king sincere in his death threat to Elisha? What induced the king's assassin to invoke God rather than carry out the royal command? The commentaries all labor to resolve these textual difficulties; see Samet, *Pirkei Elisha*, 505–10, for a summary of the opinions, and a possible reconstruction of the scene.

   Josephus reconstructs the scene in a reasonable way: "He sat in his house... with none but his disciples about him, he told them that Jehoram [the king], who was the son of a murderer, had sent someone to take away his head. 'But,' said he, 'when he that is commanded to do this comes, take care that you do not let him come in, but press the door against him, and hold him fast there, for the king himself will follow him and come to me, having altered his mind.' Accordingly, they did as they were bidden when he that was sent by the king to kill Elisha came. But Jehoram, repenting of his wrath against the prophet, and fearing that the man who had been ordered to kill him might already be doing so before he came, hastened to prevent the murder, and to save the prophet. And when he came to him, he accused him that he did not pray to God for their deliverance from the miseries they now lay under, but saw them so sadly destroyed by them. Hereupon Elisha promised that the very next day, at the very same hour in which the king came to him, they should have great plenty of food" (Josephus, *Antiquities* IX, 4:4).
9. The Talmud (Taanit 14b, and Rashi there) rereads II Kings 6:33 as suggesting that the king turns to God in prayer: "This calamity is from the Lord. Now I must implore the Lord." It is in response to his prayer then, that Elisha delivers his prophecy of

> "I am black but comely" (Song. 5:1). The people of Israel said before God: Even though I am black, I am also comely.... There was no king more evil than Jehoram son (of Ahab). About him the verse states: "And the people looked, and behold, he had sackcloth beneath, upon his flesh." When he witnessed the distress of Israel, he could not contain himself... *evil on the outside, but integrity within.*[10]

SALVATION

Elisha responds to the king by predicting a swift end to the siege and a return to normality. Just as the hunger is illustrated by means of the pricing and choice of foodstuffs, likewise is the relief from starvation:

> Listen to the word of the Lord. So says the Lord: Tomorrow at this time, a *se'ah* of fine flour shall be sold for a shekel, and two *se'ah* of barley for a shekel, at the gate of Samaria. (II Kings 7:1)[11]

Elisha's prophecy sounds like an improbable prediction of someone who plainly underestimates the situation. Indeed, this skepticism is expressed by the city captain (*shalish*). And yet Elisha's words have been made with full divine authority.[12] At this point in the story, "three matters now lie in the balance: the fate of the city, Elisha's fate, and God's prediction."[13]

---

consolation and relief (II Kings 7:1). Of course this is not the impression from the *peshat* of the text, in which the king seems to vent his frustration in a blusterous threat against Elisha.

10. *Midrash HaGadol*, Exodus, 35:5–6.
11. Cogan and Tadmor, *II Kings*, 81, point out: "A *se'ah* in Israel in the age of the monarchy was approximately 7.3 liters.... In Babylonia, in ordinary times, one shekel of silver could buy ten *satu* of barley (approximately 100 liters).... Thus if the shekel in Israel was of comparative value, which is still to be proven, Elisha's prediction of abundance was only relative; the cost of choice flour was still many times its normal price. But even that seems to have been taken as a blessing to the siege-weary residents of Samaria."
12. The divine nature of this pronouncement is given central impact by the sevenfold variations of the phrase *davar/dibber* and *devar Hashem*; see II Kings 7:1, 2, 16, 17 (twice), 18, 19, in reference to this prediction.
13. Rofé, *The Prophetic Stories*, 51.

At this juncture the story takes a shift to a group of four lepers in a seemingly disconnected, slow, and meandering sequence, a substory with not insignificantly comic overtones, as the simple, self-interested lepers unknowingly stumble upon Samaria's deliverance. In accordance with Torah law, lepers must reside outside the community, banished from the urban habitat.[14] These anonymous lepers sit at the "entrance to the gate"[15] of Samaria outside the city, and as such they have opportunities of which the besieged inhabitants of Samaria cannot avail themselves; they can approach the Aramean army camp. In the face of the dire starvation which has engulfed the city they try their luck by venturing to the enemy camp:

> Why should we sit here waiting for death? If we decide to get into the town, we shall die, and if we sit here, we shall die. Come, let us desert to the Aramean camp; if they let us live, we shall live, and if they put us to death, we shall die. (7:3–4)

The chances look slim, but the lepers exploit the sole opportunity for survival. To their utter surprise, they discover that the siege camp is absolutely deserted. God had intervened:

> God caused the Aramean army to hear a sound of chariots, a sound of horses,[16] a din of a huge army. They said to one another, "The king of Israel must have hired the kings of the Hittites and the kings of Egypt to attack us!" (7:6)

Aram had panicked and abandoned their positions. Initially, the self-absorbed lepers eat, drink, and bury whatever loot they had managed to

14. Lev. 13:45–46; Num. 5:1–4.
15. The gate of the city (*shaar*) plays a prominent role in the chapter (II Kings 7:1, 3, 10, 11, 17, 18, 20). The words *se'or* (barley) and the measure of a *se'ah* are all alliterations of this word.
16. The flight of Aram seems unrelated to Elisha. However, we can't help but wonder regarding the possibility of a connection between the sound of chariots and horses here with Elisha's horses and chariots in II Kings 6:15.

carry away.[17] But though they are societal outcasts, their communal conscience irks them: "We do not well: this day is a day of good tidings, and we hold our peace" (7:9). They announce the good news to the city, the king sends scouts to verify that the troops of Aram have indeed fled, the siege is lifted, and supplies are restored to the city. The word of God as expressed in Elisha's prediction is proven true.

A LEPROUS REDEMPTION

This astounding deliverance emerges from an unexpected source. Ironically, the prophet is not the instrument of salvation; he may know the timing of the collapse of the siege but he seems unaware precisely how it will conclude and who will be the instrument of relief. The Aramean retreat is discovered accidentally, by a group of unsuspecting lepers. What is the story telling us by granting these inglorious outcasts the historic role of heralding the nation's freedom?

The modern Hebrew poet Rachel[18] wrote a poem based upon this chapter. It is a bold statement of refusal to accept a tainted miracle. She writes:

> For a long while, the dreadful enemy
> Brought Samaria to siege;
> Our lepers to her brought tidings.
> To her brought the tidings of freedom.
>
> As Samaria besieged, the entire land,
> The famine is unbearable.
> But I do not want to receive news of redemption
> From the lips of a leper.
>
> The pure will bring news and the pure will redeem,
> And if his hand won't be there to redeem,
> Then I will choose to die from the suffering of the siege,
> On the eve of the day of the great tidings.

---

17. *Ḥazal* identify the four lepers with Gehazi and his sons (see Rashi 7:3). The connection point might be the taking of the loot, both here and in II Kings 5:23–24.
18. Rachel Bluwstein (1890–1931). In Israel she is simply known by her first name.

Rachel is an idealist. She dreams of a pure, unblemished redemption, and she prefers to die in the suffering and squalor of the siege rather than receive the tidings of salvation from the unworthy.

Does Rachel's poem express a classic Jewish perspective? Fascinatingly, the Talmud relates a scene in which the Messiah himself is a leper sitting at the gates of the city:[19]

> R. Yehoshua b. Levi met Elijah standing by the entrance of R. Shimon b. Yochai's tomb.... He asked him, "When will the Messiah come?"
>
> "Go and ask him," was his reply.
>
> "Where is he sitting?"
>
> "At the entrance to the city."
>
> "And by what sign may I recognize him?"
>
> "He is sitting among the poor lepers. All of them untie [their bandages] all at once, and reapply them together, whereas he unties and reapplies each [bandage] separately, thinking, 'Should I be called [if it is time for my appearance as the Messiah], I must not be delayed [through having to reapply all the bandages].'" (Sanhedrin 98a)

On this basis we would say that Judaism does not always present redemption as pristine or flawless. For the Talmud, unlike for the poet Rachel, redemption may arrive precisely by means of a leper![20]

---

19. The Talmud (Berakhot 54a–b) tells another story in which lepers, precisely because of their vantage point outside of society, perceive God's salvation, which would otherwise have been missed by the nation.
20. In an article entitled "Israel's Independence Day: Reflections in Halacha and Hashkafa," Rabbi Ahron Soloveitchik addresses the question of the religious significance of the State of Israel, and the claim that if the State of Israel was established by nonobservant Jews it may not be seen as religiously worthy – certainly not a redemptive occurrence. He cites the story of the leprous salvation referred to in to this chapter:

    > We thus see that the miracle of the deliverance of all the inhabitants of Samaria was carried out through the medium of four lepers: physical lepers, yes; but above all, spiritual lepers....
    >
    > The first argument, as to how any relief for the Jewish people could be realized through the medium of *apikorsim* (heretics), can easily be rebutted by

QUESTIONS

At first glance this chapter is a wonderful tale of transition from mortal crisis to sudden resolution, of prophetic prediction and fulfillment, of death to life. That is the way the story is told. But when we reconsider the context, the grand picture is disturbing. This story narrates a mere twenty-four-hour period on the eve of the national turnaround from siege to relief. But what of the previous weeks, months, and years? It is apparent that Elisha resides in the city throughout the duration of the siege. Where are his powers? Could he not bring the hostilities to a close or mitigate its dreadful impact? We read the chapter and celebrate the relief and the miracle of salvation, but how many people died before the relief came? How much suffering did the nation endure?

> the precedent of the deliverance accorded the people of Samaria through the medium of the four lepers. This episode shows that no Jew can be excluded from the grace of God, that "*Yisrael, af al pi she-chata, Yisrael hu*" (a Jew, even though he has sinned, remains a Jew), and that there is an innate tendency toward altruism even in the heart of spiritual lepers.
>
> It also shows that God does not exclude any Jew from salvation and He may therefore designate even spiritual outcasts as the messengers of relief and deliverance for the people of Israel. Consequently, we cannot ignore the significance of the establishment of the State of Israel simply because Jews who stand a substantial distance from any form of observance of mitzvos were at the forefront of founding the State. Perhaps the fact that nonobservant Jews are in the forefront today is a penalty for Orthodox Jewry's failure to play the most important part in the formation of the state.

In one of Rabbi Yehuda Amital's celebrated *siḥot* (sermons) for Yom HaAtzma'ut, Israel Independence Day, he relates to the same theme. See http://etzion.org.il/en/reishit-tzemichat-geulatenu:

> The Chatam Sofer (*Parashat Shoftim*) comments that several times during the course of history, the Holy One wanted to redeem Israel with an incomplete redemption, such as during the period of the Second Temple, but the Nation of Israel refused, for we have no desire for an incomplete redemption.... The Chatam Sofer wrote this prior to the Holocaust, but after that terrible period... we understand that there was never any *ḥillul Hashem* (desecration of God's Name) like the Holocaust, nor any *kiddush Hashem* (sanctification of God's Name) like the establishment of the state. There can be no doubt that praise and thanks should be offered for the establishment of the state, even if it is not a messianic redemption, the "revealed end."

As the poet Rachel states quite clearly, the story presents highly tainted characters; no personality escapes unscathed. All the characters are flawed; the salvation is flawed:

- We witness the king's royal outer robes and his inner sackcloth. Who is this king? Is he righteous or evil?
- The prophet knows when the relief will come; can he not save the city before its time?
- The woman on the wall seeks justice, but she has eaten her own child.
- The lepers, banished from the city, undergo a transformation as the story progresses. At first they are selfish; they eat and drink and hide trinkets while the nation continues to starve. After some time they begin to consider the starving masses, and they recognize their self-centeredness. Are the lepers worthy? What are we to make of this story?
- Even God seems to be hidden in this story. There is no direct imagery of chariots and horses of fire as in our earlier chapter. Instead we hear obliquely how "God caused the Aramean army to hear a sound of chariots, a sound of horses," but the scene of salvation is hidden from view.

The events of the next chapter will give some explanation to the peculiarly undistinguished salvation of this chapter.

II Kings 8:7–15

Elisha's Tears

VISIT TO DAMASCUS

> Then Elisha came to Damascus. Ben-Hadad, king of Aram, was sick, and it was told him, saying, "The man of God has come here." The king said to [his attendant] Hazael, "Take a gift in your hand and go to meet the man of God, and inquire of the Lord by him, saying, 'Will I recover [lit., live] from this sickness?'" Hazael went to meet him and took a gift in his hand, every kind of good thing of Damascus, forty camel-loads; and he came and stood before him and said, "Your son Ben-Hadad, king of Aram, has sent me to you, saying, 'Will I recover from this sickness?'" Then Elisha said to him, "Go, say to him, 'You will surely recover,' but the Lord has shown me that he will certainly die." The man of God kept his face expressionless as long as he could, and then he wept.[1] Hazael said, "Why does my Lord weep?" Then he answered, "Because I know the harm that you will do to the sons of Israel:

1. This translation follows Rashi, Radak, Ralbag, and *Metzudat David*. Many other translators translate it as: "He [Elisha] fixed his gaze steadily on him until he [Hazael] was ashamed." Whereas the text supports this reading, the context fits best with the reading of the traditional commentators.

> You will set their strongholds on fire, and you will kill their young men with the sword, and you will dash their little ones in pieces, and you will cut open their pregnant women." Then Hazael said, "But how can your servant, who is a mere dog, perform such a mighty deed?"[2] And Elisha answered, "The Lord has shown me a vision of you as king of Aram." So he departed from Elisha and returned to his master, who said to him, "What did Elisha say to you?" And he answered, "He told me that you would surely recover." On the following day, he took the cover and dipped it in water and spread it on his face, so that he died. And Hazael became king in his place. (II Kings 8:7–15)

This dramatic scene closes the sequence of Elisha stories.[3] Up to this point in time Elisha has functioned exclusively within Israel, engaging with various groups: the common folk, the *Benei HaNevi'im*, and royalty. But now Elisha steps into foreign territory. Why does Elisha visit Damascus, a foreign capital? Did the prophet intend to meet with the king, Ben-Hadad, and did Elisha alert the king's court to his arrival? And if so, what message did he intend to communicate?

On a first reading, this is yet another episode in the series of vignettes which demonstrate the prestige Elisha enjoyed in Aram,[4] a relationship of respect that is evidenced by the manner in which Ben-Hadad expresses his esteem for Elisha by calling himself "your son"[5]

---

2. Hazael views these vicious acts as a "mighty deed" or "great thing" – a reflection of military prowess. His reference to himself as a dog is an expression of self-disparagement, a reflection of his self-perception as an ordinary commoner (Kiel, *Daat Mikra*), or possibly a loyal servant of his master, the king – a dog usually follows his master. So he is saying, "How would I, a mere commoner, have the power to enact such incredible devastation?" Elisha replies that he will indeed become king.
3. There are still a few remaining stories: The anointing of Jehu in II Kings 9:1–6 and King Joash's visit to Elisha on his deathbed in ibid., 13:14–19, followed by the resurrection of the soldier (ibid., 13:21). However, this is the final segment of the uninterrupted sequence of the Elisha stories.
4. Previous episodes would be the story of Naaman (ibid., 5:17), and the story of Ben-Hadad's army and the foiled capture of Elisha (ibid., 6:8–23).
5. The corollary of "your son, Ben-Hadad," is voiced by the king of Israel referring to Elisha as "my father" in ibid., 6:21; 13:14.

and sending Hazael with bountiful gifts. Furthermore, Ben-Hadad's question, "Will I recover from this sickness?" evokes a parallel with II Kings 1. There Ahaziah, the injured king of Israel, sends the identical inquiry to the Philistine god, Baal-Zebub – an appeal to a foreign deity that was viewed as a betrayal and public disgrace to the God of Israel. Here we have the inverse scene, in which a foreign, idolatrous sovereign views Elisha, the "man of God," with such prestige that in his sickness he seeks his counsel and that of his God. If the tale of Ahaziah is an affront to God's honor, this story is a magnificent *kiddush Hashem*, a testimony to the way that Elisha spreads reverence for God.

INSTIGATING ASSASSINATION

Elisha's dialogue with Hazael, Ben-Hadad's attendant, is intriguing. In the first instance Elisha says to Hazael: "Go, say to him, 'You will surely recover,'[6] but the Lord has shown me that he will certainly die" (8:10). And the second time: "The Lord has shown me a vision of you as king of Aram" (8:13). Elisha's first communication seems almost duplicitous, as it contains two conflicting statements. Initially he instructs Hazael to console the king that he will live, but then he informs the king's courtier that in fact, Ben-Hadad will die. His second statement goes a stage further in that it explicitly announces that Hazael will assume the throne. Why does the prophet hide the truth from Ben-Hadad but expose it to Hazael? Why the double message?

Metzudat David suggests that the positive prognosis addressed to Ben-Hadad, although untrue, was intended to console him, to prevent adding to the stress of a dying man.[7] Malbim, bothered by the prophet's untruth, suggests a technical resolution of the language: "'You will… recover' with regard to this illness; however, 'he will… die' of another cause, because in fact Hazael killed him." But my feeling is that the Radak

---

6. The Hebrew here is awkward, as there is a critical disparity between the written text and the chanted text (*kri-ketiv*). The written text reads: "You shall not live" and the chanted text reads: "You will surely live."
7. This finds its way into the *Shulḥan Arukh, Yoreh De'ah* 338:1, which rules that one must be very careful not to use startling language with the dying, as it might expedite their death.

is closest to the mark when he suggests that Elisha's prevarication was aimed at instigating Ben-Hadad's assassination:[8]

> "You will recover *from the illness*...but the Lord has shown me *that you will be killed*." Thus, when Elisha informed Hazael that he would be king over Aram and he said, "The Lord has shown me that he will certainly die," Hazael understood that he wished to inform him that [Hazael] should assassinate [Ben-Hadad], but he didn't say it explicitly.

Elisha was essentially laying out a murder plot to Hazael. By having Hazael issue the deceitful reassurance to the king, Ben-Hadad would be misled into a false sense of security and would be off guard when Hazael came to kill him.[9] If the Radak is correct and Elisha is igniting a royal assassination, we need to probe the prophet's motives.

ELIJAH'S THREE TASKS

Why is Elisha getting involved in an Aramean royal coup? To appreciate this, we must return to I Kings 19. There at Mount Horeb, God had issued a series of instructions to the prophet Elijah:

> And the Lord said to him, "Go, return on your way to the desert of Damascus, and you shall come and anoint Hazael as king over Aram. And you shall anoint Jehu son of Nimshi as king over Israel, and you shall anoint Elisha son of Shaphat, from Abel Meholah, to be prophet in your stead." (I Kings 19:15–16)

Elijah was to perform three acts of anointing:[10]

8. The Radak's approach is shared by Long, *II Kings*, 105. See Cogan and Tadmor, *II Kings*, 92. Aramean historical records verify Hazael's seizure of the throne, as they address Hazael as "son of a nobody"; in other words, not of royal descent.
9. See Yael Shemesh, "Lies by Prophets and Other Lies in the Hebrew Bible," *Journal of the Ancient Near East Society* 29 (2002).
10. Elijah fails to accurately follow God's instructions; he performs only the third of the three tasks assigned to him: appointing his successor, Elisha. What of the other two tasks? Those are left for Elisha to perform, and it would seem that even Elisha

- Hazael as king of Aram
- Jehu as king over the Israelite (northern) kingdom
- Elisha as prophet in his stead.

What is the background to this series of leadership appointments? In that scene, Elijah had protested to God about the terrible idolatrous regime of the house of Omri, led by King Ahab and his wife, Jezebel. God responds to Elijah's outrage with these three acts of appointment, a threesome of leadership figures who become a three-pronged, synchronized plan to violently punish the northern kingdom and end the Omride hegemony:

> Those who escape the sword of Hazael, Jehu will kill, and those who escape the sword of Jehu, Elisha will kill." (1 Kings 19:17)

Hazael is the force of punishment from the outside; his kingdom will deliver a crushing blow to Israel.[11] Jehu is the force of destruction that emerges from within Israel. Jehu is an officer in Ahab's army. As depicted in the upcoming chapters, he betrays and assassinates the king, the son of Ahab, and executes the evil Jezebel.[12] The daunting mission spelled out to Elijah on Mount Horeb is the decimation of the house of Omri and the punishment of Israel, as enacted by Hazael and Jehu.

ELISHA'S TEARS

But what then is the role of Elisha? He is also singled out by God as the third of the figures whose sword will bring an end to the house of Omri. We have followed him for some time now. He generally seems to be a nonvindictive figure,[13] offering assistance of one sort or another to

delays these acts for an extended period. Moreover, Elisha's appointments are done by proxy: a disciple of Elisha anoints Jehu, and since Elisha lacks the legal power to anoint Hazael, he incites Hazael to assassinate the king and usurp the throne.

11. II Kings 10:32; 13:6–7.
12. Ibid., chs. 9–10.
13. Exceptions are the forty-two children killed by the bears (ibid., 2:23–25), his outburst to Jehoram (ibid., 3:13), the treatment of Gehazi (ibid., 5:26–27), and the trampling of the *shalish*, the king's aide (ibid., 7:17–20).

individuals, groups, or the nation. Can we envisage Elisha as a partner to the malicious figures of Hazael and Jehu?

Let us return to the scene in which Elisha talks to Hazael. Elisha glimpses an image in which Hazael will ravage Israel: "You will set their strongholds on fire, and you will kill their young men with the sword, and you will dash their little ones in pieces, and you will cut open their pregnant women" (II Kings 8:12). At this thought, Elisha becomes emotional and cries. The phrase "the Lord has shown me," expressed twice during the encounter (8:10, 13), suggests that while Elisha is speaking with Hazael, he views the powerful scenes before his eyes, experiencing prophecy in real time. The visions he beholds are so dreadfully horrifying that he is overwhelmed by emotion and cannot contain his tears.

Rabbi Elchanan Samet contends that Elisha's weeping deeply affected Hazael:

> This weeping communicates not merely the prophet's unfathomable pain, but also a critique of the cruel potential latent in Hazael's personality.
>
> Just as Hazael will be cognizant, throughout his tenure as king over Aram, that he owes his monarchy to the Israelite prophet... he will also live in the shadow of the prophet's tears... it will be a moral restraint upon Hazael's actions, and a proscription of his more monstrous acts. When Hazael battles his enemy Israel, he will fulfill his sovereign responsibility and lead his nation to victory after victory, however, he will not actualize his potential for absolute victory and cruelty. Even though he almost destroys the Israelite army... we have not heard of Hazael attacking women and children in Israel, and as such, the dreadful prophecy of Elisha: "You will dash their little ones in pieces, and you will cut open their pregnant women," never transpired.[14]

Samet suggests that Elisha's tears influenced Hazael to limit his heartless violence, but it is difficult to sustain this reading. Hazael is depicted as

14. Samet, *Pirkei Elisha*, 597.

pulverizing Israel (II Kings 10:32; 13:6–7), and there is no ready evidence that Hazael mitigates his aggression due to Elisha.

Let us try to depict Elisha's tears as connected to a wider context, as a function of his role in the particular circumstances and events through which he lives.

ELISHA'S HISTORICAL CONTEXT: ARAMEAN SUPPRESSION

Elisha leads Israel through a period that exceeds sixty years.[15] This is an era characterized more than anything else by Aramean intimidation, invasion, and suppression. Elisha's incumbency is uncannily aligned with this period of Aramean agitation and control, and it would seem that his mission serves as a willful response to it.

The escalating hardship that is associated with this era is carefully detailed in the chapters of II Kings:

- Chapter 3 describes Elisha's participation in a war against Moab, a result of Israel's waning influence in Transjordan. This campaign ends inconclusively, as Israel fail to defeat Moab.
- The aggression of Aram begins as we encounter Naaman, the Aramean general, who leads sporadic military incursions into Israelite territory, taking Israelites as war captives (5:2).
- In the next stage (see 6:8) Aramean military infiltrations have become a matter of routine, a part of an ongoing war of attrition against Israel.
- Chapters 6 and 7 narrate a full-scale assault and lengthy siege against Samaria by Ben-Hadad's entire army, a siege that is broken only by divine salvation.
- Chapter 8, verses 7–14, describe Elisha's prophecy to Hazael, warning of an intensification of Aramean aggression whereby Hazael will

15. Elisha starts his tenure under the reign of Jehoram and dies during the reign of Jehoash. Jehoram ruled for twelve years, Jehu for twenty-eight years, Jehoahaz for seventeen years, and Jehoash for sixteen years; this comes to seventy-three years. If we include Elisha's apprenticeship under Elijah, which probably began during Ahab's reign, we are most certainly dealing with sixty years of public service.

"set their strongholds on fire, kill their young men with the sword, and dash their babes in pieces" (8:12), among other atrocities.

- This prediction materializes in full. We read how in the period of King Jehoahaz, "the king of Aram ... decimated them and trampled them like dust under his feet" (13:8).

Elisha's role is intimately connected to the predominance of Aram, and it is then not coincidental that Elisha's final act is to pronounce the fall of Aram and the restoration of Israel's northern border,[16] a strategic reversal in which Aram lose power and Israel restore their security and territorial integrity. In his deathbed scene, Elisha heralds a turnabout in the national fortunes:

> Elisha had been stricken with the illness of which he was to die, and King Joash of Israel went down to him, and wept over him .... Then [Elisha] said ... "An arrow of victory for the Lord! An arrow of victory over Aram! You shall rout Aram at Aphek, until you destroy them." (13:14–17)

ELISHA'S POWERLESSNESS

It is now time to redefine Elisha's role. He is the prophet whose role is to guide Israel through a dark period of defeat, invasion, siege, and famine,[17] navigating arduous times.

---

16. II Kings 14:25.

17. Ibid., 4:38; 8:1. The Talmud (Taanit 5a) discusses this seven-year famine explicitly:

> R. Nachman said again to R. Yitzchak: It is written [ibid., 8:1]: "For the Lord has called for a famine, and it is also coming on the land for seven years." What was eaten during those seven years? And he answered: So said R. Yoḥanan: In the first year they ate the reserve store that they had in their houses; in the second year they ate the reserve store they had in the fields; in the third they ate the flesh of ritually clean animals; in the fourth, the flesh of ritually unclean animals; in the fifth year they ate reptiles; in the sixth year the famine was so severe that people had to eat their own children; and in the seventh it reached a stage where some had to eat the flesh from off their own arms. And the saying [Is. 9:19]: "They shall eat every man the flesh of his own arm," was proven true.

See also Ralbag on ibid., 6:24, who sees the devastating siege on Samaria in which

One particularly irksome aspect of Elisha's prophetic tenure is that with all his remarkable miracle-making – healing springs and lepers, procuring food, resurrecting the dead – he is unable to use his supernatural powers to repel the Aramean aggressor and to defend the nation. This is highly pronounced during the siege of Samaria (6:24–7:20) where the narrative celebrates Elisha's premonition of the siege's end, and yet absurdly, despite Elisha's amazing foreknowledge, he is absolutely powerless to overpower the enemy. Likewise, when he blinds the Aramean force who surround Dothan, his chariots of fire and horses of fire protect him personally, but he never intends to destroy the power of the Aramean military.

Why is Elisha denied the wherewithal to save Israel?

ELISHA'S MISSION[18]

In God's original instruction to Elijah (I Kings 19:15–16), which is issued after Elijah's failure to reform Ahab and to draw his regime away from its

people were eating the flesh of their children as overlapping with the seven-year famine referenced in 8:1. Perhaps this also relates to the statement in 7:2 referencing "windows in the sky," giving the sense that the years of siege were also years of famine.

18. The general approach taken in this chapter was heard from Rabbi Yoel Bin-Nun. Rav Yoel adds a further point as he makes a distinction between popular prophets and national prophets. The Talmud in Megilla 14a suggests that whereas Tanakh has only forty-eight prophets who we can identify, there were many more: "Were there no more prophets than these [forty-eight]? ... There were actually very many, as it has been taught: 'Many prophets arose for Israel, double the number of [the Israelites] who came out of Egypt'; only the prophecy that contained a lesson for future generations was written down, and that which did not contain such a lesson was not written." In other words, many thousands of prophets were spiritual men and women who assisted people in need but did not engage in national issues. They addressed the classic issues that agitate people – "length of life, children, and sustenance" (Moed Katan 28a) – and for which people, even today, will seek a spiritual address. We find Saul visiting Samuel to find his lost donkeys (I Sam. 9), and Jeroboam's wife asking the prophet whether her son will live (I Kings 14:2–3), and each time the expectation is that they will bring a gift. Similarly, Elisha deals with a lost object (II Kings 6:5); has people bringing him gifts – "A man came from Baal-shalishah and he brought the man of God ... twenty loaves of barley bread" (II Kings 4:42); and deals with a sick child (4:18–37). Similar to Samuel (I Sam 7:16–17), Elisha seems to circuit the country preaching to the people, especially on holy days such as Rosh Ḥodesh and Shabbat (II Kings 4:8, 23, 25, 38). This is the "popular"

commitment to idolatry, He decrees the fall of Ahab's kingdom. Hazael and Jehu were the agents to deliver that bitter pill. As such, during this time, Israel was destined to be overrun and controlled by Aram. Both Elisha and the king of Israel were incapable of impeding that momentum, denied the capacity to alter Aram's relentless military assault that would terminate the Omride dynasty and punish Israel.

Although initially it seemed that Elisha was the third agent of divine punishment alongside Hazael and Jehu, an instrument of God's wrath and retribution, Elisha adopts a very different role. During this time of phenomenal hardship for the kingdom of Israel, Elisha serves as something of an antidote, a counterbalance. His miracles serve individuals or small groups, offering benevolent assistance and a palpable sense of God's presence. In the international arena, his impressive powers never

---

or we might call it plebeian guise of prophecy. Very different to this model is the Samuel who acts as a national leader as he establishes the monarchy, and certainly prophets such as Elijah, Isaiah, and Jeremiah who function on the national stage, interacting with royalty in an advisory or critical capacity, frequently delivering direct divine oracles; these prophets are the seers whose prophecy "contains a lesson for future generations," whose words were recorded for posterity, and whose prophetic messages were recorded in books, sometimes known as the literary prophets. Those national prophets function very differently to the popular, plebeian prophets, men of the people, who address individuals in their moments of distress.

Interestingly, it seems as if Samuel functioned in both capacities. Where does Elisha fit? Let us recall that Elisha is appointed during the reign of Ahab and Jezebel, when prophets were under severe persecution, and living in fear and hiding (I Kings 18:4, 13; 19:10). Other than Elijah, were there prophets of the caliber to function upon the national stage as a state-prophet? In the view of Rav Yoel Bin-Nun, Elisha is fundamentally a popular prophet who, by virtue of circumstances, was compelled to rise to the occasion and function as a national prophet. This explains at some level the manner in which Elisha's prime function is the performance of miracles to the common folk and his local preaching. It might also explain why, with exception of the anointing of Hazael and Jehu, he never pronounces grand national oracles or high literary messages. It also offers a possible rationale for Elijah's reticence in nominating Elisha as his successor. Elisha's fundamental character is that of the popular prophet, but in a world in which there are few prophets, he finds himself serving in a wider and higher function than his norm. This distinction might also go some way to understanding Elisha and his role.

The distinction between popular prophets and national prophets has already been made by Yehezkel Kaufman; see Y. Kaufman, *The Religion of Israel*, translated and abridged by Moshe Greenberg (Chicago: University of Chicago Press, 1960), 275.

extend to eliminating the enemy forces; instead they generate reverence for the God of Israel, as expressed by Naaman and even Ben-Hadad.

Elisha, far from being the instrument of God's rage, is a symbol of protection, relief, consolation, support, assistance, and comfort. Throughout the years of foreign occupation and attack, domestic hardship and suffering, Elisha uses all his God-given powers in the service of keeping faith in God alive. Rather than confronting the king of Israel, he allies with him. Even the king of Israel asks the prophet's attendant to relate to him "the wonderful things that Elisha has done" (II Kings 8:4). In a generation in which faith might have been lost, Elisha is a beacon communicating God's steadfast presence, even during moments of punishment and military defeat. Elisha doesn't overpower the enemy, he cannot break the siege, but he befriends king and commoner alike, helping them understand that despite the adversity, God is still the God of Israel and He will not abandon His people.

II Kings 2–8 retrospective

Chronology and Structure in the Elisha Stories

> On the basis of the years of the kings, Elisha served Israel from the nineteenth year of Jehoshaphat until his death – a period of sixty-six years.[1]

As we close our study of Elisha, we should draw attention to his extraordinarily long career. He became an apprentice to Elijah in the days of Ahab, and assumed the full status of prophet close to the advent of King Jehoram, Ahab's son. He died during the reign of Jehoash.[2] This lengthy tenure raises questions regarding the historical context of the Elisha stories (II Kings 2–9).

Any attentive reader of II Kings 5–8 will have noticed that the king of Israel is always referenced in anonymity. This is curious, given

1. Abarbanel, II Kings 13:17.
2. This view is first found in *Seder Olam* 19, which speaks about "over sixty years" starting in the nineteenth year of Jehoshaphat's reign until the tenth year of the reign of Jehoash of Israel. The nineteenth year of Jehoshaphat's reign is the second year of Jehoram's reign. The length of the kings' reigns are as follows: Jehoram, twelve; Jehu, twenty-eight; Jehoahaz, seventeen; and Jehoash, sixteen. From the nineteenth year of Jehoshaphat's reign to the tenth year of Jehoash's reign is about sixty-six years.

that the monarch features prominently in virtually every episode. Why is the king unnamed, and which king is being referenced throughout these stories?

The standard approach adopted by many midrashic sources and followed by the traditional commentators is to assume that the nameless king is Jehoram. This accords with the flow of the chapters. Jehoram's ascent to the throne is recorded in chapter 3. Jehoram's assassination by Jehu features in chapter 9. If the flow of the text follows simple chronology, then undoubtedly, the king in question is Jehoram. The anonymous referencing of the king, however, raises other possibilities. Several factors support this alternative:

1. King Jehoram reigns for a mere twelve years. Could it be that all of Elisha's miracle stories are concentrated into twelve years of a sixty-year career, or might they be more evenly spread?[3]
2. Several of the Elisha stories depict the king and the prophet in a warm and positive relationship.[4] This seems discordant with the acerbic attitude exhibited by Elisha toward the idolatrous Jehoram: "What have you to do with me? Go to your father's prophets or your mother's prophets" (3:13–14). A relationship of respect and cooperation would make more sense if the king in question were Jehu, a God-fearing king, or his son, Jehoahaz.
3. The siege of Dothan (ch. 6), followed by Aram's entire army besieging the capital Samaria in an extended campaign (6:24–7:20), testify to the ease with which Aram penetrate central Israel. These stories suggest that Israel's northern border has entirely collapsed. However, this picture does not match up with the national security situation during Jehoram's

3. Kiel, *Daat Mikra*, suggests this option. See his comments in the summaries on pp. 538, 542, and 547–48.
4. For example, note the reference to Elisha as "my father" in II Kings 6:21.

> reign. The Israel-Aram border was drawn at Ramoth Gilead in Transjordan during Jehoram's reign (see 8:28; 9:1), and, as such, it is unlikely that the Aramean army could have so easily penetrated Jehoram's defenses, deep into the heartland of Israel's territory.
>
> This state of affairs would seem to reflect more accurately the dreadful crumbling of Israel's military in the later period of Jehu and his son Jehoahaz, during which Aram devastates the Israelite provinces of Transjordan (10:33), penetrates the heartland as far as the city of Gath (12:18), and humiliates the northern kingdom: "For the king of Aram had decimated them and trampled them like the dust under his feet" (13:7).

In summary, the evidence suggests that Elisha indeed functioned under Jehoram but that several of the episodes involving the prophet transpired later, during the reign of the kings who succeeded Jehoram: Jehu, Jehoahaz, and Jehoash.[5]

THE SEQUENCE OF THE ELISHA STORIES

If the chronology is disrupted, why are the Elisha stories grouped in a single collection? Why does the Tanakh arrange all the stories one after the other rather than narrating them in their historically appropriate, i.e., chronological, context?

The answer is as follows: the ordering principle of the Elisha stories is not historical but associative. Each episode is hinged onto the preceding one by dint of a commonality of theme or language which furnishes a linkage between stories.[6] Here are some of the connection points:

---

5. Kiel, *Daat Mikra*, 548; Rofé, *The Prophetic Stories*, 53–56.
6. See Y. Shemesh, "The Stories of Elisha: A Literary Analysis," 14–32, for a thorough analysis of the organizational principles of the Elisha stories. Kiel, *Daat Mikra*, adopts this approach as well. See his chapter summaries.

Reference	Story	Link to previous story
II Kings 1	Elijah and Ahaziah's delegates	—
2:1–18	Elijah's ascent – transition from Elijah to Elisha	• Both chapters 1 and 2 relate to groups of fifty soldiers (II Kings 1:9–13) and prophets (2:7, 17). • The root SH-L-KH (1:2, 6, 9, 13, 16 / 2:2, 4, 6, 16, 17) • Repeated use of a vertical theme • The roots A-L-H and Y-R-D
2:19–22	Healing the spring at Jericho	• The story is a continuation of the previous one geographically (Jericho) and chronologically • The chiasm of the chapter (Bethel/Jericho/Jordan/Transjordan/Jericho/Bethel) supports the placement of this story
2:23–25	Bears	• "And he left [Jericho]" (2:23) establishes this as a continuation of the previous story, as does the aforementioned chiastic pattern
3:1–27	War against Moab	• "He returned to Samaria" (2:25) / "in Samaria" (3:1) • *vatibakana* (2:24) / *lehavkia* (3:24) • The killing of children concludes both stories
4:1–7	The widow and the oil	• The filling (*yimaleh*) of the empty wadi with water (3:17, 20) / the filling (*hamaleh*) of the empty jugs with oil (4:4, 6) • "Elisha…poured water" (3:11) / "pour" (4:4) • The root N-S-A: "So they withdrew (*vayisu*)" (3:27) / "Remove each one as it is filled (*tasi'i*)" (4:4)

Reference	Story	Link to previous story
4:8–37	The Shunammite	• In both stories Elisha assists a woman who refers to herself as his "maidservant" (4:2 / 4:16) • Both are stories of a woman and her children: the danger to the child (or children) is averted, and life is restored • "What can I do for you?" (4:2) / "What shall be done for her?" (4:14)
4:38–41	"Death in the pot"	• "And he died" (4:20) / "death in the pot" (4:40)
4:42–44	The bread	• Both are stories of Elisha providing food for the *Benei HaNevi'im* • Both stories have a similar structure[7] • "Give to/pour for the people that they may eat" (4:41 / 42, 43)
5:1–27	Naaman	• In both stories gifts are brought to the prophet (4:42 / 5:5, 15)[8]
6:1–7	The floating ax-head	• The Jordan River features in both stories • Similar language: "*ho'el na*" (5:23 / 6:3); "*Hinnei na*" (5:15 / 6:1); "has not gone anywhere [*aneh vaanna*]" (5:26) / "Where [*ana*] did it fall?"(6:6)
6:8–23	Dothan – chariots of fire	• The word *makom* features three times in each story • "Alas, Master!" (6:5 / 6:15)

7. Samet, *Pirkei Eliyahu*, 291.

8. There are few parallels to the story that immediately precedes chapter 5, but many more between the Naaman story and the episode of the Shunammite and her son: "*isha gedola*" (II Kings 4:8) / "*ish gadol*" (5:1); "She stood before him" (4:12) / "He stood before him" (5:15); Gehazi is present in both stories; the number seven: "The boy sneezed seven times" (4:35) / "bathe seven times" (5:10, 15); the greeting "*Hashalom*" and the response "*Shalom*" (4:26 / 5:21-22).

Reference	Story	Link to previous story
6:24–7:20	Siege in Samaria	• Chronological connection: "And it was, afterward" (6:24) • "Horses and chariots" (6:13–14 / 7:14) • Both stories have the Arameans surrounding a town
8:1–6	The king and the Shunammite	• In both stories, women cry out to the king (6:26 / 8:3) • Both stories include the king's courtiers: the *shalish* (7:2, 19) and the *saris* (8:6) • "*Kedabber ish HaElokim*" (7:18) / "*kidevar ish HaElokim*" (8:2)

Looking at this list, we observe that the entire Elisha unit is organized under the principle of "*semikhat parashot*" – connections from one section to the next. On this basis of a literary connection between stories we are free to propose that the pieces of the Elisha story form a literary sub-unit extending over a wider historical span than the twelve years of Jehoram's reign, as may appear at first glance from the sequence of the chapters here in Kings.[9] Since all the Elisha stories are grouped within

9. Some oppose this entire theory. Samet, *Pirkei Elisha*, 638–45, supports the rabbinic identification of the king as Jehoram and asserts that the stories are indeed chronological. After all, Elisha's earlier stories (the healing of the waters in Jericho, the bears, and the war with Moab; II Kings 2–3) are incontestably from the start of Jehoram's reign. Likewise, the later stories – the anointing of Hazael and the appointment of Jehu – are clearly dated from the close of the Jehoram period. As for the middle episodes, Samet assumes that the veneration for Elisha, expressed by the royal court of Aram when Elisha visits Damascus, is a product of his fame in the episodes of Naaman (ibid., ch. 5) and Elisha's blinding of the troops in Dothan (ibid., ch. 6). On this basis, the stories are indeed ordered chronologically. Elisha's description of the king as "the son of the murderer" (ibid., 6:32) merely confirms the king's identity as Jehoram, son of Ahab. (Ahab is a "murderer" on the basis of I Kings 21:19.) As for the singular identity of the king, Samet contends that these stories display a consistent characterization of King Jehoram as a man animated by pessimism, despair, and fearfulness.

Yet Samet must still account for the huge historical lacuna in Elisha's patronage of the nation: Why does Elisha disappear after the anointment of Jehu, only to return in

the segment that depicts Jehoram's reign, the insertion of an alternative monarch at this juncture would confuse the reader. As a result, the only solution is to leave the king as an unnamed, generic "king of Israel."

ELISHA REFLECTING ELIJAH

An alternative interpretation of the chapter ordering is also particularly attractive. The table below demonstrates the manner in which the Elisha narratives reflect the structural paradigm of the Elijah stories.

Elijah Narratives: I Kings 16–II Kings 1	**Elisha Narratives: II Kings 2–8**
I Kings 16:34 Jericho	II Kings 2:18 Elisha in Jericho
17:2–6 Elijah drinks the water in the wadi	3:9–20 Soldiers of Israel drink the water in the wadi
17:8–16 Elijah and a widow; oil and flour miraculously multiply	4:1–7 Elisha and a widow; oil miraculously multiplies 4:38–44 Flour in the pot; loaves extend themselves to provide food
17:17–24 Resuscitation of a widow's child	4:8–37 Resuscitation of a widow's child
18:20–39 The miraculous spectacle at Mount Carmel induces recognition of God: "The Lord alone is God!" (18:39)	5:1–27 Elisha miraculously cures Naaman, who responds: "Now I know that there is no God in the whole world except in Israel!" (5:15)
19:1–3 Elijah's life is threatened	6:8–14 Elisha's life is threatened
chs. 20 and 22 Two military campaigns of Israel against Aram	chs. 6–7 Two military campaigns of Aram against Israel
II Kings 1 Elijah delivers God's word to a dying king	8:7–15 Elisha delivers God's word to a dying king

In this schematic structure of the Elisha chapters, the Elisha stories are modeled after those of Elijah, his master. In the same manner,

one final appearance, on his deathbed, during the reign of Joash? To this Samet turns to the model of the prophet Samuel, who anoints King Saul, interacts with him, and yet after the king fails, anoints David as Saul's successor as his final act. He then disappears from public life. Similarly, Samet suggests that Elisha was particularly designated to work with King Jehoram. He obeyed God and had Jehu anointed, but he never sought to work alongside Jehu. As the national prophet, his allegiance lay with Jehoram.

the proclamation: "My father, my father! Israel's chariot and horsemen!" is made both at Elijah's death and at the death of Elisha (II Kings 2:12; 13:14). The student who requested "a double portion" of his master's spirit finds the narrative of his miracles and interactions constructed upon the paradigm of the master himself.

* * *

We began by noting that Elisha's lengthy prophetic career is unlikely to fit into the historical window in which it is placed by the book of Kings. We also observed that all references to the king of Israel throughout II Kings 5–8 are uncharacteristically anonymous. Our analysis has led us to suggest that these chapters are in fact a collation of the Elisha stories which transpired over the entire span of Elisha's life. We suggested two different methods of organization of the sequence of stories. The first orders them using a literary and thematic linkage, an attempt by the author of Kings to telescope the stories of Elisha into a concentrated sequence.[10] The second arranges Elisha's stories upon the pattern set by his master, Elijah, generating two symmetrical units, aligning Elijah and Elisha in succession as well as in parallel to each other.

We might propose a single rationale in both of these systems as we stand back and consider the structure of this book. The question might be asked as to why Kings, a book whose framework is the royal chronologies of the kings of Israel and Judah, includes two lengthy segments about prophets, the first centered around Elijah (I Kings 17–II Kings 2) and the second around Elisha (II Kings 2–9). The answer might be found in the book of *Ben Sira* (*Ecclesiasticus*), where it reviews the period of Israel's tenure in the land. It evaluates certain leaders:

---

10. Some have suggested that the author of Kings merely copied a segment of a preexisting book of the miracles of Elisha. This may explain the origins of this collection and the anonymity of the king. A similar phenomenon may be found in Is. 36–38, which imports an entire segment of II Kings 18–20. But one still needs to explain why the editor of Kings chose to insert the collection without reorganizing it. Moreover, since we know of no such written source regarding Elisha, this thesis is highly speculative, and as a result we can only relate to the text as we know it.

> Joshua was loyal as long as Moses lived.... Then there were the judges...who never fell into idolatry and never abandoned the Lord.... All the kings, except David, Hezekiah, and Josiah, were terrible sinners, because they abandoned the law of the Most High... surrendered their power and honor to foreigners, who set fire to the holy city and left its streets deserted, just as Jeremiah had predicted.[11]

Sandwiched in between David and Hezekiah, we hear about Elijah and Elisha:

> Then there arose the fiery prophet Elijah, whose words blazed like a torch....
>
> When Elijah was hidden by the whirlwind, Elisha was filled with his spirit. As long as he lived, he was not afraid of rulers, and they could not make him do as they wished.... In life and in death he performed amazing miracles.
>
> *But in spite of all this*, the people did not abandon their sinful ways until they were taken from their land as prisoners and scattered all over the world.[12]

The book of Kings seeks to explain the *Ḥurban*. Enveloped by regnal chronologies, two lengthy sections of Kings describe the great prophets Elijah and Elisha: Elijah, "the fiery prophet," and Elisha, the prophet of miracles. These were God's emissaries to the northern kingdom to warn the people and avert national disaster. However, "*in spite of all this*, the people did not abandon their sinful ways." We now easily identify the message of the book. The nation cannot claim they had not been cautioned, cannot complain that God failed to send guidance. Two prophets, each with divergent temper and style, were dispatched. Israel was afforded every chance to reform itself, but it failed to heed the divine warnings.

11. *Ben Sira* 47–49.
12. Ibid., 48:1, 12, 14, 15.

II Kings 8:16–29

Jehoram (Judah)

Up to this point, the narrative of II Kings has described events relating to the northern kingdom of Israel. Its style has been a flowing series of dramatic legends with the prophet as the key figure and the kings of Israel featured only as secondary characters. Now we return southward to the kingdom of Judah, and the literary rhythm of the book shifts pace; Kings resumes its formulaic format of interlocking royal summaries which give the book its historical continuity and its literary scaffolding.

In this schema, the kings of Judah and Israel are presented by a standard introduction: a regnal summary that gives the name of the king, his age at his ascent to the throne, the name of his father and mother, and the duration of his rule. The monarch is assessed on a binary spiritual gauge regarding his ritual allegiance to God ("good in the eyes of God") or his worship of foreign deities ("evil in the eyes of God"). Kings synchronizes the succession of kings in the northern and southern kingdoms in order to generate a single historical continuum.

KING JEHORAM OF JUDAH

The last Judahite king we encountered was the righteous monarch Jehoshaphat,[1] a man characterized by deep religious devotion and a penchant for justice and national unity. His firstborn son, Jehoram, is appointed by his father and ascends the throne in his father's lifetime, which might lead us to anticipate a similarly God-fearing monarch. Instead, Jehoram represents a national downturn in virtually every domain:

> He followed the practices of the kings of Israel – whatever the house of Ahab did, for he had married a daughter of Ahab – and he did what was evil in the eyes of God. However, the Lord refrained from destroying Judah for the sake of His servant David in accordance with His promise.... During his reign Edom rebelled against Judah's rule and set up a king of their own... and Libnah likewise rebelled at that time. (II Kings 8:18–22)

Spiritually

Jehoram is influenced not by his pious father but by his evil wife, Athaliah, daughter of Ahab and Jezebel,[2] who is as ruthless[3] as she is idolatrous. As a result, the degenerate moral and ritual norms of the northern kingdom infiltrate the administrative culture of Judah. When the verse speaks of Jehoram turning to "the practices of the kings of Israel" (II Kings 8:18), this indicates Baal worship – a terrible religious downturn for the southern kingdom. The statement that "the Lord refrained from destroying Judah" (8:19) ominously implies that Judah's religious betrayal made it deserving of destruction.

1. I Kings 22:41–51, and see more of his achievements in II Chr. 17–20. For his interests in national unity, see I Kings 22:4; II Kings 3:7; II Chr. 18:2.
2. There is some ambiguity here. II Kings 8:18 indicates that Jehoram married Ahab's daughter; 8:26 seems to indicate that Athaliah was Omri's daughter. Most commentators assume that the reference in 8:26 identifies Athaliah by her grandfather Omri, and not by her father, Ahab.
3. II Kings 11:1.

Politically

The precise circumstances of Jehoram's rise to power are rather elusive. It would seem that a rivalry developed between Jehoshaphat's sons as they vied for power during their father's twilight years, triggering Jehoram's premature coronation.[4] In Chronicles, we read:

> He had brothers, sons of Jehoshaphat: Azariah, Jehiel, Zechariah, Azariahu, Michael, and Shephatiah.... Their father gave them many gifts of silver, gold and [other] gifts, as well as fortified towns in Judah, but he gave the kingdom to Jehoram because he was the firstborn. Jehoram proceeded to take firm hold of his father's kingdom and put to the sword all his brothers, as well as some of the officers of Israel. (II Chr. 21:2–4)

This scenario of a leadership battle between contending brothers is familiar to us; Kings opened with Solomon and Adonijah contending for King David's throne. Once a rivalry of this sort erupts, the king is compelled to name one of his heirs as his successor. In King David's case, Solomon was designated, anointed, and seated upon the royal throne, all while David

4. Jehoram (son of Ahab) of Israel ascends the throne in Jehoshaphat's eighteenth year (II Kings 3:1). Jehoshaphat reigns for twenty-five years (I Kings 22:42). On this basis, Jehoshaphat's son Jehoram of Judah should have ascended the throne in the eighth year of Jehoram of Israel. However, II Kings 8:16 records that he ruled in the fifth year of Jehoram son of Ahab. There is a three-year disparity. This indicates that Jehoram of Judah was crowned in his father's lifetime and served as coregent with his father. Such is the theory proposed by *Seder Olam* 17, and this opinion is adopted by Rashi and Radak, as well as by Cogan and Tadmor, *II Kings*, 95. This may explain the insertion of Jehoshaphat's name into the title line of II Kings 8:16, which indicates the overlap between the two kings (Kiel, *Daat Mikra*).

One difficulty in the timeline relates to the verse in II Kings 1:17 (end of verse), which suggests that the rule of Jehoram of Judah predated that of Jehoram of Israel, contradicting all the other chronological indicators in Kings 3:1 and elsewhere. To resolve the discordant verse, Ralbag offers a theory based on a joint confederacy between the north and south, whereas Rashi and Radak (ibid., 8:16) cite a midrashic tradition (Tosefta Sota 12:2) suggesting that Jehoshaphat's death was decreed at that point, but due to prayer God granted him a seven-year reprieve.

remained in office.[5] However, whereas Solomon executed his rival only after Adonijah's attempt to depose him, Jehoram secures his position by murdering every one of his brothers and other "officers of Israel," presumably civil servants and politicians who sided with other candidates.

This systemic political violence casts Jehoram in the worst company, as a murder of this sort has been wielded only by the Bible's most ignominious and debaucherous of leaders.[6] Quite possibly this pitiless butchery was learned from Jehoram's mother-in-law, the wicked Jezebel, who had no compunction when it came to murder.[7]

National Security and Foreign Control

A third sphere in which Jehoram fails is in national defense. Under his rule, Edom overthrows Israelite control. Israel had controlled Edom ever since the heyday of King David, but now Jehoram fails to suppress their uprising such that Judah loses control over Edom "to this day."[8] Whether the failure was military or diplomatic, Jehoram is rendered as a weak leader. More devastating than the loss of foreign colonies, Chronicles details a calamitous invasion by forces of "the Philistines, the Arabs who were neighbors of the Kushites":

> They marched against Judah, breached its defense, and carried off all the property that was found in the king's palace, as well as his sons and wives. (II Chr. 21:17)

Taking the royal family captive seems to be the ultimate indignity, and proof of an abject failure of national defense.

---

5. Solomon also executed his half brother and rival, Adonijah. But in the account in I Kings 2, Adonijah was initially granted a reprieve; his execution followed his scheme to depose Solomon. See discussion of this in Israel, *I Kings: Torn in Two*, 30–45.
6. For example, Abimelekh (Judges 9:5), Baasha (I Kings 15:29), and Athaliah (II Kings 11:1).
7. I Kings 18:4, 13; 19:2; 21:7–16.
8. Edom was returned to Israelite control during the reign of King Amaziah (II Kings 14:6; II Chr. 21:4), and his successor Uzziah built Eilat, which implies Judahite control of Edom. When Kings uses the phrase "to this day" it seems that "this was the original language of the source that predated [the book of Kings]" (Kiel, *Daat Mikra*, 554).

The final detail that completes this mosaic of national weakness is a revolt in Libnah, a Judahite city on the coastal plain. What events or disagreements led the city to resist Jehoram's authority? Was it stimulated by political rivalry against Jehoram due to his military collapse?

Perhaps Libnah, a Levite city, may have been demonstrating its inhabitants' religious opposition to Jehoram's idolatrous orientation.[9] We do not know, but we may certainly summarize his dismal eight-year reign as a period of national disintegration: religious deviation, internecine royal infighting, a collapse of regional influence, and failure to defend his country's borders. Judah is in decline on all fronts.

If we recall that in the north, Jehoram of Israel had lost control of Moab and was suffering from ongoing Aramean aggression, we gain the sense that the entire Land of Israel, both the northern and the southern kingdoms, has hit a severe downturn, and that the heyday of the Ahab-Jehoshaphat era, characterized by Israel's regional hegemony and financial prosperity, has come to a close.

THE BOOK OF CHRONICLES

Chronicles describes an extraordinary prophetic communiqué:

> A letter from Elijah the Prophet[10] came to [Jehoram] which read, "Thus says the Lord, God of your father David: 'Since you have not followed the practices of your father, Jehoshaphat, and the practices of Assa, king of Judah, but have followed the practices of the kings of Israel, leading Judah astray and the inhabitants of Jerusalem ... and have killed your brothers of your father's house, who were better than you, therefore the Lord will inflict a great blow upon your people.'" (II Chr. 21:12–14)

9. Kiel, *Daat Mikra*. For Libnah's Levite affiliation, see Josh. 15:42–44. The city was under Israelite control in the time of Hezekiah (II Kings 19:8).
10. How could Elijah have sent a letter posthumously, many years after his own death? Some commentators suggest that Elijah appeared to a prophet of that time (Radak), or that since it refers to the house of Ahab, Elijah had written the letter in a spirit of prophecy before his death (Malbim). Alternatively, it was miraculous and not explainable rationally (Abarbanel).

This eerie condemnation issued from the deceased prophet Elijah clearly articulates divine censure of Jehoram's moral and religious deviation. The text depicts the terrible illness that led to Jehoram's untimely death. That he was denied a royal burial[11] is a sure sign that his successor perceived him as a deviant monarch.

KING AHAZIAH OF JUDAH

Jehoram's son, Ahaziah, reigns in Jerusalem for only a year until he is assassinated in the Jehu revolt. During his short reign, however, northern religious influence prevails,[12] as he continues to follow idolatrous norms. Ahaziah allies with his northern counterpart, Jehoram of Israel, in a campaign against Aram, a battle in which Jehoram is severely injured.

The scene in which Ahaziah makes his way to Jezreel to visit the ailing Jehoram, king of Israel, will provide the backdrop to the revolt of Jehu, which we shall address in the next chapter.

11. II Chr. 21:20.
12. Ibid., 22:5.

II Kings 9–10

Jehu's Revolt

Jehu's revolt is a gripping tale of conspiracy and murder, divine justice and religious zeal. With tempestuous force, Jehu kills two royal families: the king of Israel and his mother, Jezebel, as well as the king of Judah. He then proceeds to eliminate the cult of Baal, which had flourished under royal sponsorship for an entire generation.

We begin our presentation with a brief summary of the storyline. Jehu, a senior army officer, is stationed at Ramoth Gilead, the border between Israel and Aram. He commands his troops in an ongoing war of attrition against the Syrian forces of Hazael.[1]

Most unexpectedly, a prophet arrives, sent by Elisha, and singles out Jehu from the group of senior ranking offices. They retire to a side room, where the prophet anoints Jehu as king over Israel and charges him to destroy the house of Ahab and avenge the lives of all the prophets killed under the regime of Jezebel.

Losing no time, Jehu rides down to the royal palace in Jezreel and is greeted by both the king of Israel (Jehoram) and the king of Judah (Ahaziah). He promptly assassinates them both.[2] In a scene rich with

1. See II Kings 8:28; 9:1, 14.
2. A remarkable recent archaeological find raises fascinating questions about this chapter. On the one hand, it corroborates the assassination of these two kings

recompense for Ahab's sins, Jehoram is killed in the field of Naboth; Jezebel, the king's mother, is hurled from the palace window, and the wild dogs of Jezreel consume her body.

Following this, Jehu commands the officials of the capital city, Samaria, to execute the entire royal family – seventy sons of King Jehoram. The city leaders, highly fearful of Jehu (II Kings 10:4), comply with his orders. Jehu and his followers make their way from Jezreel to Samaria; en route, they encounter a group of forty-two royals from the kingdom of Judah and slaughter them all.

Finally, Jehu acts against illicit worship. He proclaims a festival to Baal, but this is a trap: Jehu's men surround the idolaters and execute the entire throng. He then proceeds to obliterate all the monuments and temples dedicated to the Baal deity.

ACTING FOR GOD

Jehu's revolt is a triumphant moment in the book of Kings. Elijah had battled the infamous dynasty of Omri and their ardent support of the cult of Baal, yet even Elijah's fiery miracles and his passionate appeal to God seemed unable to shift the power paradigm. Until now.

At Elijah's greatest moment of despair, Jehu had been designated as the instrument of divine retribution (I Kings 19:16). Now, years later,

---

and identifies their names. Moreover, it is the earliest reference to the "house of David." However, it attributes their deaths to an Aramean king, probably Hazael. We refer to the Tel Dan Stele, two fragments of a royal victory plaque found at Tel Dan in 1993. It reads:

4. ...[And] Hadad made me king.
5. And Hadad went in front of me, [and] I departed from [the] seven [...-]
6. s of my kingdom, and I slew [seve]nty kin[gs], who harnessed thou[sands of cha-]
7. riots and thousands of horsemen. [I killed Jo]ram son of [Ahab]
8. king of Israel, and [I] killed [Ahaz]iahu son of [Jehoram kin-]
9. g of the house of David. And I set [their towns into ruins and turned]
10. their land into [desolation ...]

See A. Biran and J. Naveh, "An Aramaic Stele Fragment from Tel Dan," *Israel Exploration Journal* 43 (1993): 81–98; A. Biran and J. Naveh, "The Tel Dan Inscription: A New Fragment," *Israel Exploration Journal* 45 (1995): 1–18.

As can be seen, the fragments are certainly incomplete. They are on display at the Israel Museum Jerusalem.

Jehu's moment arrives. His appointment by the young prophet[3] charges him with an unequivocal divine assignment:

> Thus says the Lord, the God of Israel: "I anoint you king over the Lord's people, over Israel. You are to strike down the house of Ahab your master.... The whole house of Ahab shall perish. I will cut off from Ahab every last male – bond and free – in Israel. I will make the house of Ahab like the house of Jeroboam ben Nebat and like the house of Baasha son of Ahiah. The dogs shall devour Jezebel in the field of Jezreel, and no one will bury her." (II Kings 9:6–10)[4]

Jehu acts under divine agency. This is a point that Jehu takes care to emphasize at several points in the story:

1. When he kills Jehoram in Naboth's field:

   > Jehu said to Bidkar, his chariot officer, "Pick him up and throw him on the field that belonged to Naboth.... Remember how you and I were riding together in chariots behind Ahab his father *when God made this prophecy* about him.... Now then, pick him up and throw him on that plot, *in accordance with the word of God*." (9:25–26)

2. When Jezebel's body is eaten by the dogs:

   > It is just *as the Lord spoke*.... "The dogs shall devour the flesh of Jezebel in the field of Jezreel." (9:36)

3. When Jehu commends the officers of Samaria after they kill the seventy progeny of Ahab:

---

3. II Kings 9:1–3.
4. These lines echo Elijah's pronouncement of the termination of Ahab's royal line (I Kings 21:20–24). Similar terminology marks the demise of earlier royal houses of the deviant northern kingdom monarchs, Jeroboam (ibid., 14:10–11) and Baasha (ibid., 16:3–4, 11).

> Know then that nothing that *the Lord has spoken* concerning the house of Ahab shall remain unfulfilled." (10:1–11)

The final summation of the chapter confirms this assessment:

> The Lord said to Jehu, "Because you have acted well and done what is right in My eyes ... to the house of Ahab, your descendants will sit on the throne of Israel to the fourth generation." (10:30)

MADNESS

We have identified Jehu as an emissary of religious retribution. His confident, rapid, and aggressive style is a perfect fit for this divine reckoning. The sentry accurately identifies Jehu's chariot (II Kings 9:20) because "he drives as a madman (*beshigaon*)." In what way is Jehu seen as "mad"? Is this a mode of personality – Jehu as a man who bucks the rules, a maverick? Or could it possibly express ideology – Jehu as the quintessential zealot, an idealist, driven by the rage of truth and responsibility? Or maybe his "madness" lies in his strength and speed; after all, he is a military officer. The text fails to offer sufficient clarity to fully define Jehu's "madness," but certainly the "deranged" flight of the prophet (9:10–11) and Jehu's furious riding (9:20) indicate the wild force and brute velocity of this entire episode. If we combine the prophetic mandate with Jehu's vehemence, we identify Jehu as the tool of divine fury.

ELIJAH'S ZEAL

From this perspective, we can easily see Jehu as Elijah's successor. Elijah testifies about himself: "I am moved by zeal for the Lord" (I Kings 19:14), and Jehu views himself as a zealot in the image of Elijah.[5] When he meets Jehu's associate, Jonadab son of Rechab, he says: "Come with me and see my *zeal* for the Lord" (II Kings 10:16).

Jehu and Elijah seem to embody a kindred spirit, and indeed Jehu makes frequent reference to Elijah:

> It is just as the Lord spoke through *His servant Elijah the Tishbite.* (9:36)

5. For a full treatment of the Elijah-Jehu connection, see Samet, *Pirkei Elisha*, 628–37.

> The Lord has done what He announced *through His servant Elijah.* (10:10)

> Arriving in Samaria, he struck down all the survivors of the house of Ahab until he wiped it out, fulfilling the word *the Lord had spoken to Elijah.* (10:17)

Jehu's slaughter of the worshippers of Baal is highly reminiscent of Elijah's public execution of the Baal prophets at Mount Carmel. They both regard the idolatrous house of Ahab with equal hatred and contempt, and they are uncompromising in their opposition to idolatry even when it is supported in the highest echelons. As indicated above, Jehu was named as the man who would complete Elijah's war against Baal (I Kings 19:16).

FLEE WITHOUT DELAY!

We have depicted Jehu as the agent of God, a man in the image of the great Elijah. Further examination, however, raises some disquieting questions about him.

Let us take a moment to examine the opening scene, which triggers the revolt. Its clandestine atmosphere is thick with intrigue and subversion. Why does Elisha abdicate his personal mission and instead select a subordinate, one of the *Benei HaNevi'im,* to anoint Jehu? After all, Elisha traveled to Damascus to instigate Hazael's rise to power (II Kings 8:7–15). If the national prophet can travel unhindered and unharmed to appoint an enemy king, what impedes his active role in this instance? Furthermore, the subordinate prophet's instruction "to flee without delay" (9:3) suggests highly irregular behavior; even Jehu's colleagues observe the prophet's erratic behavior and presume that he is insane![6] What do we make of this unorthodox conduct?[7] Abarbanel offers an explanation:

---

6. The use of the root SH-G-A, meaning loss of sanity, is familiar from Deut. 28:34; I Sam. 21:15–16.
7. Prophets were occasionally labeled as crazy, possibly due to strange acts in which they would engage. See the root SH-G-A in reference to various prophets; for example, "Every man that is mad, and makes himself a prophet" (Jer. 29:26), and "The prophet is a fool, the spiritual man is mad" (Hos. 9:7). In our story, the use of this same root

> [Elisha] could not travel to Ramoth Gilead to anoint Jehu, as the excitement of his arrival would disclose the event [of Jehu's anointing.] He thus performed the act by proxy, giving instructions to one of the prophets who sat before him … to enact [the anointing] in an inner room so that the king not be informed … and to ensure that the prophet not be endangered; and he commanded [the prophet] to flee so that he not remain there.

Treason is risky business. One cannot openly spur a loyal army officer to revolt without endangering one's life.[8] In our story, the prophet is about to interrupt a meeting of the joint chiefs of staff – a group of men who are by definition loyal to the king – and to anoint one of them as a traitor, a mutineer against his commander-in-chief, the king. We appreciate Abarbanel's point. Elisha's public profile precludes him from inciting the rebellion. The youthful prophet, who rushes in and exits quickly, may just get away, even if the plan backfires.

The privacy of the anointing affords Jehu the option of keeping the clandestine message secret for the time being, allowing him time to think and plan. His initial response when questioned about the prophet's purpose – "You know the man and the way he speaks" (II Kings 9:11) – feigns refusal to divulge the secret, but in fact, it invites further inquiry. When his comrades press him for the truth, he readily reveals the prophet's purpose. An ad hoc coronation is staged, the event so hurried that the nearby staircase is turned into an impromptu podium on which to "enthrone" Jehu. The group's spontaneous backing of the mutiny is indicative of a discernable dissatisfaction with King Jehoram. Possibly this was a pervasive sentiment in the military after Jehoram failed in his military campaign against Moab (ch. 3), and was defeated in his conflict with Aram (8:28–29). The

---

is either a pejorative label for the prophet, corroborated by "You know the man and the way he speaks" (II Kings 9:11), or his behavior in this circumstance was outlandish and strange.

8. In a similar situation, when the prophet Samuel is commanded by God to anoint the young David as king, he is also concerned for his personal safety: "How can I go? If Saul hears of it, he will kill me" (I Sam. 16:2).

unanimous and instantaneous response of these high-ranking officers reveals a deep loss of confidence in the national leadership.[9]

A RELUCTANT PROPHET

Elisha's reluctance to personally anoint Jehu could stem not from fear of the king, but rather from deep reservations that the prophet might have regarding the mission itself. Rabbi Elchanan Samet sees Elisha's hesitation as grounded in his congenial personality:

> The legacy that is placed upon Jehu is a harsh and cruel one. The command to eliminate the house of Ahab, when issued from the merciful Elisha, will be insufficiently caustic, less brutal than it must be. Moreover, Elisha, unlike his master Elijah, has never confronted the house of Ahab, and has barely rebuked Jehoram, Ahab's son... in these circumstances it is hard for Elisha to restate Elijah's prophecy of the decimation of the house of Ahab directly to Jehoram without his voice wavering, without tearing up. This mission goes against Elisha's personality.[10]

Samet suggests that Elisha is a willing conspirator, but fears that he will not be able to perform the task with the requisite determination. As such, he passes the mission to a subordinate.

But we shall propose an alternative understanding: that the prophet's reluctance to anoint Jehu relates to fundamental reservations regarding Jehu's character and conduct.

On the one hand, Jehu is clearly the instrument of God's vengeance. Yet the narrative contains a powerful and contrasting subtext. The manner and style of the depiction of Jehu's revolt demonstrates an emphasis on Jehu's furious and violent methods,[11] which both Elisha and the biblical text shun. Let us explain how this is manifest.

---

9. Kiel, *Daat Mikra*, 589; Samet, *Pirkei Elisha*, 624.
10. Samet, *Pirkei Elisha*, 625.
11. My approach here follows that of Prof. Yisrael Rozenson, "The Story of Jehu and the Question of Mixed Messages," *Megadim* 25 (5756): 111–24 [Hebrew]; Y. Rozenson, "A Plotter or the 'King of God's People'? Jehu Compared to David," *Megadim* 32 (5760): 69–82 [Hebrew]. See also Kiel, *Daat Mikra*, 589.

THE SUBTEXT: AN AVERSION TO BRUTALITY

Jehu's actions are replete with highly detailed descriptions of violent death. Kings is no stranger to military coups,[12] yet not one of these mutinies revel in the explicit gore and detailed descriptions of murder that we find with Jehu. The narrative's detail communicates Jehu's barbarism.

First is the sheer scope of the killing. Jehu kills King Jehoram of Israel, King Ahaziah of Judah, Jezebel, seventy of Ahab's sons, and forty-two members of the royal family of Judah (II Kings 10:14). There are constant references to the totality of slaughter: "He left none remaining" (10:11), "neither left he any of them" (10:14), "Go in and slay then, let none come forth" (10:25).[13] The grim body count conveys Jehu's intense appetite for killing and raises questions as to whether Jehu has possibly exceeded the reasonable limits of his prophetic mandate. If the killing of idolatrous King Jehoram[14] is mandated, one wonders as to the justification in assassinating Ahaziah, the king of Judah – whose death was not commanded by God. If somehow Ahaziah is guilty, possibly for having married Jezebel's daughter and adopting the religious orientation of the "house of Ahab" (8:27), should forty-two of his relatives also be slaughtered? Was the execution of every one of Ahab's seventy sons necessary?

The second problematic aspect is the graphic depictions of excessive gore and ruthlessness. We read of the manner in which Jehu's arrow pierces Jehoram's heart and his dead body is unceremoniously dumped in Naboth's field (9:24–25). Jezebel is hurled to her death from an upstairs window, "and her blood [is] spattered on the wall and on the horses, and they trampled her" (9:33). When they come to bury her, they find that she has been consumed by wild dogs "other than her skull, her feet, and her hands" (9:35).

---

12. I Kings 2:25, 31; 15:26–29; 16:11–12.
13. George Savran, "I and II Kings," in *The Literary Guide to the Bible*, ed. Robert Alter and Frank Kermode (Cambridge, MA: Harvard University Press, 1987), 153.
14. At the death of Jehoram, the text takes pains to repeatedly state Jehoram's ailments (II Kings 8:29; 9:15), galvanizing sympathy for him as a war hero and raising the reader's concern for the king's welfare. Furthermore, the text gives voice to his shock and panic at the betrayal of his close army officer ("Treason, Ahaziah!"[9:23]).

Next is the scene in which Jehu forces the administration of Samaria to send the heads of Ahab's seventy sons in baskets to the palace at Jezreel, the grisly image of their heads arrayed in two piles at the gates (10:6–8). The terror that he instills in the elders of Samaria is startling: "They were overcome by fear, for they thought, 'If two kings could not stand up to him, how can we?'" (10:4). The forty-two Judahite royals are deliberately captured alive and then slaughtered into a single cistern. The final scene of the revolution is a giddy bloodbath in which Jehu's men lure the unsuspecting Baal devotees to a celebration and then massacre them all.

One may see this as a celebration of God's retribution against a ruthless idolatrous regime; Jezebel, after all, persecuted and killed God's prophets and threatened Elijah's life.[15] Yet this slow-motion description of an ever-widening circle of carnage has no equal in the books of the Prophets and seems to exceed the reasonable limits of zealous action. By contrast, in the very next chapter we encounter the overthrow of the murderous queen Athaliah. When she is apprehended and deposed, the text merely states: "They took her away by force... she was put to death" (11:16). No blood, no explicit violence; this is the standard style of the books of the Prophets.

Whereas Jehu's elimination of Baal is lauded, the subtext of this literary style is seen as critical of his methods.

---

15. Rofé, *The Prophetic Stories*, 70, suggests that the ancient biblical writer saw the violence as the veritable fulfillment of God's fury and that only the modern reader is sensitive to the dissonance: "His actions are a classic example of Machiavellianism – the cynical use of religion as a political tool in order to win over public opinion and to legitimize the wielding of brutal violence. However, these disenchanted assessments are just the modern historian's critical response to the biblical narrative. *The ancient historian who opened the story with the anointing of Jehu by God's prophet, and closes with the expungement from Israel of the Baal cult... perceived the renegade officer as a divine messenger whose hands enacted God's deeds and through whom the divine word was realized.*" We shall beg to differ and shall suggest that the dissonance is inherent in the biblical text for readers both ancient and modern. This approach is shared by Rozenson (see footnote 11 above); Savran, "I and II Kings," 153; Robert L. Cohn, "II Kings," in *Berit Olam Studies in Hebrew Narrative & Poetry* (Collegeville, MN: The Liturgical Press, 2000), 73–76; and Kiel, *Daat Mikra*, 612–13, among others.

The associations drawn by the imagery of this chapter conjure up some of the Bible's most infamous images. To take a few examples, Jehu executes Jezebel, leaving her mangled corpse outside the city walls, and proceeds to sit and eat a meal. His eating and drinking following such violence draws immediate association with Joseph's brothers, who thrust Joseph into a pit and then calmly and nonchalantly "sat down and ate bread" (Gen. 37:25). Moreover, Jehu's "He entered, he ate, and he drank" is reminiscent of Esau's "He ate, he drank, he got up, he left" (Gen. 25:34).[16] When we examine Jehu's execution of Ahab's seventy sons, we note that the only other biblical instance of the killing of seventy sons of a single man is the story of the despotic Abimelekh (Judges 9:5), a tale of tyrannical abuse of power. These intertextual allusions project a far from positive appraisal. Jehu is a revolutionary desperately insensitive to the trail of blood that he is leaving in his wake.

"PEACE" AND OTHER WORDS

As Jehu charges toward Jezreel, the following threefold exchange ensues:

> The horseman went to meet him, and he said, "The king inquires, is all well [*Hashalom*; lit., Is it peace]?" And Jehu replied, "What have you to do with peace [*ma lekha ulshalom*]?" (9:18)

This conversation – the appeal "*Hashalom*" and its rejection by Jehu – repeats twice, but the third time it is King Jehoram who greets Jehu in the name of peace, only to be rebuffed by the man who will become his assassin. Yehuda Kiel comments:

> Jehu resorts to a strategy of "falsehood" (9:12), "betrayal" (9:23), and "chicanery" (10:19). The word *shalom*, which appears ten times in this section, loses its normal meaning, and its intent is absolutely inverted: cold-blooded murder.[17]

16. Rashi (Gen. 25:29) quotes Genesis Rabba that Esau had just come in from an act of murder.
17. Kiel, *Daat Mikra*, 589.

We might say that beyond the overt story that informs us of Jehu's prophetic mandate to eliminate the house of Ahab is a covert subtext suggesting that Jehu took his path of zealotry too far, relishing the tool of violence.[18]

PROPHETIC DISAPPROVAL?

When we examine the finer details of the story, we gain the impression that Jehu might have had some early association with the community of prophets. For instance, when Elijah is initially instructed to anoint Jehu son of Nimshi (I Kings 19:16), he needs no further identifier; Elijah already knows him.[19] A prophetic background may be corroborated by Jehu's frequent quoting of Elijah. Jehu clearly views Elijah as a role model; is it possible that he was actually Elijah's student?

> We may presume that Jehu had some prior knowledge of Elijah's prophecy. This impression is sharpened by the incredible speed of the anointing; it is difficult to imagine that the prophet who anointed him managed to communicate so much of Elijah's teachings in so short a time span! Thus there is some basis to say that Jehu was affiliated with the circles of the *Benei HaNevi'im* who were close to Elijah and Elisha, and it was there that he internalized the fundamentals of their prophecy, at the very least with regard to the house of Ahab. God ... chose a leader who identified with the mission that was to be cast upon him.[20]

If this assertion is true, Elisha would have been aware of Jehu's hotheaded style – but for all the reasons counted above was opposed to his fanatical mode of operation. When Elisha passes the anointing of Jehu to a young subordinate, when he tells him to deliver his speech and then "open the

18. Gen. 49:5–7.
19. By contrast, God needed to inform Elijah of Elisha's place of residence. Apparently at this stage Elisha was unknown to Elijah, in contrast to the familiar Jehu. See II Kings 9:25, where it sounds as if Jehu and Bidkar witness Elijah's reproof of Ahab, as pronounced in Naboth's vineyard. Was Jehu a military man only, or did he also have prior experience in the community of prophets? Of this we have no direct evidence.
20. Rozenson, "The Story of Jehu," 120.

door and flee; do not delay," Elisha is expressing his reservations regarding Jehu. If God had named Jehu, then Elisha will fulfill his duty, but it is almost as if he could not bring himself to empower a man who was so extreme. It is fascinating that we never witness Elisha interacting with Jehu, even after he becomes king:

> Elijah, who was commanded to anoint Jehu, was instructed at the selfsame time to anoint Elisha as his successor.... A certain expectation emerges that there will be a connection between them. However, throughout Jehu's tenure we hear nothing of Elisha.[21] The anointing of Jehu is performed by proxy and with maximal speed; from this point onward, Jehu emerges almost as a prophet in his own right."[22]

But why is Jehu so unsuitable for leadership? Even if we can appreciate how Elisha's personal style may bristle at Jehu's zeal, would Elijah not be proud of his disciple? Would Jehu not seem to be the ideal candidate to complete Elijah's unfinished mission? Prof. Rozenson suggests that the king and the prophet inhabit different worlds – one represents government, the other its critic and detractor – and as such they are driven by contrasting temperaments and divergent principles:

> The text alludes to Jehu's attempt to emulate Elijah: "Come with me and see my zeal for the Lord" (II Kings 10:16), and the next verse ends: "As the word of God which He spoke to Elijah" (10:17). Zeal in its essence is not open to emulation... Elijah – a man who stood alone against an entire society – and his actions, cannot be simplistically duplicated to the function of a king who holds the entire establishment and national governance in his hands. It is incompatible with the entire conception of Israelite kingship, an

21. The absence of a prophet alongside Jehu is unsettling. This void is so problematic that in II Kings 11:30, it seems that God speaks directly to Jehu, a most irregular situation, seemingly because there is no prophet accompanying him. Paradoxically, in his violent revolt, Jehu views himself as some sort of prophet: "He conveniently has a divine oracle ready to defend his every action" (Savran, "I and II Kings," 153).
22. Rozenson, "The Story of Jehu," 122.

> institution which champions justice and law.... National rule by a king and systematic zealousness stand in absolute contradiction to one another; there is no bridging the abyss between them."[23]

A SUMMARY OF JEHU'S REIGN (II KINGS 10:29–36)

We have presented ambivalent strains in this chapter. We have discovered that Jehu is God's instrument in eliminating the evil rule of the house of Ahab and Jezebel; at last the regime of Baal has been uprooted from the northern kingdom. But we have also identified several exceedingly problematic aspects of Jehu's mode of operation.

This ambivalence is highlighted in the closing lines of the chapters dedicated to Jehu. On the one hand, the Tanakh testifies about him:

> The Lord said to Jehu, "Because you have acted well and done what is right in My eyes ... to the house of Ahab, your descendants will sit on the throne of Israel to the fourth generation." (10:30)

On the other hand, Jehu is flawed in his service of God:

> Jehu was not careful to follow wholeheartedly the teaching [*Torah*] of the Lord, God of Israel; he failed to abandon the sins of Jeroboam who led Israel astray. (10:31)

In other words, Jehu removed Baal, but still retained icons and illicit shrines. His heart was not "whole" with God, not fully committed to God. Of course, this is deeply problematic. If Jehu is impassioned to enact a bloody purge of idolatry, he better ensure that his religious integrity is flawless, impeccable. This point is made in the opening lines of the book of Hosea which declares vengeance on the royal house of Jehu:

> I will soon punish the house of Jehu for the blood of Jezreel, and I will put an end to the kingdom of Israel. (Hos. 1:4)

Why should Jehu be punished for the "blood of Jezreel?" Rashi explains:

---

23. Ibid., 120.

> Because Jehu and his children also worshipped idolatry, thus I [God] consider the blood of the house of Ahab to have been spilt in vain.

The biblical narrative has focused upon Jehu's rise to power, but what of Jehu's twenty-eight-year rule? The closing lines of II Kings 10 offer only a scant[24] but representative glimpse of Jehu's era, a period of national decline:

> In those days, the Lord began to reduce Israel. And Hazael smote them throughout the territory of Israel east of the Jordan, all the land of the Gilead – the Gadites, the Reubenites, and the Manassites – from Aroer by Wadi Arnon up to Gilead and Bashan. (II Kings 10:32–33)

What we witness here is a total capitulation on Israel's eastern front, in which Hazael's forces absolutely dominate the Israelite tribes on the east side of the Jordan. "The Lord began to reduce Israel" sounds very much like divine displeasure with Jehu.

The waning of Israel's power may have political underpinnings. Jehu's assassination of Jezebel and his removal of Baal engendered a rupture of ties with Phoenicia; his execution of the royals of Judah left him without a southern ally. This situation damaged the kingdom military and economically, leaving Jehu vulnerable and weak.[25] And yet it is not without some irony that Jehu, the swashbuckling military captain,

---

24. Archaeology has provided evidence of a short-lived Assyrian attack into the northern kingdom. The Shalmaneser III obelisk, a black limestone monument seven feet in height that was discovered by Layard in 1846 and is now on display at the British Museum, depicts Jehu bowing to Shalmaneser (858–824 BCE). It records his tribute in the following inscription: "The tribute of Jehu, son of Omri: I received from him silver, gold, a golden bowl, a golden vase with pointed bottom, golden tumblers, golden buckets, tin, a staff for a king [and] spears." The Tanakh is not interested in recording every historical event, and it offers only details that contribute to the agenda of the book. Such is the function of the frequently stated line: "The other events of Jehu's reign and all his actions and all his exploits are recorded in the Annals of the Kings of Israel" (II Kings 10:34).
25. *Olam HaTanakh*, 85.

proved inept at defending his people, unable to succeed on the battlefield where his predecessor failed. In these final lines of the chapter, Jehu is not a success story.

We leave this dramatic episode with a complex understanding of Jehu: on the one hand a zealot for God, but on the other hand a man who failed to adopt for himself the high standards that he demanded from others. As shall be seen, his is the longest-ruling dynasty of the northern kingdom, and yet he presides over the beginning of a period in which Israel will suffer greatly from Aramean dominance.

II Kings 11

A Murderous Queen

Following Jehu's stormy revolt in the northern kingdom, our attention turns southward to Judah and Jerusalem as we read of yet another tale of murder, mutiny, and leadership upheaval:

> When Athaliah, the mother of Ahaziah, learned that her son was dead, she promptly killed off all who were of royal stock. But Jehosheba, daughter of King Joram and sister of Ahaziah, secretly took Ahaziah's son Joash away from among the princes who were being slain and put him and his nurse in a bedroom. And they kept him hidden from Athaliah so that he was not put to death. He stayed with her for six years, hidden in the house of the Lord, while Athaliah reigned over the land. (II Kings 11:1–3)

Jehu's assassination of King Ahaziah[1] and many of his close family members[2] left a gaping leadership vacuum. It is Athaliah, the king's mother, daughter of Ahab and Jezebel,[3] who seizes power with shocking cruelty.

1. II Kings 9:27–8.
2. Ibid., 10:13–14.
3. Ibid., 8:26.

She kills the entire royal family, including, we presume, many of her own children and grandchildren, in order to secure her rule. However, unbeknownst to her, baby Joash, the youngest of Ahaziah's sons and heir to the line of David, is secretly snatched from the massacre and raised in secret, until he will be able to ascend the throne.

A PASSION FOR POWER

Athaliah's position as queen is inherently illegitimate, as the throne of Judah can be occupied by the line of King David only (see II Kings 8:19). This violation is expressed in the narrator's omission of a formulaic regnal summary; the daughter of Jezebel may administrate the kingdom, but her name will never be recorded in the roster of Judahite kings.

Athaliah's behavior bears witness to the corrupting influences of the northern kingdom, such as the execution of the deposed royal line[4] and the adoption of Baal worship – norms that have now seeped into the political culture of Judah due to the intermarriage between the royal houses of David and Omri.

Unlike Jehu's revolution in Israel, Athaliah's motive in massacring her own family is inexplicit. Why did she do it? Is it because if her son cannot rule, no other person from the Davidic line may rule either? Is it because, as sole remaining member of the house of Ahab, she seeks to preserve her dynastic legacy in Judah?[5] The killing of her children does certainly suggest an absolute, tyrannical desire to govern, sweeping away even the primal instinct of motherhood:

> Athaliah, like Jezebel, was not just a strong personality but a woman who yearned to rule; a woman with a real ambition, an intense passion for power.... Her passion was simply for power itself, and this drive of hers was so strong that it caused her to carry out a series of extreme acts, even to the point of destroying the royal heirs.... She did not even make any serious political or religious changes

4. I Kings 15:27–29; 16:11; II Kings 10:11.
5. R. L. Cohn, *II Kings*.

> within the country. She became simply a manifestation of this one drive: to rule.[6]

Rabbi Adin Steinsaltz suggests an almost pathological hunger for power. If we had any doubt, she is the sole female biblical figure to be awarded the moniker: "the Wicked" – *hamirshaat* (II Chr. 24:7).

Some commentators assign Athaliah less pathological motives. Yehuda Kiel dwells upon her political motivations:

> "When Athaliah, the mother of Ahaziah, learned that her son was dead" – slain by Jehu. She was concerned that Jehu would co-opt and annex the kingdom of Judah to his kingdom, and would execute her since she was from the house of Ahab.... Thus she decided on her course of action.
>
> The construction of the temple of Baal in Jerusalem had national-economic significance beyond its religious import; the builders sought to establish the historic ties of the kings of Israel with the kings of Tyre.[7]

But we do not need to select one reading over the other. As with today's realpolitik, even the most despotic and murderous leaders may combine malicious ambition with a sophisticated political strategy; both approaches may be true at the same time.

THE GREAT REVERSAL

In the midst of Athaliah's bloodbath, Joash's aunt, Jehosheba, saves his life, snatching him away from the massacre and concealing the little prince and his wet-nurse. This would have been a dangerous and highly secretive affair; after all, the baby's body would have had to be accounted for. Almost certainly, only a small team of conspirators were involved in hiding the young heir, possibly limited to Jehosheba's close family; Jehosheba's husband[8] is Jehoiada the high priest, who allows Joash to be raised in the confines of

6. Adin Steinsaltz, *Biblical Images*, 193.
7. *Daat Mikra*, 591, 601.
8. II Chr. 22:11.

the Temple,[9] and it is Jehoiada who will leverage this opportunity, not merely to restore the royal line but to instigate a process of religious renewal.

For seven years Jehoiada bides his time, until the designated day upon which the young heir is publically revealed. The mutiny is staged within the Temple courtyard. The logistics are planned meticulously: the Temple is guarded and secured, and the young king is presented to the invitees; special mention is made of the young king's protection. Joash is crowned with full ceremony. The trumpets sound, and the people applaud and acclaim their new king. By the time Athaliah realizes what is happening, it is too late. Joash is the sovereign, and Athaliah is led to her execution.

Jehoiada uses this coronation as a springboard for a national and spiritual reorientation, enacting no less than three covenants: the first, between the king and God; the second, between the people and God; and the third, between the king and the nation (II Kings 11:17). Far from the brutal coup which occurred in Israel, this uprising becomes a celebration, with joy, cheering, fanfare, and clapping.[10] It becomes a day of restoration of legitimate kingship and religious monotheism. One of the features of this revolt is the central part played by the rank and file priests, in collaboration with the *Am HaAretz* (11:13, 14, 18, 20), a social group of high standing within Judahite society.[11] One senses the relief with which the nation greets this moment.

9. The text of II Kings is unclear regarding the precise identification of Joash's hideaway. His initial escape is to one of the bedrooms (11:2), but it seems that later he is hidden in the Temple compound (11:3). Were there secret chambers in the Temple itself? See the rabbinic discussion as to whether he was kept in the attic of the Temple or the side chambers (Song of Songs Rabba 1:66; *Midrash Shoḥer Tov* 18:23, and see Rashi and Radak ad loc.). The *Targum Rabbi Yosef* to II Chr. 22:11 suggests that he was kept in the Holy of Holies (*Kodesh HaKodashim*) itself, but possibly he means the attic above the Holy of Holies (*Daat Mikra*).
10. There are many ways in which this revolt is similar to Jehu's: A ruler from the house of Ahab, dedicated to Baal, is deposed and killed in a rebellion led by a religious figure. Subsequently, the followers of Baal are executed. But the differences are stark as well. Here only Queen Athaliah and Matan the priest of Baal are executed. Here there is joy, not fear. Here the rebellion spans wide strata of the nation; there it was a rebellion of a single man. Here the revolt is orderly; there it was chaotic and furious. See Kiel, *Daat Mikra*, 612–13.
11. We meet the group identified as the *Am HaAretz* – "people of the land" – several times in II Kings, always associated with the appointment of royalty in situations

After the coronation, the throngs proceed to the temple of Baal, which stood nearby. The people dismantle the altar, destroy the images and accoutrements of the Baal cult, and kill Matan, the priest of Baal.

When had this shrine to Baal been constructed? Baal had held sway in Jerusalem under kings Jehoram and Ahaziah as well as under Queen Athaliah. As such, it is likely that the structure predated Athaliah. And yet the fact that even during this idolatrous period the Temple retained its status as Judah's central religious institution, its sacrificial rite unobstructed,[12] is a testament to the robust place of monotheism in Judahite culture.

---

of dynastic crisis. We find them here with Joash; at the coronation of Uzzariah/Uzziah (14:21); at the coronation of Josiah after the assassination of Amon (21:23–24; 23:30); and at the burial of Josiah and appointment of Jehoahaz, his son. The group, who are identifiable from this historical point onward and are mentioned a total of thirty-seven times in the books of II Kings, II Chronicles, Jeremiah, and Ezekiel, have inspired much research and speculation. Many have suggested that they are a Judahite aristocratic group, possibly landowners or senior military figures, close to the monarchy (see II Kings 25:18–21; Jer. 1:18; 37:2), and it is unclear whether they were an ad hoc association or an organized political forum. Prof. Shemaryahu Talmon describes them as "not an institution at all but a fairly loosely constituted power group in the kingdom of Judah ... which does not function continuously but always goes into action ad hoc when extraordinary political conditions make action imperative." Ezekiel (22:29) accuses them of having abused the poorer classes.

In the Torah, the phrase *am haaretz* has a less specific application, merely referring to the "people of the land," a regional or national population; see Gen. 23:7, 12, 13; 42:6; Ex. 5:5; Num.14:9. At times (Lev. 4:27; 20:2, 4) it refers to the totality of Israelite society. See *Olam HaTanakh*, 91–93; S. Talmon, "The Judean *'Am-ha'ares* in Historical Perspective," *Proceedings of the Fourth WCJS* (Jerusalem, 1967), 71–76.

12. II Chr. 24:7 records how Athaliah would poach funds from God's Temple and dedicate them to the temple of Baal.

II Kings 12–13

Joash of Judah: Accountability and Betrayal

Joash has a colorful and rich biography. His youthful years are dedicated to the Temple, but late in life his religious orientation shifts. Why does Joash repudiate a lifelong commitment to God and His Temple? We shall follow his story in an attempt to identify Joash's priorities, and to uncover the motivation behind his surprising about-face.

JOASH'S EARLY LIFE

As the sole survivor of Queen Athaliah's royal massacre, Joash, the child-heir, is raised in secrecy, only to be crowned at age seven in a dramatic and unprecedented priestly coup. Throughout his childhood and youth, the priesthood are his backers, protectors, and advisers (II Kings 12:3). A seven-year-old is hardly capable of personally administering a nation; Jehoiada, the high priest, was essentially the national chief executive.

RENOVATIONS

Joash dedicates his first adult project to the Temple's renovation. This is hardly a surprise given Joash's strong Temple affiliation. It has been 150 years since King Solomon constructed the Temple,[1] and a refurbishment is long overdue. Possibly Athaliah's Baal affiliations had contributed to the neglect and deliberate defacement of the Temple.[2]

The story of the Temple refurbishment centers upon the procurement of financing for the project. At the initial stage, the fundraisers are none other than the priests:

> Jehoash[3] said to the priests, "All the money...brought into the house of the Lord as sacred donations[4]...let the priests receive

1. *Seder Olam Rabba* 24 says 155 years.
2. II Chr. 24:7.
3. Kings refers to this king of Judah as Jehoash; Chronicles calls him Joash. We have adopted the more familiar form of Joash, but biblical quotations will follow the Hebrew in Kings, i.e., Jehoash.
4. The sources of these "sacred donations" originate in Torah law. Three donation categories are detailed:

   i. *Kesef ovver*. This seems to refer to the half-shekel poll tax: "This is what everyone who is entered the records (*kol **ovver** al hapekudim*) shall pay: a half-shekel" (Ex. 30:13). In addition, II Chr. 24:6, 9 explicitly talks about collecting the "tax imposed on Israel in the wilderness by Moses, servant of God." This, and the scene later in the chapter whereby the people pay their money into a chest, led to this chapter's selection as the *haftara* for *Shabbat Shekalim*.

   ii. *Kesef nafshot erko*. Lev. 27 issues a fixed scale of monetary amounts that are to be contributed to Temple funds when a vow is made to donate the value of a human being to God. These are known in halakhic literature as *arakhin*.

   iii. The third group is simply donations made by a person who wishes to support the Temple.

   Radak (II Kings 12:5) asks the following question: If all these funds – monies that were usually used to fund the budget of daily sacrifices – were designated for the Temple renovations, then how were those routine sacrifices purchased? He offers a creative solution: During the idolatrous years of Athaliah and her Baal-inclined predecessors, the daily Tamid sacrifice had been suspended. The pious among the community set aside their annual contribution, hoping to donate it when the national religion turned away from Baal and returned to God. Now these extra funds were funneled to the routine sacrifices, and new funds were earmarked for the renovations.

> it, each from his benefactor; they in turn shall make repairs on the house,[5] wherever damage may be found." (12:5–6)

The initial plan had been to fund the renovation by private donations channeled through the priests. However, this strategy proves ineffective and unsuccessful. After some time, the king discovers that repairs have not been made. Joash summons his mentor, Jehoiada, and accuses him of negligence:

> But in the twenty-third year of King Jehoash, [it was found that] the priests had not made the repairs on the house. So King Jehoash summoned the priest Jehoiada and the other priests and said to them, "Why have you not kept the house in repair? Now do not accept money from your acquaintances anymore, but deliver it for the repair of the house." The priests agreed that they would neither accept money from the people nor make repairs on the house. (12:7–9)

A careful reading of this passage suggests that Joash is not merely berating Jehoiada for neglecting to get the job done. There is an insinuation here of monies that are being misdirected. Joash reverses his earlier instructions; he removes financial control from the priesthood and puts a different system in place. A chest with a hole (the first *tzedaka* box!) is placed alongside the Temple altar into which donations will be deposited, monies that can be withdrawn only by the joint supervision of the Crown – the royal scribe – together with the priesthood:

> And the priest Jehoiada took a chest and bored a hole in its lid. He placed it at the right side of the altar as one entered the house of the Lord, and the priestly guards of the threshold deposited there all the money that was brought into the house of the

5. The phrase used here is *bedek habayit*. In the course of time it came to be the name for the Temple treasury funds, but in its original form the word *bedek* comes from Aramaic and means a breach or crack in a wall or a piece of wood. See also Ezek. 27:9, 27.

> Lord. Whenever they saw that there was much money in the chest, the royal scribe and the high priest would come up and put the money accumulated in the house of the Lord into bags, and they would count it. Then they would deliver the money that was weighed out to the overseers of the work, who were in charge of the house of the Lord. These, in turn, disbursed it to the carpenters and the laborers who worked on the house of the Lord. (12:10–12)

At first glance, this is merely an interesting vignette about the Temple finances, but if we read it closely, we notice that it harbors a great deal of information about Joash and his relationships. Let us try to probe deeper; why did the priests and Levites fail in their responsibility? What was the flaw in the original system?

THE FIRST PLAN – PRIESTLY FUNDRAISING[6]

The priests' initial method of collection was to solicit funds, "each from their acquaintance": from personal contacts, friends, and benefactors. What was the concept here? Possibly, after years in which Baal-oriented kings had ruled the kingdom, enthusiasm for the Temple was at a low ebb. The priests, who were impassioned for the Temple, would be its most enthusiastic advocates, not merely waiting passively for Temple worshippers to contribute but rather collecting door-to-door in each town and village:

> [Joash] assembled the Priests and the Levites and charged them as follows: "Go out to the towns of Judah and collect money from all Israel for the repair of the house of your God. Do it quickly!" (II Chr. 24:5)

And so the priests solicited the requisite finance from their circles of neighbors, friends, associates, and colleagues. This should have proven an effective fundraising technique if each priest had fulfilled his duty.

6. My analysis here has been influenced by Rabbi Mosheh Lichtenstein's reading. See http://hatanakh.com/sites/herzog/files/herzog/pdf._13.pdf.

However, this method is not without its problems. It is reminiscent of a charity board or a school committee in which each member must fill a table for the annual dinner by appealing to friends and relatives. It can work well for small communal organizations, but it is a disaster for public institutions. Why?

First, there is apathy; second, there is conflict of interest. With regard to the apathy, perhaps the priests simply resented being the sole fundraising mechanism for the Temple renovations. Regarding the conflict of interest, what incentive would the priests have had to fundraise for the Temple? The priests themselves subsisted by collecting tithes – *teruma* and *maaser.* They would likely have been reluctant to appeal to benefactors for further money, possibly fearing that a generous Temple donation would harm their personal livelihood. Whatever the cause, Chronicles informs us the fundraising campaign became protracted and eventually fizzled out:

> But the Levites did not act quickly. And the king summoned Jehoiada … and said to him, "Why have you not demanded that the Levites collect the tax[7] … from [the people of] Judah and Jerusalem?" (II Chr. 24:5–6)

CORRUPTION?

Some commentaries suggest that the king suspected corruption on the part of the priests.[8] When he shifts the plan: "Now do not accept money *from your acquaintances anymore, but deliver it* for the repair of the house" (II Kings 12:8), he is essentially insinuating that significant sums have been pocketed by the priests. And certainly, the original priestly financing system opens a distinct temptation of corruption. It encourages certain priests to become lobbyists, procuring extra donations and acquiring powerful benefactors and backers. These priests may then have a greater

7. This is called, "the tax of Moses, the servant of God," and would seem to refer to the annual half-shekel donation to the Temple. See Ex. 31:11–16. In that passage, it seems that the money was used in order to take a national census, with the silver donated to the Tabernacle. However, Chronicles supports the tradition as detailed in Tractate Shekalim of an annual half-shekel tax for Temple purposes even in the absence of a national census.
8. Radak and Abarbanel, II Kings 12:8.

influence in allocating those funds. Financing through personal favors opens the door to paybacks, bribery, and ethical abuses.

Were the suspicions true or misplaced? Rashi (12:6) suggests that the priests took the role of professional fundraisers, drawing expenses from the funds they collected. With a lack of oversight or accountability it is hardly surprising that the priests were exposed to accusations of misappropriation. When the king changes the system, they are quite relieved:

> The king suspected that they were taking money for themselves, and so he instructed ... to pass funds immediately to the Temple. "*The priests agreed that they would neither accept money from the people...*" at all, so that they would be above suspicion. (Radak, 12:9)

Whereas Chronicles attributes the failure to mere apathy and conflict of interest, implying that the fundraising effort was an amateur system rather than a fraudulent one, Kings suggests financial impropriety. Whatever the case, we may conclude that the collection system was deeply flawed and the Temple paid the price.

THE SECOND STAGE – CENTRALIZATION AND REGULATION

How long had this dismal situation continued? We do not know in which year Joash had issued the original instruction, but now, at age thirty, in the twenty-third year of his reign, the king issues the new, direct method of taxation. Effectively, he is instituting an admission fee, or sacrifice-levy, for all visitors to the Temple. This fresh financing strategy proves vastly more effective:

> All the officers and all the people brought it joyously and threw the money into the box until it was full. (II Chr. 24: 10)

Joash's innovation improves the situation in several ways:

- Control: Management of the money is withdrawn from the exclusive control of the priests.
- Direct and Anonymous Donations: The anonymous and unmediated donation method precludes the possibility of middlemen

garnering power by means of fundraising potential and curbs the influence of wealthy donors, thereby limiting priestly corruption.

- Equitability: Each visitor to the Temple has to give.
- Accountability: A representative of the government *and* the high priest each have to be present as the money is counted.[9]

Chronicles remarks that the people gave this tax "joyously." Who gives taxes with glee? Might we suggest that Temple adherents were relieved at the transparent and honest monetary system?

JOASH'S RELIGIOUS DEVIATION

In contrast to the book of Kings, to which we will soon return, Chronicles offers a deeply disturbing record of the closing years of Joash's reign, recording a fundamental religious transformation:

---

9. One line here seems to contradict this tight system of accountability: "No check was kept on the men to whom the money was delivered to pay the workers; for they acted in good faith" (II Kings 12:16). Despite the prior mismanagement of Temple funds, the administrators of the Temple craftsmen are given budgeting license and are not closely scrutinized or regulated. Interestingly, this becomes the talmudic model for administration of charity funds:

> Our Rabbis taught: The collectors of charity are not required to give an account of the monies entrusted to them for charity, nor the treasurers of the Temple of the monies given for holy purposes. There is no explicit [biblical] proof text, but it is hinted at [in the verse]: "No check was kept on the men to whom the money was delivered to pay the workers; for they dealt honestly." (Bava Batra 9a)

The Talmud treads carefully between supervision and over-suspicion. Talmudic legislation mandates two, and preferably three, charity treasurers, people of impeccable repute, to preclude fraud and to secure financial integrity. But "collectors of charity are not required to give an account of the monies entrusted to them for charity." Is this not excessive license? It would seem that if every charity official is cross-examined over each budgetary decision, over every misplaced receipt, then few people would be willing to undertake the task. At some level, along with the safeguards and the accountability, there must be some element of trust and integrity. When is trust appropriate and when is it negligent? When can one rely on the integrity of public officials and when must one be suspicious and wary? How does one decide? These are difficult dilemmas facing any public sector, and a balance is needed between regulation and people's honesty and integrity – "for they acted in good faith" (II Kings 12:16).

> But after the death of Jehoiada, the officers of Judah came, bowing low to the king; and the king listened to them. They forsook the house of the Lord God of their fathers to serve the sacred posts and idols; and there was wrath upon Judah and Jerusalem because of this guilt of theirs. The Lord sent prophets among them to bring them back to Him; they admonished them but they would not pay heed. Then the spirit of God enveloped Zechariah, son of Jehoiada the priest; he stood above the people and said to them, "Thus God said: Why do you transgress the commandments of the Lord when you cannot succeed? Since you have forsaken the Lord, He has forsaken you." They conspired against him and pelted him with stones in the court of the house of the Lord, by order of the king. King Joash disregarded the loyalty (*ḥesed*) that his father Jehoiada had shown to him, and killed his son. As he was dying, he said, "May the Lord see and require it." (II Chr. 24:17–22)

Jehoiada's death engenders a total religious reformation for Joash. At the very moment in which Jehoiada's son Zechariah reprimands the king for his sinful actions, he is murdered in the Temple courtyard.[10] Joash

10. There is no small sense of irony in the location of this murder. In the scene of Joash's coronation, Athaliah was hurried out of the Temple so that her execution could not defile the holiest of places (II Kings 11:15). Now Joash demonstrates flagrant disregard for the most basic of Temple regulations.

Interestingly, Kings fails to mention Joash's turn away from God and his murder of Zechariah. In fact, it assesses Joash favorably: "Jehoash did that which was right in God's eyes, all his days that Jehoiada instructed him" (ibid., 12:3).

The interconnection between Kings and Chronicles is complex, and the precise relationship between the books is elusive. The Septuagint called Chronicles *Paraleipomenon*, meaning "a supplement to things omitted," indicating that the historical traditions of Chronicles were authentic but for some reason not included in Kings. Abarbanel shares this view, suggesting that Chronicles explicates and augments historical traditions that were becoming lost in the course of time:

> I have already written in my introduction to this book [Kings] that the book does not intend to relate all the biographical and national details of the kings… for this was recorded in the [royal] annals… with Joash it states, "Joash did that which was right in God's eyes, all his days that Jehoiada instructed him" (12:3), and thus it indicates that after Jehoiada's death, he did not perform that which was right in God's eyes, and served the Baal… but Ezra [author of Chronicles]

displays absolute disregard for God and contempt for the memory of his adopted father, Jehoiada.

What led to this turning of Joash's religious affiliation? Rabbi Yigal Ariel weaves the variant strands of our chapter together:

> Joash's sins did not begin with the death of Jehoiada. Their origins are to be found even in his righteous acts performed in the Temple during his mentor's lifetime.
>
> Joash was dependent on Jehoiada, who rescued and raised him, and was inestimably indebted to both Jehoiada and the Temple. This feeling of beholdenness was deeply sensed by Joash and weighed heavily upon him. Quite naturally, Joash longed to be a man and a king in his own right, to free himself of the yoke of the elderly Jehoiada and his controlling influence... but he dared not rebel against Jehoiada in the latter's lifetime, while his saintly demeanor and his great personage dominated. Joash found a positive avenue to maneuver [away from Jehoiada's influence] – acting more pious than even his mentor...: "Why have you not kept the house in repair?"
>
> After the death of his teacher, Joash sought independence and freedom, a new path, at all costs. To achieve this, he introduced new advisors, the officers of Judah, whose policies differed from those of his mentor, Jehoiada. In place of Jehoiada's rebuke and criticism, Joash now employed courtiers who groveled to him, who praised him and admired his every move."[11]

We have watched as Joash is discovering his own independence. Whereas the king's early agenda overlapped with the priestly interest, we have

---

> saw that in the course of time, the royal annals had been lost. To ensure that the events not be entirely forgotten, he wrote details that were essential to comprehend the text of Kings, and in such a case, Chronicles... acts as an expansion of the book of Kings. (Commentary on II Kings 12)

See also Sara Japhet, *The Ideology of the Book of Chronicles and Its Place in Biblical Thought* (Jerusalem: Mossad Bialik, 1977), 153 [Hebrew]. With all this having been said, the variance between the "parallel" books is considerable.

11. Yigal Ariel, *Mikdash Melekh* (Hispin: Midreshet Golan, 1994), 322–23 [Hebrew].

seen how at age thirty, Joash confronts and reprimands Jehoiada. In that uncomfortable scene, we already sense the king shifting from his youthful persona. Now, upon the death of Jehoiada, Joash's independence gains full momentum. He redirects his affiliations away from the priesthood to new "advisors" who offer a fresh political and religious direction.[12] The introduction of idolatry into the kingdom indicates that the new officials advocated a political reorientation, opening the country to other cultures and nation-states, a policy that advocated a relaxed approach to foreign worship rather than a strict monotheistic regime. Obviously, this sharp national cultural turnabout led Joash into a direct clash with the priests who had controlled the agenda up to this point.[13] Consequently, we have a frontal collision between two rival political factions: the religious right wing, an inward-looking, priestly group; and the left-wing advisors, more cosmopolitan, with its Ahab-ite leanings. Joash rejects the first faction, his childhood fraternity, with whom he has now lost patience, and allies with the second group and their more internationalist agenda.[14]

The priests refuse to be deflected, and they continue to wrangle with Joash. At first, he merely ignores their religious reproach, but as they become more vociferous, the tension and animosity intensifies. When the high priest, Zechariah, publically admonishes the king, the new administration has him executed, silencing their most influential opponent and critic. The priestly groups are not slow to retaliate;

---

12. The Midrash presents a different dynamic:

> Why did they bow to the king? They turned him into a god. They said, "If it were not for the fact that you were a god, how could you have emerged unscathed after residing in the Holy of Holies for seven years?" He replied, "Indeed!" and willingly assumed the role of a deity, and caused his own destruction. (Exodus Rabba 8)

The text in neither Kings nor Chronicles portrays Joash as a king-deity. Kiel, *Daat Mikra*, suggests that the courtiers' genuflection is no more than royal protocol, not an act of worship. Alternatively, we might discern this midrash as portraying norms of other Near Eastern kingdoms in which the king was perceived as a deity, thereby alluding to Joash's adoption of foreign religious paradigms. A further possibility is to read the midrash psychologically. Precisely because Joash was raised in the Temple, he felt he could disregard its sanctity and discard its authority.

13. H. Reviv, *The Society in the Kingdoms of Israel and Judah* (Jerusalem: Mossad Bialik, 1993), 161–63 [Hebrew].
14. Kiel, *Daat Mikra*, 611 (chapter summary).

Chronicles pins the motive for Joash's assassination as vengeance for "the blood of the sons of Jehoiada"[15] (II Chr. 24:25).

EPITOME OF INGRATITUDE

Chronicles views the murder of Zechariah as Joash's ultimate betrayal, a cruel suppression of the human instinct for gratitude, ignoring and repudiating Jehoiada's *ḥesed* – his selflessness and loyalty to Joash. Joash callously murders the son of the man who raised him!

The classic commentators note several ways in which Joash's own death is indicative of reciprocal justice (*midda kenegged midda*), reflecting precisely Joash's ingratitude and disloyalty to the family of Jehoiada:

- "He [Joash] was punished reciprocally: He killed Zechariah, whose position was safe and secure as son of Jehoiada ... and so [Joash] was killed when he was calm and secure – in his bed" (Rashi).
- "Joash violated God's Temple and commanded that Zechariah the priest be executed in the house of God; and [Joash's] own servants violated his [royal] authority, killing him in his bed .... Just as Joash repudiated the kindness done to him by Jehoiada, similarly his servants ignored the kindness performed by their sovereign; Joash had no qualms regarding the execution of a priest, son of a prophet, and his servants were undeterred at killing a king, son of a king" (Abarbanel).
- Joash's death in his bed is reminiscent of his being hidden as a baby in a bedroom (*ḥadar hamittot*).[16]
- "Let the nation of ingrates take vengeance from he who is ungrateful" (*Mekhilta, Amalek* 1). The *Mekhilta* proposes that Joash's assassins are a Moabite and an Ammonite,[17] two national identities singled out by the Torah for their historical ingratitude: "No Ammonite or Moabite ... may be admitted to the assembly of

15. Note that Chronicles talks about the "sons" of Jehoiada, in the plural, indicating that several of Jehoiada's sons were killed. This suggests a more comprehensive battle waged against the priesthood than is evident from the story in Kings.
16. II Chr. 22:11.
17. Ibid., 24:25.

> God. These nations did not welcome you with food and water when you came out of Egypt. Instead, they hired Balaam…to curse you" (Deut. 23:3–4).

In this damning epitaph, Joash's ingratitude becomes his enduring legacy, his hallmark.

JOASH'S DEMISE

The alternative account in Kings has Joash meet his end in the wake of a military attack by Hazael of Aram, who rampages through the country, threatening Jerusalem (12:18–22). Joash is forced to pay a huge bribe to avert a military clash. He finances the tribute from the royal treasury, but also from the gold reserves of the Temple, even dispatching Temple artifacts to Hazael.[18] Whereas Joash's sidestepping of armed conflict[19] may be viewed as a skillful maneuver on the king's part, some of his inner circle seem to have thought otherwise. Joash's courtiers who conspire and assassinate him are possibly government or military figures outraged at his capitulation to the Arameans.[20]

"MAY THE LORD SEE AND REQUIRE IT"

The Talmud pictures Zechariah's grotesque murder as unforgivable, a crime that remains unavenged, an open wound, a perpetual travesty:

18. This is not without some irony, as he is undoing the very Temple treasury that he had so carefully established. These *kodashim*, or consecrated objects, are not defined. In David's time (see II Sam. 8:11–12) *kodashim* seem to be war trophies, installed later by Solomon in the Temple (I Kings 7:51, although we fail to discern the role they might have played there; some commentators simply explain the *kodashim* as wealth from the era of King David). David and Solomon's *kodashim* were looted by King Shishak (I Kings 14:25–26). The verse here specifies that even Joash's idolatrous father and grandfather made sacred donations of this sort to the Temple, evidence that though Jehoram and Jehoahaz worshipped Baal, they did not totally abandon the Temple. We may conclude, then, that the Judahite monotheistic tradition was sufficiently strong to demand that even deviant kings follow the royal norm of God-worship in the Temple.
19. See II Chr. 24:25, where it seems that he was injured in battle or possibly captured and tortured. Indeed, Y. Kiddushin 1:7 talks of Joash being brutally raped in Aramean captivity.
20. The men responsible for the assassination appear to be officials of high standing, as they remain in government long after Joash's death. His son, Amatziah, succeeds in executing these assassins only when "the kingdom is strong in his hands" (II Kings 14:5). In other words, he had to muster considerable political clout in order to get rid of them.

> As [Zechariah] was dying, he said, "May the Lord see and require it [*veyidrosh*]." (II Chr. 24:22)

This language deliberately evokes associations with other heinous crimes. First, we hear the echo of God's warnings about murder in the aftermath of the Flood:

> "But for your *lifeblood*, I will *require* a reckoning; I will *require* it of every beast; of man too will I *require* a reckoning for human life." (Gen. 9:5)

Similarly, Reuben's comment, after the sale of Joseph:

> "And now comes the *reckoning* for his *blood*." (Gen. 42:22)

The implications of these verses are clear: An act of murder is a moral outrage which must be redressed and avenged; the blood of the murdered victim cries out for justice.[21]

This could be the reason that the Talmud imagined Zechariah's blood as enduring, bubbling madly in the Temple, perpetually unappeased, even until the Temple's destruction.[22] It depicts the Babylonian aggressor Nebuzaradan as transfixed by Zechariah's blood, which he tries to avenge, without success. Zechariah's indelible blood endures in the national consciousness as a perpetual symbol of the most reprehensible of murders:

> [Nebuzaradan] saw the blood of Zechariah bubbling.
>
> "What is this?" he cried.
>
> "It is the blood of sacrifices, which has been spilled," they answered.

21. Gen. 4:11; Num. 35:33–34.
22. *Sifrei, Beḥukotai* 6:3 connects the story of Zechariah with the verse in Lamentations 2:20: "Should priest and prophet be killed in the sanctuary of the Lord?" The talmudic midrash from Tractate Sanhedrin cited above makes the same connection.

> "Then bring [some animal blood] and I will compare them, to see whether they are alike," he said. So he slaughtered some animals and compared them, but they were dissimilar.
>
> "Disclose [the secret] to me, or if not, I will tear your flesh with iron combs," he threatened.
>
> They replied: "This is [the blood of] a priest and a prophet, who foretold the destruction of Jerusalem to the Israelites, and they killed him."
>
> "I will appease him," he said.
>
> So he brought the scholars and slew them over him, yet [the blood] did not cease [to boil]. He brought schoolchildren and slew them over him. Still it did not rest. He brought the young priests and slew them over him, and still it did not rest, until he had slain ninety-four thousand, and still it did not rest.
>
> Whereupon he approached him and cried out, "Zechariah, Zechariah, I have destroyed the flower of them: Do you desire that I massacre them all?"
>
> Immediately [the blood] rested.
>
> Thoughts of repentance came into his mind: If they, who killed only a single person, have been so [severely punished], what will be my fate? So he fled, sent his testament to his house, and became a proselyte. (Sanhedrin 96b)

Joash is a king with great promise. Succeeding the evil Athaliah and raised in the Temple by the high priest, he follows God devotedly. However, when he grows up he repudiates the priestly influence in affairs of state, turning to idolatry and a different national agenda. One sin causes another, as events swiftly lead to the murder of the high priest, Zechariah. In the final account Joash has all the potential but he fails to live up to these high expectations.[23]

---

23. The figure of King Joash burst in to the public limelight some years ago when a tablet surfaced, said to have been excavated on the Temple Mount, which quoted, almost verbatim, certain lines from Chronicles that relate to Joash. Unfortunately, the expert assessment was that the tablet had been forged. See http://en.wikipedia.org/wiki/Jehoash_Inscription.

II Kings 13–14

The Fall and Rise of Israel

Our previous two chapters depicted the southern kingdom, Judah, under Athaliah and Joash. We now return northward to Israel, where we last witnessed Jehu's dramatic and violent revolt, to discuss four successive kings of the Jehu dynasty:

- Jehu (28-year reign)
- Jehoahaz son of Jehu (17 years)[1]

1. The chronology here is difficult. Jehoahaz is said to have ascended the throne in the twenty-third year of Joash of Judah's reign and to have reigned seventeen years. But Jehoahaz's son Joash ascends the throne in the thirty-seventh year of Joash of Judah's reign. This gives Jehoahaz a fourteen-year reign. This discrepancy is solved in a variety of ways by the classical and modern commentaries. Rashi (II Kings 13:10) admits that he cannot find a resolution. Radak (ibid., 13:1) adopts an unorthodox approach already suggested by Josephus (*Antiquities* IX, 173), suggesting that Jehoahaz in fact became king in the twenty-*first* year of Joash of Judah's reign. His basis for this is that Athaliah seizes the throne at the time of Jehu's revolt. Jehu is king for twenty-eight years (ibid., 10:36). Joash of Judah is crowned in the seventh year of Jehu's reign, so the twenty-first year of his reign coincides with Jehu's death and the ascent of Jehoahaz. This resolves the problem – the only catch is the problematic biblical text!

- J(eh)oash son of Jehoahaz (16 years)
- Jeroboam son of Joash (41 years)

PRESSURE FROM ARAM

The central factor that dictates this historical period is the overwhelming dominance of Aram under Hazael. These turbulent times, predicted by Elijah[2] and ordained by Elisha,[3] witness Hazael's devastating forces ascendant over Israel, eventually controlling the northern kingdom in its entirety and advancing along the coastal plain to the strategic southern city of Gath,[4] threatening even Jerusalem.

Our chapter charts this crushing military campaign. It begins during the reign of Jehu, with Hazael's control of Transjordan:

> In those days, the Lord began to reduce Israel. And Hazael smote them throughout the territory of Israel east of the Jordan, all the land of the Gilead – the Gadites, the Reubenites, and the Manassites – from Aroer by Wadi Arnon up to Gilead and Bashan. (II Kings 10:32–33)

During the reign of Jehoahaz, Jehu's son, a king who "did that which was evil in God's eyes," Hazael, and his son Ben-Hadad, make further inroads into Israelite territory, crippling the Israelite military forces:

> The Lord was angry with Israel and He repeatedly delivered them into the hands of King Hazael of Aram and into the hands of Ben-Hadad, son of Hazael…. Jehoahaz was left with a force of only fifty horsemen, ten chariots, and ten thousand foot soldiers. For

---

2. I Kings 19:16–17.
3. II Kings 8:7–15.
4. Ibid., 12:18–19. Regarding archaeological evidence of Hazael's attack, we refer the reader to an online lecture by Prof. Aren Maeir, the archaeologist responsible for the dig at Tell-es-Safi, the ancient site of Gath. The lecture was delivered at the fifteenth World Congress of Jewish Studies (2009): "Hazael in Southern Israel: The Campaign to Philistia and the Conquest of Philistine Gath." View it at http://multimedia.huji.ac.il/video/congress09/05.html.

> the king of Aram had decimated them and trampled them like the dust under his feet. (13:3, 7)[5]

The desperate situation in which Aram permits Israel only fifty cavalry and ten chariots indicates Hazael's absolute domination of Israel, to the point where he can impose a full demilitarization of the kingdom – save a ceremonial guard. The Israelites are too weak to resist Aramean control: "King Hazael of Aram had oppressed the Israelites throughout the reign of Jehoahaz" (13:22).

But during the period of Ben-Hadad and the next Israelite king, Joash, we begin to identify a turnaround:

> When King Hazael of Aram died, his son Ben-Hadad succeeded him as king; and then Jehoash son of Jehoahaz recovered from Ben-Hadad son of Hazael the towns which had been taken from his father Jehoahaz in war. Three times Joash defeated him, and he recovered the towns of Israel. (13:24–25)

The new Aramean king evidently lacks the military prowess of his predecessor. Consequently, Joash of Israel musters the force to repel the invaders, restoring territories previously lost to Aram.

The process of the fall of Aram and the restoration of Israel reaches its peak with Jeroboam II, Joash's son:

> He restored the border of Israel from the entrance of Hamath to the sea of the Arabah, according to the word of the Lord, the God of Israel, which He spoke by the hand of His servant, the prophet Jonah son of Amittai from Gath-Hepher. (14:25)

In other words, in Jeroboam II's era, Israel restores its fortunes and its border with Aram, even making inroads into Aramean territory as far as Hamath!

5. The KJV translation is "like the dust by threshing." See a similar phrase referencing the threshing sled as a tool of destruction in Is. 41:15. Dust or earth is often used as a metaphor in reference to Aram; see I Kings 20:10; II Kings 5:17.

HISTORICAL BACKGROUND

What caused this reversal in Israel's fortunes? Here we may offer two explanations. One is to chart the geopolitical shifts that befell the region during this period. Aram was able to exhibit regional strength when its enemies were weak. Historians[6] chart the upswing in Aram's hegemony under Hazael to a corresponding lull in Assyrian regional power. This Aramean ascendency continued under Ben-Hadad III until the rise of the Assyrian king Adad-Nirari III (806–782 BCE), who attacked Aram, besieging Damascus and subjecting Aram to continued military pressure and heavy taxation. With Aram paralyzed, Israel was free to expand, extending her northern and eastern borders to a size not witnessed since the era of David and Solomon.

THE PROPHETIC PERSPECTIVE: GOD'S MERCY, LOVE FOR ISRAEL

And yet Kings is a prophetic composition and not a chronicle of political-military history. It explains historical events in spiritual terms: Sin breeds war, poverty, and invasion; fidelity to God stimulates economic prosperity and peace. Thus, when we witness a dramatic reversal from domestic collapse under foreign domination to secure borders and military victory, we might anticipate the national turnabout to be attributed to a repudiation of idolatry, a popular revival of religious devotion, or a process of nationwide repentance. Curiously, it seems that in our situation a different dynamic was underway.

> Jehoahaz pleaded with the Lord, and the Lord listened to him, *for He saw the suffering that the king of Aram inflicted upon Israel. So the Lord granted Israel a deliverer,*[7] and they gained their free-

6. See S. Yeivin, "The Foreign Policy of Judah and Israel in the Jehu Dynasty," in *Studies in Kings*, vol. 2 (Jerusalem: Kiryat Sefer, 1985), 299–305 [Hebrew]; *Encyclopedia Mikrait* (The Biblical Encyclopedia), vol. 1, cols. 597–8; Avraham Grossman, "Kings II, chapter 14: The Conquests of Jeroboam son of Joash," http://www.daat.ac.il/daat/tanach/rishonim/grosman7.htm [Hebrew].
7. Who was this "deliverer," or "savior," a term that is reminiscent of the period of the Judges (see Judges 2:14–16; 3:9)? The classic commentaries suggest that it refers to Joash (see Rashi). Kiel, *Daat Mikra*, however, proposes that it alludes to the period

> dom from Aram, and Israel dwelt in its homes as before. However, they did not depart from the sins which the house of Jeroboam had caused Israel to commit; they persisted in them. Even the sacred post stood in Samaria. (II Kings 13:4–5)

> King Hazael of Aram had oppressed the Israelites throughout the reign of Jehoahaz. But the Lord was gracious and merciful to them, and He turned back to them for the sake of *His covenant with Abraham, Isaac, and Jacob.* He refrained from destroying them, and He still did not cast them out from His presence. (13:22–23)

> He restored the border of Israel.... For the Lord saw the very bitter plight of Israel, with neither bond nor free left, and with none to help Israel. *And the Lord resolved not to blot out the name of Israel from under heaven;* and He delivered them through Jeroboam son of Joash. (14:25–27)

The kingdom's long arc of slump and restoration bears no evidence of significant religious improvement on the part of royalty or the people. Certainly, Jehoahaz beseeches God, but the Ashera persists in Samaria (II Kings 14:6), and illicit worship continues at the shrines of Bethel and Dan. Under this dynasty, we witness no fundamental reorientation in Israel's religious direction.

So why does God assist? Why does He rescue Israel? The three passages quoted above reveal three explanations for this divine relief.

First, "And the Lord listened to him, for He saw the suffering that the king of Aram inflicted upon Israel" (13:4). Israel's helplessness stimulates God's merciful rehabilitation. The nation is saved not because it deserves salvation, but rather out of divine concern for its welfare.

---

of Jehoahaz, in which the story (II Kings 6–7) of the devastating Aramean siege of Samaria takes place, and specifically to the miraculous flight of the Aramean army (ibid., 7:6–7). In that episode, Elisha refers to the unnamed king of Israel as "the son of the murderer" (ibid., 6:32). Might that be a reference to Jehoahaz son of Jehu, who assassinated two kings? If so, the "savior" alluded to by our verses is God Himself and the salvation is the supernatural manner in which He caused the foreign army to take flight. This is also the interpretation of Rav Yaakov Medan.

A second rationale underpins the national reprieve during the reign of Jehoahaz: "the covenant with Abraham, Isaac, and Jacob." The power of God's ancient relationship with Israel, sealed with the forefathers, saves the nation.[8]

Finally, under Jeroboam, He "would not blot out the name of Israel from under heaven." God saves Israel because its very survival is in jeopardy. If the alternative to salvation is exile and Israel's decimation, God here demonstrates His interest in Israel's continuity and perpetuity.[9]

The process charted here might denote even an incremental deterioration. Initially, God's assistance is stimulated by the king's prayer. Next, it is the recollection of the patriarchs and their merits that save the nation. But in the final stage, the positive ingredient is absent; Israel's salvation is earned neither by prayer nor by merit; the nation's survival is merely an expression of God's aversion to destroying Israel.

But God's patience, caring, and mercy do not last indefinitely. The reference in Kings to the potential "blotting out" of Israel sounds a cautionary note, suggesting that Israel's demise is not in the realm of the impossible; it is a real and present option! Indeed, we shall see how, after the heady reign of Jeroboam II, son of Joash, the northern kingdom swiftly crumbles under Assyrian pressure – a dynamic which leads to exile. This period of Joash and Jeroboam then, stimulated by a lull in international pressure, signifies the last opportunity for the success of

---

8. Jewish tradition sees *zechut avot* (the protective merit of the national patriarchs: Abraham, Isaac, and Jacob) as a potent force; see, for example, Ex. 32:13; Lev. 26:42; Deut. 29:12; I Chr. 16:15–22. But how long into Jewish history may the protection of the patriarchs endure? The first opinion in Leviticus Rabba 36:6, based on II Kings 13:22, suggests that the reign of Jehoahaz is the closing moment in which the national-historical memory and good deeds of the forefathers have the power to protect Israel. See also Shabbat 55a; Y. Sanhedrin 10:1. Traditional liturgy, which frequently appeals to *zechut avot,* evidently adopts the dissenting opinion of Rav Acha that "the merit of the patriarchs is in effect for all time."
9. These lines echo the Song of *Haazinu,* in which God saves his people, even in the absence of repentance, so as to obviate national destruction and to minimize *ḥillul Hashem.* See especially the literary parallel of "bound and free" in II Kings 14:26 and Deut. 32:36, as well as A. Bazak, "The Uniqueness of the Song of Haazinu," Yeshivat Har Etzion: Virtual Beit Midrash, http://www.vbm-torah.org/parsha.64/53haazinu.htm, which cites these verses.

the north! God exercises forbearance now, but soon even God's abundant tolerance and patience will be stretched beyond the breaking point.

THE PROPHET'S ROLE – A CALL TO CHANGE

As we read of the reversal in Israel's fortunes, we hear of two prophets who predict the national upswing. The first is Elisha,[10] who foresees the victory of Israel against Aram. Later (II Kings 14:23), a prophet called Jonah son of Amittai (possibly the prophet of the book that bears his name) predicts Israel's return to independence and security.

Why does God send two prophets to herald Israel's victory against Aram? What effect should this foreknowledge generate? This relates directly to our earlier observation. Spiritually, Israel is at an all-time low and is veritably undeserving of salvation. And yet, God has instigated the rehabilitation of the kingdom and the breaking of the shackles of Aram.

But the critical question is this: How will the king and the nation perceive these victories? What effect will this turnabout have on the national psyche? Will it be perceived as a fluke, a random regional fluctuation, or even evidence of Israel's military prowess? Could it lead Israel to appreciate God? Will a new period of peace and prosperity merely lead to a rise in the standard of living, with an ensuing atmosphere of hedonism, corruption, materialism, and continued abuse of the poor; or will people take advantage of prosperity, calm, and security to better the ills of society?

The role of the prophet is to convey that the upcoming victory is God-given, not a product of the winds of chance. This awareness might stimulate a positive religious response from the nation. Possibly the carrot will work instead of the stick; the good times as heralded by the prophet will draw people closer to God. And so, in charting the fall and rise of the northern kingdom, Kings seeks to generate appreciation for God, His love for Israel, and His great mercy.

10. There is a certain poetic irony here, as Elisha visited King Ben-Hadad as the latter was on his deathbed. That led to Hazael's rise to power. Now on Elisha's deathbed, he predicts the decline and fall of Aram (Hazael).

ELISHA AND SYMBOLIC ACTIONS

The final scenes of Elisha's life impress us with their dramatic power:

> Elisha had been stricken with the illness of which he was to die, and King Joash of Israel went down to him, and wept over him and cried, "My father, my father! Israel's chariot and horsemen!" Elisha said to him, "Get a bow and arrows," and he brought him a bow and arrows. Then he said to the king of Israel, "Grasp the bow!" And when he had grasped it, Elisha put his hands over the king's hands. "Open the window toward the east," he said; and he opened it. Then Elisha said, "Shoot!" and he shot. Then he said, "An arrow of victory for the Lord! An arrow of victory over Aram! You shall rout Aram at Aphek, until you destroy them." He said, "Now pick up the arrows." And he picked them up. "Strike the ground!" he said to the king of Israel; and he struck three times and stopped. And the man of God was angry with him and said, "If only you had struck five or six times! Then you would have annihilated Aram; as it is, you shall defeat Aram only three times." (II Kings 13:14–19)

The king visits the dying Elisha and cries at the prospect of the prophet's death, proclaiming Elisha as "Israel's chariot and horsemen" – in other words, the protector of the nation. This echoes Elisha's lament at the moment of Elijah's passing (I Kings 2:11).

At this point Elisha demands that the king perform some peculiar drama: the shooting of the "arrow of victory" eastward, and the dashing of the arrows on the floor. Why does the prophet demand this strange behavior, almost a theatrical performance? Is it a magic ritual? What place does this activity have in the world of prophecy?

Looking through the stories of biblical prophets, we witness a rich tradition of prophetic theater: Jeremiah is instructed to wear a yoke on his shoulders to demonstrate subservience to Babylonia (Jer. 27); Isaiah walks barefoot and undressed, simulating a prisoner of war (Is. 20). Hosea is commanded to marry a harlot (Hos. 1) to express Israel's infidelity to God; Ezekiel acts out a scene of exile by breaking the wall of his house and leaving with a small bag of essential items (Ezek. 12), and he makes a show of grafting separate branches into a single branch to communicate a lesson of national unity (ibid., 37:16–17). Prophets of Israel were frequently commanded to dramatize God's message.

Are these actions merely theatrics, or do they generate an otherworldly mechanism? In thinking about the instances listed above, several are clearly designated to be a signal, to act out the divine message and animate it.[11] However, in our story with Joash, the prophet criticizes the king, and says: "If only you had struck five or six times!" The implication is that these actions can manipulate and determine future events!

Nahmanides adopts precisely this approach:

> Know that once a decree delivered by angels emerges from the potential to the actual via symbolization, this decree will be fulfilled in all cases. Therefore, the prophets perform an act of prophecy, as Jeremiah ordered Barukh (Jer. 51:63–64): "When you finish reading this book, tie a stone to it and cast it into the midst of the Euphrates, and say, 'Thus shall Babylonia sink,'" etc. *This is the issue of Elisha's putting his hand on the bow* (II Kings 13:17): "Then Elisha said, 'Shoot!' and he shot. And he said, 'An arrow of victory for the Lord! An arrow of victory over Aram!'" And it says there (13:19): "And the man of God was angry with him and said, 'If only you had struck five or six times; then you would have annihilated Aram; as it is, you shall defeat Aram only three times.'"[12]

Nahmanides perceives prophetic symbolic drama as a means of transforming God's will from a potential decree to fulfillment. He believes that the acts of the prophet have a spiritual-mechanical effect, genuinely

11. Maimonides took a radical view that most of these actions transpired in a prophetic dream, but not in reality. See *Guide for the Perplexed*, II:46.
12. Nahmanides, Gen. 12:6.

determining the future. Elisha's laying of hands upon the king invests the figurative action with prophetic aura, and the precise performance of the act is critical; a mistake in the choreography engenders a flaw in the outcome. This view, while highly nonrational, reflects Nahmanides' mystical wisdom regarding the machinations of prophecy. Despite the difficulty in comprehending the relationship between cause and effect, this supernatural interpretation seems a highly appropriate explanation for this scene.

By contrast, Rabbi Joseph ibn Kaspi[13] suggests that the king's behavior as expressed in this scene is a psychological reflection of his resolve:

> If the king had struck [the ground with the arrows] several times, as the man of God intended...this would demonstrate his success in battle, for it would reveal his enthusiasm and determination, his mood regarding the war... and when he failed to do this, it highlighted his tepid enthusiasm and his foolishness. This is what angered the prophet.

In other words, striking the floor three or six times will not alter the nation's fate, but a passionate and desperate king may strike the floor with more gusto. Joash's lukewarm response exposes an absence of rage and urgency, emotions that have the capability of motivating the troops with a determination that could seriously influence the military campaign.

Ibn Kaspi's approach may be given greater credence as we discern the modular way in which the story is constructed and identify two distinct segments, each with their own dynamic.[14] We may chart the scene and its composite segments as follows:

13. 1297–1340. He was a Provençal exegetical commentator, grammarian, and philosopher.
14. See Rabbi David Sabato, "The Death of Elisha," Yeshivat Birkat Moshe, http://www.ybm.org.il/Admin/uploaddata/LessonsFiles/Pdf/5503.pdf.

Segment 1: 13:15–17	**Segment 2: 13:18–19**
"Get a bow and arrows"; *and he brought him a bow and arrows.*	"Now pick up the arrows." *And he picked them up.*
"Grasp the bow!" *And when he had grasped it,*	—
Elisha put his hands over the king's hands.	—
"Open the window toward the east" ... *and he opened it.*	—
"Shoot!" *and he shot.*	"Strike the ground!" ... *and he struck three times and stopped.*
Message: "An arrow of victory for the Lord!" ... You shall rout Aram at Aphek, until you destroy them."	Message: "If only you had struck five or six times! ... you shall defeat Aram only three times."

The first segment contains a series of specific actions, very carefully instructed, and fulfilled to the letter. Only one arrow is fired; there is not much to go wrong. The prophet waits patiently at each stage to ensure that his instructions are followed. But the second segment allows more room for the king's initiative. The instruction by the prophet is general, not specific, and all the activity is performed by the king. The prophet is inactive.

The first segment in which God's "arrow of victory" is shot toward the east symbolizes God's action and His decision to turn the tables and begin Aram's decline. The laying of the prophet's hands upon the king's hands invests the action with divine power.

By contrast, the second segment presents the king's independence. It is reflective of the human activism in God's plan. As Ibn Kaspi notes, it exposes the king's inner attitude and determination. It seems that the king was to follow the instruction, "Strike the ground!" and not to stop until he was instructed to do so; but in this instance, "he stopped." The king's halfhearted fulfillment is seen by Elisha as a deficient implementation of God's pronouncement.

Prof. Avraham Grossman suggests a political motivation for Joash's lack of resolve:

> Perhaps Joash's reluctance to strike several times expresses his hope and aspiration to return to the ancient Ahab-ite alliance between Israel and Aram, uniting to repel Assyria, a mutual aggressor which could threaten both Israel and Aram.[15]

Of course, the "arrow of victory" predicted by Elisha will wait a generation until it is fully fulfilled; the kingdom's borders are restored only in the period of Joash's son, Jeroboam.

RESURRECTION

The deathbed scene ends with a report of Elisha's burial, followed by the enigmatic anecdote of Elisha's bones causing a man to come back to life.

> Then Elisha died and was buried. Groups of Moabite raiders used to invade the land each spring. Once, when some Israelites were burying a man, they spied a band of these raiders. So they hastily threw the corpse into the tomb of Elisha and fled. But as soon as the body touched Elisha's bones, the dead man revived and jumped to his feet. (II Kings 13:20–21)

So much about this story is incoherent: Why are there Moabite troops in Israel – the foreign invader in these chapters is Aram! And is the identity of the raiders relevant to the story of the dead man? Who is the individual being buried; is it significant?[16] Why did the man come to life? And what became of him afterward? Most important, we desire to comprehend why this story is an essential element to our knowledge of Elisha. The commentaries search for answers. Ralbag (13:21) suggests:

> It was unlike the [resurrection of the] son of the Shunammite who gradually returned to life. Here, he suddenly arose and

15. See A. Grossman, "Kings II, chapter 14."
16. This question stimulates a wide discussion. See the Talmud in Sanhedrin 47a and Rashi there, s.v. "*vayḥi vayakom al raglav,*" who identifies the man as the "old prophet" in I Kings 13. Radak on 13:21 identifies him as Shalum son of Tikva, the husband of Hulda the prophetess.

> stood up.... But this was not to return home to his previous life, but merely to have him leave Elisha's grave for the honor of Elisha.

Radak disagrees:

> The Rabbis said that he lived and had children, and the reason that he was revived was to fulfill Elijah's blessing to Elisha that he be granted a double portion of [Elijah's] spirit (2:9). Elijah resurrected one person, and [Elisha] resurrected two: one in his lifetime – the Shunammite's son, and one in his death – this man.[17]

For Ralbag, the story demonstrates how even after Elisha's death, miracles are wrought to ensure that the prophet's bones are left undisturbed. For Radak, it is a fulfillment of Elijah's promise that his student be granted a double portion of his power; only at Elisha's death do we discover that he had been granted Elijah's blessing.

It is possible that neither of these answers fully explains the elements of this story, but we will suggest two somewhat speculative thoughts that may add a dimension to this enigmatic scene. First, when Joash addresses Elisha as "Israel's chariot and horsemen," we hear the echo of Elijah's death scene. But of course, Elijah was not buried; he flew heavenward, and tradition continues to identify Elijah's power, even after his mortal body has departed this world. If we are looking to identify this as a parallel scene, we might propose that this story comes to inform us that Elisha, just like his mentor Elijah, also retained some of his miraculous potency, even after his death.

Second, this scene suggests that Elisha's role is one of resurrection in the larger sense – the revival of the nation.[18] The combination of the threatening troops, and the man who is revived, not through merit but merely by proximity to the prophet, encapsulates in some way

17. Radak, II Kings 13:21, based on Sanhedrin 47a.
18. Cogan and Tadmor, *II Kings*, 150, suggest, "Thus the Elisha cycle is closed; it opens with a tale about his deadly curse (2:23–25) and ends with one about life-giving contact with his bones."

the work of Elisha. Elisha never calls for repentance. He simply offers assistance and healing to the people with whom he comes into contact. His life ends by announcing the restoration of Israel's fortunes after an extended period of foreign dominance and national hardship. The idea of the revival of the dead is fitting to Elisha's legacy.

UNDERSTANDING ELISHA

This chapter concludes Elisha's life, and it would seem that there is no coincidence that Elisha reenters the story at this juncture, if only to bid farewell. As we have contended,[19] Elisha's tenure has overlapped with a period in which Israel has been plagued by national weakness, including extended military defeat and foreign invasion. It was Elisha who gave divine sanction to Hazael, Israel's Aramean aggressor. God's initial announcement of Elisha's appointment signified Elisha's era as one in which the nation was subjected to punishment for the sins of the house of Omri. And certainly, as we have read the Elisha stories, we have witnessed famine, foreign invasion, siege, and foreign domination.

In this environment Elisha loomed, larger than life, with the ability to perform miracles at whim. He exuded an optimism, a deep faith, and a sense that God was with Israel – even as the national evidence pointed otherwise. When he had to anoint Hazael as the oppressor of Israel he burst into tears; here was no prophet of doom.

Now with the restoration of Israel's fortunes on the horizon, Elisha's final act is to announce that the national collapse had terminated and that better days were ahead. This final scene cements our sense of Elisha as the prophet who chaperoned Israel through its slump, and whose legacy was to invigorate faith in God, even in the darkest of times.

19. See the end of the chapter "Elisha's Tears."

II Kings 14

Amaziah (Judah)

During the two-hundred-year duration of the divided monarchy, Judah and Israel rarely clashed in armed conflict.[1] At times, the two kingdoms joined in warm partnership and even marital ties; during other times, relations appeared to be calm and cordial. But in rare circumstances, the two kingdoms became bitter aggressors. Our chapter depicts the reign of King Amaziah of Judah, during which violence erupted between north and south, the sole instance in which Jerusalem was penetrated and a Judahite king taken captive by a king of Israel. If our previous chapter told the tale of Israel's relief from foreign domination – a respite for the beleaguered kingdom – sadly, this story demonstrates how favorable regional conditions can breed an environment of in-fighting, turning brother against brother.

1. Military engagement is recorded after the split of the kingdom between Aviam (Judah) and Jeroboam (Israel), and between Assa (Judah) and Baasha (Israel); see I Kings 14:30; 15:6, 16. See also the war, before the fall of the northern kingdom, between Pekah and Ahaz, in II Kings 16:1–9; Is. 7:1–9.

THE ACCOUNT IN KINGS

Amaziah becomes king after his father, Joash, is assassinated.[2] He ascends the throne in difficult times; after all, Hazael of Aram had only recently directly threatened Jerusalem! And yet, Amaziah's early reigning years see the tables turn.

The new king has to tread carefully, slowly garnering power and consolidating his rule. After all, his father was assassinated by "his servants" in a conspiracy hatched in government circles. Once he stabilizes his position, he executes the men who killed his father (II Kings 14:5).

Religiously, Amaziah follows the path of God. The book of Kings consolidates our positive impression of him in that sector in a rare citation of an earlier biblical book – Deuteronomy (24:15) – evidence that Amaziah knows the Torah and adheres to its dictates:[3]

> But he did not put to death the children of the assassins, in accordance with what is written in the Book of the Teaching of Moses, where the Lord commanded, "Parents shall not be put to death for children, nor children be put to death for parents; a person shall be put to death only for his own crime." (II Kings 14:6)

With regard to foreign policy, Amaziah's era presents a sea change for the entire region. Aram was defeated by Adad-Nirari III of Assyria,[4] and with the waning of Aramean pressure Amaziah is free to reassert Israelite control over Edom for the first time in four generations.[5] He captures the strategic city of Sela, renaming it with a Judahite name – Joktheel. The location of Sela commanded important trade routes and copper

2. In the northern kingdom the assassin usually ascends the throne, quite frequently murdering the heirs of the previous royal house. This is the pattern with Jeroboam, Baasha, Omri, Jehu, and Athaliah. In Judah the legacy of the house of David held such commanding stature that even in circumstances of assassination, the royal heir succeeded his murdered father rather than the assassin.
3. For more on this verse in Deuteronomy, see Rabbi Prof. Yonatan Grossman, "A Man Shall Be Put to Death Only for His Own Crime," Yeshivat Har Etzion: Virtual Beit Midrash, http://www.vbm-torah.org/parsha.59/48kitetz.htm.
4. Cogan and Tadmor, *II Kings*, 158.
5. Judah had lost control over Edom during the reign of Jehoram, Amaziah's great-grandfather; see II Kings 8:20.

mines.[6] It is probable that the attack on Edom was aimed primarily to open the way southward to the southern port city of Eilat and the trade routes that it controlled. Amaziah never reached Eilat, but his son, Uzziah, completed his objective and established a successful port there (14:22).

THE CEDAR IN LEBANON

Up to this point all seems to go well for Amaziah. The story continues, however, with a disastrous military embroilment:

> Then Amaziah sent envoys to King Jehoash son of Jehoahaz son of Jehu of Israel, with this message: "Come, let us confront each other [lit., meet face to face]." King Jehoash of Israel sent back this message to King Amaziah of Judah: "The thistle in Lebanon sent this message to the cedar in Lebanon: 'Give your daughter to my son in marriage.' But a wild beast in Lebanon went by and trampled down the thistle. Because you have defeated Edom, you have become arrogant. Stay home and enjoy your glory, rather

6. See Kiel, *Daat Mikra*; *Olam HaTanakh*. There is some uncertainty as to the identification of Sela. Whereas Josephus identifies it as Petra, it more likely ought to be identified as es-Sela, an imposing natural rock fortress that still carries the name, east of Tafilleh (Tofel) and near the Edomite city of Bozrah (Buseirah) in the rugged highlands of today's southern Jordan. Surrounded on all sides by deep ravines, es-Sela rises more than six hundred feet above the surrounding valleys, culminating in a broad, flat summit. It can be reached only by an ancient, well-hidden staircase that follows a narrow cleft in the eastern face of the mountain. This would fit the account in II Chr. of ten thousand men being hurled from "the Sela."

   Rav Yaakov Medan, however, contends that Sela (Judges 1:36) is located at the Ascent of Akrabim on the southern border of Judah. This would also fit nicely with the battle in the Valley of Salt, which might be Tel el-Malah, today's Tel Malhata near Beer Sheba. This identification, though ignored by academic sources, fits well into the narrative. There is wide academic consensus that Amaziah failed to take control of the region of Edom as a whole. According to Rav Medan's approach, this war took place on Judah's southern border. If the Edomites had expanded into the southern edge of Judah, seizing lands previously regarded as Judahite territory, we can well imagine that there was constant friction between the rival populations. This would explain the extreme violence exhibited by Israel toward Edom, and the renaming of Sela with a Judahite name. That this region commands the road to Eilat is evidenced in II Kings 14:22.

> than provoke disaster and fall, dragging Judah down with you." But Amaziah paid no heed; so King Jehoash of Israel advanced, and he and King Amaziah of Judah confronted each other at Beth-Shemesh in Judah. Judah was routed by Israel, and they all fled to their homes. King Jehoash of Israel captured King Amaziah son of Jehoash son of Amaziah of Judah at Beth-Shemesh. He marched on Jerusalem, and he made a breach of four hundred cubits in the wall of Jerusalem, from the Ephraim Gate to the Corner Gate.[7] He carried off all the gold and silver and all the vessels that there were in the house of the Lord and in the treasuries of the royal palace, as well as hostages; and he returned to Samaria. (II Kings 14:8–14)

What triggered this war? Why did Amaziah instigate a clash with the northern kingdom? Why did Israel react so fiercely to Judah's provocation? And what is the meaning of the riddle that speaks of the cedar and the thistle of Lebanon?

Some suggest that Amaziah instigated an alliance, a peaceful union, as indicated by Joash's metaphor of marriage (14:9). In this reading, the offer "let us meet face to face" (14:8) should be read in a positive light. It is possible that after his conquest of Edom, Amaziah sought open access to key Mediterranean ports to control trade routes, and thus his motive in seeking a northern alliance was economic.[8] Joash rejects this union. He views himself and the kingdom of Israel as the cedar in the Lebanon, in contrast to Amaziah

---

7. This is probably on the northern side of Jerusalem. This is evidenced by the naming of the "Ephraim Gate," which leads north toward the territory of Ephraim, much like today's Damascus Gate, which leads northward on the ancient route to Shekhem (Nablus) and then Damascus. The west, south, and east of ancient Jerusalem are protected by deep valleys, whereas the north is exposed. As such, historically, Jerusalem has been most vulnerable on its northern flank. Even today, with walls that date to the sixteenth century, Damascus Gate is the most heavily fortified.
8. Shmuel Yeivin, "Foreign Policy of Judah and Israel in the Era of the Jehu Dynasty," in *Studies in the Book of Kings: Proceedings from The Bible Study Circle at the Residence of David Ben-Gurion*, vol. 2, ed. B. Z. Luria (Jerusalem: Kiryat Sefer, 1985), 303–4, and the ensuing discussion on 308–10.

and Judah, who are depicted as the lowly thistle – a stark and deprecating imbalance.

This reading poses several difficulties. If Amaziah is indeed proposing an alliance, what would explain Joash's belligerent and disdainful rebuttal? Joash's quip, "You have become arrogant. Stay home and enjoy your glory, rather than provoke disaster and fall," demonstrates that Amaziah's approach is a threat, an act of aggression! As such, his "let us meet face to face" should read: "Come, let us confront each other in battle."[9]

Some have speculated that Amaziah instigated a war to shift the border northward and gain more territory for his kingdom.[10] Josephus goes further, suggesting that Amaziah, whose ego had become inflated after his Edomite victory, seeks to dominate and incorporate the north, forcibly reuniting Israel with Judah:

> Now upon the victory which Amaziah had won, and the great acts he had done, he was puffed up…in a vein of insolence he wrote to Joash, the king of Israel, and commanded that he and all his people should be obedient to him, as they had formerly been obedient to his progenitors, David and Solomon; and he let him know, that if he would not be so wise as to do what he commanded him, he must fight for his dominion.[11]

THE NORTHERN RAMPAGE

These theories rest on some interpretation but also on a good deal of conjecture. The text does not reveal enough information to verifiably determine the cause of war. But the correlative story in Chronicles provides just enough information to explain the catalyst to the flare-up:[12]

9. Rashi; Radak; Ralbag. This reading rests on Amaziah's initial approach of *nitra'eh panim* – a phrase that is ambivalent on its own – being mirrored by *vayira'u panim*, which describes a military clash, and clarifies the intent behind the language of Amaziah's initial approach.
10. *Olam HaTanakh*, 107.
11. Josephus, *Antiquities* IX, 9.
12. This interpretation is adopted by Abarbanel and Malbim.

> Amaziah assembled the men of Judah ... 300,000 chosen men, fit for service, able to bear spear and shield. *He hired 100,000 warriors from Israel for 100 talents of silver.* Then a man of God came to him and said, "O King! Do not let the army of Israel go with you, for the Lord is not with Israel – all these Ephraimites. But go by yourself and do it.... So Amaziah detached the force that came to him from Ephraim, [ordering them] to go back to their place. *They were greatly angered against Judah and returned to their place in a rage.*
>
> Amaziah took courage and, leading his army, he marched to the Valley of Salt. He slew 10,000 men of Seir.... The men of the force that Amaziah had sent back ... made forays against the towns of Judah from Samaria to Beth-Horon. They slew 3,000 of them, and took much booty. (II Chr. 25:6–10, 13)

Originally Amaziah had indeed proposed "a marriage," a military alliance against Edom. And Joash had accepted his offer when he sent his 100,000 troops to boost the Judahite army. However, as the troops mobilized, Amaziah, on prophetic instruction, discharged the northern troops and sent them home. The infuriated soldiers responded by rampaging through Judahite territory, killing three thousand people and despoiling the towns and villages en route. Here we understand the second clause of the parable; if one had to express it in poetic form, one might say: "A wild beast in Lebanon went and trampled down the thistle."

Why did the northern troops react with such ferocity? Their violent reprisal was presumably motivated by a dual factor. First is the king's insulting rejection of the northern troops, on the prophet's proclamation: "The Lord is not with Israel." Second is the financial aspect. The mercenaries were hired for a sum of one hundred talents of silver. It would seem that this modest payment was to be supplemented by looting and despoiling the enemy. But now, as Ahaziah relieves them from active duty, their anticipated income, the spoils of war, had been taken away. When the Israelite troops loot Judahite towns, they are unleashing their frustration while also recouping what they perceived as their financial loss.

Amaziah hears about this rampage and declares war on the north. Joash warns him that their forces are mismatched; he is the "cedar" compared with the lowly "thistle." This explanation shifts some of the weight off Amaziah. After all, he was responding to a northern provocation.

Amaziah made a dreadful tactical miscalculation; his indignation blinding his better judgment. There is little doubt that this civil war was a total blunder for Amaziah. The southern army is defeated, Jerusalem is penetrated, and Amaziah and members of his clan are taken captive.

AFTER THE WAR

> King Amaziah son of Joash of Judah lived fifteen years after the death of King Jehoash son of Jehoahaz of Israel.... A conspiracy was formed against him in Jerusalem and he fled to Lachish; but they sent men after him to Lachish, and they killed him there. They brought back his body on horses, and he was buried with his fathers in Jerusalem, in the City of David. (II Kings 14:17–20)

The details of Amaziah's fate after the war are elusive. Kings records the capture of Amaziah (14:13), but we lack information as to when he returned to Jerusalem. The unusual language, that "Amaziah... *lived* fifteen years after the death of Jehoash" (14:17) – "lived" rather than "reigned" – is commonly taken to indicate that his son, Uzziah, assumed the throne in his father's lifetime, while his father was incarcerated in Samaria.[13] Further obscurity surrounds the circumstances of Amaziah's assassination. The conspiracy originated in Jerusalem but transpired in Lachish. Had Amaziah reassumed the throne in Jerusalem? What were the motives of the assassins? The details are withheld. And when all is said and done, the book of Kings issues negligible criticism of Amaziah.[14]

---

13. See Kiel, *Daat Mikra*; Cogan and Tadmor, *II Kings*, 159.
14. Amaziah is depicted as a king who "did what was pleasing [*yashar*] to the Lord" (II Kings 14:3), and Kings specifies no particular transgressions. One could claim that his sins are implicit: Amaziah was "not like his ancestor David, he did just as his father Joash had done," and he was accused of arrogance in Joash's verbal jibe (14:10). However, many classical commentators were disturbed as to why God would allow the strict monotheistic Amaziah to be defeated by a king of the idolatrous northern kingdom. Ibn Kaspi answers that the biblical text fails to present all the evidence

THE VIEW FROM CHRONICLES

As we have seen, Chronicles offers alternative perspectives which can supplement and enrich our readings of Kings. However, frequently the new information added by Chronicles radically alters our perception of key personalities. Amaziah is certainly one such example. Let us refer to some details that illustrate this:

Amaziah's Brutality against Edom

When Amaziah conquers Sela, he "captured ten thousand men alive, took them to the top of a cliff, and threw them down so that all were dashed to pieces" (II Chr. 25:11). It is possible that this violence was merely reflective of the norms of ancient warfare.[15] However, one midrashic source condemns this action as highly immoral and a cause of national exile:[16]

---

and that God has His criteria even if they elude human judgment: "Even if [Judah] had been good, what is to say that they did not sin in the course of the war campaign, transgressing God's covenant, whether by action or by thought? For God knows all… and there is no presumption that all details are recorded in the [biblical] books." As we shall see, Chronicles accuses Amaziah more directly of idolatry, which may provide some explanation for the reader bothered by the divine calculus.

15. See another difficult episode in II Sam. 8:2, or the mass killing in I Kings 11:15–16.
16. This malicious violence seems extreme, and yet the history of Edom and Judah is filled with spite and butchery. I Kings 11:16–18 depicts David's military campaign which describes how Joab "killed every male in Edom" in a six-month massacre. Amos 1:11, written in the same period as Amaziah but reflecting on the past, condemns Edom for wanton bloodshed against Israel: "Because he pursued his brother with the sword and repressed all pity, because his anger raged unceasing and his fury stormed unchecked." Notably, Edom and Israel are seen as brothers, descending from Esau and Jacob – reflected in the injunction: "You shall not abhor the Edomite, for he is your kinsman" (Deut. 23:8). Later history, as we know, is not brotherly in any way.

    The book of Obadiah is entirely dedicated to a diatribe against Edom, probably connected to Edom's part in the destruction of the First Temple. See also Is. 63:1–10; Mal. 1:1–5; Ps. 137:7; Lam. 4:21–22 for evidence of a vendetta against Edom, in recompense for their ruthlessness toward Judah. This malevolence was seen in retrospect as rooted in the rivalry between Esau and Jacob, but in truth we lack the information to gain an accurate history of this ferocious and bloodstained saga.

> At that time the Holy One Blessed be He said: "I decreed death upon the descendants of Noah only by the sword,"[17] but these people "threw them down, so that all were dashed to pieces." … At that time, the Holy One Blessed be He said, "Since they acted thus they shall go into exile."[18]

Amaziah's Idolatry and Opposition to the Prophet

In Chronicles, it is not Amaziah's arrogance but rather his turn to idolatry that serves as the key determinant of his demise:

> After Amaziah returned from defeating the Edomites, he had the gods of the men of Seir brought and installed them as his gods; he prostrated himself before them and he made sacrifice to them. The Lord was enraged at Amaziah, and sent a prophet to him who said to him, "Why are you worshipping the gods of a people who could not save their people from you?" As he spoke to him, [Amaziah] said to him, "Have we appointed you a counselor to the king? Stop, else you will be killed!" The prophet stopped, saying, "I see God has counseled that you be destroyed, since you act this way and disregard my counsel." (II Chr. 25:14–16)

In this passage we read how Amaziah adopts Edomite deities, worships and sacrifices to them, and then threatens the prophet who berates him for his transgression.

The contrast between Kings and Chronicles is striking. Kings presents Amaziah as a religiously devoted king, successful in expanding his empire. It was his miscalculated aggression against Israel that brought about his downfall.

Chronicles details two distinct stages of Amaziah's religious biography.[19] Prior to embarking on the campaign against Edom, Ama-

---

17. The punishment for a non-Jew's transgressing the Seven Noahide Laws is death by the sword, a method that was considered less brutal than stoning. See Maimonides, *Mishneh Torah*, Laws of Kings 9:14; Mishna Sanhedrin 7:3.
18. Lamentations Rabba, *Petiḥta* 14.
19. Japhet, *The Ideology of the Book of Chronicles*, 410–11, notes that whereas Kings generally depicts a king in a static way, as either a sinful or a righteous king (as a function

ziah complies with the prophet and is faithful to God; he demonstrates compassion (against his father's assassins) and seeks national unity. During and after his successful campaign against Edom, he worships idols, intimidates the prophet and resists his message, exhibits extreme cruelty to Edom, and engages in a bombastic war campaign. Chronicles sees Amaziah's downfall as engendered by his turn to idolatry. It is his direct affront to God that arouses divine punishment.[20]

In the Chronicles account, it is difficult to understand what generated the drastic shift in Amaziah's behavior. In some ways, Amaziah's biography mirrors that of his father, Joash of Judah,[21] whose early life was marked by ardent devotion to God but who altered radically in later life, rejecting the priesthood and turning to idolatry. Both kings disastrously mismanaged a war which resulted in Jerusalem's being penetrated by the enemy, and both kings were assassinated by political opponents.

* * *

This is a challenging historical period. After years of Aramean pressure, the Land of Israel, both north and south, experiences a lull in foreign domination, a power vacuum. This invites local kings to vie for domestic and regional control. It offers opportunities, but also pitfalls and dangers. In this environment, we see Judah regaining control over Edom. However, in Amaziah's attempt to dominate Israel, he instigates his own downfall.

---

of his idolatry or opposition to it), Chronicles will frequently present a more complex biography, with vacillations in the religious affiliation of the king. This is true regarding kings Rehoboam, Assa, Jehoshaphat, Joash, Amaziah, Uzziah, Hezekiah, Manasseh, and Josiah.

20. The application of a strict correlation between actions and their reward or punishment is a distinctive feature of Chronicles. See Japhet, ibid., 145–54.

21. See Kiel, *Daat Mikra*, 839–40.

II Kings 14:23–15:7

The Best of Times: Jeroboam II and Uzziah

The period of Jeroboam II (Israel), and Uzziah[1] (Judah), may truly be described as the best of times; the kingdoms, both north and south, experience power and prosperity unknown since the period of David and Solomon, and unseen hereafter.

But what does the nation and its leadership do with these years of good fortune? How does this national flourishing affect Israel and Judah? Are these years of collective accomplishment, societal cohesion, and religious commitment, or is the opportunity squandered?

The histories of Jerobam son of Joash and Uzziah as described in the book of Kings are presented in formulaic, undramatic lines, giving little of the outstanding accomplishments of the age. Our task will be to explore their worlds with greater depth and color.

1. He is called Azariah in II Kings 15:1, 6, 7, 8, 17, 23, 27; he is called Uzziah in II Kings 13:30, 32, 34; Is. 1:1; 6:1; Hos. 1:1; Amos 1:1; Zech. 14:5; II Chr. 26–27. The two names have the same meaning: Azariah is derived from the Hebrew root A-Z-R, indicative of strength (see Ps. 89:20). It is similar to *oz,* or the root A-Z-Z, which invests the name Uzziah with the same meaning. In a lovely touch, II Chr. 26:7, 15 mixes the two names: "[Uzziah's] fame spread, for he was helped (*lehe'azer*) wonderfully."

JEROBOAM II (II KINGS 14:23–29)

During his long and impressive forty-one-year reign, Jeroboam son of Joash of the northern kingdom takes full advantage of a regional power vacuum. Aram, Israel's prime enemy of the past decades, has waned, while the Assyrian empire has yet to extend its reach westward. Jeroboam restores and expands the northern border beyond Damascus, to Hamath, establishing Israel's hegemony to the borders in place during King Solomon's heyday (14:25), a territorial expansion preordained by God's prophet.[2]

Notwithstanding Kings' terse account of Jeroboam's reign, other sources enrich our understanding of the period. Archaeology reveals enormous building works at Hazor, Dan, Megiddo, and Samaria during this era.[3] However, the most insightful assessment of the mood and pulse of this period may be gleaned by reading the powerful words of the prophet Amos,[4] who prophesied during the reign of Jeroboam.[5]

THE VIEW FROM AMOS

The book of Amos depicts a society of wealth, complacency, and security, and yet it bears startling inequalities of income and outrageous exploitation of the poor by the rich. Amos addresses the wealthy upper class of

2. The prophet who foretold this event is named Jonah son of Amittai. This could be the prophet of the biblical book of Jonah, an approach adopted by most medieval commentators but questioned by Ibn Kaspi. Interestingly, *Seder Olam* 18 identifies him as the selfsame prophet who anointed Jehu. The Jehu story focuses on a period of Aramean influence, while the prophet of the book of Jonah who visits Nineveh, the capital of Assyria, would be connected to a different Assyrian historical dynamic – although that certainly does not preclude the prophet from engaging in variant tasks.
3. Ostraca found at Samaria and dated to the ninth, tenth, and fifteenth years of Jeroboam II reveal huge revenues based on wine and oil, as well as expensive ivory plaques or furniture inlays. Archaeologist Israel Finkelstein records significant building at Megiddo, Hazor, and Gezer in this period, See I. Finkelstein and N. Silberman, *The Bible Unearthed* (New York: Simon and Schuster, 2002), 206–9.
4. For a very useful summary of the themes of Amos, see A.J. Heschel, *The Prophets*, vol. 1 (New York: Harper and Row, 1962), 27–38. For more on the themes we raise regarding Amos's prophetic-societal critique, see Y. Cherlow, *Looketh on the Heart*, 31–44.
5. The book is dated to the period of Jeroboam; see Amos 1:1–2; 7:11.

Samaria with their lavish homes, expensive ivory furniture, and a decadent preoccupation with food, drink, and entertainment:

> They lie on ivory beds,
> Lolling on their couches,
> Feasting on lambs from the flock
> And on calves from the stalls.
> They listen to song to the tune of the lute –
> They account themselves musicians like David,
> They drink straight from wine bowls
> And anoint themselves with the choicest oils. (Amos 6:4–6)

Luxury is not a sin, but Amos describes how this high life is financed by the exploitation of the poor:

> Hear this word, you cows of Bashan
> On the hill of Samaria –
> Who defraud the poor,
> Who rob the needy,
> Who say to their husbands,
> "Bring, and let's party." (4:1)

This gilded flamboyance is sustained by oppression of the peasantry. Amos depicts the rich feasting on wines collected as penalties for late payment of credit, and celebrations in which the moneylenders recline on ornate fabrics seized from the hardworking poor as security for loans.[6] God sends Amos to warn the people that the abusive behavior – "You… trample the heads of the poor" – will warrant the punishment of exile:

> … they have sold for silver
> Those whose cause was just,
> And the needy for a pair of sandals.
> [Ah,] you who trample the heads of the poor

6. Another example is Amos 8:4–8, which describes people who cannot wait for Shabbat to end so that they can continue with their fraudulent financial affairs.

> Into the dust of the ground,
> And make the humble walk a twisted course!
> Father and son go to the same girl,
> And thereby profane My holy name.
> They recline by every altar
> On garments taken in pledge,
> And drink in the house of their God
> Wine bought with fines they imposed. (2:6–8)

While Kings dwells almost exclusively on the struggles associated with the sin of idolatry, Amos highlights the crime of social injustice and oppression within the northern kingdom. With the dramatic rise in national fortunes, the influx of wealth and prosperity has enriched the leadership exclusively. Society is starkly divided into the haves and the have-nots in an economy riddled with loan-sharking systems that make the rich richer and leave the poor in desperation:

> My Lord swears by Himself;
> I loathe the pride of Jacob,
> And I detest his palaces.
> I will deliver (to the enemy) the city and its inhabitants alike. (6:4–8)

COMPLACENCY

But it is nearly impossible to frighten a smug, complacent society. In Jeroboam's era, the national military successes have engendered a zeitgeist in which people are certain that Israel is invincible:[7]

> They boast:
> "Destruction shall never overtake us,
> Nor approach us." (Amos 9:10)
> Those who rejoice with no substance,[8]

7. See also Amos 5:18.
8. This is a subtle pun about the victory over the town of Lo-Dabar in Transjordan, so it may be read, "rejoice about [the victory over] Lo-Dabar" (NJPS).

> Who exalt, "By our might we have captured Karnaim!"
> But I, O house of Israel,
> Will raise up a nation against you,
> Declares the Lord, God of Hosts,
> Who will harass you from Lebo-Hamath
> To the Wadi Arabah. (6:13–14)

Some were most probably convinced that the Israelite military was unbeatable. But others couched their confidence of the national invincibility in a religious belief; that as the chosen people, God would never abandon Israel. As such, if and when the day of the Lord's retribution and reckoning ("The Day of the Lord" – *Yom Hashem*[9]) would arrive, Israel as God's chosen people would escape unscathed. Amos sets his mind and rhetoric to challenge this perspective:

> You alone have I known of all the families of the earth;
> Therefore I will punish you for all your iniquities. (3:1–2)

The people of Samaria assumed that God's special relationship with Israel would guarantee them protection. The prophet warns that the relationship offers no privileges but rather demands a higher ethical standard. Instead of offering unconditional safety it will heighten their liability, accentuating sins and exacerbating punishment.[10] Again and again, Amos dispels popular optimistic misconceptions, offering instead foreboding warnings of Israel's exile, as punishment for its abusive society.

WARNINGS

Amos takes his message to the Temple in Bethel, but he is ejected by the high priest for his dire predictions to the king and his people. Among his repeated threats of war, exile, and drought, Amos consistently predicts that the earth will turn over; maybe a metaphor, but possibly an

9. This phrase recurs throughout the latter prophets. See Is. 13:6, 9; Ezek. 13:5; Joel 1:15; 2:6, 11; 4:14; Amos 5:18, 20; Ob. 15; Zeph. 1:7; 2:2; Zech. 14:1.
10. See also Amos 9:7.

earthquake.[11] Indeed, an earthquake shakes the kingdom a mere two years after Amos begins his prophecy.[12] Yet even with a national disaster of this proportion, the king fails to heed the prophet.

More severe and disappointing is that in these fortunate times, in which Israel existed as an island of calm and prosperity in a stormy region, it could not have found a way to harness its peace and wealth toward kindness, justice, and national cohesion.

UZZIAH (II KINGS 15:1–7)

King Uzziah of Judah ruled alongside Jeroboam II for a lengthy and stable fifty-two years. Yet again, Kings furnishes little information besides generic statements of Uzziah's positive religious commitment and indications of his expanded borders and extensive building. One detail is his conquest and restoration of Eilat to Judah (II Kings 14:22) and its reestablishment as a port city, an achievement shared by only the greatest of Judahite kings – Solomon, Jehoshaphat, and Hezekiah. This outpost brought both opportunity and challenge. On the one hand, a seaport at Eilat ensured access to Arabia and Africa, opening up new sources of revenue. On the other hand, maintaining and supplying a settlement in that arid, inhospitable terrain, far from Judahite centers of power and population, necessitated full military control of the Arava, the desert lands between Beer Sheba and Eilat through which the supply and trade caravans would travel, as well as

11. Ibid., 4:11; 8:7; 9:1.

12. See ibid., 1:1; Zech. 14:6. "Masonry walls best display the earthquake, especially walls with broken ashlars, walls with displaced rows of stones, walls still standing but leaning or bowed, and walls collapsed with large sections still lying course-on-course. Debris at six sites – Hazor, Deir 'Alla, Gezer, Lachish, Tell Judeideh, and 'En Haseva – is tightly confined stratigraphically to the middle of the eighth century B.C., with dating errors of ~30 years.... The earthquake was at least magnitude 7.8, but likely was 8.2" (Steven A. Austin, Gordon W. Franz, and Eric G. Frost, "Amos's Earthquake: An Extraordinary Middle East Seismic Event of 750 B.C.," *International Geology Review* 42 (2000): 657–71). Yigael Yadin and Prof Israel Finkelstein date the earthquake to around 760 BCE. See Y. Yadin, *Hazor: The Rediscovery of a Great Citadel of the Bible* (New York: Random House, 1975); I. Finkelstein, "Hazor and the North in the Iron Age: A Low Chronology Perspective," *Bulletin of the American Schools of Oriental Research* 314 (1999): 55–70.

the infrastructure to support a large logistical center in that remote location. As such, the very building of Eilat is evidence of considerable power and resources.

Chronicles again supplements the missing details. Among them:

- Uzziah's military conquests of Philistia, Ammon, and the Sinai, all the way to Egypt, essentially granting him wide regional hegemony. Historians have noted that Uzziah reached a position in which he controlled both major highways between Egypt and Mesopotamia, the *Via Maris* (*Derekh HaYam*) and the King's Highway (*Derekh HaMelekh*), an achievement which gave him enormous influence and procured significant national revenues[13] (II Chr. 26:6–8).
- His extensive building. In Jerusalem Uzziah strengthens the city's walls and constructs towers. On the desert frontier he establishes border fortifications (26:9-10).
- Uzziah's love of farming and agriculture. He invests in irrigation, which in turn generates new pastureland and arable areas (26:10). Uzziah is the only king in Tanakh who is described as a "lover of the land."
- His large and powerful army, fully supplied with uniforms and weaponry. Among the armaments, we read of *ḥeshbonot maḥshevet ḥoshev*; in our language, new missile technologies. Uzziah's development and manufacture of new weaponry secures his military advantage against new developments in the Assyrian military arsenal.

---

13. II Kings 14:28 refers to how Jeroboam "fought and recovered Damascus and Hamath for Judah in Israel," indicating that there was a military alliance between the northern and southern kingdoms. Uzziah's conquest of Ammon, an area usually affiliated with the northern kingdom, also indicates Judahite influence in the north and possibly an alliance between the two states. See also I Chr. 5:17 which speaks of a joint census between Israel and Judah. The theory of a north-south alliance is upheld by M. Haran, "The Rise and Decline of the Empire of Jeroboam ben Joash," *Vetus Testamentum*, vol. 17, Fasc. 3 (July 1967), 280–82, 297; and H. Tadmor, "Azriyau of Yaudi," in *Scripta Hierosolymitana* 8, ed. Chaim Rabin (Jerusalem: Magnes Press, 1961), 248.

As we can see, the composite picture is of a kingdom that is thriving in every area.

PRIDE COMES BEFORE A FALL

Uzziah's story takes a startling turn when he is stricken with leprosy. In Kings, this event is left unexplained:

> The Lord struck the king with a plague and he was a leper until the day of his death; he lived in isolated quarters while Yotam, the king's son, was in charge of the palace and governed the people of the land. (II Kings 15:5)

Chronicles offers a more detailed account:

> When he was strong, he grew arrogant [lit., his heart was lifted up] to the point of destruction. He trespassed against the Lord, his God, and entered the Temple of the Lord to offer incense on the incense altar. The priest Azariah, with eighty other brave priests of the Lord, followed him in, and confronting King Uzziah, said to him: "It is not for you, Uzziah, to offer incense to the Lord, but for the Aaronite priests who have been consecrated to offer incense. Leave the sanctuary, for you have trespassed; there will be no honor in it for you from the Lord God." Uzziah got angry as he held the censer and made ready to burn the incense, and as he became enraged with the priests, leprosy broke out on his forehead in front of all the priests in the house of the Lord beside the incense altar.... So they rushed him out of there; he too made haste to get out, for the Lord had struck him with a plague. Uzziah was a leper until the day of his death; he lived in isolated quarters as a leper, for he was banned from the house of the Lord. (II Chr. 26:16–21)

Why did Uzziah offer incense in the Temple? And why was he punished by leprosy (*tzaraat*) in particular? Chronicles pinpoints Uzziah's arrogance or overblown pride: his "heart was lifted up."[14]

If we place Uzziah's formidable accomplishments in context, his hubris is quite understandable. Uzziah had inherited a humiliated and destitute kingdom. His two forebears – Joash and Ahaziah – both suffered disastrous military campaigns, leaving their kingdom impoverished and weak, and both kings were assassinated by their courtiers. Uzziah generated a spectacular turnaround both domestically and internationally. Possibly it was precisely this eminence that generated the idea:

> One day [Uzziah] came to the beit midrash. He asked them: What are you discussing? They replied: The law that "any outsider who encroaches shall be put to death" (Num. 1:51). Said Uzziah: God is a King, and I am a king. It is appropriate that the king serve the King by offering incense before Him. Immediately, "He entered the Temple of the Lord to offer incense." (*Midrash Tanḥuma, Noaḥ* 13)

Uzziah views himself as citizen number one, as the figure most fitting to represent the nation before God. He can approach God because he, like God, embodies sovereignty, and as such, is the appropriate designate to encounter God!

CHALLENGING THE PRIESTHOOD

Uzziah's attitude is certainly presumptuous, and it reflects a foreign way of thinking. What he is essentially proposing is the ascendancy of the monarchy over the priesthood. Rabbi Prof. Yonatan Grossman remarks:

---

14. Echoed in the Talmud (Arakhin 16a): "R. Samuel b. Nahmani said in the name of R. Yoḥanan: Because of seven things the plague [of leprosy] is incurred: slander, the shedding of blood, taking and oath in vain, incest, arrogance, robbery, and envy.... Because of arrogance, as it is written: But when he [Uzziah] was strong, he grew arrogant to the point of destruction. He trespassed against the Lord, his God ... leprosy broke out on his forehead."

> Uzziah is not motivated by a religious awakening or religious emotion, he is seeking to acquire total social authority. Aside from the political power that is in his possession, Uzziah also wants the religious authority held by the priests.[15]

Judaism perceives the Temple as an institution independent of the king. From a certain perspective, the Temple and royalty function as two parallel environments. Both king and high priest are elevated to high office by means of anointing oil;[16] both palace and Temple have royal livery, an honor guard, and a treasury.[17] Yet the unification of king and priest in a single personality are proscribed.[18] The priests are God's representatives engaging with the sacred, whereas the king embodies the nation and is preoccupied with its management. When the king acts as high priest, he is fusing these disparate institutions in a manner in which both will be compromised. Uzziah is stepping beyond his jurisdiction.

This encroachment of priestly authority, an infringement upon the divine order of the Temple, would explain Uzziah's punishment – the affliction of leprosy-*tzaraat.* To understand this particular divine response, we recall the famous episode of Miriam who sees herself on a par with Moses as she challenges his preeminent status as chief-prophet.

She is struck swiftly and unexpectedly by leprosy:

> Miriam and Aaron spoke against Moses … "Has the Lord indeed spoken only through Moses? Has he not spoken through us also?" … And suddenly the Lord said … "Hear My words: If there is a prophet among you … I speak with him in a dream. Not so with My servant Moses. He is faithful in all My house. With

15. Y. Grossman, "The Plague of Tzara'at," Yeshivat Har Etzion: Virtual Beit Midrash, http://etzion.org.il/en/plague-tzaraat. See also Cherlow, *Looketh on the Heart*, 228. Leviticus Rabba 16:1 asserts that Uzziah "sought to discredit the high priesthood."
16. High priest, Lev. 4:3; 21:10; king, I Sam. 10:1; 16:13; I Kings 1:39.
17. See, for example, I Kings 14:26; II Kings 14:14.
18. See Nahmanides' discussion on Gen. 49:10 where he suggests that the Hasmonean monarchy met a swift demise due to its violation of this separation between palace and Temple.

> him I speak mouth to mouth, clearly, and not in riddles, and he beholds the likeness of the Lord. Why then were you not afraid to speak against My servant Moses?" And the anger of the Lord was kindled against them, and He departed. When the cloud removed from over the tent, behold, Miriam was leprous, like snow. (Num. 12:1–10)

Prof. Yair Zakovitch comments:

> All the stories of leprosy deal with non-recognition of authority, whether prophetic authority or priestly authority, and if the person fails to learn the message he will remain unhealed, much like Uzziah who was a leper until his death, and Gehazi whose leprosy extended for generations.[19]

This understanding was instinctual and elementary to the priests, who felt empowered to warn the king to "leave the sanctuary!" "It is not for you, Uzziah, to offer incense to the Lord, but for the Aaronite priests who have been consecrated to offer incense" (II Chr. 26:18). When we appreciate that the offense here is not mere arrogance but rather Uzziah's seeking to usurp the domain of the priests, his punishment rings with deep irony. The affliction of leprosy can be diagnosed and cured only by means of an attendant priest who pronounces the plague and recovery from it.[20] Thus the man who wished to act as a priest finds himself in need of their services.[21]

---

19. http://mikrarevivim.blogspot.co.il/2011/03/blog-post_29.html. In this article, Zakovitch is referring to Miriam, Naaman, Gehazi, and Uzziah. Rabbi Prof. Yonatan Grossman engages in a comparative study of the narratives of Uzziah and Miriam in his article cited in footnote 15, above.
20. Lev. 13–14; Mishna Nega'im 3:1.
21. King Uzziah lived out his days in a leper's quarantine while his son ruled the country. In 1931 a stone was unearthed in Jerusalem by Prof. Eliezer Sukenik. It read: "The bones of Uzziah, King of Judah, rest here.... Do not open!" However, it was found off-site and dated at 70–30 BCE, some six hundred years after Uzziah. Some speculate that Uzziah's gravesite was renovated in Second Temple times, and that this is the "new" headstone. See *Olam HaTanakh*, 117–19.

EARTHQUAKE

During Uzziah's reign, a historic earthquake shook the kingdom. It was an event so devastating as to be recalled by the prophet Zecharia some three hundred years later.[22] Josephus cites an intriguing tradition[23] connecting this earthquake with Uzziah's illicit offering of the Temple incense:

> While Uzziah was in this state … he was corrupted in his mind by pride, and became insolent … he put on the holy garment, and went into the Temple to offer incense to God upon the golden altar…. *In the meantime, a great earthquake shook the ground and a rent was made in the Temple,* and the bright rays of the sun shone through it, and fell upon the king's face, insomuch that the leprosy seized upon him immediately. And before the city, at a place called Erogel, *half the mountain broke off* from the rest on the west, and rolled itself four furlongs, and stood still at the east mountain, until the roads, as well as the king's gardens, were spoiled by the obstruction.[24]

That same tradition[25] links yet a third strand to this. The great prophet Isaiah records the moment in which he receives his inaugural prophecy. In that scene, "the doorposts shook … and the house filled with smoke." Isaiah proclaims:

> "Woe is me; I am lost! For I am a man of unclean lips and I live among a people of unclean lips; yet my own eyes have beheld the King, Lord of Hosts." … Then I heard the voice of my Lord saying, "Whom shall I send? Who will go for us?" And I said, "Here I am; send me." (Is. 6:5, 8)

Rashi links the shaking doorposts with Uzziah's earthquake. This prophecy, dated to "the year that King Uzziah died," is in fact the year he was

22. Amos 1:1; Zech. 14:5.
23. *Seder Olam* 20; *Avot DeRabbi Natan* 9.
24. *Antiquities* IX, 10:4.
25. Rashi, Amos 1:1 and Hos.1:2; Radak, Is. 6:4.

stricken with leprosy.[26] Both Uzziah's act and Isaiah's prophecy are scenes that transpire in the Temple. As such, Isaiah's prophetic initiation coalesces with Uzziah's great downfall, an event which portends disaster on a national scale.

Why was Uzziah's offering incense so severe as to warrant an earthquake of enormous proportions? We might say that this midrashic linkage suggests that Isaiah, who identifies Judah as "people of unclean lips," indicates that the sin lies as much with the nation as with the king. The verses in Isaiah[27] suggest that the earthquake was recompense and a corrective measure for a callous and socially indifferent society. In Judah, much like in Israel, national prosperity had cultivated a moneyed, libertine, aristocratic culture:

> Those who chase liquor from early in the morning and until late in the evening are inflamed by wine! Who, at their banquets, have lyre and lute, timbrel, flute, and wine; but who never give a thought to the plan of the Lord.... Assuredly, My people will suffer exile for not giving heed; its multitude victims of hunger, and its masses parched with thirst. Assuredly, *Sheol has opened wide its gullet and parted its jaws in a measureless gape; and down into it shall go that splendor and tumult, that din and revelry.* Yea, man is bowed, and mortal brought low; brought low is the pride of the haughty. And the Lord of Hosts is exalted by judgment, the Holy God proved holy by retribution. Woe to those... who acquit the guilty in return for a bribe, but deny justice to the innocent.... Therefore the Lord's anger burns against His people; His hand is raised and He strikes them down. *The mountains shake,* and the dead bodies are like refuse in the streets. (Is. 5:11–26)

Uzziah's self-centered arrogance is endemic of a wider national disposition. His presumptuousness in overstepping his position as

26. Following the rabbinic tradition that the leper is considered as dead; see Nedarim 54a; Avoda Zara 5a.
27. See Rabbis Yoel Bin-Nun and Binyamin Lau, *Isaiah* (Tel Aviv: Miskal–Yedioth Ahronoth / Chemed, 2013), 53–93 [Hebrew].

monarch is reflective of a decadent nation that has lost sense of its boundaries. Isaiah's mission is to bring God's word to his generation and to explain the dynamic that brought about the catastrophic national earthquake.

* * *

This chapter illustrated the heyday of Kings Jeroboam II of Israel and Uzziah of Judah. They were times of good fortune, peace, and prosperity. In a period such as this, the challenge for the nation is to retain their moral standards amidst the wealth and the high standard of living. The words of Amos and Isaiah indicate that the sins in this period were not idolatry but excessive indulgence on the part of the upper class, along with extreme abuse of the poor. Every blessing brings its unique challenges. Here, the prophets alert us to the pitfalls of a peaceful, affluent society. We would do well to heed their words.

II Kings 15:8–38

Tumult and Decline (Israel)

Two new dangerous processes merge in II Kings 15. The first is an unremitting series of political assassinations in the northern kingdom of Israel, one revolt swiftly followed by the next mutiny such that five kings rule the country in tumultuous succession. The second is the rise and advance of Assyria, a vast, intimidating imperial power that threatens the very future of the kingdom.

These two currents unite in grim coalescence. The story opens as Zechariah, son of the great Jeroboam II (Israel), is assassinated after a mere six months in power, an act of political violence that is particularly disturbing when we consider the stability and prosperity of the Jeroboam era. His assassination triggers a culture of relentless political opportunism, as coup and counter-coup bring the kingdom into rapid decline and eventual collapse. At the same time, constant buffeting by foreign aggressors weakens Israel and leads to her demise. In a mere generation after Jeroboam, Samaria falls to Assyria and its population are exiled.

The Kings of Israel during this period are:

Zechariah son of Jeroboam – 6 months

Revolt

Shallum son of Jabesh – 1 month

Revolt

Menahem son of Gadi – 10 years

Pekahiah son of Menahem – 2 years

Revolt

Pekah son of Remaliah – 20 years

Revolt

Hosea son of Elah – 9 years

Chapter fifteen consists of brief passages, regnal summaries, standard to Kings, which list and assess the succession in both kingdoms. For the casual reader, these detail-heavy, formulaic summaries offer little of interest other than the monotony of names and dates. Yet this assemblage of data reveals more than meets the eye, as both the cumulative impression of the passages and the novel details regarding each sovereign open the door to an assessment of both the personalities concerned and the state of the nation in this period.

REGNAL INSTABILITY

With the demise of Zechariah, the stable dynasty of Jehu comes to its end. Jehu's royal line ruled for ninety-two years, the longest succession among the northern dynasties, and although it had known some difficult times, Zechariah's public assassination at the hands of Shallum comes as something of a shock after the substantial rule of Jeroboam. This violent termination of the house of Jehu is marked by a statement of divine providence: "This was in accord with the word that the Lord had spoken to Jehu ... so it came about" (II Kings 15:12).[1]

Shallum murders Zechariah after a mere six months on the throne. This mutiny sends the kingdom into a state of political mayhem, as only a month later Shallum is assassinated by Menahem. Menahem is depicted as a warlord but even his dynasty lasts little more than ten years. His sole accolade is his brutal attack of Tiphsah, a foreign colony near the Euphrates under Israelite control. It seems that Tiphsah witnessed the political unrest in Samaria and seized the opportunity to renounce their subordination to Israel.[2] Menahem douses the flames of the rebellion by attacking Tiphsah, where he "tore open its pregnant women" – savagery that evokes memories of the cruel Aramean king Hazael.[3] Menahem passes the throne to his son Pekahiah after a ten-year reign, but this succession is swiftly terminated in another bloody coup (15:25), and the latest usurper, Pekah, loses his own life at the hand of a third assassin, Hosea (15:30).

The sheer violence and shameless ambition for power[4] signals the ominous breakdown of governmental authority and stability in this period.

ASSYRIA'S ADVANCE

Against the backdrop of this destructive and unstable royal carousel, a second feature may be distilled from the regnal summaries – the menacing advance of Assyria. First, "Pul, king of Assyria, came against the land" (II Kings 15:19), threatening Menahem who stymies the attack

1. See also II Kings 10:30.
2. Kiel, *Daat Mikra*. There are several problems with II Kings 15:16. First is its awkward positioning, prior to the introduction of Menahem. Second is the ambivalence as to whether Menahem's base is Tirzah (ibid.) or Samaria (ibid., 15:17). Third is the question of the identity of Tiphsah. Whereas Kiel relies upon I Kings 5:4, placing it in the Euphrates area, others doubt Israel's ability to wage a campaign at such a distance, and suggest instead that Shallum attacks a local town – Tappuah – on the Ephraim-Manasseh border (Cogan and Tadmor, *II Kings*).
3. Cf. II Kings 15:16 with 8:12. See also Amos 1:13; Hos. 14:1.
4. See the prophet Hosea's critique in Hos. 7:3–7. See also Is. 9:19–20: "The people became like devouring fire; no man spared his countryman. They snatched on the right, but remained hungry – Manasseh Ephraim's and Ephraim Manasseh's."

with a huge monetary payment,[5] which he finances by taxing the aristocracy.[6] Pul is the nickname in late sources for Tiglath-Pileser III (745–727 BCE), and its usage here is testimony to the degree to which he was a household name at the time in which the book of Kings was written.

The reign of Pekah sees a more damaging Assyrian attack in which Tiglath-Pileser penetrates and overruns the entire Galilee panhandle, a major swathe of the kingdom: "Ijon, Abel-Beth-Maachah, Janoah, Kedesh, Hazor – the Gilead and the Galilee – all the territory of Naphtali; and he deported [the population] to Assyria" (15:29). Records from Assyria mention 13,520 exiles.[7]

Read in a larger context, these events foreshadow a sad and violent conclusion yet to be told: the conquest by Assyria and Israel's exile and dispersion. The composite picture here is of a nation in disarray, turbulent, weak, and self-destructive.

FOUR CONCURRENT PROPHETS

In our previous chapter we referenced Amos and Isaiah, who in their own books delivered a biting critique of the thriving kingdoms of Jeroboam and Uzziah. Amos (7:9–10) warned of Samaria's destruction; Isaiah (6:11–12) prophesies the ruin of Judah.

The Talmud suggests that these two prophets – Amos and Isaiah – were not alone: "R. Yoḥanan said: Four prophets prophesied

---

5. This tribute is recorded in the annals of Assyria. See *Olam HaTanakh*, which suggests that the payment was made by Menahem to procure Assyria's backing of his regime against his political opponents. If this assessment is correct then this is an instance in which an Israelite king, in a narrow and self-centered political calculation, tragically invites his kingdom's eventual destroyer into its own borders.
6. II Kings 15:20. The word for aristocracy here is *gibborei hachayil*. Sometimes it indicates military prowess, but it frequently suggests social standing, as in I Sam. 9:1; II Kings 24:14; Ruth 2:1. Cogan and Tadmor, *II Kings*, translate it as "every man of means." Assyrian documents relay that the value of a slave was fifty shekels. In that case, we have some sense of the three thousand shekels that were levied upon the aristocracy (Cogan and Tadmor ad loc.).
7. This campaign is dated at 733–732 BCE and is well documented in Assyrian sources; see *Olam HaTanakh*; Cogan and Tadmor, *II Kings*.

concurrently: Hosea, Isaiah, Amos, and Micah."[8] The source for this rabbinic statement may be found by simply examining the opening lines of the prophetic books:

> The prophecies of Isaiah son of Amoz, who prophesied concerning Judah and Jerusalem in the reigns of *Uzziah, Jotham, Ahaz, and Hezekiah,* kings of Judah. (Is. 1:1)

> The word of the Lord that came to Hosea son of Beeri, in the reigns of *Kings Uzziah, Jotham, Ahaz, and Hezekiah* of Judah, and in the reign of King Jeroboam son of Joash of Israel. (Hos. 1:1)

> The words of Amos, a sheep breeder from Tekoa, who prophesied concerning Israel in the reigns of *Kings Uzziah of Judah and Jeroboam son of Joash of Israel.* (Amos 1:1)

> The word of the Lord that came to Micah the Morashtite, who prophesied concerning Samaria and Jerusalem in the reigns of *Kings Jotham, Ahaz, and Hezekiah of Judah.* (Mic. 1:1)

In other words, starting with the Jeroboam-Uzziah period and continuing throughout the reigns of Judahite kings Jotham, Ahaz, and Hezekiah, we witness a veritable burst of prophetic voices. Typically, Tanakh features the prophet as a lone figure; only a single prophet occupies the national stage at any given moment in time. A historical epoch in which multiple prophetic voices sound in parallel suggests a message that must be urgently heard, as God funnels His guidance through multiple channels, determined that the message penetrates. God's sending of prophet after prophet indicates an impending catastrophe.

The looming danger is the ascent of the Assyrian Empire, a superpower the likes of which the Middle East has never seen, a regime that will fundamentally change the region. Assyria is the aggressor that will destroy the northern kingdom. In Judah, forty-six walled cities will be

8. Pesaḥim 87a.

invaded and burned, and Jerusalem will survive only by dint of a miracle. The storm is approaching.

What sort of message does the prophet offer to a country that will soon be threatened by a devastating empire? The final chapter of Hosea offers two: "Assyria will not save us; we will not mount horses" (14:4). Hosea's statement is more than a prophet's directive; he is critiquing and contesting opinions in contemporary society.

What strategy should be employed in the face of a huge superpower that threatens to overwhelm your nation? One obvious policy is to ally with the superpower, serving as a vassal kingdom. Hosea rejects this policy as ill-fated. He says, "Assyria will not save us!" Fealty of this sort generally exacts a heavy cultural and religious price, as will be aptly demonstrated by King Ahaz's treaty with Assyria, a pact that brought the deities of Assyria and their worship into the heart of Jerusalem.

A second alternative would be to organize a resistance, a coalition of states which could fight and fend off the foreign aggressor. Again Hosea warns against this: "We will not mount horses."[9] Hosea warns that a direct confrontation with Assyria could threaten the very existence of the Judahite state.

These messages recur, as we shall see, in the prophecies of Isaiah. Everyone agrees concerning the threat. Everyone wants to save the country. The question is the appropriate policy. As we progress through this challenging era, we shall identify God's call to Judah to maintain its neutrality and to avoid alliances. For now, let us simply take note of the enormous challenge on the horizon.

KING JOTHAM OF JUDAH: A FLAWLESS MONARCH

Against the chaotic backdrop of the northern kingdom, King Jotham's reign shows remarkable vitality. It appears that Jotham ruled the kingdom in his father's lifetime, following Uzziah's being stricken with

9. Rashi sees this as a reference to Egypt, as Egypt was the lynchpin of a military alliance to counter Assyria. See Is. 30–31.

leprosy,[10] and he rules for another sixteen years in his own right.[11] He continued his father's uncompromising devotion to God and his regional control.[12] Jotham fortified the kingdom, perhaps in preparation for the Assyrian advance, renovating the Ophel in Jerusalem – the fortified area on the southern edge of the Temple precinct – and constructing defense installations in the hill country of Judah.

But it is his religious prowess that seems unprecedented. Chronicles states, "Jotham was strong because he kept a faithful course before God his Lord" (II Chr. 27:6). In an impressive summative piece, Rashi surveys every king of Judah, identifying each one's sin; he concludes regarding Jotham, "He had not a single flaw."[13] This assessment finds its origin in the Talmud:

> Ḥizkiya quoted Rav Yirmeya in the name of R. Shimon b. Yochai: "I could save the world from judgment from the time I was born to the present moment; and together with my son Eliezer from the moment of creation until the present time; and in conjunction with Jotham son of Uzziah we could exempt the world from judgment from Creation until the end of time." (Sukka 45b)

One wonders as to the biblical origin of this glowing appraisal of Jotham as the epitome of piety. One particular detail arouses our curiosity: "He did that which was pleasing to the Lord as his father Uzziah had done, but *he did not enter the Temple of the Lord*" (II Chr. 27:2). Why did Jotham not enter the Temple? Radak comments: "Because

10. II Chr. 26:21.
11. The chronology is complicated to say the least. In II Kings 15:33 we read that Jotham had a sixteen-year reign, but 15:30 talks about Hosea son of Elah rebelling against Pekah in the twentieth year of Jotham's reign. Rashi and Radak interpret this as occurring twenty years after Jotham's ascent, and in fact the fourth year of Ahaz, suggesting that the biblical text prefers to ignore the sinful Ahaz. But in truth, the more problematic issue is the resolution of the biblical timeline with the chronology of Assyria. See *Encyclopedia Mikrait* (The Biblical Encyclopedia), vol. 3, cols. 623–24, "Jotham, Chronology," or *Olam HaTanakh*, 124–6, for details.
12. II Chr. 27:1–8.
13. Rashi attributes this commentary to Rabbi Eliezer ben Moshe.

his father had stumbled in this matter, he refrained from entering the Temple to pray or sacrifice. Instead he offered sacrifices on the local altars (*bamot*)."

Jotham withdraws from the Temple, steering clear of the Temple service that caused the downfall of his father, Uzziah. Let us be specific. Jotham venerates the Temple: "He built the Upper Gate of the house of the Lord" (II Kings 15:35), but worships God outside its gates. This is a mark of penitence, as Maimonides states:

> One of the ways to repent is...to remove oneself as far as possible from the original sin. (*Mishneh Torah*, Laws of Repentance 2:4)

Or, as Maimonides writes in *Mishneh Torah*, Laws of Personal Development (2:1):

> So too should a person behave regarding all character traits. If he finds himself on one extreme, he should move to the opposite extreme and accustom himself to such behavior...until he may return to the proper middle path.

Jotham removes himself from the environs of the Temple to impede any temptation to repeat his father's sin. This is a sure sign that he invested considerable thought and effort in his dedication to God. Ironically, this entangles him in the prohibition of worshipping at local altars (*bamot*), and yet rabbinic tradition grants him the accolade of the flawless monarch; such is the power of repentance.

II Kings 16

King Ahaz: Religious Capitulation

The moment King Ahaz of Judah[1] comes to power he finds himself under foreign attack,[2] besieged by a military alliance of the kingdoms of Aram and his northern neighbor, Israel.

What is the background to the assault on Jerusalem? The key to the regional unrest was the looming advance of Assyria, a menacing superpower that threatened to overwhelm the entire region. Small nation-states knew they could retain their independence against such a large, powerful, and aggressive empire only by forging a regional alliance, a conglomerate of smaller kingdoms whose united front could defeat Assyria's imperial war machine. Two kings – Pekah of Israel and Rezin of Aram – are key players in this united resistance. However, they need comprehensive regional support,

1. Ahaz's name, as evidenced by archaeological evidence, was Yeho-Ahaz. The Tanakh removes the prefix, which bears God's name. Why? It is possible that the divine association with his name was deliberately omitted due to his idolatrous affiliation.
2. It appears that this attack was gaining momentum already in the period of King Jotham. See II Kings 15:37.

and Ahaz of Judah, one of the most powerful local rulers, refuses to collaborate with the anti-Assyrian coalition. Pekah and Rezin attack Jerusalem to remove Ahaz from power and to replace him with an anti-Assyrian, pro-alliance sovereign. They plan to "march against Judah and invade and conquer it, and we will set up as king...the son of Tabeel" (Is. 7:6).[3]

They attack Judah and besiege Jerusalem. This military force is no small threat in itself, but it is merely the spearhead of a coordinated attack by all the kingdoms of the anti-Assyrian alliance. In addition to Israel and Aram, Chronicles records invasion from the west by Philistia and from the east by Edom.[4] The battle statistics reinforce our understanding of the magnitude and severity of the attack: 120,000 casualties in a single day of fighting, 200,000 Judahite women and children captured as prisoners of war, and the king's son as well as other key government figures among the dead.[5]

The huge siege of Jerusalem throws King Ahaz into a panic: "His heart and the heart of his people trembled as trees of the forest shake in the wind" (Is. 7:2). What can he do? He risks losing his kingdom. For Ahaz, the only recourse is to appeal to Assyria for protection:

> Ahaz sent messengers to Tiglath-Pileser, king of Assyria, to say, "I am your servant and your son; come and deliver me from the hands of the king of Aram and from the hands of the king of Israel who are attacking me." Ahaz took the gold and silver that were in the house of God and in the treasuries of the palace and sent them as a gift (*shoḥad*)[6] to the king of Assyria. The king of Assyria consented; he marched against Damascus and captured

3. Is. 7–10 deals with the period of the siege by Pekach-Rezin against Jerusalem.
4. See also II Kings 16:6: "At that time king Rezin of Aram recovered Eilat for Aram... and Edomites came to Eilat and settled there." We are talking about an invasion on every front.
5. II Chr. 28:6–8, 17–18. See the dramatic story of the return of the captives in ibid., 28:9–15.
6. This word is not standard terminology for a royal tribute, and it reflects disapproval. *Shoḥad* certainly bears pejorative implications, as it is an act forbidden by the Torah; see Ex. 23:8; Deut. 16:19. It is seen by Prov. 17:23 and Ps. 15:5 as an ethical perversion.

> it. He deported [its inhabitants] to Kir and put Rezin to death. (II Kings 16:7–9)

Ahaz signs a vassal agreement, voluntarily surrendering Judahite independence to Assyria. One imagines that Assyria is only too happy to accept the offer. They are securing an ally, a foothold, in a sought-after region, and undermining the enemy coalition.

THE VOICE OF PROPHECY

Does the prophet approve of Ahaz's appeal to Assyria? At the critical juncture, in the thick of the siege, Isaiah had approached King Ahaz to convey God's displeasure, warning Ahaz that a strategic alliance with Assyria would prove disastrous. In that scene, the prophet's initial message to the king is that the attack by Aram and Israel will soon cease:[7]

> Be firm and be calm. Do not be afraid, do not lose heart on account of those two smoldering stumps of firebrands, the raging of Rezin of Aram and Son of Remaliah.... Thus says the Lord God: "It shall not succeed, it shall not come to pass." (Is. 7:4–7)

When Isaiah calls Pekah and Rezin "smoldering stumps of firebrands," he is saying that these aggressors make a great deal of smoke but are not nearly as threatening as they appear. God assures Ahaz that the attacking armies would soon retreat. The prophet continues by urging Ahaz to appeal directly to God[8] for guidance:

> The Lord spoke further to Ahaz: "Ask for a sign from the Lord your God, anywhere down to Sheol or up to the sky." But Ahaz replied: "I will not ask, and I will not test the Lord." (Is. 7:11–12)

---

7. See also Is. 8:1–5.
8. An example of such a test would be that of Gideon (Judges 6:36–40) or of Moses (Ex. 4:8).

Ahaz's refusal to "test" God should not be viewed as an expression of humility, a devout gesture.[9] It is possible that the king doubts the effectiveness of prophecy, but more likely, Ahaz is simply indifferent to God, and disdainful of the message communicated in His name:

> "I have no desire to contribute to God's veneration." (Rashi)

> Ahaz's intent is to say: "I don't believe in the prophet's divine message, and I have no interest in hearing it whatsoever." (*Daat Mikra*)

Or deeper still, we might suspect that Ahaz has already taken the decision to appeal to Assyria, and that his interest in an Assyrian protectorate entails a willing acceptance of their religious norms.

THE DANGERS OF ALLIANCE

The prophet advises against the pact with Assyria: *Hishamer vehishaket* – "Stand back and stay quiet," he advises, essentially advocating a policy of diplomatic neutrality and political quietism, neither to join the coalition nor to ally with Assyria. This is a difficult request. A small kingdom such as Judah is reliant upon its allies. Assyria's backing will save Judah from invasion and foreign control! And we should not minimize Ahaz's predicament. In a crisis of this magnitude, sitting still, adopting a passive stance, seems like a sign of weakness and paralysis. We understand why Ahaz refuses to follow Isaiah's advice.

But what does Isaiah see as the problem with the pact? What harm will it cause?

His first objection is that Assyria is unreliable. She has her own interests, and one never knows when she will turn against Judah:

> Because that people has spurned the waters of Siloam, which flow gently, my Lord will assuredly bring up against them the mighty

9. Ahaz uses the language of Deut. 6:16. A.J. Heschel, *The Prophets*, vol. 1, 64, suggests that "we have no right to question the king's sincerity. His refusal to ask for a sign was motivated by piety." However, the majority of commentators read his response as we have presented it.

> waters of the Euphrates, the king of Assyria in his multitude. It shall rise above all its channels ... and swirl over Judah like a flash flood, reaching up to the neck. (Is. 8:6–8)

Isaiah contrasts the water source of Jerusalem – the Siloam Spring – with the mighty Euphrates River in Assyria. The magnificent Euphrates looks more reliable that the paltry Siloam Spring. But, says Isaiah, entanglement with a power of Assyria's magnitude can bring unforeseen results. When one associates with the "mighty waters," the water might unexpectedly overwhelm Judah, "reaching up to the neck," drowning the kingdom. It is preferable to rely upon the slow, steady waters of Siloam than to meddle with the mighty forces of the Euphrates.

Isaiah's prophecy will indeed come to bear. A few years hence, Assyria will destroy and exile the people of the northern kingdom and then proceeded southward to attack Jerusalem. When you invite a powerful aggressor as your ally, you never know when the firepower might be turned against you.

THE RELIGIOUS PRICE

But there is a second concern to oppose an accord with Assyria, an issue that goes to the core of Kings, relating to the cultural-religious sphere:

> The Assyrians were fanatically devout. In military campaigns the king assumed the role of deputy of the god. The prowess and victories of the army were thought to reflect the power of the god Assyria. Assyria imposed the recognition of her gods as the overlords of the gods of the conquered peoples. Political subservience involved acceptance of her religious institutions. It was nearly impossible for a small vassal state to keep from being flooded with the idolatrous and superstitious practices under royal Assyrian protection. This explains the infiltration into Judah of all sorts of foreign cults and superstitions in the period she was a vassal of Assyria.[10]

10. Heschel, *The Prophets*, vol. 1, 72.

In other words, reliance upon the military might of Assyria would engender a parallel religious capitulation. The most severe price would be felt in the sphere of religion. Indeed, Ahaz's association with Assyria will become the catalyst for a wholesale engagement with Assyrian worship.

IDOLATRY

We have discussed Ahaz's difficult decision in the face of the debilitating siege on Jerusalem, but we have said very little about the manner in which Kings depicts him. The lines that introduce Ahaz describe his unprecedented embrace of idolatrous norms with a litany of religious abrogations:

> He followed the ways of the kings of Israel. He even consigned his son to fire, in the abhorrent fashion of the nations which the Lord had dispossessed before the Israelites. He sacrificed and made offerings at the shrines on the hills and under every leafy tree. (II Kings 16:3–4)

We do not know what triggered Ahaz's departure from the ways of God; after all, his father and grandfather had devotedly adhered to monotheistic standards. It is impossible to accurately pinpoint the extent to which Ahaz's penchant for idolatrous culture was stimulated by the alliance with Assyria, or whether it reflected the king's personal religious predilections, but his religious violations are so flagrant that the Talmud personifies Ahaz as "evil from start to finish" (Megilla 11a).

First, Ahaz institutes worship outside the Temple compound – a biblical offense[11] – as he promotes sacrifice to the forces of nature as represented by the "leafy tree" and the impressive "hills." Next, he "consigned his son to fire," practicing the *Molekh*, an ancient Canaanite pagan rite,[12] the first time it is practiced by a king of Judah.[13] If we wish

11. Deut. 12:1–14. See the intertextuality in ibid., 12:2, "on the high mountains and on the hills and under every green tree," and see especially ibid., 12:13, for the prohibition of worship beyond the Temple walls.
12. Lev. 18:20; 20:2.
13. Woefully, this practice, adopted here by Ahaz, endured in Jerusalem, such that it featured during the period of Manasseh (II Kings 23:10) and afterward in the era of

to understand how Kings assesses these transgressions, the phrase "in the abhorrent fashion of the nations which *the Lord had dispossessed before the Israelites*"[14] warns how this foreign worship would lead to national exile.

THE ASSYRIAN ALTAR

But Ahaz's worst offense was his adoption of Assyrian religion, a product of his vassal agreement with Assyria:

> When King Ahaz went to Damascus to greet Tiglath-Pileser, king of Assyria, he saw the altar in Damascus. King Ahaz sent the priest Uriah a sketch of the altar and a detailed plan[15] of its construction. The priest Uriah did just as King Ahaz had instructed him from Damascus; Uriah the priest built the altar before King Ahaz returned from Damascus. When the king returned from Damascus and when the king saw the altar, the king approached the altar, ascended it, and offered his burnt offering and meal offering; he poured his libation and he dashed the blood of his peace offering against the altar. As for the bronze altar which had been before the Lord, he moved it from its place in front of the Temple. (II Kings 16:10–14)

Jeremiah (Jer. 7:31; 32:35 – practiced in the Hinnom Valley, today's Sultan's Pool in Jerusalem). The precise manner of its rituals is open to debate: It is possibly a symbolic fire ritual whereby a father leads his child between flaming pyres, although the child is unharmed as indicated by the language of "passing your son through fire" (Maimonides, *Mishneh Torah*, Laws of Idolatry 6:3). Alternatively, the child is sacrificed in a grotesque burning ceremony; such is the view of Nahmanides (commentary on Lev. 18:21). When describing Ahaz's carryings on, II Chr. 28:3 subtly shifts the Hebrew root letters from A-V-R to V-A-R, changing the meaning from "pass through" to "burn." The Hebrew is similar in Jeremiah (see references above in this footnote). See also Jer. 19:5 and Ezek. 16:20–21, which mention burning or sacrificing the child.

14. This line references the Torah's depiction of the Canaanites' illicit worship in Lev. 18:21; 20:2 (and by implication, the warnings of Lev. 18:25–28; 20:22–24) and Deut. 12:2. These passages instruct Israel to obliterate the degenerate religious culture of Canaan, replacing it with a society built around a single worship site and a moral culture (as depicted in Lev. 19).
15. The word used here is *tavnit*. It has particular resonance, as it features prominently in the description in Exodus of the Tabernacle furniture. Cf. Ex. 25:9, 40.

King Ahaz travels to Damascus to personally greet and swear allegiance to his royal protector. He sees the Assyrian sacrificial altar and demands that an identical model be installed, without delay, at the Temple in Jerusalem. The text does not indicate that Tiglath-Pileser had demanded that the altar be built to express Ahaz's vassalage. Rather, it appears to reflect Ahaz's ready adoption of Assyrian mores.

> The construction of a new altar of striking dimensions (the "great altar," II Kings 16:15) should be viewed as motivated rather by a spirit of assimilation to the current international fashions. Syrian art and architectural styles are reported even within Assyria proper.... The voluntary innovation of Ahaz was thus the first wave in the larger movement of acculturation to the practices of the Assyrian empire.[16]

Ahaz initially appeals to the Assyrian ruler with the words, "I am your servant and your son" (16:7). By implication then, Tiglath-Pileser is his king and his father, or as we express it in traditional liturgy: *Avinu Malkeinu*! Ahaz knowingly and calculatingly replaces his Judaism with the Assyrian religion. Moreover, he appears to revel in it.

The verses here emphasize Ahaz's royal title: "The *king* returned... the *king* saw the altar, the *king* approached," etc. *Daat Mikra* views the royal emphasis as an indicator that the altar is inaugurated with majestic pomp and ceremony. Alternatively, it calls attention to the expansion of the royal role, as the king ascends the altar, adopting the role of priest – yet another embrace of foreign ritual protocol.

REMOVING THE PEDESTALS

But Ahaz's desecration of the Temple has yet to reach its climax. Several cryptic verses describe his dismantling of some of the Temple furniture:

> King Ahaz cut out the insets – the laver stands (*mekhonot*) – and removed the laver (*kiyor*) from them. He also removed the tank

16. Cogan and Tadmor, *II Kings*, 193.

> (*yam*) from the bronze oxen that supported it and set it on the stone floor – on account of the King of Assyria. (II Kings 16:17)

Why does Ahaz remove these insets and stands? Whereas some have suggested that the metal bases are part of the payment to Tiglath-Pileser (16:8), this is difficult to sustain seeing that Ahaz's payment was "silver and gold" whereas these are bronze and not particularly valuable. Radak views this as an act of vandalism and desecration:

> Everything he did was in a spirit of provocation and debasement, as we witnessed with the altar, as with his extinguishing of the [Temple] lights[17] and the closing of its doors....[18] He defaced the vessels of God's house.

But perhaps we can explain this Temple alteration in a theological context. What was the idea of the removal of the Temple water reservoirs from their pedestals? Why cut out the insets on the lavers? These items had been fashioned on Solomon's instructions and decorated with animal imagery. The *yam* stood on twelve oxen, and the *mekhonot* were inlaid with insets of "lions, oxen, and cherubs."[19] What was the meaning of these images and what relevance did they have to the Temple?

> These [images of lions, oxen, and cherubs] are the images seen by Ezekiel in his vision of the divine chariot. (Ralbag)
> [The crafting of these wheels was in the form of] the wheels of the chariot (I Kings 7:33) – the holy chariot that was seen in the vision of Ezekiel. (Radak)

These commentators are referring to the vision of Ezekiel, in which "the heavens opened and I saw visions of God" (Ezek. 1:1). The angelic figures depicted by Ezekiel have the faces of a cherub, an ox, and a lion (1:5, 10; 10:14). Accordingly, Solomon was drawing upon this mystical imagery.[20]

---

17. II Chr. 28:7.
18. Ibid., 27:24; 28:7.
19. See I Kings 7:25, 29, 36.
20. See analysis in Alex Israel, *I Kings: Torn in Two*, 98–102.

This Ezekiel imagery is the representation of God's "chariot," His angelic entourage, His mode of movement. The images do not depict God Himself, as God has no image, but rather God's mobility, His power. If Ahaz is taking pains to remove the *yam* and the *kiyor* from their ornate pedestals, he is deliberately removing this angelic imagery. If these carvings and moldings do in fact portray God's mobility and strength, then their removal is a deliberate attempt to symbolically paralyze God. Ahaz seeks to depict God as stagnant, not merely immobile but incapacitated – a deep insult to God's honor.[21] II Chronicles (29:7) records the cessation of the Temple service during Ahaz's reign: Israel "shut the doors of the [Temple] entrance and put out the lights; they did not offer incense and did not make burnt offerings."

POISONING YOUNG MINDS

The biblical depiction limits Ahaz's offenses to the sphere of idolatry and the Temple; the sages, however, spread the net farther afield.[22] In a vivid image, the Midrash pictures Ahaz as closing the national education system:

> "And it came to pass in the days of Ahaz." This may be compared to the son of a king against whom his tutor plotted, desiring to kill him. He said to himself, "If I slay him now, my life will be forfeit to the king. Rather, I will withdraw his wet-nurse from him and he will die of himself."
>
> Ahaz ... reasoned thus to himself:
> "If there are no children, there will be no students;
> if there are no students, there will be no scholars;
> if there are no scholars, there will be no elders;
> if there are no elders, there will be no prophets;

21. I heard this approach from Rav Yaakov Medan.
22. Sanhedrin 103b: "Ahaz permitted incest." The Talmud also debates as to whether Ahaz had a place in the World to Come: "R. Shimon b. Eleazer said on the authority of R. Meir: Ahaz, Ahaziah, and all the kings of Israel of whom it is written: 'And he did that which was evil in the sight of the Lord,' will neither live [in the future world] nor be judged [there]."

> and if there are no prophets, the Holy One Blessed be He will not cause His *Shekhina* to rest upon them" ....
>
> R. Hunia said in R. Eleazer's name: "Why was he called Ahaz? Because he closed (*ahaz*) the synagogue and houses of study."[23]

The above passage paints Ahaz as intent on destroying Judaism. In this creative portrayal, his strategy is not a frontal attack upon the religious establishment[24] but rather a ploy to divert the younger generation from their engagement with Judaism. This midrash is intriguing, but where do the sages see this in the biblical story?[25]

How might the notion that Ahaz seeks to eliminate God's presence by denying a religious education to schoolchildren be understood within the storyline of Kings? The Midrash might be suggesting that Ahaz made Assyrian norms and fashions so attractive, so desirable, that the younger generation found Judaism dull and outdated. With Assyria as a superior military and economic power – the national patron – and with the adoption of Assyrian culture at every level – "altars on every hill and under every tree" – pagan alternatives seemed far more enticing for the average person than worship of God. Schools taught Assyrian myths, history, and literature rather than the parochial Judahite lore. In this way Ahaz eroded loyalty to God at the popular level. The effect of such a shift would certainly have been devastating.

***

The entrance of the Assyrian empire sends enormous pressure throughout the region. For Ahaz, Assyria is a source of strength and enlightenment; he is attracted to everything Assyrian. This attitude seeps into the

23. Genesis Rabba 42:3.
24. Interestingly, the Talmud (Sanhedrin 104a) indicates that Ahaz had some respect for, or at least shame in the face of, the prophet Isaiah.
25. The Midrash relates this to Is. 8:16–18, where Isaiah appears to state that he and his students will have to seclude themselves, studying Torah and waiting for more hospitable times. The book and biography of Isaiah is beyond the scope of our presentation, but see Rabbis Yoel Bin-Nun and Beni Lau, *Isaiah*, 145–46, 164–66.

public sphere as idolatrous worship becomes the norm and the Temple is transformed into an Assyrian shrine. The story of Ahaz underscores the powerful impact of strategic and political alliances in the cultural and religious realm. Ahaz's military pact with Assyria significantly altered the cultural texture of society. In consequence, he may be seen as one of the most damaging kings of Judah that we have yet encountered in the book of Kings.

The Expanse of the Ancient Near East

Route of the Exiles from Samaria and the Influx of the Samaritans (ch. 17)

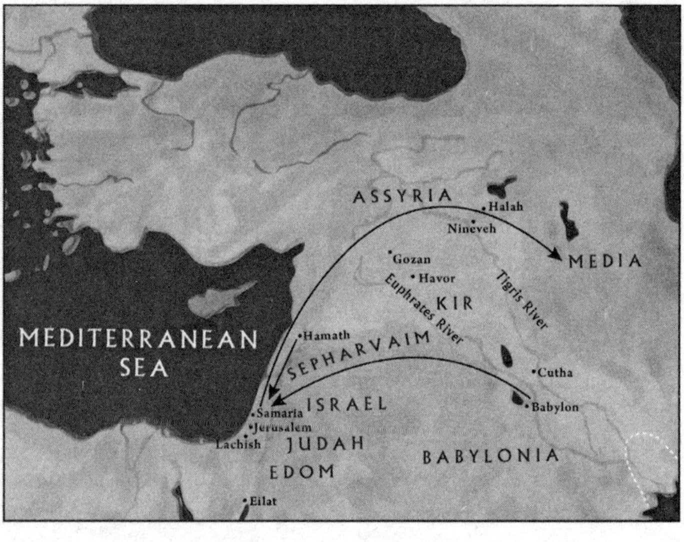

II Kings 17: 1–23

The Fall and Exile of Samaria

This painful chapter recounts the catastrophe of the fall of Samaria and the exile of its people. Surprisingly for a tragic event of this importance, Israel's defeat and dispersion at the hands of Assyria is narrated in a terse, factual manner. The brief account is followed by two expansive sections: The first explains Samaria's fall as divine punishment and details the religious sins that led to its demise. The second narrates the story of foreigners brought to Israel by Assyria to replace the exiles, as it critiques their syncretic religious practices. The theme that unites these two segments is religious deviance from pure and unadulterated worship of God.

The chapter is structured in the following manner:

1. The reign of Hosea son of Elah (17:1–2)
2. The fall of Samaria
   a. Report of the exile of Samaria (17:3–6)
   b. Religious causes of the exile (17:7–23)
3. The aftermath
   a. Resettlement of Samaria and syncretic religion (17:24–33)
   b. Persistence of syncretism (17:34–41)

THE REIGN OF HOSEA (II KINGS 17:1–2)

> In the twelfth year of Ahaz king of Judah, Hosea son of Elah became king over Israel in Samaria, and reigned nine years. He did evil in the sight of God *only not like the kings of Israel who were before him.*

King Hosea is viewed as less sinful, his guilt somehow lighter than previous kings of Israel. What did he do to deserve this judgment? Prof. Gershon Galil offers an interesting theory:

> The author of Kings wanted, it seems, to stress that the kingdom didn't fall due to the sins of Hosea or his generation, but rather as a result of the cumulative sin[s] which began in the days of Jeroboam son of Nebat.[1]

For Galil, Hosea's sins are downplayed to shine the spotlight on the history that preceded his reign.

The early rabbinic work *Seder Olam* offers an alternative perspective. If the primal sin of the northern kingdom is the golden calves and the cultic shrines instituted by Jeroboam at Bethel and Dan, *Seder Olam* suggests that at this point in history, during the period of Hosea, the offensive icons had already been seized by Assyria:

> In the twentieth year of Pekah, Tiglath-Pileser of Assyria came and conquered Ijun and Dan and took the golden calf which was in Dan.... In Ahaz's twelfth year, the spirit of God awakened King Pul of Assyria[2] and he took the golden calf in Bethel... in fulfillment of the verse (Hos. 10:6), "This too [the calf] will be carted away to Assyria as tribute for the king."
>
> Once Hosea ben Elah saw that the golden calves had been exiled, he removed the guards that Jeroboam son of Nebat had

1. *Olam HaTanakh.*
2. *Seder Olam* telescopes II Kings 15:29–30; 17:1 and I Chr. 5:26 into a single event, dating to the year of Pekah's defeat and Hosea's coronation.

> positioned on the highways to restrict pilgrimage of [the northern tribes] to Jerusalem, and hence for all other northern kings it is written: "He walked in the path of Jeroboam son of Nebat," and concerning Hosea: "He was not like the kings of Israel who were before him."[3]

Hosea's era benefits from two distinct advantages. The first is the absence of the noxious calves of Jeroboam. The second is Hosea's active decision to open the border and allow Israel access to celebrate and worship at the Temple in Jerusalem. This decision allows Kings to perceive Hosea in a manner more favorable than his forebears.

UNITED IN JERUSALEM

There seems to be some biblical evidence for this latter assertion. King Hezekiah of Judah, who is crowned in Hosea's third year, stages a huge Passover celebration at the Temple in Jerusalem in his inaugural year. It is an opportunity to renew national commitment to God after the idolatrous regime of his father, Ahaz. Hezekiah invites the northern tribes to the festive rededication:

> Hezekiah sent word to all Israel and Judah and also wrote letters to Ephraim and Manasseh, inviting them to come to the house of the Lord in Jerusalem and celebrate the Passover to the Lord, the God of Israel.... So they sent a proclamation throughout all Israel, from Beer Sheba to Dan.... The runners went from town to town throughout Ephraim and Manasseh and as far as the territory of Zebulun. But most of the people just laughed at the runners and mocked them. However, some people from Asher, Manasseh, and Zebulun humbled themselves and went to Jerusalem.... The entire assembly of Judah rejoiced, including...all who came from Israel.... There was great joy in the city, for since the days of Solomon, son of David king of Israel, there had been nothing like this in Jerusalem. (II Chr. 30:1, 5, 10–11, 25–26)

---

3. *Seder Olam* 22.

Why had Jerusalem not experienced a celebration of this magnitude "since the days of Solomon"? Because Solomon's era was the last time that north and south had been truly united! After centuries of separation, suddenly, in Hezekiah's first year in power, Israelites from the northern tribes of Ephraim, Manasseh, Zebulun, and Asher could attend the paschal sacrifice at the Temple, en masse! This could happen only under northern royal sanction. As *Seder Olam* asserts, Hosea ben Elah had removed the legal restrictions of passage to Jerusalem, allowing northerners to visit the Temple, and for this reason he is granted special praise.

But this religious shift is too little too late for the north. Assyria's pressure weighs heavily upon the region, and Israel is facing its demise.

THE CONQUEST OF SAMARIA (II KINGS 17:3–6)

> King Shalmaneser marched against him, and Hosea became his vassal and paid him tribute. But the king of Assyria caught Hosea in an act of treachery: he had sent envoys to King So of Egypt, and he had not paid the tribute to the king of Assyria, as in previous years. The king of Assyria arrested him and put him in prison. Then the king of Assyria marched against the whole land. He came to Samaria and besieged it for three years. In the ninth year of Hosea, the king of Assyria captured Samaria. He deported the Israelites to Assyria and settled them in Halah, at the [River] Habor, at the River Gozan, and in the towns of Media.

The text here raises many questions. How many times did Shalmaneser travel to the region? What stimulated Hosea's sudden rejection of Assyrian control, shifting his allegiance from Assyria to Egypt? How did he not anticipate the Assyrian reprisal?

Fortunately, the evidence provided by Tanakh, along with a wealth of Assyrian records that have survived, enable us to reconstruct the events.

Hosea came to power by deposing Pekah. Assyrian records show that Tiglath-Pileser III appointed him. It is likely that the rise to power of a pro-Assyrian king in Israel saves the north from a fate similar to that which befell Aram, in which the king was executed and the capital city, Damascus, was overrun. Hosea comes to power in 730 BCE as an Assyrian vassal. However, in his fourth year, Tiglath-Pileser dies and is replaced by Shalmaneser V (727–722 BCE). In contrast to Tiglath-Pileser, who was famed as a cruel and determined warmonger, Shalmaneser initially fails to establish power[4] and is perceived as a weak leader. This stimulated regional efforts to overthrow Assyrian domination, with Egypt serving as the fulcrum of the revolt.[5] This is the "treachery" referred to by the verses above.

Shalmaneser returns to the region to restore control. Hosea travels to meet and appease the Assyrian sovereign, but he is rebuffed, incarcerated, and deported to Assyria as a disloyal vassal.[6] Meanwhile, Samaria is besieged, and the city elders administer the city in the absence of their sovereign.

After three years, the city falls. Assyrian cuneiform documents attribute the conquest of Samaria to two kings – some texts list Shalmaneser and others list his successor, Sargon II. It is likely that Shalmaneser reigns for the majority of the siege's duration, whereas the city falls during the reign of Sargon, who rises to power in 722 BCE.

How many Israelites are exiled from Samaria? Sargon inscribes his record of the campaign on the palace walls at Dur-Sharrukin (Khorsabad):

> In my first year of reign... [I fought] the people of Samaria... to the number of 27,290... I carried away. Fifty chariots for my royal equipment I selected. The city I rebuilt. I made it greater than it

4. His three-year siege against Samaria possibly testifies to his military weakness. See A. Malamet, "The Wars of Assyria and Israel," in *The Military History Land of Israel in Biblical Times*, ed. J. Liver (Jerusalem: Israel Defense Force Publishing, 1964) [Hebrew].
5. The Egyptian king mentioned here by the name of So is unknown to scholars of ancient Egypt. Albright suggests that it is the Hebrew translation of the city Sais, which would make its ruler Tefnakht, Hosea's ally. The prophet Hosea critiques this political zigzagging and the general heady atmosphere in Samaria; see Hosea 7 and Bin-Nun and Lau, *Isaiah*, 178–84.
6. Josephus, *Antiquities* IX, 14.

> was before. People of the lands I had conquered I settled therein. My official (Tartan) I placed over them as governor.[7]

With regard to the number of exiles, 27,290 may not seem like a huge number; after all, there was likely a far larger population in the northern kingdom. But if we recall that in the first wave of exiles from Jerusalem to Babylonia,[8] ten thousand of Jerusalem's leadership were exiled, we can appreciate that this deportation probably includes the entire population of the city of Samaria and also areas outside the capital, such that the Israelites who remained would have had to live under foreign domination, without an Israelite leadership of any sort. The north had been dealt a debilitating blow. Furthermore, the widespread killing and mutilation inflicted by the kings of Assyria, "who were cruel destroyers and who pursued world domination with a ruthlessness they never tire of describing in their inscriptions,"[9] may imply that the death toll in Israel was frighteningly high.

THE THEOLOGICAL EXPLANATION OF EXILE (II KINGS 17–23)[10]

Our chapter has, thus far, offered a political explanation for Samaria's demise: Hosea's political vacillation. However, at this point Kings shifts from politics to historiosophy, as it presents the exile's causes as spiritual in nature rather than political.[11] The verses offer a detailed reckoning of the nation's degenerate actions, listing crimes incurred over centuries, from the time that God "freed them from the land of Egypt from the hand of

7. Daniel David Luckenbill, *Ancient Records of Assyria and Babylonia*, vol. 2 (Chicago: University of Chicago Press, 1927), 2, para. 4.
8. II Kings 24:14.
9. Prof. Yehezkel Kaufmann, *The Religion of Israel*, transl. Moshe Greenberg (New York: Shocken, 1972), 383.
10. The structure of this section is very difficult to discern. For one attempt, see M. Z. Brettler, "Ideology, History and Theology in II Kings xvii 7–23," *Vetus Testamentum* 39 (1989): 268–82.
11. In an interesting symmetry, both the political and the historiosophical readings of the lead-up to Samaria's fall end with a similar phrase: "And Israel was exiled to Assyria" Cf. II Kings 17:6 with 17:23.

Pharaoh" (17:7) until the northern exile.[12] This is an uncharacteristic departure for Kings, as it is generally a book that focuses almost exclusively on royal sin and responsibility, and yet here, when reflecting upon the demise of the northern kingdom, the lens is widened to a collective, national guilt:[13]

> When the Children of Israel sinned... [they] feared other gods and followed the practices of the nations... they built for themselves shrines in every settlement... and set up pillars and Ashera on every high hill and under every leafy tree.... The Lord warned Israel and Judah by every prophet and every seer... but they did not obey... they spurned His laws and the covenant... they rejected all the commandments of the Lord their God, they made molten idols for themselves, two calves... bowed down to all the host of the heaven, worshipped Baal. They consigned their sons and daughters to the fire, they practiced augury and divination. (17:7–17)

WARNINGS

The text emphasizes that God warned Israel, through the prophets, to repent and abandon their evil ways, but they were ignored. The sense of divine forewarning is inherent in the very phraseology of this painful spiritual condemnation. In a clever intertextual technique, phrases from the Torah, Moses' warnings portending the tragic consequences of idolatry, are woven into this grim homily. We will bring but a few examples.[14]

---

12. One question that is raised both by classical commentary and by modern scholarship is the degree to which Israel had abandoned God and traditional Jewish practice. See Radak, II Kings 17:28, and see the discussion in Israel, *I Kings: Torn in Two*, 166–69. See also Jonathan Greer, "Cultic Practices at Tel Dan: Was the Northern Kingdom Deviant?" *Biblical Archaeology Review* 38:2 (March/April): 26, 67, who proves from evidence at Tel Dan that the cultic practices at the northern altar reflect several of the Torah's unique ritual and sacrificial laws.
13. See *Yalkut Shimoni* 234, which suggests that after Hosea had opened access to Jerusalem, "the noose was removed from his neck and placed on the neck of the nation." Whereas this midrash fails to reflect the scope and depth of the national guilt, which is presented in our chapter as persistent and pervasive, it nonetheless accurately reflects the attribution of responsibility to the nation at large rather than the leadership alone.
14. See Kiel, *Daat Mikra*, where he explores each and every phrase for its biblical antecedent.

- **The practices of the nations (*ḥukot hagoy*)** (II Kings 17:8).[15] This expression appears in Leviticus explaining the causes of exile:

  > You shall faithfully observe all My statutes and all My regulations, and fulfill them, lest the land, to which I am bringing you to settle in, vomit you out. You shall not follow *the practices of the nations* (*ḥukot hagoy*) that I am driving out before you, for they committed all these [sins], and I was disgusted with them. And I said to you: "You shall possess their land." (Lev. 20:22–24)[16]

- **"They feared other gods"** (II Kings 17:7). This phrase is reminiscent of verses in Deuteronomy, such as "Thou shall not serve *other gods*," in the Ten Commandments. But there is an additional interplay with its linguistic corollary – *yirat Elokim* – the instruction that Israel fear God.[17] As such, this phrase raises the manner in which Israel have vividly redirected their "fear" – a word which is also indicative of reverence and obedience – away from God and toward other deities, abandoning the teachings of Torah and inviting destruction:

  > *Fear the Lord your God,* worship Him *alone,* and swear by His name. Do not follow *other gods,* any gods of the peoples about you.... Lest the anger of the Lord your God blaze forth against you and He wipe you off the face of the earth. (Deut. 6:15–17)

- **"They made *molten idols* for themselves,** *two calves*...the Lord was *incensed* [*vayitanaf*] at them" (II Kings 17:14, 16). This echoes the language of the story of the Golden Calf in Deuteronomy, particularly: "At Horeb you so provoked the Lord that the Lord was angry [*vayitanaf*] enough with you to have destroyed you" (Deut. 9:8).[18]

---

15. Similarly, see II Kings 17:19, "the practices of Israel."
16. See also Lev. 18:1–5, 24–30.
17. This phrase appears as a refrain later in our chapter. See II Kings 17:24, 28, 33, 35–39, 41. For references in Deuteronomy for the command to fear God, see, for example, 4:10; 5:26; 6:2, 13, 24; 8:6; 10:20; 13:5.
18. Ex. 32:4, 8; 34:17; Deut. 9:12. The echoes of the Golden Calf can also be felt here in

- **"They spurned His laws"** (II Kings 17:15) evokes the key word of the *tokhaḥa*, the "rebuke" in Leviticus, which portends national ruin and exile: "If you spurn My laws (*Im beḥukotai timasu*)" (Lev. 26:15).[19] Our chapter again invokes this word to affirm that Israel's "spurning" of God has generated a reciprocal gesture: "The Lord spurned (*vayimas*) all the seed of Israel" (II Kings 17:20).

The lengthy list of crimes – the Ashera;[20] the pillars;[21] the worship of molten images, particularly calves; the worship of the heavenly host;[22] the passing of children through fire; augury and divination[23] – all resonate intertextually in that they reflect the Torah's warnings regarding the pernicious culture of Canaan and the heavy national price of nonadherence to God's covenant.[24]

LAND, EXILE, AND GOD

We shall comment on two final points. First is the phrase of rejection, unique to our chapter, that God "removed Israel from *before His face*" (II Kings 17:18, 20, 23). Is this harsh expression similar to that of God's "hidden face,"[25] the imagery which connotes divine punishment and withdrawal of protection? Or is it simply a metaphor for exile, not of God's withdrawal but rather of Israel's banishment from God?

We would like to offer a third understanding. The Land of Israel itself is where God's presence is most manifest. Ejection from the land is tantamount to banishment from God's domain.[26] We may recall the description of God's continual gaze, focused on the Land of Israel:

---

the vocabulary that reflects Exodus and Deuteronomy, for example, the depiction of Israel as "stiff-necked" (II Kings 17:14; Ex. 32:9; 33:3, 5; 34:9; Deut. 9:6, 13).

19. See also Lev. 26:43–44.

20. Deut. 16:21.

21. Ibid., 16:22, and Rashi there.

22. Ibid., 4:19.

23. See Lev. 19:26; 20:1–6; Deut. 18:9–15.

24. There is a wealth of parallel phrases in the book of Jeremiah. For example, II Kings 17:15: "They went after delusion and were deluded," finds a precise parallel in Jer. 2:5. Linkages such as this may bolster the rabbinic attribution of Kings' authorship to Jeremiah.

25. Deut. 31:17–18; 32:20.

26. Of course, geographically transcribed deities were also common in other cultures; see I Kings 20:23. Similarly, it is possible that Naaman takes earth back to Aram with

> But the land into which you go to possess it, is…a land which the Lord your God cares for; the eyes of the Lord your God are always upon it, from the beginning of the year to the end of the year. (Deut. 11:10–12)

As such, the Land of Israel and God's presence are synonymous. This is expressed in the following manner by Maimonides:

> A person should always dwell in the Land of Israel, even in a city where most of the residents are gentiles, rather than live outside of the Land in a city where most of the residents are Jewish. For anyone who leaves the Land is considered as if he worships idols, as it says (I Sam. 26:19): "For they have driven me out this day that I should not cleave to the inheritance of the Lord, saying, 'Go serve other gods.'" (*Mishneh Torah*, Laws of Kings 5:15)

The verse cited from Samuel quotes the young outlaw, David, as he is banished from Israel's borders by King Saul. In this verse, he views the Land of Israel as "the inheritance of the Lord," and his banishment from the kingdom as equivalent to serving a foreign god.

If we may return to its implication for our chapter, exile is not merely a geographical displacement. The people of Israel have betrayed God's covenant. In response, their exile is not merely ejection from their historic homeland and from self-governance; it is an act of being ousted from association with God and His watchful eye. This has already been spelled out in God's warning to Solomon, expressed earlier in Kings:

> But if you turn aside from following Me, you or your children, and do not keep My commandments and my statutes that I have set before you, but go and serve other gods and worship them, then *I will cut off Israel from the face of the land* that I have given them, and the house which I have consecrated for My name *I will cast*

---

him (II Kings 5:17) because he sees God as connected to Israelite soil. Perhaps Elijah organizes the contest with Baal at Carmel because it is a lush, green region in which Baal was perceived as strong (I Kings 18).

> *out of my sight* [lit., face], and Israel will become a proverb and a byword among all peoples. And this house will become a heap of ruins. (I Kings 9:6–9)

JUDAH

The second observation regards a textual fluctuation, an awkward aberration in the smooth flow of the text. The dominant subject of our chapter is the fall of the northern kingdom; how and why it happened. Yet this concentration upon Israel's exile is interrupted by the interjection of a "preview" of the fate of Judah, the southern kingdom:

> Nor did Judah keep the commandments of the Lord their God; they followed the practices of Israel. The Lord spurned all the seed of Israel and He afflicted them and delivered them into the hands of plunderers, and finally He cast them out from His presence [lit., face]. (II Kings 17:19–20)[27]

Why do the sins and ultimate fate of Judah feature in the middle of the reflection upon the northern exile? Kings is written in retrospect. Composed after Jerusalem's fall, it surveys the history of the kings, all the time highly cognizant of a destroyed Jerusalem, the Temple in ruins, and the Babylonian exile.[28] As it narrates and reflects upon Israel's deportation to Assyria and the sins that led to it – some 140 years before the destruction of Jerusalem – the book cannot remain silent. It reminds us, the reader, that Judah was guilty of the same errant practices as its northern neighbor, with the exception of the sins of Jeroboam (17:16, 21–23), and in this way the northern exile foreshadows a second exile still to come. It leads us to ask ourselves why Judah didn't learn from the mistakes of its northern counterpart.

27. See also reference in 17:13. Verses 13–15 could be read as applying to both Israel and Judah, and the ambiguity may be deliberate. However, verses 16–17 and 21–23 refer exclusively to Israel.
28. Samaria falls in 722 BCE; the Temple in Jerusalem is destroyed in 586 BCE. The Talmud (Bava Batra 14b–15a) identifies Jeremiah as the author of Kings; academic opinion also points to a post-exilic (and pre-return) authorship of this book. As such, the Judahite exile is more contemporary, more painful and raw, than the exile of Samaria.

II Kings 17

Lost Tribes and Samaritans

Samaria is vanquished by the Assyrians and its inhabitants are deported. This historical juncture precipitates the demise, or disappearance, of the ten "lost" northern tribes. How did these tribes lose their Israelite identity? Was the entire population exiled in one fell swoop? Assyrian records speak of only 27,290 deportees from Samaria, certainly a mere fragment of the population. Even if we factor in a high casualty toll from military engagement with the Assyrians, the bulk of the civilian population is still intact at this point. What then befell the population of the north, and why did their identities erode to the point of oblivion?

Logically, we might speak of three populations:

1. The exiles to Assyria.
2. Israelites migrating to Judah.
3. Israelites who remained in the north.

Let us discuss each of these groups in turn.

THE EXILES: LOST IDENTITIES

The Assyrian policy of population transfer was a means of crushing hostile nations. By dispersing the exiles to far-flung locations: "Halah, at the [River] Habor, at the River Gozan, and in the towns of Media"

(II Kings 17:6), Assyria sought to punish, destabilize, and disorient their defeated adversaries. This technique of geographic transfer and dispersion thoroughly dismantles the internal cohesion of the exiled community and exhausts its force as a political threat.

Scattered and dispersed, leaderless and severed from the heartland of the Jewish people, the exiles disappeared as a coherent Jewish unit. This policy was employed against other populations conquered by Assyria. The effect of the deportations and mass population transfers during this period generated a fascinating halakhic ramification:

> When Sennacherib, king of Assyria, came [i.e., conquered the region], he transferred all the populations and mixed them, exiling them from their original lands. Thus, the Egyptians in Egypt are other people [than the original biblical Egyptians] and similarly the Edomites who reside in Edom. And since these four forbidden nations [Ammon, Moab, Edom, and Egypt] have all become mixed among the nations of the world that are permitted [to convert and marry into the Jewish people] ... all nations are permitted, because we assess a potential convert as emerging from the majority group.[1]

This passage from Maimonides' legal code addresses laws of conversion. Torah law restricts four nations from conversion and marriage into Judaism: Ammon, Moab, Edom, and Egypt.[2] Do today's Egyptians hail from the same nation as ancient Egyptians? The halakha asserts that Sennacherib jumbled all the regional ethnic groups, such that local Egyptians, Edomites, and Moabites are unlikely to be genetic descendants of those indigenous biblical nations. This simple legal rule opens the door to accepting converts without fear of contravening a biblical law because any given convert, despite ignorance of his or her ethnic background, is assumed to emerge from the majority group, and as such is permitted to convert.

For our purpose, this legal curio is clear evidence of the absolute racial chaos and national confusion effected by Sennacherib, such that all national-ethnic lines were disrupted. Against this backdrop, we begin to understand how the historical identity of the ten tribes eroded.

---

1. Maimonides, *Mishneh Torah,* Laws of Forbidden Relations 12:19.
2. Deut. 23:4–9.

This disintegration was a gradual affair; it seems that the original ethnic identities endured for some time. Prophets, even a century and a half after this exile, continue to hope for the return of "Ephraim"[3] – evidence that these tribes were still identifiable. Yet with time, they became lost as independent groups.[4]

SOUTHERN MIGRATION

But only a minority of the Israelite population were exiled. For those who remained, the northern kingdom under the Assyrians was irrevocably changed. Assyrian political control combined with a huge influx of alien populations into Samaria made it impossible for the north to reinstate itself as an independent Israelite political entity.

As a result, much of the northern population migrated south to Judah. Archaeology shows a burgeoning of the population in Judah during this period, presumably migrants from the northern tribes, indicative of a desire to remain under Israelite governance.[5] These emigrants, notwithstanding their original tribal origins, merged with the majority culture. In time they became known simply as "Yehudim" – Judahites, or Judeans – or as we now refer to ourselves, Jews![6]

ISRAELITES WHO REMAINED IN THE NORTH

What happened to the remaining Israelites who continued to reside in their farms and villages in the north? During both the era of Hezekiah[7] and the

---

3. Is. 11:13; Jer. 31; Ezek. 37. Ezekiel is the latest of this group.
4. The Mishna and Talmud in Sanhedrin 110b discuss whether the ten tribes will eventually return. Yet none of the *Tanna'im* or *Amora'im* express any firsthand familiarity with these groups, indicative of the fact that they had already disappeared and the discussion is being held at a conceptual level.
5. Archaeologists identify a fourfold expansion of Jerusalem in this period. See M. Broshi, "The Expansion of Jerusalem in the Reigns of Hezekiah and Manasseh," *Israel Exploration Journal*, 24:1 (1974): 21–26.
6. A wonderful example may be found in the book of Esther (2:2): "In Shushan, the capital, lived a *Jew* (*Judean/Yehudi*) by the name of Mordecai, son of Jair, son of Shimei, son of Kish, a *Benjaminite*." He is ethnically-tribally from Benjamin, but is identified as a Judean, or simply a Jew!
7. II Chr. 30:1–12 talks of Hezekiah inviting people from Beer Sheba to Dan; and Jews from Ephraim, Manasseh, Zebulun, and Asher attending the Passover celebration at the Temple. This takes place shortly after the fall of Samaria.

era of Josiah,[8] we have evidence of an Israelite presence in the north who still retained their connection to the Temple and were known by their original tribal identity. Even some 135 years after Samaria falls, in the wake of Jerusalem's destruction, we read of "eighty men... from Shechem, Shiloh, and Samaria" (Jer. 41:5) who travel to sacrifice in Jerusalem, sure evidence of the persistence of a strong loyalty to the faith of Israel on the part of the northern population.

In the course of time, however, the retention of a distinct Israelite identity became more complicated. A key factor in the evolution and assimilation of northern Israelite identity was the arrival of the foreigners who became known as the *Shomronim*[9] or Samaritans (because they came to Samaria), and by their mishnaic title, *Kutim* (Cutheans – because they hail from Cutha). It is to this story that we now turn.

THE SAMARITANS[10]

The latter half of II Kings 17 is structured in a composite manner:[11]

8. II Chr. 34:6–7 talks of Josiah destroying idolatry as far north as the tribe of Naphtali, north of the Sea of Galilee. Temple taxes are taken from Ephraim and Manasseh (ibid., 34:9).
9. The sole instance of this appellation in Tanakh is here in II Kings 17:29, but it could well refer to the Israelite inhabitants of Samaria.
10. There seems little doubt that the Samaritans splintered from Israel, or merged with them at some point. We can identify at least four options as to the historical inception of the Samaritans:
    (1) The history espoused by the Samaritans themselves, that they are the true representatives of the Israelite faith as it was practiced in the pre-monarchical period at Shechem (1300–1100 BCE).
    (2) The view from Kings that Samaritanism is a heresy derived from a corrupt worship of God. It developed after the Assyrian conquest in 722 BCE.
    (3) An opinion, based on Ezra, Nehemiah, and Josephus, that the Samaritans broke away from the Jews in the Persian period.
    (4) That the Samaritan schism occurred during the early Greek period. *Encyclopedia Mikrait* (The Biblical Encyclopedia), vol. 8, cols. 166–68, "*Shomronim*"; J. D. Purvis, *The Samaritan Pentateuch and the Origin of the Samaritan Sect* (Cambridge, MA: Harvard University Press, 1968), and E. Stern and H. Eshel, eds., *Sefer HaShomronim* (Jerusalem: Ben-Zvi Institute, 2002) [Hebrew].
11. This mirrors the structure of the first half of the chapter which offers: (1) 17:1–6 – A historical description of the exile from Samaria; and (2) 17:7–23 – A religious-philosophical analysis of the sins that led up to that exile. Both religious-philosophical segments end with the phrase "until this day."

17:24–33 – A historical account of the Samaritans
17:34–41 – A philosophical-religious assessment of the post-exilic situation.[12]

The historical account is as follows:

> The king of Assyria brought people from Babylonia, Cutha, Avva, Hamath, and Sepharvaim, and placed them in the cities of Samaria instead of the people of Israel. And they took possession of Samaria and lived in its cities. At the beginning of their dwelling there, they did not fear God. Therefore, God sent lions among them, which killed some of them. So the king of Assyria was told, "The nations that you have carried away and placed in the cities of Samaria do not know the law of the God of the land; therefore he has sent lions among them, and behold, they are killing them, because they do not know the law of the God of the land." Then the king of Assyria commanded, "Send there one of the priests whom you carried away from there, and let him go and dwell there and teach them the law of the God of the land." So one of the priests whom they had carried away from Samaria came and lived in Bethel and taught them how they should fear God. (17:24–28)

Corresponding to the Israelite dislocation from Samaria, the Assyrians exiled other ethnic populations and transported them to Samaria and Israel – foreigners from "Babylonia, Cutha, Avva, Hamath, and Sepharvaim." Kings describes an epidemic in which lions attack and intimidate this new populace, a phenomenon interpreted as rage on the part of the

12. As we mentioned in our previous chapter, this passage (17:34–41) is almost certainly a retrospective assessment, written from the vantage point of the composition of Kings (after the destruction of the First Temple) as a survey of the last 150 years, "to this very day" (17:34, 41). This is further evidenced by referencing the Judean exile. Prof. Shemaryahu Talmon sees the focus upon the illegitimacy of the Samaritans as reason to view this segment as an early Second Temple insertion to the book of Kings, emerging from that period in which there was a bitter struggle with the Samaritans. See S. Talmon, "Biblical Traditions in Samaritan History," in E. Stern and H. Eshel (eds.), *Sefer HaShomronim* (Jerusalem: Ben-Zvi Institute, 2002), 25–27 [Hebrew].

"God of the land." Consequently, a priest from Bethel is returned from exile. He educates the newcomers about the religion of the land and the lion attacks ceased.

Two questions arise from this story:

1. Why would God send lions to attack a group of non-Jewish émigrés? Is there some anticipation that a gentile population will adhere to the religion of Israel?
2. The priest who is imported to teach these newcomers is one of the priests of Bethel. But as we have seen, the religion of Bethel is the worship of the golden calves, denoted as a cause of Israel's exile (17:22–23) and led by priests who were not from the tribe of Levi.[13] And yet, paradoxically, the teachings of this priest sufficed to remove the plague of lions! Why should the errant religion of an illegitimate priest resolve the problem?

THE LIONS

The idea of animals functioning in a punitive divine role is familiar to the reader of Kings. I Kings 13:24–28 tells the story of a prophet of God who contravened an explicit divine instruction and paid with his life; he was killed by a lion. Similarly, in the Ahab stories, a prophet's defiance incurs a swift death by means of a lion (20:36).[14]

But this animal punishment is not limited to the sinful individual. The Torah features several instances in which wild beasts implement divine providence on the national stage:

> If you walk in my statutes and observe My laws, I will send you the seasonal rains. The land will then yield its crops, and the trees of the field will produce their fruit.... I will give you peace in the land, and you will be able to sleep with no cause for fear. *I will rid the land of wild beasts* and keep your enemies out of your land. (Lev. 26:3–6)

13. I Kings 12:31. This is echoed here in II Kings 17:32.
14. Elisha bellows at some children and they are killed by two bears. See II Kings 2:24.

Conversely, if Israel does not observe the laws of Torah:

> *I will unleash wild beasts against you,* and they shall bereave you of your children and wipe out your cattle. They shall decimate you, and your roads shall be deserted. (Lev. 26:22)

The power of the animal kingdom is harnessed to enforce God's regime.[15]

THE LAND

Of course, the verses quoted above are applicable to the people of Israel. Why then were a group of foreigners suddenly plagued by wild animals upon their arrival in Samaria? The Radak answers:

> The punishment was inflicted upon these nations who came to Samaria, although they were not afflicted in their original land. This is because the Land of Israel is sanctified above other lands and will not tolerate abominations of this sort.

Radak is drawing upon several instances in which the Torah indicates that the very Land of Israel is susceptible to defilement engendered by murder or sexual perversion effected upon its soil. These pernicious behaviors may risk ejection from this special territory:

> The land became defiled, and I visited its sin upon it, and the land vomited out its inhabitants. (Lev. 18:25)

> And you shall not corrupt the land in which you live, for the blood corrupts the land. (Num. 35:33)

For the Radak, the Land of Israel is sensitive and reactive to spiritual wrongdoing, and doesn't discriminate in this regard between Jew and

15. Another example may be the divine assistance in conquering the land of Canaan: "And I will send hornets before you, which shall drive out the Hivites, the Canaanites, and the Hittites from before you" (Ex. 23:28). For more on these verses and the wild beasts in Ex. 23:29, see my article at http://www.alexisrael.org/ekev---gradual-conquest.

non-Jew. This perspective is reflected as well in the writings of Nahmanides, who presents the Garden of Eden as the prototype for this dynamic:[16]

> The Torah began with the story of Creation in the Garden of Eden and the creation of man; how God invested man with dominance over the world and control of it. The Garden of Eden – the choicest of places in the world – was his dwelling place. But his sin prompted his banishment. The generation of the Great Flood were banished from the face of the globe and only the righteous among them (Noah) was rescued.... *It is the way of God, then, from time immemorial, that when a nation continues to sin, it will lose its place and home and another nation will replace it.*

Nahmanides explains that what was true for Eden becomes the reality in the Land of Israel, the "choicest of all places":

> He expelled those who rebelled against Him from the Land of Israel and placed His loyal servants there. Israel must know that they merit the land only through their loyal service to God. If they sin the land will vomit them out.[17]

In this perspective, the Land of Israel demands higher standards of conduct than other locations.[18] What was legitimate for the émigrés in their homelands is not tolerated in the Holy Land.

DOUBLE STANDARD

Why would a priest from Bethel be successful in teaching the new inhabitants of Samaria how to serve God? And why would the selfsame syncretic worship of which Israel was found guilty be sufficient for the Samaritans? The Malbim comments:

---

16. Nahmanides' commentary on Gen. 1:1. See also Lev. 26:34, and Yael Ziegler, "Paradise Regained: Eretz Yisrael and the Garden of Eden," in *The Koren Mahzor for Yom HaAtzmaut and Yom Yerushalayim* (Jerusalem: Koren Publishers, 2015), 101–9.
17. Commentary on Gen. 1:1.
18. In the previous chapter we discussed the notion of a particular divine presence in the Land of Israel as reflected in II Kings 17:18, 20.

> One of the priests – he was a priest of the images worshipped by Israel; however, Israel believed in the existence of God and beheld Him as a supreme deity; [Israel] perceived the calves as intermediaries. For Israel, this was a transgression of the law, as Israel were commanded to practice unadulterated and exclusive monotheism because they are under God's direct control and not those of the stars. But with regard to the Cutheans, it was sufficient that they acknowledge that they feared God... that they called Him the "God of gods." In this regard he [the priest from Bethel] "taught them how they should fear God."[19]

The Malbim is essentially suggesting that God tolerates a theistic double standard.[20] The strict monotheism mandated for Jews is different from that required of other nations. For Israel, icons are absolutely forbidden, even when they serve as intermediaries to God. This fundamental sin was the impetus for the exile of Samaria. However, for other peoples, idolatry and other gods were tolerable as long as God was seen as the supreme deity, even while other gods were worshipped alongside Him:

> So they feared God but also served their own gods, after the manner of the nations from among whom they had been carried away. (II Kings 17:33)[21]

---

19. Abarbanel shares this approach, as does *Daat Mikra.*
20. Cf. Rabbeinu Tam in *Tosafot,* Sanhedrin 63b, s.v. "*assur.*"
21. Among the classic commentators there is a deep divide as to which group is addressed in the subsection of 17:34–40. Rashi, R. Avraham ben HaRambam, and the second opinion in Radak assume that it addresses the Samaritans. Rabbi Yosef Kara and the first opinion in Radak are of the opinion that it describes the religious corruption of Israel in the lands of their dispersion. Ralbag and Ibn Kaspi suggest that this passage refers to the Israelites who remained in place in the northern kingdom.

    There is certainly reason to see this passage as addressed to Israel, in that it mentions "God who brought you up from the land of Egypt... the Torah which He wrote for you... the covenant He made with you" (17:36–39). On the other hand, the passage opens and ends with lines which seem to refer to the gentile émigrés.

    The target group addressed in this segment is similarly debated by academics. Cogan suggests that it addresses Israel in exile, whereas Eshel sees it as aimed at the remaining

GENUINE CONVERTS?

How should these émigrés be assessed? Are they perceived as Jews who practice idolatry, or gentiles who have adopted some Jewish observances? Eventually the Samaritans emerged as a distinct group with independent beliefs and practices, but for a considerable period their identity was indeterminate, and their proximity to or distance from the Jews and their religious observance was subject to fluctuation. Due to this ambivalence, there were *Tanna'im*[22] who considered Samaritans as Jews in many aspects, and others who viewed them as gentiles. In a discussion regarding *teruma* (tithes) we read:

> Rebbi says: A Cuthean (Samaritan) is like a gentile.
> Rabbi Shimon ben Gamliel says: A Cuthean is considered as Israel [a Jew].[23]

The talmudic debate regarding classification of the Samaritans as authentic Jews returns frequently to the history of their deportation as narrated in Kings: Did the émigrés convert in a sincere manner (*gerei emet*) and as such are full Jews, or was it a disingenuous and invalid conversion, enacted "[due to the fear of] the lions" (*gerei arayot*)?[24]

IN SECOND TEMPLE TIMES

The earliest recorded clash between the Samaritans and the Jews transpires when Jews return from Persia by royal permission of the emperor Cyrus.[25] The Samaritans made a request to participate in the construction of the Second Temple: "Let us build with you, since we too worship your God" (Ezra 4:2). However, the Jewish leadership in Jerusalem rebuffed them, as they viewed the Samaritans as not part of Israel.[26] Once rejected,

---

Israelites in the Land of Israel. See M. Cogan, "Israel in Exile: The View of a Josianic Historian," *JBL* 97 (1978): 40–44 and H. Eshel, "The Samaritans in the Persian and Hellenistic Periods" (PhD diss., The Hebrew University of Jerusalem, 1994), 6–56 [Hebrew].

22. Scholars who are cited by the Mishna.
23. Tosefta Terumot 4:10, 12.
24. Bava Kamma 38b.
25. Ezra 1–2.
26. The book of Ezra supplies more information about this group. They claim that they arrived in Israel in the days of "Esarhaddon, king of Assyria, who brought us here"

the Samaritans respond fiercely and use every means at their disposal to obstruct the construction of the Temple and Jerusalem's walls.[27] They are designated as "the adversaries of Judah and Benjamin" by the book of Ezra-Nehemiah. And yet the son of the High Priest marries a Samaritan, much to Nehemiah's disapproval (Neh. 13:28). Evidently, opinion within the Jewish community was divided as to the degree to which the Samaritans could adopt Jewish status.

Second Temple post-biblical sources such as *Ben Sira*, Josephus, and the New Testament feature the Samaritans. The book of *Ben Sira* (50:25–26) expresses antipathy toward the Samaritans, who are "not a people." Josephus articulates the inconsistency and opportunism of this group:

> When they see the Jews in prosperity, they pretend that they are changed, and allied to them, and call them kinsmen, as though they were derived from Joseph, and had by that means an original alliance with them.
>
> But when they see them falling into a low condition, they say they are in no way related to them, and that the Jews have no right to expect any kindness or marks of kindred from them, but they declare that they are sojourners, that come from other countries.[28]

These vacillations are reflected by fluctuations and ambivalence in the rabbinic attitude to the Samaritans as portrayed in the Mishna.[29] On the one hand, R. Shimon b. Gamliel (mid-second century) proclaims: "All religious obligations (mitzvot) observed by a Cuthean are observed with greater

(Ezra 4:2). Esarhaddon was Sennacherib's son, and his reign is dated at 680–669 BCE, some forty years after the exile of Samaria (722 BCE). We can therefore surmise that following Samaria's exile there were further waves of emigration, and consequently the evolution of Samaritan identity is a long process.

27. See Ezra 4–5. The character by the name of Sanballat seeks to obstruct the building of the walls of Jerusalem (Neh. 4–5), to assassinate Nehemiah (ibid., ch. 6), and to overtake the Temple (ibid., 13:5–11). Sanballat is identified as a Samaritan in Neh. 3:34, and external sources suggest that he was governor of the province of Samaria.
28. Antiquities IX, 14.
29. See Y. Elitzur, "The Cutheans in the Writings of the *Tanna'im*," in Y. Elitzur and A. Frisch, eds., *Israel and the Bible* (Ramat Gan, Israel: Bar Ilan University, 1999), 393–414 [Hebrew].

stringency than Israel,"[30] and the Mishna records their loyal observance of Shabbat.[31] But at the close of the mishnaic period, there seems to have been a rupture between the Jews and Samaritans. They were banned from marrying Jews, either due to their non-Jewish status or their nonobservance of the marital laws.[32] Their circumcision[33] was viewed as suspect, as were their ritual blessings,[34] because these were directed to "Mount Gerizim" rather than to God. Under the mishnaic scholar, R. Meir (late second century), Samaritan wine and cheese were banned, as was their *sheḥita* (ritual slaughter), due to accusations of idolatry: "An image of a dove, which they worshipped, was found on Mount Gerizim."[35]

* * *

For nine hundred years, from the fall of Samaria until the period of the Mishna, the Samaritans inhabit a liminal space, living alongside Israel but never classified as insiders. Frequently, relations become strained and oppositional. The sense that they "worshipped the Lord, but they also served their idols. To this day their children and their children's children do as their ancestors did"[36] never dissipates. Eventually, the groups diverge and the Samaritans are declared idolaters.

---

30. Berakhot 47b; Gittin 10a; Kiddushin 76a.
31. Nedarim 3:10.
32. Kiddushin 75b; Y. Gittin 1:5.
33. Tosefta Avoda Zara 3:13.
34. Mishna Berakhot 8:8.
35. Ḥullin 6a. Mishna Rosh HaShana 2:2 describes the Samaritans as disrupting the message system that communicated the advent of the new moon from Jerusalem to Babylonia. Was this a deliberate attempt to sabotage the rabbinic tradition? When exactly did this disruption transpire: in Temple times or a century afterward? Leiberman suggests that since the Samaritans used a different calendar, they lit bonfires to publicize their new moon, an act which de facto sabotaged the message system from hilltop to hilltop all the way from Israel eastward. See Rabbi Prof. Saul Lieberman, *Tosefta Ki-fshuta: A Comprehensive Commentary on the Tosefta* (Jerusalem: JTS, 1992), 1029 [Hebrew].
36. II Kings 17:41.

II Kings 18:1–6

Hezekiah's Religious Restoration

King Hezekiah heralds an exciting period of religious renaissance in the kingdom of Judah. Hezekiah's loyalty to God, his responsiveness to prophecy, and his efforts to heal the rift between the Israelites of the north and the southern kingdom of Judah make him among the greatest of Judahite kings.

And yet the challenges that he faces are far from easy. Hezekiah assumes the leadership after the death of his father, the idolatrous king Ahaz. Ahaz had adopted a pro-Assyrian orientation, and under his rule Judah had functioned as an Assyrian vassal, enjoying the benefits of affiliation with the regional superpower. But an alliance with Assyria meant acceptance of its gods. Under Ahaz the Temple had become a pagan shrine. How could Hezekiah restore the nation's undivided loyalty to God, purify the kingdom of its idolatry, and still keep his kingdom safe from the Assyrian threat? If he needed any reminder of the dangers that loomed ahead, his northern neighbor, the kingdom of Israel, was vanquished and exiled in the sixth year of his reign, palpable evidence of the menacing power of Assyria. How does a small kingdom navigate in such a perilous environment? Let us follow Hezekiah and watch how he confronts the formidable tests of his reign.

REPUDIATING IDOLATRY

The account of Hezekiah's reign opens with an exceedingly positive assessment in the book of Kings:

> He did what was right in the eyes of the Lord, according to all that David his father had done. He removed the high places (*bamot*) and broke the pillars and cut down the Ashera. And he broke in pieces the bronze serpent that Moses had made, for until those days the people of Israel had made offerings to it, and called it Nehushtan. He trusted in the Lord, God of Israel, so that there was none like him among all the kings of Judah after him, nor among those who were before him. For he held fast to the Lord. He did not depart from following Him, but kept the commandments that the Lord commanded Moses. And the Lord was with him; wherever he went out, he prospered. (II Kings 18:3–7)

These introductory verses employ an impressive sequence of superlatives to denote Hezekiah's unwavering devotion to God. He is compared to David, he "does not depart" from the laws of Moses, he "trusts" in God and "holds fast" to Him. These are unusual accolades. What actions earn Hezekiah this glowing assessment?

Primary seems to be Hezekiah's ardent campaign to eradicate idolatry. He dismantles the illicit altars and expunges the Ashtoret cult. One curious detail is his disposal of Moses' copper serpent, an implement of divine healing in the wilderness.[1] Evidently the country had become so overwhelmingly idolatrous that even the copper serpent had been adopted as an object of worship. Hezekiah's offensive against national idolatry is so sweeping that he is prepared even to remove and dismantle that historic artifact in his campaign.

1. Num. 21:4–9.

A BED OF ROPES

Hezekiah's war against idolatry begins from the moment he ascends the throne. *Ḥazal* offer a fascinating image for Hezekiah's rejection of his father's religious affiliation; they say that he "dragged his father's coffin on a bed of ropes."[2] The textual basis for this comes from Chronicles. There we read that Hezekiah denied his father's body access to the royal tomb:

> Ahaz slept with his forefathers, and they buried him in the city, in Jerusalem, but they *did not bring him to the graves of the kings of Israel,* and Hezekiah his son reigned in his stead. (II Chr. 28:27)

Rabbis Yoel Bin-Nun and Binyamin Lau dramatize the scene of Ahaz's state funeral and the shock that Hezekiah's act would have generated:

> We can only try to imagine the scene of that funeral, choreographed by the heir to the throne, Hezekiah, under the supervision of the prophet Isaiah. The officials of Judah and its national leadership stand, lined up for the royal procession. The protocol dictates that the heir apparent lead the royal coffin of the deceased sovereign to the official burial tomb of the monarchs of the house of David.
>
> Meanwhile, a heated discussion was being held in Isaiah's study. Isaiah refused to approve the funeral proceedings. For almost twenty years, Hezekiah had grown up under Isaiah's tutelage. His grandfather had put him under Isaiah's guidance – his father barely noticed – and he had become one of the prophet's finest students.... Now Isaiah and the royal heir sat hatching the spectacle of the king's departure, his final journey. He must demonstrate to the people of Jerusalem that the days of paganism have ended, and his father's evil era had come to a close.
>
> ... At the key moment, the courtiers laid the coffin of the deceased sovereign in the palace courtyard, a coffin fit for a king.

2. Mishna Pesaḥim 4:10.

> Official royal convention dictated a silken burial shroud and a hearse encrusted with precious stones. Around the head of the king were spices and sweet-smelling branches. All the elder statesmen and the members of the government stood waiting for the heir to emerge and approach the bier.
>
> Suddenly, an official announcement sounded: "By order of Hezekiah, son of Ahaz; remove the body from the carriage, and place it on a bed of ropes!" A shocked murmur was heard from the crowd: "A bed of ropes? Like a wretched pauper?"
>
> Suddenly the figure of Hezekiah emerged, erect, standing tall at the gateway of the palace. Nobody dared defy the royal pronouncement. Slowly, the body was removed from the royal hearse onto the bed of ropes and the funeral procession began on its way.[3]

This shocking rejection of protocol was an inaugural act that powerfully conveyed the young king's intent to reverse the national religious orientation.

REOPENING THE TEMPLE

Hezekiah's religious revolution takes another step forward as he reestablishes the Temple as a national center:

> In the first month of the first year of his reign, he opened the doors of the Temple of the Lord and repaired them. He brought in the priests and the Levites, assembled them in the square on the east side, and said: "Listen to me, Levites! Consecrate yourselves now and consecrate the Temple of the Lord, the God of your ancestors. Remove all defilement from the sanctuary. Our parents were unfaithful; they did evil in the eyes of the Lord our God.... Therefore, the anger of the Lord has fallen on Judah and Jerusalem.... Now I intend to make a covenant with the Lord, the God of Israel." (II Chr. 29:3–6, 8, 10)

3. Bin-Nun and Lau, *Isaiah*, 170–72.

This they do. It takes eight days to clean out the Temple of its idolatry, and then they rededicate the Temple in an eight-day consecration ceremony.[4]

NATIONAL UNITY

Next, Hezekiah invites the northern tribes to join him in celebrating Passover in Jerusalem.[5] Due to the time needed to purify the Temple, the official date for the Passover sacrifice had passed, and consequently, the holiday was scheduled a month later:[6]

---

4. Possibly based on the eight-day *Miluim* ceremony in Lev. 8–9.
5. Some question whether Hezekiah's Passover could have transpired in his inaugural year. They assume that it would have taken some time for the new king to gain the political capital to invite the northern tribes, especially in his first year, prior to the conquest of Samaria. Furthermore, Hezekiah talks of the captivity of the northern tribes (see II Chr. 30:9; Bin-Nun and Lau, *Isaiah*, 96). But the text can be read without difficulty, as in II Chr. 30, as referring to the first year of Hezekiah's reign. *Ḥazal* (*Seder Olam* 22) assume that the northern tribes had already begun making pilgrimages to Jerusalem during Hosea's reign. The "captives" spoken of may have been from the Assyrian attack which preceded the fall of Samaria (see II Chr. 15:29), or the exiles of Reuben and Gad (I Chr. 5:26).
6. The Talmud (Sanhedrin 12a–b) debates the meaning of the "second month" (II Chr. 30:2) referenced here. One opinion suggests that it is the second month of Hezekiah's reign, and that he added a month to the calendar, effectively creating a second Nisan – an act criticized by the Rabbis, since a leap year may be enacted exclusively in the Hebrew month of Adar and not during the month of Nisan. An alternative opinion sees the second month as the calendrical month of Iyar, and they were celebrating a mass *Pesaḥ Sheni*. See the various proofs in the classical commentaries on Chronicles.

   See also Zev Erlich, "To Perform Passover in the Second Month," *Hazofeh* (11 Iyar 5741): 5–6 [Hebrew], or at http://www.vbm-torah.org/vtc/0033968.html. Erlich suggests that the rescheduling of Passover to "the second month" was also a measure directed at tribal unity. We might recall how Jeroboam enacted the celebration of Sukkot at a month's remove from the southern kingdom: "And Jeroboam established a festival on the fifteenth day of the eighth month, in imitation of the festival in Judah" (I Kings 13:32). Some understand that Jeroboam shifted the calendar a month behind to ensure that the population in the north would not migrate to the Temple for its festive celebrations. Since Sukkot was celebrated in the north a month after it was celebrated in Jerusalem, there would be no opportunity to attend the festival in Jerusalem because it had been celebrated a month earlier. Now Hezekiah synchronizes the southern and northern calendars, allowing all of Israel to celebrate at the same time!

> Hezekiah sent word to all Israel and Judah and also wrote letters to Ephraim and Manasseh, inviting them to come to the house of the Lord in Jerusalem and celebrate the Passover to the Lord, the God of Israel. The king and his officials and the whole assembly in Jerusalem decided to celebrate the Passover in the second month. They had not been able to celebrate it at the regular time because not enough priests had consecrated themselves and the people had not assembled in Jerusalem. (II Chr. 30:1–3)

The appeal to the tribes of the north, "from Beer Sheba to Dan" (II Chr. 30:5) – Ephraim and Manasseh, Asher and Zebulun (30:10–11) – emphasizes Hezekiah's interest in unifying the nation for this inaugural celebration. However, a problem arose. Many of the northerners were ritually impure:

> Although most of the many people who came from Ephraim, Manasseh, Issachar, and Zebulun had not purified themselves, yet they ate the Passover, contrary to what was written. But Hezekiah prayed for them, saying, "May the Lord, who is good, pardon everyone who sets their heart on seeking God – the Lord, the God of their ancestors – even if they are not clean according to the rules of the sanctuary." And the Lord heard Hezekiah and healed the people. (II Chr. 30:18–20)

The people are impure and yet they celebrate Passover![7] Ordinarily this would be an insurmountable obstacle, and yet Hezekiah prays for them and God forgives them. Clearly Hezekiah was determined to bring the nation together for this event. The atmosphere was euphoric:

> There was great joy in Jerusalem, for since the days of Solomon, son of David king of Israel, there had been nothing like this in Jerusalem. (II Chr. 30:26)

---

7. See Maimonides, *Mishneh Torah*, Laws of Entering the Temple, 4:16–18, who allows the public to offer the paschal lamb in a state of impurity.

Immediately after the reign of Solomon the kingdom had split into two. This was the first religious moment in over two hundred years in which the nation had celebrated as one at the Temple. Hezekiah wanted Jerusalem and its Temple to be a national center and not merely the shrine of a single tribe. The "great joy" of this Passover reflects the delight of a nation reunited.

TEACHING TORAH

We have demonstrated Hezekiah's repudiation of his father's regime, his battle against idolatry, his rehabilitation of the Temple, and his hopes for national unity. But both the Tanakh and *Ḥazal* highlight a further passion of this righteous king: his fervor for Torah study.

> [The Talmud speaks of] the oil of Hezekiah, which burned in the synagogues and schools. What did he do? He planted a sword by the door of the schoolhouse and proclaimed, "He who will not study the Torah will be pierced with the sword." Search was made from Dan to Beer Sheba, and no ignoramus was found; from Gabbath to Antipatris – no boy or girl, man or woman was found who was not thoroughly versed in the laws of ritual purity and impurity.[8]

Hezekiah enforces national Torah study. His methods are admittedly violently coercive, but the product is a civilian population that is thoroughly versed in the minutiae of Jewish law.

Of course, this is an aggadic tradition. But what are its roots? Is there any biblical evidence of Hezekiah's interest in spreading Torah knowledge? The book of Proverbs provides some evidence of Hezekiah's commitment to study: "These following are *also* the proverbs of Solomon, compiled by the men of Hezekiah king of Judah" (25:1).

This verse introduces chapters 25–31 of the book of Proverbs, and indicates that the "original," pre-Hezekiah book of Proverbs comprised only twenty-four chapters. But Hezekiah published an "expanded edition" of the book, including as yet unpublished writings of Solomon. The conclusion we should come to is that Hezekiah invested in the publication of wisdom literature, such as Proverbs. His interest was the promotion of

8. Sanhedrin 94b.

national Torah education. Similarly, the Talmud states: "Hezekiah and his company wrote Isaiah, Proverbs, Song of Songs, and Ecclesiastes" (Bava Batra 15a).

The impression is that Hezekiah actively pursued the writing, publication, and distribution of manuscripts that predated his time. The works mentioned are all literature that delve deeply into the religious experience. Hezekiah's legacy is a profound enthusiasm for religious observance and study.

But Hezekiah's religious commitment will be severely tested as he confronts a national challenge that imperils the very survival of the kingdom – the Siege of Sennacherib.

II Kings 18–19

Hezekiah under Siege

Hezekiah's religious enthusiasm conveys a favorable impression, but as the international environment quickly becomes complicated and perilous, the king's true challenge begins. In Hezekiah's fourth year Samaria is besieged by Assyria, and in his sixth year Samaria falls (II Kings 18:9–12).[1] The powerful Assyrian empire is the dominant regional force; clearly Hezekiah should exercise caution. Yet we read that "he rebelled against the king of Assyria and would not serve him" (18:7). What prompted Hezekiah to challenge Assyria?

Hezekiah's insurgency incites Assyria to attack the southern kingdom and to besiege Jerusalem. The devastation wrought by Sennacherib

1. There is a significant disparity between the internal biblical timeline and the Assyrian timeline that is adopted by historians. Samaria falls in the sixth year of Hezekiah's reign. Historians date this event at 722 BCE. But the siege of Jerusalem is dated at 701 BCE, some twenty-one years later. This is problematic because the books of Kings, Isaiah, and Chronicles all agree that the Assyrian siege coincides with the fourteenth year of Hezekiah's reign. The *Olam HaTanakh* commentary suggests dating the fourteen years from another event. Bin-Nun and Lau, *Isaiah*, 195–96, propose that Hezekiah was recrowned over all Israel in the eleventh year of his reign at the celebratory Passover celebration. The fourteenth year is marked from the second coronation and coincides with the twenty-fifth year of Hezekiah's reign. Despite scant textual support for this approach, it succeeds in resolving the disparity.

is unprecedented. Forty-six walled cities, "all the fortified cities of Judah" (18:13),[2] are attacked and defeated, including the impressive fortress city of Lachish (18:14),[3] second only to Jerusalem in strength. The victorious Assyrian war machine then marches against Jerusalem and besieges it. The prophet Isaiah depicts the capital city, vulnerable and isolated, as a "hut in a vineyard," an unsteady, flimsy structure, surrounded by a devastated land:

> Your land is a waste, your cities burned down; the yield of your soil is consumed by strangers before your eyes – a wasteland, like Sodom overthrown. And Zion is left like a hut in a vineyard, as a lodge in a field; like a city beleaguered. (Is. 1:7–8)

This imagery drives home the question with greater acuity: Why did Hezekiah provoke Assyria? Was he not aware of the ruinous consequences he was bringing upon his kingdom?

To answer this question we would do well to understand the historical background to the period.

---

2. The Assyrian attack on Jerusalem is one of the most extensively documented events in biblical history. Beyond the biblical account in the books of Kings, Isaiah, Micah, and Chronicles, there is a wealth of archaeological and Assyrian records that verify, enrich, and sometimes challenge aspects of the biblical account. The statistic of forty-six cities is recorded in Sennacherib's own annals documenting his war prowess, written in cuneiform on a baked terracotta prism, just 38 cm in height, discovered in ancient Nineveh. Three identical clay prisms have been discovered inscribed with the same text: the Jerusalem Prism in the Israel Museum, the Taylor Prism (discovered in 1830 and now in the British Museum), and the Oriental Institute Prism (Chicago).
3. Sennacherib's throne room in Nineveh was decorated with an incredibly elaborate and detailed relief, a series of thirteen huge panels picturing the siege, the attack, and eventual conquest and enslavement of Lachish. It is evident that this victory was an outstanding mark of pride for Sennacherib. It is amazing to behold how a small province like Judah could muster such resilient opposition to a colossal empire such as Assyria. The panels are on display in the British Museum. When Lachish was excavated by Starkey in 1932–38, the defenses and attack ramps uncovered matched the Sennacherib relief quite accurately.

FROM SARGON TO SENNACHERIB

The Assyrian king Sargon II (722–705 BCE) was a cruel and determined ruler. It is likely that he began his reign by presiding over the despoiling and exile of Samaria.[4] Notwithstanding the distastefulness of being a vassal to Assyria and the substantial annual tribute to its king, Hezekiah appreciated that to throw off the Assyrian yoke meant courting disaster.[5] But in 705 BCE Sargon was killed in battle and his body was never found nor given a royal burial. The death of an emperor always presented an opportunity for revolt, but the circumstances of Sargon's death, widely seen as a bad omen for Assyria, exacerbated the unrest. Rebellion broke out at both extremities of the sprawling empire. East of Assyria, in Babylonia, Merodach-baladan (known in Kings as Berodach-baladan)[6] crowned himself as ruler. In the West, Judah allied itself with Philistia and Egypt in rejecting Assyrian power. Since Kings records that Berodach visited Hezekiah in Jerusalem (II Kings 20:12–13), it is probable that the resistance efforts in the East and West were coordinated. We can appreciate that for Hezekiah, the death of Sargon seemed the opportune moment, after two decades, to overthrow foreign domination.

For four years, Hezekiah prepares assiduously for war. He carves a magnificent water tunnel through the bedrock,[7] a marvel of ancient

4. II Kings describes Shalmaneser as the conqueror of Samaria (18:9), whereas Assyrian records chart Sargon II as responsible for exiling its inhabitants. Most likely the fall of Samaria transpired during the period that spanned the death of Shalmaneser and the ascent of Sargon. II Kings 18:11 might hint to this by referencing the "king" without explicit reference to Shalmaneser.
5. An insurrection was attempted by Azuri, king of Ashdod, in 711 BCE. Spurred by power shifts in Egypt, there was a feeling that Egypt could succeed in repelling Assyria. The prophet Isaiah cautions Hezekiah against joining the alliance (Is. 20). Although Assyrian records document a conspiracy of "the kings of Philistia, **Judah**, Edom, and Moab," Hezekiah withdrew in a timely manner, as Ashdod and Philistia were devastated under Tartan, Sargon's official, whereas Judah escaped unscathed.
6. Marduk-apla-iddina II. In Kings he is referred to as Berodach-baladan; consequently, that is the name used in this volume. However, Isaiah 39:1 calls him as Merodach-baladan. See more historical information in footnote 12 of the chapter "Tests of Faith."
7. I highly recommend a tour of the City of David in Jerusalem where one can wade, flashlight in hand, through the water channel of Hezekiah's Tunnel. It winds for 533 meters, deep in the bedrock with only a 30 cm (0.6%) gradient. A tablet written in

engineering, rerouting the waters of the Gihon spring away from the exposed outer wall of Jerusalem into the center of the city (20:20).[8] The city walls are raised and fortified, arms and foodstuffs are stockpiled,[9] and the army is trained.

Sennacherib fights back. In 703–702 BCE he puts an end to the Babylonian revolt. In 701 BCE he invades Judah, crushing the rebellion. He defeats the Egyptian and Ethiopian forces, and then sends his army to besiege Jerusalem.

Initially, Hezekiah attempts to pay Sennacherib a tribute:

> Hezekiah, king of Judah, sent this message to the king of Assyria at Lachish: "I have done wrong. Leave me, and I will pay whatever tribute you impose on me." The king of Assyria exacted three hundred talents of silver and thirty talents of gold from Hezekiah, king of Judah.[10] Hezekiah paid him all the funds there were in the Temple of the Lord and in the palace treasuries. At that time

---

ancient Hebrew script, now housed at the Istanbul archaeology museum in Turkey, records the method of construction in which teams started from opposite ends and met in the middle!

Recently there has been some debate as to the period in which the tunnel was constructed. See R. Reich and E. Shukron, "The Date of the Siloam Tunnel Reconsidered," *Tel Aviv* 38 (2011): 147–57; H. Shanks, "Will King Hezekiah Be Dislodged from His Tunnel?" *Biblical Archaeology Review* (September/October 2013).

8. See II Kings 20:20; Is. 22:10; II Chr. 32:3. For the assessment of the four-year period of war preparations, the death of Sargon II was in 705 BCE and the Assyrian attack is dated at 701 BCE. See also A. Sneh, E. Shalev, and R.Weinberger, "The Why, How, and When of the Siloam Tunnel Reevaluated," *Bulletin of the American Schools of Oriental Research* 359 (2010): 57–65.
9. Excavations in Lachish demonstrate an unusually large concentration of handles from earthenware storage jars stamped with a *LaMelekh* ([Belonging] to the king) seal, indicative of their status as royal property. These are dated to the period of Hezekiah. One theory for this phenomenon suggests a stockpiling of food to withstand an extensive siege.
10. Sennacherib's records testify that Hezekiah paid "thirty talents of gold, eight hundred talents of silver, precious stones, antimony, large cuts of red stone, couches inlaid with ivory, nimedu chairs inlaid with ivory, elephant hides, ebony wood, boxwood, and all kinds of valuable treasures, his own daughters and concubines." This is a more generous bribe than mentioned in Kings, but it is possible that in light of his defeat at Jerusalem, Sennacherib made the bribe look more attractive to save face.

> Hezekiah cut the doors of the Temple of the Lord which King Hezekiah had overlaid with gold, and gave them to the king of Assyria. (II Kings 18:14–16)

Despite Hezekiah's remorse and the extensive bribe, no response is heard from the king of Assyria. Instead, the narrative turns to an expansive and dramatic enactment of Sennacherib's official delegation to Jerusalem.

THE NARRATIVE IN KINGS

We have outlined the political and military background to the Assyrian siege, a campaign which threatened the very existence of Judah. Kings, however, adopts an entirely different angle to narrate this clash, presenting the military attack and the political negotiations as a religious and theological drama, more a verbal offensive and religious disputation than a military attack. It transforms Sennacherib's aggression and Hezekiah's defense into a discourse about man's hubris versus his reliance on God, just as the tense conflict will become a direct challenge to God's power.

The structure of the narrative is highly complicated. This schema should provide a framework for reading the text.[11]

1. **Report of Invasion** **18:13–16**
   - a. Invasion of Judahite cities (18:13)
   - b. Hezekiah's response: apology and tribute (18:14–16)
2. **Sennacherib's Threat to Jerusalem from Lachish** **18:17–19:7**
   - i. Threat
     - a. Setting (18:17–18)
     - b. Rabshakeh's 1st address (18:19–27)
     - c. Rabshakeh's 2nd address (18:28–36)
   - ii. Coping with the Threat – Prayer and Prophecy
     - a. Hezekiah's ascent to the Temple (19:1)
     - b. Isaiah's reply: prophecy of salvation (19:2–7)
3. **Sennacherib's Threat to Jerusalem from Libnah** **19:8–34**
   - i. Threat

11. Loosely based on the structure presented in Long, *II Kings*, 199.

a. Setting (19:8–9)
b. 3rd address, to Hezekiah (19:10–13)
ii. Coping with the Threat – Prayer and Prophecy
a. Hezekiah's ascent to the Temple and prayer (19:14–19)
b. Isaiah's reply: prophecy of salvation (19:20–34)

4. Salvation: Assyrian Threat Is Eliminated **19:35–7**

a. The miraculous elimination of the Assyrians (19:35–36)
b. Sennacherib assassinated (19:37)

The first scene takes place as Sennacherib has dispatched a heavily armed force from Lachish to Jerusalem. In a dramatic standoff as the Assyrian army stands poised outside Jerusalem's wall, three Assyrian high officials[12] convene in a tense negotiation with three senior Judahite government figures.[13] The spokesman, Rabshakeh, launches into an artful oratory,

12. Tartan – military commander and deputy to the king; the Rab-saris (head eunuch) – the chief official; and the Rab-shakeh – the head wine butler, possibly a title for a central government position. However, he might have a lower official stature, but he speaks Hebrew and thus functions as the spokesman for the group.

13. Eliakim son of Hilkiah "over the house"; Shebna the "secretary"; and Joah son of Asaph, the "recorder." For more on these government positions during earlier times, see II Sam. 8:16–18; 20:23–25; I Kings 4:1–5; 18:3. We don't know with any certainty the precise functions of these government positions.

Shebna is an intriguing character and worthy of a lengthy study. Is. 22 depicts the siege of Jerusalem as having a carefree, celebratory atmosphere: "Why have you gone up to the housetops? Celebration, a tumultuous joyous city…joy and revelry, slaughtering of cattle and sheep, eating of meat and drinking of wine! 'Let us eat and drink,' you say, 'for tomorrow we die!'" (Is. 22:1, 13). The inhabitants of Jerusalem feel that if life will be sharp and short, at least it should be enjoyed. Isaiah challenges this in God's name: "God has called for weeping, and to mourning, and to baldness, and to girding with sackcloth" (22:12); in other words, God wants to see the people turn to Him. Who is responsible for the upbeat, wild mood? The government figure singled out in that chapter is Shebna. Isaiah speaks in God's name, rebuking Shebna, and predicting, or possibly instructing, that Shebna be replaced by Eliakim (22:15–21). Evidently this is what happened, as our chapter in Kings presents Eliakim as the minister "over the house," indicating that Hezekiah was receptive to Isaiah's criticism and replaced Shebna with Eliakim.

The Talmud views Shebna as a sinister figure. His policy of revelry hides his true motive: to betray his king and instigate a surrender: "When Sennacherib besieged

aimed at humiliating and intimidating the Judahite leaders and their compatriots:

> Rabshakeh said to them, "You tell Hezekiah: Thus said the great king, the king of Assyria: What is the security (*bitaḥon*) on which you have relied (*bataḥta*)?…On whom are you relying (*bataḥta*), that you have rebelled against me? You rely (*bataḥta*) on Egypt, that splintered reed of a staff, which enters and punctures the palm of anyone who leans on it! That's what Pharaoh, king of Egypt, is like to all who rely on him. And if you tell me that you are relying (*bataḥnu*) on the Lord your God, He is the very one whose shrines and altars Hezekiah removed…. Do you think I have marched against this land to destroy it without the Lord? The Lord Himself told me: Go up against that land and destroy it." (II Kings 18:19–22, 25)

In a spirit of arrogance and ridicule, Rabshakeh strips Hezekiah of his royal title, in contrast to Sennacherib, "the great king." His speech, ostensibly directed to the king, is in reality a skillful exercise of mockery, demoralization, and religious disputation. It is truly directed at the common people of Jerusalem who mass on the wall to hear the enemy speak, as they suffer the dire effects of the protracted siege. This is evidenced in the following exchange:

> Eliakim son of Hilkiah, Shebna, and Joah replied to Rabshakeh: "Please! Speak to your servants in Aramaic, for we understand it; do not speak to us in the language of Judah in the earshot of the people on the wall." But Rabshakeh answered them, "Was it to your master and to you that my master sent me to speak those words? It was precisely to the men who are sitting on the wall, who will have to eat their own dung and drink their own urine." (18:26–27)

Jerusalem, Shebna wrote a note, which he shot on an arrow [into the enemy's camp, declaring]: Shebna and his followers are willing to conclude peace; Hezekiah and his followers are not" (Sanhedrin 26a). Shebna's motive is unclear. Does he support an alliance with Assyria? Or is he motivated by self-interest? Does he merely seek to please the population of Jerusalem?

By royal edict (18:36), the people are restricted from issuing any response or reaction to the Assyrian provocation. The formulation of a ban of this sort conveys the effectiveness of Rabshakeh's taunts as well as the importance of the psychological factor at this stage of the military standoff. It is essential that Jerusalem retain her stoic face, and her people their resilience. Let us make no mistake that this is a war of words in the most literal sense.

RABSHAKEH'S TAUNT

When we read Rabshakeh's first speech we cannot but notice the sevenfold repetition of the verb B-T-H.[14] The central theme is that of *bitaḥon* – one's source of fortitude or strength. From where does one draw confidence and endurance? From where does Judah draw its courage and the audacity to oppose and defy Assyria?

Rabshakeh raises three possibilities. First, Israel might be relying upon Egypt. Rabshakeh responds that Egypt will fail to support them.[15] Like a Nile reed, when Israel will lean on it, it will simply pierce their hand. The second source of strength, Rabshakeh suggests, might be Judah's military. He issues a wager in the name of "my lord, the king of Assyria" who offers to provide two thousand horses "if you can provide yourself riders for them" (18:23). This mockery of Israelite weakness is compounded by a third, religious attack: "And if you tell me that you are relying on the Lord your God…." Rabshakeh demonstrates impressive familiarity with Judah's religious culture[16] when he references Hezekiah's religious reforms

---

14. 18:19 (twice), 20, 21 (twice), 22, 24.
15. Isaiah has already warned of this. See Is. 30:1–5; 31:1–3.
16. Sanhedrin 60a suggests that Hezekiah's men tear their clothes in response to Rabshakeh's flagrant blasphemy. It is in this talmudic passage that Shmuel is quoted as suggesting that Rabshakeh is a Jewish apostate: "Rav Yehuda said in Shmuel's name: He who hears the divine name blasphemed by a gentile need not rend his clothes. But if you will object; what of Rabshakeh? He was an apostate Israelite." Several strands of the story lend credence to this theory. First, Rabshakeh's fluency in Hebrew and the fact that he works for the enemy. Second, his intimate knowledge of Hezekiah's abolition of the *bamot* (the local worship sites). In fact, Rabshakeh's argument in 18:22 is that God will be angry with Hezekiah due to his removal of the *bamot*. Rabshakeh accuses Hezekiah of dismantling the local sites so that all Israel would worship at the central altar in the Temple. In other words, he suggests that Hezekiah has harmed God in order to serve his own political or egotistical aspirations. Abarbanel suggests that this line of

in which Hezekiah removed idolatry from the kingdom, destroying the *bamot*, the provincial shrines. In that light Rabshakeh suggests God's anger toward Hezekiah for destroying His shrines and limiting God to a single place – the Temple. Moreover, he acclaims that it was God Himself who sent Sennacherib against Jerusalem; Sennacherib is God's agent!

In his second speech, Rabshakeh again appeals to the people of Jerusalem, ignoring Eliakim's request that he speak in Aramaic, grandstanding to the assembled throngs "loudly in the language of Judah" (18:28). He undercuts the king – "Don't listen to Hezekiah" – as he continues with his smug oratory, seeking to convince the people to prefer Assyrian rule:

> Don't let Hezekiah deceive you, for he will not be able to save (*lehatzil*) you from my hands. Don't let Hezekiah make you rely (*yavtiaḥ*) on God, saying: "The Lord will surely save (*hatzel yatzilenu*) us; this city will not fall into the hands of the king of Assyria." Don't listen to Hezekiah. For thus said the king of Assyria: "Make your peace with me and come out to me, so that you may all eat from your vines and your fig trees and drink water from your cisterns, until I come and take you away to a land like your own, a land of grain and vineyards, of bread and wine, of olive oil and honey, so that you may live and not die." Don't listen to Hezekiah, who misleads you by saying, "The Lord will save (*yatzilenu*) us." Did any of the gods of other nations save (*hahatzel hitzilu*) his land from the king of Assyria?...Did they save Samaria (*hitzilu*) from me?...Will the Lord save (*yatzil*) Jerusalem from my hand? (II Kings 18:29–35)

Rabshakeh's words endeavor to dishearten and frustrate the trapped population, enticing them to surrender. Now a new *leitwort* features: H-TZ-L – salvation, deliverance, or rescue. If the inhabitants of Jerusalem submit, they can leave the besieged city and return to their farms and villages. His rhetoric invites his listeners to imagine the peace and serenity of Solomon's era, "each man sitting under his vine and fig tree"

---

argument proves he is familiar enough with Israelite religious norms but that he adopts an attitude alien to Torah law. Third, we may suggest that his vicious vilification of king and God support a person alienated from, and filled with antipathy for, his origins.

(18:31, reflecting I Kings 5:5). Alternatively, he tantalizes them, offering them a life in Assyria, "a land like your own, a land of grain and vineyards, of bread and wine, of olive oil and honey" (18:32, echoing Deut. 8:7–8), surely a superior option to life under siege; "Stay alive and don't die" (18:32), he taunts. But after promising Assyrian salvation and relief, the focus returns to God, as Rabshakeh disparages Him, profanely mocking His inability to save His people.

Kings quotes Rabshakeh's lengthy and provocative speech verbatim.[17] We might question the necessity of presenting the offensive taunts of Israel's enemy so comprehensively. The goal of this narration, it seems, is to accentuate the smugness of the Assyrians[18] on the one hand, and their blasphemy on the other. On a human plane, Sennacherib's conceited braggadocio will be a stark contrast to Hezekiah's earnest and humble appeal to God. On a higher plane, God will enter the picture; for if the chief antagonist, Sennacherib, has challenged God Himself, claiming to act as His messenger, then the Divine protagonist will intervene to show that Hezekiah's "trust" is indeed not misplaced, and that Sennacherib's military superiority is an illusion.

THE BIRTHSTOOL

Hezekiah's men return from Rabshakeh having torn their clothes, a sign of mourning[19] and desperation.[20] Hezekiah responds by appealing directly to God. This he does in two ways. First, Hezekiah too tears his clothes, dons sackcloth, and ascends to the Temple to pray. Second, he immediately sends his delegation (also now in sackcloth) to consult with the prophet Isaiah:

---

17. In a wonderful archaeological corroboration, other original Assyrian letters from Nimrud reveal an almost identical style of intimidation and mockery in the face of their enemy. See Letters 1–3 in H. W. F. Saggs, *The Nimrud Letters, 1952: Cuneiform Texts from Nimrud V* (London: British Institute for the Study of Iraq, 2001), 24–33. See also Long, *II Kings*, 218–19, who brings further examples of religious disputation and bellicose oratory as long-standing diplomatic practice in the ancient world.
18. Some points seem designed to create an almost satirical effect on the faithful reader of Kings. When Rabshakeh claims that God is angry with Hezekiah for removing the shrines (*bamot*), the impression is comic, as the very act that Rabshakeh perceives as offensive to God is known by the reader to be one of Hezekiah's greatest accolades. Rabshakeh's words resonate as foolish bluster.
19. Gen. 37:29; II Sam. 1:11; 3:31; 13:19; 15:3 and others.
20. Gen. 44:13; Num. 14:6; I Kings 21:27; II Kings 5:8; 11:14; Joel 2:13; Est. 4:1 and others.

> This day is a day of distress[21] and rebuke and disgrace! The babes have reached the birthstool but the strength to give birth is lacking. Perhaps the Lord your God will take note of the words of Rabshakeh whom his master, the king of Assyria, has sent to blaspheme the living God." (II Kings 19:3–4)

The metaphor is a powerful one, as Radak illustrates:

> As the baby is about to emerge from the womb and the pain is greatest, if the mother cannot find the strength to push the baby out, then the mother is abandoned to the intensity of her birth pain without any hope of relief. Similarly, the great crisis is upon us and we lack the strength to escape it unless God will assist us.

For Radak, Jerusalem is like the mother who cannot extract herself from her most excruciating pain. We might instead choose to interpret the people of Jerusalem as the baby trapped in the womb, fighting for its life. Jerusalem's survival seems tenuous. The baby is waiting to be released from its "siege" but it needs an external source, a "mother" to push it out. The baby is helpless.

And this is the story of Jerusalem. Jerusalem is alone, besieged and vulnerable. In his helplessness, Hezekiah understands that it is solely upon God that he can rely, and he casts the city's deliverance at God's door.

HEZEKIAH'S PRAYER[22]

Sennacherib is persistent and continues to threaten Jerusalem, sending a third communiqué (19:10–13). This time it is in the form of a written letter, boasting of his strength, blaspheming God yet again, and seeking to demoralize Hezekiah.

---

21. *Yom tzara*. This is a fascinating phrase. In many instances it indicates God's immediate salvation in a situation of distress. See for example Gen. 35:3; Jer. 16:19–21; Nahum 1:7; Ps. 20:2; 50:15.
22. To understand the precise chronology, see the schema presented earlier in this chapter. Hezekiah's entry into the Temple is mentioned twice, in II Kings 19:1 and ibid., vv. 14–19. Similarly, Isaiah issues two different prophecies: in ibid., vv. 6–7 and 20–31. In between is Sennacherib's third communiqué from Libnah.

But Hezekiah finds his strength in God. He takes Sennacherib's letter and spreads it out in the house of God as if to show God what has been said about Him, as he prays and earnestly reaffirms his faith in God's manifest power and control:

> O Lord, God of Israel, enthroned on the *cherubim*! You alone are God of all the kingdoms of the earth. You made the heavens and the earth. O Lord, incline Your ear and hear; open Your eyes and see. Hear the words that Sennacherib has sent to blaspheme the living God! True, O Lord, the kings of Assyria have annihilated the nations and their lands, and have committed their gods to the flames and have destroyed them; for they are not gods, but man's handiwork of wood and stone. But now, O Lord our God, deliver us from his hands, and let all the kingdoms of the earth know that You alone, O Lord, are God. (II Kings 19:15–19)

Assyria has defeated other nations along with their gods, "for they are not gods," Hezekiah argues. He appeals to God to show His presence to the world.

ISAIAH

Isaiah responds to Hezekiah's prayer by speaking in God's name and addressing Sennacherib directly:

> Whom have you blasphemed and reviled? Against whom have you made your voice loud and haughtily raised your eyes? Against the Holy One of Israel! By your messengers you have ridiculed the Lord.... But I know where you are, and when you come and go, and how you rage against Me. Because you rage against Me, and because your insolence has reached My ears, I will put My hook in your nose, and My bit in your mouth, and I will make you return by the way you came. (II Kings 19:22–23, 27–28)

Sennacherib, says God, has profaned the God who empowered him, and now he will be demoted and treated as a slave, a mere horse, with a hook in his nose and a bit in his mouth. God is firmly in control.

As for the current siege on Jerusalem, Isaiah assures Hezekiah that Sennacherib will soon leave Jerusalem and return home, and what is more, not a single shot will be fired in Jerusalem. It will be over sooner than anyone anticipates:

> Thus says the Lord: "Do not be frightened by the words of blasphemy against Me that you have heard from the minions of the king of Assyria. I will put a spirit in him; he will hear a rumor and return to his land and I will make him fall by the sword." (19:7–8)

> Therefore this is what the Lord says concerning the king of Assyria: "He shall not enter this city or shoot an arrow there. He shall not come before it with shield or build a siege ramp against it. By the way that he came he will return; he shall not enter this city," declares the Lord. "I will defend this city and save it, for My sake and for the sake of David My servant." (19:32–34)

This prediction must have seemed quite improbable to Hezekiah; quite absurd. And yet, surprisingly, it is fulfilled without delay, that very night:

> That night an angel of God went out and put to death 185,000 in the Assyrian camp. And the following morning they were all dead corpses. (19:35)

The final prophecy of the chapter points to Sennacherib's assassination at the hands of his own sons, and the Tanakh records the realization of that prophecy. We now possess the Assyrian annals of Esar-haddon which report that this was precisely how Sennacherib met his death, albeit, some twenty years hence, in 681 BCE.

HISTORICAL AND ARCHAEOLOGICAL REFERENCES

It almost seems too fantastical to imagine a huge army of 185,000 just expiring in their sleep. The biblical account has always aroused skepticism. For centuries, this remarkable miracle seemed unsubstantiated by any external source. The Greek historian Herodotus (485–425 BCE) reported a similar story, although in his account the adversary is Egypt. In his version, field mice invaded the Assyrian camp and gnawed the quivers, bow strings, and leather shield handles, thus disarming the military force. As a consequence, many of the soldiers were killed and others fled. Josephus too reports the miracle of Jerusalem's reprieve in the days of Hezekiah, ascribing the death of the Assyrian troops to a devastating plague (*Antiquities* X, 21–3). These sources notwithstanding, there was little to verify the biblical version of events.

However, with the discovery of Sennacherib's own records[23] almost two centuries ago, we have greater backing for the veracity of the story described by Kings. Sennacherib's war records demonstrate a strange anomaly when it chronicles the siege on Jerusalem. As Prof. Haim Tadmor[24] has observed, Sennacherib uses a standardized formula when describing the conquest of an enemy town: "Four elements which constitute a fixed structure, without which one cannot speak of a description of battle against a renegade enemy." The four elements are: (1) Sennacherib's conquest of the kingdom (including the capital city), (2) execution of the king, (3) the appointment of a vassal in place of the former king, and (4) the imposition of heavy taxation. These are fixtures in recording each and every conquest – except one: the war against Jerusalem in 701 BCE. Sennacherib describes the siege and Hezekiah's tribute, but fails to record the fall of Jerusalem and the execution or incarceration of its king.[25] This leads Tadmor to assume

23. The Sennacherib prisms cited in footnote 2 above.

24. H. Tadmor, "Sennacherib's Campaign to Judah: Historical and Historiographical Considerations," *Zion* 50 (1985): 65–80 [Hebrew].

25. "[Hezekiah] himself, like a caged bird I shut up in Jerusalem, his royal city. I threw up earthworks against him – the one coming out of the city gate, I turned back to his misery. His cities, which I had despoiled, I cut off from his land, and to Mitinti, king of Ashdod, Padi, king of Ekron, and Silli-bêl, king of Gaza, I gave [them]. And thus I diminished his land. I added to the former tribute, and I laid upon him the surrender of their land and imposts – gifts for my majesty. As for Hezekiah, the terrifying splendor of my majesty overcame him, and the Arabs and his mercenary

that Sennacherib abandoned the siege of Jerusalem, having failed to vanquish the city.

The Sennacherib annals yield other gems which corroborate and enrich our reading of the account in Tanakh. One particular phrase sheds light upon an unusual metaphor in the book of Isaiah. Sennacherib, in his own words, boasts: "[Hezekiah] himself, *like a caged bird* I shut up in Jerusalem, his royal city." This unusual metaphor gives greater poignancy to the metaphor used by Isaiah (31:5): "*Like birds in flight*, so will the Lord of Hosts protect Jerusalem. He will protect it and deliver it, He will spare it and rescue it."

Until this Assyrian document was uncovered we didn't appreciate the significance of Isaiah's language. Now we realize that Isaiah's phraseology was a direct retort to the language of Sennacherib, one of biblical archaeology's most famous contributions to our understanding of Tanakh.

GOG AND MAGOG

The Talmud offers an intriguing critique of King Hezekiah:

> The Holy One Blessed be He wished to appoint Hezekiah as the Messiah, and Sennacherib as Gog and Magog. The Attribute of Justice said before the Holy One Blessed be He: "Sovereign of the Universe! If You did not make David the Messiah, who uttered so many hymns and psalms before You, will You then appoint Hezekiah as such, who did not praise You despite all these miracles which You performed for him?" (Sanhedrin 94a)

Why is the confrontation between Hezekiah and Sennacherib described in terms relating to the End of Days? What is the meaning behind this analogy? The Rabbis are suggesting it evokes similar biblical eschatological scenarios. We are describing an event in which the world's most destructive military force attacked Jerusalem, the city was on the verge

---

troops which he had brought in to strengthen Jerusalem, his royal city, deserted him.... To pay tribute and to accept servitude, he dispatched his messengers." This text, from Sennacherib's Rassam Prism, can be found in Cogan and Tadmor, 337–38.

of annihilation, and then suddenly and unexpectedly – miraculously – the city was saved.

The parallel used by the Talmud is the biblical account of Gog and Magog (Ezek. 38–39 and specifically 39:21–23). It depicts Gog gathering war forces to decimate Israel, and then God's devastating intervention and salvation. An overwhelming, unsurpassable war leader of Sennacherib's power and force, a man who had conquered all civilization, fulfills the character depiction of Gog. The supernatural death of the enemy forces matches God's role in the messianic vision. Consequently, the Rabbis suggest that this war had the potential to be the definitive messianic moment, the war to end all wars. For them, all that was left was for Hezekiah to recognize God's guiding hand in the victory.

But somehow, Hezekiah failed to religiously channel this moment, to generate spiritual momentum. In his distress, he desperately turned to God; in victory, he failed to praise the Almighty. We wonder why this happened.

We might offer one explanation. Despite Jerusalem's reprieve, the entire landscape of Judah was scarred and war-torn, tens of thousands of civilians had been taken as prisoner of war by Sennacherib, cities had been burnt and destroyed, and the country suffered from heavy war casualties. To Hezekiah, this may not have felt like a moment of absolute jubilation.[26]

THE INVINCIBLE CITY

Let us consider the Talmud's assertion that this event powerfully evokes messianic allusions.[27] The deliverance was beyond any expectation – no superlative could contain it. Whether the magnitude of the event was fully absorbed at the time is questionable, but as it was remembered by

26. Bin-Nun and Lau, *Isaiah*, 275.

27. See the opinion of Rabbi Hillel in Sanhedrin 98b that Hezekiah was the Messiah! For more on these messianic allusions, see A. Grossman, "*Nevua LeDorot KeBaabua LeMetziut HaHistorit*," in Y. Z. Rimon, ed., *Mussar, Milḥama veKibbush* [Ethics, War and Conquest] (Alon Shevut, Israel: Tevunot, 1994), 68–71[Hebrew].

subsequent generations, this miraculous victory made a colossal impression upon the national psyche:

> The kings of the earth did not believe, nor did any of the peoples of the world, that enemies and foes could enter the gates of Jerusalem. (Lam. 4:10)

When the Temple was eventually destroyed, kings and commoner alike were astonished. They simply failed to comprehend that Jerusalem could fall. Why? Because the victory against Sennacherib had engendered the belief that Jerusalem was under divine protection, that it was invincible.

Similarly, Jeremiah (ch. 7) seeks to persuade the people of Jerusalem to stop believing blindly that the Temple was fundamentally indestructible, that God would never abandon His Temple. Ironically, the wondrous miracle of Jerusalem's rescue from Sennacherib's attack made it almost impossible for subsequent generations to believe the words of the prophet as he threatened the impending demise of the city. The people recalled God's promise: "I will defend this city and save it, for My sake and for the sake of David My servant" (II Kings 19:34).

II Kings 20

Tests of Faith

Jerusalem has been miraculously saved from the brink of destruction. Now, Kings surprisingly returns to focus on two earlier events,[1] one personal, the other national:

1. Hezekiah's illness, his recovery, and the sign of the steps (20:1–11).
2. The state visit of Berodach-baladan and Isaiah's rebuke (20:12–19).

HEZEKIAH'S ILLNESS: THE POWER OF PRAYER

> In those days Hezekiah fell dangerously ill. The prophet Isaiah son of Amoz came and said to him, "Thus said the Lord: Set your affairs in order, for you are going to die; you will not recover." (II Kings 20:1)

1. These two stories transpired before or during the Assyrian siege. Why do they appear here? It seems that these stories would have interrupted the flow of the narrative of II Kings 18–19, but that they are important enough to offer something vital regarding the prophetic appraisal of Hezekiah, as we shall explain.

Kings offers no reason or cause for Hezekiah's illness, only that he is afflicted with a life-threatening ailment.[2] Isaiah proclaims the king's imminent demise, and advises him to prepare for death.[3] The finality of the divine decree spurs Hezekiah into desperate prayer:

> Hezekiah turned his face to the wall and prayed to the Lord, "Remember, God, how I have walked before You faithfully and with wholehearted devotion, and have done what is good in Your eyes." And Hezekiah wept profusely. (20:2–3)

In no time at all – Isaiah hardly had time to leave the palace grounds – God issues a reprieve, granting the king an additional fifteen years. Hezekiah will live!

This story becomes a powerful motif of tenacious prayer, an embodiment of the firm belief that even after the die has seemingly been cast, one may still appeal to God. In his faith, Hezekiah challenges the absolutism of prophecy and overturns the divine sentence:

> [Hezekiah said], "This tradition I have from the house of my ancestor:[4] Even if a sharp sword rests upon a man's neck he should not desist from prayer...." Immediately, Hezekiah turned his face to the wall [*kir*] and prayed unto the Lord. What is the meaning of *kir*? R. Shimon b. Lakish said: [He prayed] from the innermost chambers [*kirot*] of his heart. (Berakhot 10a–b)

2. II Kings 20:7 suggests a skin ailment, but it is impossible to know whether this was merely one symptom of the disease or the ailment itself.
3. Three other instances in Kings depict royals who fall dangerously ill and inquire of God, "Will I recover from this sickness?" In each case, the prophet predicts the demise of the royal concerned – Jeroboam's son (I Kings 14:1–18), Ahaziah (II Kings 1:2–4), Ben-Hadad (ibid., 8:9–10) – a prediction that transpires. These three stories form something of a pattern, with the fourth story – that of Hezekiah – diverging from it.
4. Which ancestor? Could it be a reference to Ahaz, to whom Isaiah suggests that he make any request of God? Ahaz refuses: "I will not test God!" (Is. 7:11). Now his son, Hezekiah, learns the lesson his father refused to learn. He *does* ask and test God!

A SIGN FROM GOD

Notwithstanding the prophet's explicit annulment of the fatal decree, the king seeks further heavenly verification:

> Hezekiah asked Isaiah, "What is the sign that the Lord will heal me and that I shall go up to the house of the Lord on the third day?" Isaiah replied, "This is the sign for you from the Lord, that the Lord will do the thing that He has promised: Shall the shadow advance ten steps or recede ten steps?" Hezekiah said, "It is easy for the shadow to lengthen ten steps, but not for the shadow to recede ten steps." So the prophet Isaiah called to the Lord, and He made the shadow which had descended on the dial of Ahaz recede ten steps. (II Kings 20:8–11)

Does the king not trust the prophet? Why does he require further evidence of God's word? Radak explains:

> After Isaiah had pronounced the decree twice – "You are going to die"; "You will not recover" – Hezekiah considered Isaiah's response, "I will heal you" (20:5), as an attempt to console him after [the prophet] had witnessed his extensive weeping. And although [Hezekiah] saw the manner in which the boils had become healed, he did not believe that he would genuinely regain his strength such that he could "go up to the house of the Lord."

Hezekiah was unsure whether the reversal of God's prophecy was in fact real; possibly the prophet was simply trying to mitigate his distress with kind words.[5] Hezekiah needed a direct and clear message from God.[6] The precise details of the divine sign elude us, but it seems that Ahaz

---

5. This false consolation is precisely what Elisha did to Ben-Hadad. See II Kings 8:10.
6. Compare this with the parallel account in Is. 38 in which Hezekiah does not request divine proof, but rather is offered this sign by Isaiah. Prof. Yair Zakovitch engages in a valuable comparison of the accounts of this story in Kings, Isaiah, and Chronicles in his book, *The Concept of Miracle in the Bible* (Tel Aviv: Ministry of Defense, 1987), 91–92 [Hebrew].

had a sundial that marked time on a series of steps.[7] Hezekiah requested that the sun shift its direction, similar to the miracle in Joshua's days.[8] The reversal of the sun's natural course extended the hours of the day, indicating that the king's life too would be prolonged. Precisely the fact that this miracle was a reversal of nature gave it veracity. Hezekiah's passionate prayer and his request for divine reassurance communicate a portrait of the king as a man gripped by firm belief in a God of salvation.

THE DIPLOMATIC VISIT OF BERODACH[9]-BALADAN

The next story, however, is critical of Hezekiah:

> At that time Berodach-baladan, son of Baladan king of Babylonia, sent Hezekiah letters and a gift, because he had heard of Hezekiah's illness. Hezekiah received the envoys and showed them all that was in his storehouses – the silver, the gold, the spices and the fine olive oil, his armory, and everything found among his treasures. There was nothing in his palace or in all his kingdom that Hezekiah did not show them. (II Kings 20:12–13)

Hezekiah's enthusiastic display triggers the prophet's ire. He censures Hezekiah and issues a chilling prophecy of doom and exile:

---

7. What are the "the steps of Ahaz" and how does the sun or shade function upon them? Josephus and the Septuagint suggested that we are dealing with a shadow on a flight of steps, and that Hezekiah requested the shadow to move backward, as if the day were reversing. Rashi, following *Targum Yonatan*, suggests that the movements are on a sundial. Yigael Yadin pointed to ancient Egyptian shadow clocks which were built using steps and shadows, thereby uniting the two lines of interpretation. See Kiel, *Daat Mikra*, for an illustration of Yadin's shadow clock.

   Ralbag, however, refuses to accept an alteration in the laws of physics: "We have not seen miracles of this sort even with Moses ... a miracle in the orbit of the sun itself!" (Note that Ralbag lived from 1288 to 1344, predating Copernicus and Galileo.) Ralbag proposes that what transpired was a sudden shift in the shade and sunlight, created by a cloud cover, not a shift in the orbit or rotation of the earth itself.

8. Josh. 10:12–13.
9. Here the name is Berodach. In Isaiah (39:1) it is Merodach – probably a hebraization of Marduk.

> The time will surely come when everything in your palace, and all that your predecessors have stored up until this day, will be carried off to Babylonia. Nothing will be left behind, says the Lord. And some of your own sons, who shall be born to you, shall be taken away, and they shall be eunuchs in the palace of the king of Babylonia. (20:17–18)

This passage raises many questions. Who is this Babylonian ruler? What is his interest in visiting Hezekiah? Is this a convalescent visit by a fellow royal, or is there more than meets the eye here? Most intriguing is Isaiah's rage as Hezekiah showcases his royal treasures and national storehouses. Is a king precluded from exhibiting his wealth? And why does this of all actions stimulate the earliest prophetic prediction of the Babylonian exile?[10]

TIMING

We mentioned at the start of our chapter that these stories predate the Assyrian assault on Jerusalem. What is the basis of this assertion? Regarding Hezekiah's illness it is simple arithmetic. Sennacherib's siege is dated to the fourteenth year of Hezekiah's reign (18:13). Here, Hezekiah, who rules for twenty-nine years (18:2), falls ill and is assured an additional fifteen years of life. By simple deduction, we may now date his illness to the fourteenth year of his reign, while Sennacherib's armies surround Jerusalem![11] Hezekiah's deadly illness mirrors the nation's looming

10. An additional prediction of exile from this period can be found in Micah 3:12. (Jer. 26:18 identifies Micah's prophecy as having been delivered in the period of Hezekiah.) According to Micah 3, the sin which engenders exile is social injustice and the thorough corruption of the ruling classes: priesthood, judiciary, prophets, and government.
11. Radak, based on the verse, "I will save you from the hand of Ashur, and this city... I will protect" (II Kings 20:6), dates the illness to the duration of the siege. Rashi and Abarbanel, following *Seder Olam* (ch. 23), propose that Hezekiah fell ill a mere three days prior to the Assyrian retreat. As such, the night on which he was healed coincided with the night of the failure of the Assyrian army. Miracle was superimposed on miracle. Even if this precise timeline is improbable, the biblical tie-in, "in those days," certainly furnishes a link between the two stories of reprieve and deliverance. Ralbag sees these events as happening after the Assyrian withdrawal.

catastrophe. In both instances the king appeals to God, and the deliverance of the two transpires concurrently.

As for the Babylonian state visit of Berodach-baladan, we have already noted that Berodach-baladan is well known from ancient Near-Eastern records[12] having staged a revolt and mustered an anti-Assyrian coalition after the fall of Sargon in battle. If so, we presume that this royal visit was an international diplomatic consultation with the objective of raising precisely such a war coalition.[13] In that case, we may date this diplomatic delegation to the years between 705 and 703 BCE, years in which there was hope of overthrowing Assyrian domination. Hezekiah's display of his treasury and stores is probably a demonstration of his financial means, showing that he had the funds to finance a costly and lengthy military campaign.[14] Berodach-baladan visits Hezekiah not to pay a courtesy visit to a sick king, but rather to further the overthrow of the Assyrian empire.

WHAT ANGERED THE PROPHET?

If these stories are chronologically displaced, then what is the purpose of their arrangement? Furthermore, why did this visit of Berodach-baladan anger Isaiah so severely?[15] Is a king precluded from forging alliances with other regional forces; is this not precisely the king's role?

---

12. Berodach-baladan, or Marduk-apla-iddina II, was a Babylonian rebel who united the Chaldean tribes to resist and overthrow Assyrian dominance. His revolt succeeded, and from 722 to 711 BCE he ruled Babylonia and sought to galvanize a broad resistance to crush Assyria entirely. However, Sargon fought back against Berodach's allies and prevented the rise of an anti-Assyrian coalition. After Sargon's death in 705 BCE, Berodach once again felt that his time had come, but Sennacherib conquered Babylonia in 703 BCE and Berodach lost power. Scholars debate whether this delegation to Hezekiah should be dated to the period of 711 BCE or the later attempt in 705–703 BCE, but the visit by Berodach's men seems highly plausible.
13. See Elitzur, *Israel and the Bible*, 201–9.
14. Cogan and Tadmor, *II Kings*, 259, note the usage of the phrase "*beit nekhoto*" (20:13), which has no parallel in Tanakh. However, in the context of Assyrian royal inscriptions, "*bit nakamti*" was a depository for the booty of foreign campaigns. This lends credence to the notion that Babylonia was negotiating a military campaign with Hezekiah.
15. II Chr. 32:24–25 suggests that Hezekiah's sin during his illness was an attitude of pride, a feeling of overconfidence after the victory against Assyria. Many midrashic sources adopt this approach in connection with our story, for example: "When Hezekiah saw

Isaiah is a prophet who repeatedly warns against alliances with foreign governments. He advised King Ahaz against a pact with Assyria; he also tries to obstruct Hezekiah's alliance with Egypt. We can readily appreciate the basis of the prophet's opposition. First, the ally can easily let you down:

> "Woe to the obstinate children," declares the Lord…"who go down to Egypt without consulting Me; who look for help to Pharaoh's protection, to Egypt's shade for refuge. *But Pharaoh's protection will be to your shame; Egypt's shade will bring you disgrace."* (Is. 30:1–3)

As we have explained, the Babylonian alliance was crushed by Assyria, and this was the catalyst for the Assyrian reprisal that endangered the very survival of Judah.

Second, Judah is simply a small player up against huge imperial forces much larger than herself. Judah would do much better to remain neutral and uninvolved. If she bets upon the wrong alliance, she can be easily overwhelmed and destroyed. Possibly this is the easiest explanation of Isaiah's gloomy prediction: "All that your predecessors have stored up until this day will be carried off to Babylonia." He means that the people who you befriend today are likely to turn against you tomorrow.

In turbulent times, Isaiah recommends a policy of political neutrality and quietism – "You shall triumph by stillness and quiet; your victory shall come about through calm and confidence" (Is. 30:15) – not brokering international treaties and geopolitical meddling. Isaiah warns that a policy based on forging rushed alliances with the strongest force in the region is too risky, and will lead to exile.

---

the delegates of Babylonia, he became exceedingly conceited. He showed them the royal treasury and the Holy of Holies, and opened the Ark [of the Covenant], and pointing to the tablets [of stone], said: "It is with these that we wage war, and achieve victory!" (*Pirkei DeRabbi Eliezer* 51). In this midrashic text Hezekiah presumes that he can rely on divine support irrespective of the ethical and religious conduct of the people. Numbers Rabba 20:6 identifies his arrogance as his lack of deference to Isaiah. When Berodach-baladan arrived to consult with the king, he should have claimed that all the power lay in the prophet.

But mostly, the prophet encourages reliance upon God rather than man.

THE STRUCTURE OF THE STORIES

The question of the placement or inner structure of the Hezekiah stories will demonstrate the prophet Isaiah's fundamental critique. If we survey the narrative structure, we find four situations in which the king interacts with the prophet:

Verses (in II Kings)	**The predicament**	**Hezekiah's response**	**God's reassurance**	**What happens?**
19:1–8	Sennacherib's first attack. Rabshakeh's speeches in Jerusalem.	Sends delegation to ask Isaiah to **pray**. (19:4)	"Do not be frightened… he will hear a rumor and return to his land." (19:7)	"Rabshakeh heard that [the king] had left Lachish; he turned back." (19:8)
19:9–37	Sennacherib's second attack. Letter from Libnah.	**Prays** in the house of God.	"He shall not enter this city or shoot an arrow there… I will defend this city and save it." (19:32–34)	A miracle happens, and the 185,000 Assyrians are smitten. Assyrians retreat.
20:1–11	Hezekiah's illness. The prophet announces Hezekiah's impending death.	"Hezekiah turned his face to the wall and **prayed** to the Lord… and [he] wept profusely." (20:2–3)	"I have heard your prayer; I have seen your tears. I will add fifteen years to your life." (20:5–6)	Hezekiah is healed.

Verses (in II Kings)	The predicament	Hezekiah's response	God's reassurance	What happens?
20:12–21	Babylonian delegation of Berodach-baladan. Isaiah condemns Hezekiah: "Everything in your palace... will be carried off to Babylonia..." (20:17)	Hezekiah said: "The word of the Lord is good... if there will be peace and security in my days." (20:19)	–	–

It is easy to see that Hezekiah's responses develop and escalate. Initially, he goes to the house of God and asks Isaiah to pray for him. Later, he goes to the house of God and offers his own personal prayer. In the third scene, the prayer is more intimate, as the narrator stresses that he prays at home: "He turned his face to the wall." Now that the reader has become accustomed to Hezekiah's routine response – prayer – in the face of the challenges that he confronts, and now that we have seen how this prayer becomes more personal, the reader anticipates that on the fourth instance, *Hezekiah* will pray when he hears the divine punishment conveyed by the prophet.

Yet for some reason, not only does Hezekiah fail to pray this time, he nonchalantly accepts the divine decree: "The word of the Lord... is good (*tov*).... If there will be peace (*shalom*) and security (*emet*) in my days." The terms *tov, shalom,* and *emet* echo from his earlier prayer: "Remember... how I have walked before You in faithfulness (*emet*) and with a whole (*shalem*) heart, and have done what is good (*tov*) in Your eyes" (II Kings 20:2). This recurrence merely emphasizes what the reader expects from Hezekiah.

How might we explain the structural composition here?

> The breaking of the familiar pattern expresses an implicit criticism of Hezekiah in the fourth iteration.... With the visit by the Babylonian delegation, Hezekiah's story becomes a diplomatic story. In other words, Judah responds to the Assyrian pressure in a political manner, supporting Babylonia to undermine the Assyrian empire.... As long as Hezekiah prayed to God he expressed his trust and reliance upon Him, and Isaiah stood by his side.... However, with the arrival of the Babylonian delegation, Hezekiah changes course, and this becomes a story that is occupied with diplomatic strategy.... In this manner a great opportunity is squandered and the fourth cycle of the story breaks the pattern of the narrative. Hezekiah's irregular response to Isaiah is similarly the inverse of what we would expect.[16]

Hezekiah's reaction to the divine decree is most surprising. In addition to his seeming indifference to Isaiah's dire prediction, his response at first glance sounds almost arrogantly self-centered. The king declares to the prophet:

> "The word of the Lord that you have spoken is good." For he thought, "Why not, if there will be peace and security in my days?" (II Kings 20:19)

Isaiah has presented an exceedingly frightening prophecy! How did Hezekiah see it as "good"? The simplest explanation is that Hezekiah rebuffs Isaiah's rebuke, saying that as king, he cannot be overly concerned with scenarios in the distant future. If the Babylonian pact will bring "peace and security in my days," it is the correct policy. Successive

16. Yonatan Grossman, *Text and Subtext: On Exploring Biblical Narrative Design* (Tel Aviv: Hakibbutz Hameuchad, 2015), 158–59 [Hebrew]. See Tractate Sanhedrin 96a, which suggests that the diplomatic note from Berodach-baladan to Hezekiah placed Hezekiah's name at the start and God's name last. This upturning of the order eventually brought about Jerusalem's destruction. Here, it seems that *Ḥazal* are commenting on Hezekiah's deflection of God.

kings will have to navigate the stormy waters of future regional conflict. But now Assyria is on the horizon and a coalition must be formed to defend the nation![17]

QUESTIONS OF TRUST: THE BOOK OF REMEDIES

As we reflect upon this narrative pattern, we wonder as to the degree to which Hezekiah should be reliant upon God. Hezekiah is caught in a complex tug of war between faith-oriented decisions on the one hand and navigating the kingdom's course on the basis of hard strategy and skilled diplomacy on the other. When should Hezekiah use the one, and when should he employ the other?

This difficult question may be reinforced with a famous rabbinic assessment of Hezekiah's successes and mistakes:

> King Hezekiah did six things. Concerning three the sages agreed with him, and concerning three they did not agree with him:
> 1. He dragged his father's corpse on a rope bier, and they agreed with him.
> 2. He crushed the bronze serpent, and they agreed with him.
> 3. He hid the Book of Remedies, and they agreed with him.
>
> And concerning three they did not agree with him:
> 1. He cut down the doors of the Temple and sent them to the king of Assyria, and they did not agree with him.
> 2. He blocked the waters of the upper Gihon, and they did not agree with him.
> 3. He intercalated the month of Nisan in Nisan, and they did not agree with him.
>
> (Pesaḥim 55b–56a)

17. Malbim adopts an alternative approach, seeing Hezekiah as expressing a religious point: "The matter which the prophet predicts can change from bad to good if the nation alter their actions from bad to good." Malbim retains the image of the faithful Hezekiah, who knows that any doom-filled prediction may be altered by an appeal to God!

The Rabbis approve of Hezekiah's war on idolatry: his humiliation of his father's hearse and his disposal of Moses's serpent. But the debate regarding the Book of Remedies will open a fascinating discussion regarding questions of faith versus self-reliance.

What is the Book of Remedies, and if, as it sounds, it is a compendium of cures, a medical almanac, why would anyone destroy it? Rashi (Pesaḥim 55b–56a) explains that the "Book of Remedies" supplied a swift medicinal solution to any ailment: "It was hidden away due to the fact that people's hearts were not subdued regarding illness, and they were healed immediately." In other words, Rashi contends the book was banned because it eliminated the need to rely upon God. Sickness is a prime opportunity to reach out to the divine, and this book was simply providing a shortcut to health, without appealing to God. Maimonides was flabbergasted at this interpretation:

> How nonsensical is this argument, and how deluded! It ascribes a degree of foolishness to Hezekiah (and to the sages who supported his efforts), the like of which one should attribute only to the basest of the masses. According to their confused and idiotic reasoning, if a person is hungry and turns to bread and consumes it, thus becoming healed from that great "sickness" of hunger, shall we say that he has lost his faith in God? Only fools would say that! For just as I thank God when I eat for that which He provided me to relieve my hunger and to sustain and preserve me, so too will I thank Him for providing me with a remedy which heals sickness. (Commentary on the Mishna, Pesaḥim, ch. 4)

Maimonides is suggesting that medicine is no more an affront to God than human nutrition. God has granted humans the intelligence to cure disease using medicine just as He has given us food to relieve hunger.

The conclusion of the mishna quoted above states that the sages disapproved of Hezekiah's rerouting of the Shiloah spring, "because he should have relied upon God" (Rashi). But again, is this line of thinking realistically acceptable? Should Hezekiah have left his city defenseless as the Assyrians prepared for war? This returns us to our central question. When is it legitimate to exercise human initiative, and when is it more appropriate to rely upon God?

If Hezekiah has license to use his initiative to guide his foreign policy, why did God censure his overtures to Berodach-baladan?

Another fascinating talmudic text highlights this tension:

> In those days Hezekiah became mortally ill. The prophet Isaiah, son of Amoz, came to him…
>
> Hezekiah said to him: "Why have I been punished so severely?"
>
> Isaiah responded: "Because you did not try to have children."
>
> He said: "The reason was because I saw by the divine spirit [*ruaḥ hakodesh*] that the children issuing from me would not be virtuous."
>
> He said to him: "What have you to do with the secrets of the All-Merciful? You should have done what you were commanded, and let the Holy One Blessed be He do that which pleases Him." (Berakhot 10a)

Hezekiah's illness is attributed here to his unwillingness to have a family.[18] Hezekiah holds back from having children out of fear that his progeny might follow a sinful path. The prophet responds that man is enjoined to fulfill his worldly duties and let God take care of the rest. Hezekiah's fears are an understatement, seeing that Hezekiah's son Manasseh was one of Judah's most evil kings, the cause of Jerusalem's eventual destruction.[19] But again, it raises the question of *bitaḥon*. May one merely rely upon God and relinquish personal responsibility? Does reliance on God always produce a desirable result?

---

18. There is some contextual support for this claim, as Hezekiah's son and heir is Manasseh, who ascends the throne at age twelve (see II Kings 21:2). In that case, Hezekiah fathers Manasseh after his illness and after the Assyrian siege. It would appear that he has no (male) children prior to his illness.
19. II Kings 21:10–16; 23:26; 24:3–4.

* * *

We leave Hezekiah with these challenging reflections. This monarch took an idolatrous kingdom and turned it around, rededicating the Temple and cleansing the country of idolatry. Furthermore, he makes every attempt to unify the kingdom, persuading the northern tribes to join him in Jerusalem.

In the leadup to Sennacherib's attack on Judah, Hezekiah is excoriated for exploring an alliance with Babylonia to create a regional resistance. Indeed, the alliance with Babylonia is crushed, and when the Assyrian war machine closes in on Jerusalem, he has no recourse except to trust God. The city's miraculous deliverance and Hezekiah's personal medical recovery both underscore God's role in history and the remarkable effect of reliance on the Almighty.

The question that looms over Hezekiah's reign is the balance between human initiative and reliance on God. Hezekiah is a man of great faith and commitment who leaves a powerful legacy as one of the greatest of the Judahite kings, and precisely a king of his stature needs to advance his nation on rational political lines. Where indeed is the correct balance between human effort and faith?

II Kings 21

King Manasseh: An Idolatrous Kingdom

Of the entire book of Kings, the period of King Manasseh is singled out for particular ignominy and divine denunciation. During these years the country becomes awash with idolatry and an assortment of deviant religious worship, divination, and magic. This era will be remembered as the religious low point of the First Temple era. The manifestations of Manasseh's idolatry overwhelm in their brazenness and scope:

> He rebuilt the shrines that his father Hezekiah had destroyed… altars for Baal… [and] Ashera…. He bowed down to all the host of heaven and worshipped them, and he built altars for them in the house of the Lord…. He consigned his son to the fire; he practiced soothsaying and divination, and consulted ghosts and familiar spirits; he did much that was displeasing to the Lord, to vex Him… and placed the image of the Ashera in the house [of God]. (II Kings 21:3–7)[1]

1. II Kings 23:4–14 gives further details of the wide range of idolatry and the depth of their dissemination in Jerusalem and its environs: "Houses of the ritual prostitutes…

What stimulated this sudden eruption of idolatry? Why would the son of a pious king become an inveterate sinner?

One answer may lie with Manasseh's strategic affiliations. Manasseh's long reign coincides with the peak of Assyrian power, wealth, and prestige. He wholly embraced his status as an Assyrian vassal, an association that gave him an unprecedented fifty-five years of international calm and domestic prosperity. However, there was a poisonous spiritual corollary: Israel was incapable of withstanding the deep cultural implications of the association with Assyria:

> It may be noted that no other period of cuneiform records has yielded any remotely comparable mass of tablets relating to magic and divination, and that the royal Assyrian letters of the time contain numerable references to astrology and magic. It was practically impossible for a small vassal state to keep from being flooded with such idolatrous and superstitious practices which were under royal Assyrian protection.[2]

The religious reader of Kings is frequently puzzled; how can a single king sway the entire national religious orientation? Was state religion so powerful? Why would a royal policy have such deep societal implications?

It is important to understand that in ancient times, religion and society were far from separate. Religion and science were synonymous; the way in which people explained their world was by means of religion. Religion permeated all life-cycle events, all national ceremony, farming,

---

women who wove coverings for the Ashera … priests from the towns of Judah … the altars … from Geva to Beer Sheba … horses that the kings of Judah had dedicated to the sun … chariots of the sun." The book of Zephaniah dates to this period as well. See its apocalyptic warnings in chapters 1 and 3, and the depictions of "those who prostrate on the roofs to the hosts of the heavens … those who enrobe in the clothing of heathens" (Zeph. 1:4–8).

2. W. F. Albright, *The Biblical Period from Abraham to Ezra* (New York: Harper and Row, 1963), 79. Interestingly, an aggadic passage (Sanhedrin 102b) corroborates Albright's sentiment that it was "practically impossible" to avoid being swept up in the idolatrous momentum: Rav Ashi encounters King Manasseh in a dream. He asks Manasseh: "Since you are so wise, why did you worship idols?" Manasseh replied, "If you were there, you would have caught up the skirt of your robe and sped after me."

commerce, and the like. Priests and prophets were political analysts as much as religious functionaries. Thus, a national alliance with a superpower, even if it was motivated by military protection and openness to its economy and culture, could precipitate a huge shift in religious orientation.

This may be difficult to appreciate from a modern perspective, but even in our times, an affiliation with NATO aligns with an openness to Western cultural norms, much as during the Cold War, an affiliation with the Soviet bloc had influence far beyond the sphere of the military, in areas of the economy, religion, government, political and cultural freedom, fashion, music, and the arts. In a similar manner, Manasseh's acceptance of Assyrian governance dictated a wide and deep cultural transformation that permeated every walk of life.

We should not presume that Manasseh's religious and political reforms were adopted without opposition. Our chapter of II Kings informs us that: "Manasseh put so many innocent people to death that he filled Jerusalem with blood from end to end" (21:16). The king's victims were probably not only political opponents, but also religious insurgents who challenged the king's odious spiritual orientation and fought to sustain the national monotheistic tradition.[3]

In a lengthy exhortation, Kings delivers a stern indictment of Manasseh's practices. The text ominously equates Manasseh to Ahab (II Kings 21:3) and to the Amorites who resided in Canaan before the entry of Israel into the land (21:2, 13), predecessors whose sinful record led to their demise. Repeatedly the Temple is referenced:

---

3. There is a rabbinic tradition that Manasseh murdered the prophet Isaiah (Yevamot 49b; Sanhedrin 103b). The assumption that his murderous policy was directed at his religious opponents is proposed by Prof. Yehezkel Kaufmann and also by *Daat Mikra* and *Olam HaTanakh*. See Y. Kaufmann, *History of the Religion of Israel*, 8th ed., vol. 4 (Jerusalem: Mossad Bialik; Tel Aviv: Dvir, 1967), 234–35. Kaufmann calls Manasseh "The 'Jezebel' of the southern kingdom" due to his ardent idolatry and the murder of the adherents of God. Prof. Yehuda Elitzur brings archaeological evidence suggesting that due to the corruption of the Temple during this period, alternative monotheistic sacrificial sites were established west of Jerusalem by loyal adherents of monotheism. See *Israel and the Bible*, 164–73; 230–34 [Hebrew].

> [It is] the house of the God, of which God had said, *"I will establish My name in Jerusalem ....* In this house and in Jerusalem *I will establish My name forever,* and I will not again cause the feet of Israel to wander from the land that I gave to their fathers if they faithfully observe all I have commanded." (21:4, 7–8).

These lines reiterate God's original intent that Jerusalem become an eternal site of God's presence and the everlasting home of the Jewish people. However, in the context of the roster of Manasseh's offences, these references resonate ironically like a foreboding ritornelle, warning that Manasseh's idolatry and violence will displace God, desecrate His name, and invite the city's destruction.

The prophecies of both Jeremiah[4] and Kings[5] repeatedly attribute the destruction of the Temple and the national exile to the evil regime of Manasseh. Our chapter in II Kings gives the clearest warning of the impending *Ḥurban*:

> Thus says the Lord, the God of Israel, "I am going to bring such a disaster on Jerusalem and Judah that both ears of everyone who hears it will tremble.[6] I will apply to Jerusalem the measuring line of Samaria and the weight of the house of Ahab.[7] I will wipe Jerusalem clean as one wipes a dish and turns it upside down. And I will cast off the remnant of My own people and deliver them into the hands of My enemies." (21:12–14)

The Mishna groups Manasseh with two other kings whose are precluded from the afterlife:

---

4. Jer. 15:1–4.
5. II Kings 23:26–27; 24:3–4.
6. See Jer. 19:3, which uses this phrase. Since the chapter there relates to the Molekh cult in the Hinnom Valley, the entire prophecy might draw strongly on the practices of Manasseh.
7. The "measuring line" is a horizontal level that guides the builder to construct the wall in a perfect horizontal. The "weight" is a string attached to a weight that allows the builder to create a perfect vertical line. Of course, with Samaria destroyed, the "measuring line of Samaria" is a metaphor for absolute wreckage. For further uses of this metaphor in the context of the *Ḥurban,* see Amos 7:8–9; Lam. 2:8.

> Three kings... have no portion in the World to Come: Jeroboam, Ahab, and Manasseh. (Mishna Sanhedrin 10:1)

The common factor shared by these leaders is their advancement of idolatrous practices. Jeroboam instituted shrines outside the confines of Jerusalem's Temple; Ahab was the first sovereign to abandon the worship of God, adopting instead Baal as the national deity; and now Manasseh has introduced idolatry to Judah on an unprecedented scale. With Manasseh's lengthy tenure these practices have plenty of time to become deeply rooted cultural realities, and even after his death, the kingdom never recovers from the damage.

CHRONICLES: A DIFFERENT ENDING

Kings presents an uncomplicated biography of Manasseh. However, when we study Chronicles, we encounter a surprisingly different account of Manasseh's end:

> The Lord spoke to Manasseh and his people, but they paid no attention. So the Lord brought the army commanders of the king of Assyria against them, they took Manasseh prisoner, put a hook in his nose, bound him with bronze shackles, and took him to Babylonia. In his distress he sought the favor of the Lord his God and humbled himself greatly before the God of his ancestors. And when he prayed to him, God was moved by his entreaty and listened to his plea; so He brought him back to Jerusalem and to his kingdom. Then Manasseh knew that the Lord alone is God. Afterward he rebuilt the outer wall of the city of David.... He got rid of the foreign gods and removed the image from the house of God.... He restored the altar of God and sacrifices of peace offerings and thanksgiving offerings upon it, and told Judah to serve the Lord, God of Israel. (II Chr. 33:10–17)

The differences are so radical that they appear almost unbridgeable:

- Kings presents Manasseh as irreparably devoted to idolatry and murder. His evil ways seal the fate of Jerusalem. In Chronicles, however, Manasseh's idolatry is a passing event; he repents and restores Jerusalem to monotheism.

- In Kings we hear nothing of Assyrian aggression against Manasseh, no mention of Chronicles' account of the capture, incarceration, and return of the sovereign.

One possible resolution might suggest that the account in Chronicles is historically accurate,[8] yet Kings chooses to omit Manasseh's repentance in favor of the dominant strain in his life, his idolatry. In fact, Kings fails to record even a single anecdote about Manasseh's life. Furthermore, even if Manasseh repented in his later days, the long-term damage his reign wrought was so extreme, the influx of idolatry into the kingdom so prevalent, and the degenerate public culture so pervasive that later attempts at rehabilitation were futile – too little, too late. Thus, Kings ignores Manasseh's repentance, late in life, preferring to present a more comprehensive picture of the king's pernicious historical legacy, even if it does some minor injustice to his personal biography.

KINGS AND CHRONICLES: DISTINCT AGENDAS

We might take this a stage further by noting the variant agendas of Kings and Chronicles. We recall that Kings' central thesis attributes the Temple's destruction and the national exile to the sin of idolatry, targeting

8. Assyrian records describe how the Egyptian Pharaoh Necho was brought to Assyria by Assurbanipal as a prisoner and then restored to his kingship (*Ancient Near Eastern Texts, Relating to the Old Testament*, ed. James B. Pritchard, 3rd ed. [Princeton, NJ: Princeton University Press,1969], 296–97). In light of this, the story of Manasseh seems like a reasonable historical possibility. The historical accuracy of this event is broadly discussed in Jacob Liver's lecture, "The Reign of Manasseh," in Luria, *Studies in the Book of Kings*, 323–48.

One logical problem raised against the Chronicles account is that if Manasseh was indeed captured by the Assyrians, it is probably due to Assyrian concerns of rebellion or disloyalty. In that scenario, it is unlikely that he would have been able to build Jerusalem's wall or to undertake a religious revolution upon his return without again arousing Assyrian suspicions. Liver suggests that the order be reversed. The return to God and the construction in Jerusalem predated his incarceration in Assyria. Manasseh had come under the influence of anti-Assyrian opinion which affected religion and national policy. This policy reversal was precisely the red flag that attracted Assyrian suspicion and led to his imprisonment.

specifically the monarchy as the key culprits. Kings is a prophetic work, not a historical record that recounts each and every detail. As such, it is uninterested in rehabilitating the character of the worst royal offender, conveying a balance between his early sins and his later repentance. Kings looks to condemn Manasseh's idolatry in the harshest terms. A focus upon his repentance can only obscure the message.

The philosophy of Chronicles, on the other hand, reflects other emphases. Chronicles is a Second Temple book that revels in repentance and seeks its promotion.[9] Chronicles wishes to send a message that no matter how bad a person's past, the option of rehabilitation is available. Moreover, it expresses a particular perspective on divine reward and punishment. Prof. Sara Japhet explains:

> The destruction of the kingdom of Judah is explained by [II] Kings in two ways, both articulated in the prophetic speech of 21:11–15....
>
> 1. Jerusalem's destruction was caused by the sins of Manasseh....
> 2. The destruction of the land and the exile are the product of the cumulative sins of all the generations from the Exodus until the present.[10]
>
> Why does God defer the execution of the punishment and not penalize the sinners themselves?...Why is a person punished if they did not sin? Why is there no correlation between the depth of sin and the degree of punishment? This is the basis of the question: "The fathers have eaten sour grapes, and the children's teeth are blunted" (Jer. 31:29). The point is not, why did the fathers eat sour grapes and their teeth were not blunted, but rather, why were the children's teeth blunted for grapes they did not eat.... The main discussion of this topic may be found in the book of Ezekiel. His answer is: "The righteousness of the righteous shall be upon himself, and the wickedness of the wicked shall be upon himself"

9. This is noted by Y. Elitzur in Luria, *Studies in the Book of Kings*, vol. 2, 339.
10. II Kings 21:15.

> (Ezek. 18:20). Actions do not accumulate [intergenerationally], and no generation is punished for the sins of its forebears.
>
> The concept of divine justice in Chronicles is fundamentally identical to that of Ezekiel...the theoretical option that a father sins and that not he but his sons will be punished is deemed inconceivable; every action receives its recompense. And thus in Chronicles, it is unimaginable for the *Ḥurban* to be justified upon the actions of prior generations.... The destruction of the Temple in the reign of Zedekiah is perceived by Chronicles as punishment for the sins of Zedekiah and his generation exclusively. Neither the sins of Manasseh nor the iniquities of other generations were responsible.[11]

According to Japhet, Second Temple society felt condemned by the sins of the past: "Our ancestors sinned and are gone; but we bear the weight of their guilt" (Lam. 5:7). Jeremiah already expresses a shift in the mechanics of divine justice; a "new covenant" is announced in one of the book's most hopeful chapters:

> See, a time is coming, declares the Lord, when I will sow the house of Israel and the house of Judah with seed of men and seed of cattle; just as I was watchful over them to uproot and to pull down, to overthrow and to destroy and to bring disaster, so will I be watchful over them to build and to plant, declares the Lord. In those days, they shall no longer say, "Parents have eaten sour grapes and children's teeth are blunted." But *everyone shall die for his own sins: whosoever eats sour grapes, his teeth shall be blunted.* See, a time is coming, declares the Lord, when I will make a new covenant with the house of Israel and the house of Judah. (Jer. 31:27–31)

As Japhet contends, this philosophy is articulated by the prophet Ezekiel (ch. 18) and later championed by the book of Chronicles, which upholds an ideology that promotes the opportunity for repentance and repair, while maintaining a sense of divine justice in which no generation carries the

11. Japhet, *The Ideology of the Book of Chronicles*, 140–44.

sins of their forebears. As such, Chronicles, in contrast to Kings, reports Manasseh's sins and his punishment. Manasseh's incarceration by the Assyrians is retribution for his idolatry; on the other hand, his long reign represents the reward for his repentance. Everything is balanced and fair.

THE EXTREMES OF GOD'S FORGIVENESS

Following the account in Chronicles, rabbinic tradition presents Manasseh as the most extreme exemplar of the principle that no penitent, however evil, is beyond acceptance and repair. The Talmud relates a dramatic account of Manasseh's humiliation and torture at the hands of his Assyrian captors, and his reluctant rediscovery of God, as a desperate last resort:

> R. Levi said: [The Assyrians] filled a copper cauldron and placed Manasseh inside it and lit a fire under it. When he saw his plight, he called out to every idolatrous deity. When none assisted him, he said, "I remember that my father read me a verse in the synagogue: 'When you are in distress and all these things befall you in the latter days, you shall return to the Lord your God, and listen to His voice… He will not fail you nor destroy you' (Deut. 4:30–31). Now I will cry out to God. If He listens to me, well and good; if not, then all kinds of gods are alike." The angels barricaded the windows of heaven that the prayer of Manasseh would not ascend to God, and they said: "Lord of the world! Are You willing to give gracious hearing to one who has worshipped idols and set up an idol in the Temple?" "If I did not accept the penance of this man," replied God, "I should be closing the door in the face of all repentant sinners." God made a small opening under the throne of His glory and received the prayer of Manasseh through it. (Y. Sanhedrin 10:1)[12]

12. Whereas this passage focuses on God's expansive mercy, see Sanhedrin 101a–b, where R. Akiva sees Manasseh as a paradigm of forgiveness through suffering. For more about the rabbinic view of Manasseh, see H. Mack, "*Ḥazal*'s Manasseh the King of Judah: An Enlightened Biblical Critic," in *B'einei Elohim VeAdam*, ed. Y. Brandes, T. Ganzel, H. Deutsch (Jerusalem: Beit Morasha, 2015), 377–85 [Hebrew].

And on the basis of Chronicles, the great *Amora* R. Yoḥanan contests the statement of the mishna mentioned earlier which lists Manasseh as one of the three evil kings who were denied the afterlife: "R. Yoḥanan said: Anyone who said that Manasseh has no share in the afterlife weakens the hands of repentant sinners."[13]

Paradoxically, the most sinful Judahite king in the book of Kings becomes the archetype of the penitent!

AMON

Amon, Manasseh's son, continues the idolatrous course trod by his father. Kings presents him as "walking in all the paths that his father had walked, serving the idols that his father had served" (21:21). Ḥ*azal* view Amon's actions as an intensification of the wrongdoings of his father: "Manasseh placed [the idolatrous image] in the Temple ... Amon introduced it into the Holy of Holies" (Sanhedrin 103b).

On the basis that Manasseh did indeed repent, Chronicles asserts that Amon failed to learn from his repentance:[14] "[Amon] did not submit to God as his father Manasseh had submitted" (II Chr. 33:23).

Rav Yaakov Medan goes further, basing himself on the Talmud to suggest that Amon forcibly usurped his father's power in order to maintain Manasseh's idolatrous path:

> Amon violated his mother, as it is written, "For [Amon] sinned very much" (II Chr. 33:23). R. Yoḥanan and R. Eleazer [dispute]: One maintained, He burned the Torah; the other, he violated his mother. His mother remonstrated with him: "Do you, then, have any pleasure in the place from where you emerged?" He replied: "Do I do this for any other purpose than to provoke my Creator?" (Sanhedrin 103b)

In our assessment, the talmudic scholars are not necessarily in disagreement. Amon's retort to his mother – "Do I do this for any other purpose than to provoke my Creator?" – may be explained

13. Sanhedrin 103b.
14. Abarbanel. See also L. Ginzburg, *Legends of the Jews*, vol. 4 (Philadelphia: Jewish Publication Society, 1968), 281.

> as a statement of rebellion against his father, and not merely against God. When Manasseh returned from his incarceration [in Assyria] to Jerusalem, and naturally sought to reclaim the reins of power from his son, who ruled in his place during his imprisonment, Amon revolted against his father. The tension between father and son manifested itself in Amon's burning of the Torah, continuing his father's idolatrous policy during his earlier rule.... His rebellion expressed itself further in [Amon's] sexual violation of his mother... in the same manner that Absalom, when he wished to rebel against his father David, was intimate with his father's concubines (II Sam. 16:21–22)... as a statement of his inheritance of his father's rule.[15]

Amon rules for a mere two years, until he is assassinated by his courtiers.[16] His son Josiah will bring the kingdom back to monotheism, making every effort to remove Manasseh's and Amon's idolatry.

* * *

We have offered two divergent images of Manasseh. The first, from the book of Kings, portrays the king as an ardent idolater and a ruthless murderer, akin to the evil King Ahab. The second, from the book of Chronicles, captures a moment, late in life and under duress, in which Manasseh repents and returns to Judaism. We cannot overstate the dramatic difference of perspectives between Kings and Chronicles. For Kings, Manasseh's devastating capitulation to Assyrian religious norms, his full embrace of the "abhorrent practices of the society,"[17] flooding society at every level with idolatry, magic, and superstition, is irrevocable, indelible, and ultimately unforgivable. Manasseh is the king who sends Israel on a direct course toward exile.

---

15. Rav Yaakov Medan, *The Word Is Very Near: Shemot* (Tel Aviv: Miskal-Yedioth Ahronoth / Chemed Books, 2014), 320–21 [Hebrew].
16. See Cogan and Tadmor, 275–76, where they survey academic literature and raise three possible motives for Amon's assassination: political, religious, and royal infighting.
17. *Toa'vot hagoyim*, the practices of the pre-Israelite nations of Canaan. See Lev. 18; Deut. 18:9–14.

II Kings 22–23

Josiah's Religious Revolution

Previous chapters have charted the dramatic twists and turns that characterize the kingdom of Judah in the latter First Temple period: Ahaz's capitulation to Assyrian idolatry is reversed by Hezekiah, who restores national religious purity. Manasseh and Amon dramatically overturn Hezekiah's religious accomplishments, flooding the country with idolatry yet again. And now with Josiah the pendulum swings back once more toward monotheism and loyalty to God.

Of all the kings we have encountered in the book of Kings, Josiah is unsurpassed as a champion of God-worship, cleansing the kingdom of its idolatry and returning the nation to God. No accolade is spared in the enthusiastic assessment of this religiously impassioned king, as reflected in the opening and closing lines of II Kings 22–23:

> He did what was correct in God's eyes…he did not deviate to the right or to the left. (22:2)

> There was no king like him who turned to God with all his heart and soul and might, in full accord with the teachings of Moses, nor afterward did any arise like him. (23:25)[1]

RELIGIOUS ORIENTATION

Josiah rises to the throne at the age of eight, after his father's assassination. Little is documented of his early life. Kings records his religious activity as concentrated in the eighteenth year of his reign, when the king was twenty-six years of age. Chronicles, however, details a more protracted timeline:[2]

> In the eighth year of his reign, while still young, [Josiah] began to seek the God of his father, David, and in the twelfth year he began to purge Judah and Jerusalem of the shrines (*bamot*), the sacred posts, the idols, and the molten images. (II Chr. 34:3)

We don't know what spurred Josiah's devotion to God in contrast to his idolatrous father and grandfather. Did he have an instinctive personal aversion to idolatry and an attraction to monotheism? Or was his religion a new discovery made at age sixteen,[3] a teenage interest that grew into a passion as he matured?

---

1. Note how this verse echoes the *Shema*. These accolades are unique within the royal assessments of the book of Kings, applied exclusively to Josiah. Moreover, Josiah is the only king whose name is predicted, centuries before his birth. See I Kings 13:2; II Kings 23:16. See also David's charge to Solomon in I Kings 2:1–5, where David warns Solomon: "Keep the charge of the Lord your God … as recorded in *the Teaching of Moses* …. Then the Lord will fulfill the promise that He made concerning me: 'If your *descendants* are scrupulous in their conduct, and walk before Me faithfully, *with all their heart and soul*, your line on the throne of Israel shall never end!'" The echo of these verses regarding Josiah suggests that whereas Solomon failed to act faithfully to God and worshipped idolatry in his old age, Josiah succeeded, remaining absolutely loyal to the Law of Moses.
2. Chronicles differs in its order of events. Whereas the story of Josiah in Kings opens with Josiah's Temple renovation, it is the discovery of the *Sefer HaTorah* that stimulates the purge of idolatry. In Chronicles, however, the cull of idolatry predates the finding of the scroll and is merely a product of Josiah's independent commitment to God.
3. See Shabbat 56b, where according to one opinion the word *shav* in II Kings 23:25 indicates that Josiah was a "penitent" who sinned in his early life and then turned to God and even repaired his earlier sins. By contrast, Ralbag (ibid., 22:2) is one of the medievalists who maintain Josiah's righteousness throughout his life.

Who influenced Josiah?[4] When a child-king comes to power, he is not independently managing the kingdom; a group of advisors are effectively in charge. Who are these figures? Are they from the group known as *Am HaAretz* (II Kings 21:24)[5] – the political faction that executed Amon's assassins, possibly an aristocratic association that supported the monarchy in times of instability? One aspect of his guardians' priorities certainly influenced his adult decisions. Josiah gets married, at age fourteen, to Zebudah from the northern town of Rumah (23:36).[6] The choice of a queen from a northern province reflects a policy of national reunification, demonstrating the administration's aspiration to return the northern Israelites to the jurisdiction of Judah, a policy that Josiah later embraces.

A further factor that aids Josiah's religious turnabout is the waning of Assyrian power.[7] The decline of Assyrian influence releases Judah from that kingdom's hefty cultural impact.

RELIGIOUS REVOLUTION

Josiah instigates the most comprehensive and intensive purge of idolatry witnessed in the book of Kings. It begins with the cleansing of the Temple precinct from all idolatrous accoutrements. What follows is a comprehensive disposal of every form of idolatry in the kingdom: Baal,

---

4. Josiah's story resembles that of Joash, another Judahite child king – their names are even similar – who also sets to repairing the Temple. Compare the language of II Kings 11:13, 16, for example, with the identical phrases in 22:6–7. Both stories narrate the downfall of an evil, idolatrous regime, to be replaced by a loyal, monotheistic king. One image common to both stories is of the king standing on an *amud*; see II Kings 11:14; 23:3.

   Joash was raised by the high priest. On the basis of the parallel stories, it may be possible that Josiah's courtiers, Hilkiah the high priest and Shaphan son of Etzaliah, were the God-fearing men who raised the child king. See Yigal Ariel, *Mikdash Melekh* (Hispin, Israel: Midreshet Golan, 1994), 395n15 [Hebrew].
5. See, for example, II Kings 23:30, and also 11:17–19; 15:5. We discuss this group in the chapter entitled "A Murderous Queen," footnote 11.
6. Jehoiakim is their son. He rises to the throne at the age of twenty-five, following Josiah's death. Seeing that Josiah is killed in the thirty-first year of his reign, Jehoiakim would be born in the sixth year of Josiah's reign, when the king is just fourteen years old.
7. Josiah rises to power in 640 BCE. The Assyrian king Assurbanipal dies in 627 BCE, a date that marks the decline of Assyrian power. Nineveh falls into Babylonian hands in 612 BCE.

Ashera (II Kings 23:4), Kadesh (23:7), the sun, moon, and all the hosts of the heaven (23:5), Molekh (23:10), and necromancy and soothsayers (23:24). We read how Josiah dismantles worship sites that had endured in Israel for hundreds of years and no loyal king had dared to expunge: First, the idolatrous shrines of Solomon's wives (23:13–14) in Jerusalem, and then Jeroboam's altars at Bethel (23:15) and Samaria (v. 19). One wonders why these had not been removed in previous royal purges of idolatry, but the thoroughness of Josiah's campaign is impressive and unprecedented. Josiah takes purity of religion a stage further as he destroys the *bamot*, the regional sacrificial altars (23:5, 8). These are dedicated to God, but their location outside the Temple makes them illicit. At no point in Kings have they ceased to function in Judah; here, however, in yet another unrivaled action, Josiah removes them.

This destruction of idolatry culminates in a jubilant celebration of God-worship. Reflecting Hezekiah before him, Josiah instigates a mass observance of Passover in Jerusalem. This festival of God is depicted in terms that indicate its historic significance:

> There had not been a Passover celebration like that since the time when the Judges ruled in Israel, nor throughout all the years of the kings of Israel and Judah. (II Kings 23:22)

What made this event so unique? Rashi points to the sheer numbers of people worshipping and sacrificing to God, a gathering of a size unseen since the days of the prophet Samuel (the tail end of the Judges period). Radak focuses on the combination of national unity – the populations of the north and south together – along with the repudiation of idolatry, another feature of the period of Samuel. This, along with Josiah's destruction of the idolatrous cult of the north, reflects his passion for national unity and cohesion.[8]

JOSIAH FINDS A SEFER TORAH

The catalyst for Josiah's extensive religious campaign is a mysterious occurrence – the discovery of a Torah scroll. How does this come about?

8. Rabbi Binyamin Lau, *Jeremiah* (Jerusalem: Maggid Books, 2013), 17–32.

Josiah's first act as king is the renovation of the Temple. The Temple had fallen into disrepair due to the long period in which God-worship had been neglected;[9] alternatively, the removal of Manasseh's idolatrous icons from the Temple caused quite some damage to the decor.

In the course of the repairs, Hilkiah, the high priest, discovers a Torah scroll. He hands it to Shaphan, a senior government minister:

> Shaphan read it in the presence of the king. When the king heard the words of the Book of the Law (*Sefer Torah*), *he tore his clothes.* Then the king commanded Hilkiah the priest, Ahikam the son of Shaphan, Achbor the son of Michaiah, Shaphan the scribe, and Asaiah the king's servant, saying, "Go, inquire of God for me and the people and all Judah concerning the words of this book that has been found, for great is *the wrath of God that burns against us,* because our fathers have not listened to the words of this book, to do according to all that is written concerning us." (II Kings 22:10–13)

The senior delegation consults with Huldah, a prophetess, and she confirms God's anger as incurred by the people's religious transgression, as specified by the scroll.

The scroll's discovery stimulates Josiah to read the scroll publically, staging a covenantal ceremony in which the people renew their religious commitment. Josiah then proceeds to lead the people in the aforementioned nationwide elimination of idolatry.

But what is the Torah scroll, or *Sefer Torah,* that they discovered? Why did it elicit such alarm among all those who encountered it? And how did this book or scroll communicate the message that God was furious with Israel?

LOST TORAH, LOST RELIGION

Radak suggests that the Torah had been lost to Israel during the period of Manasseh and Amon:

---

9. *Seder Olam* 22 asserts that it had been 218 years since the last renovation of the Temple, in the days of Joash. Indeed, that is the last explicit citation of Temple renovations, but it is difficult to imagine a building of this importance without some constant upkeep and repair.

> Manasseh was a king for an extended period, fifty-five years, and he "did evil in God's eyes, as the abominations of the nations" (II Kings 21:2)...and he caused Torah to be forgotten from Israel. No one was interested in it, for they all turned to other gods and practices of the nations. In those fifty-five years the Torah was forgotten.[10]

Radak asserts that upon the discovery of the *Sefer Torah*, "they realized how they had forgotten the Torah, which prohibits all the evil practices that Israel was engaged in." According to Radak, the shock that gripped Josiah and his officials was a result of their sudden exposure to areas of Jewish law of which they were entirely unaware.

In order to put this reading in a realistic context, let us appreciate that with Manasseh's fifty-five-year reign, followed by Amon's two year rule and the sixteen years of Josiah's reign until the Torah's discovery, we have seventy-three years in which foreign religious norms held sway in mainstream Judahite society. A period of this length can certainly result in a total erosion of any real Jewish knowledge and practice. If we can give a contemporary example, we may want to consider Soviet Jewry, a community with a rich and vibrant Jewish heritage of scholarship and observance, which was starved of its Judaism from the Russian Revolution until the fall of the Soviet Union in 1991 – seventy-four years! After a duration of that length, how much endured of substantial Judaism? How many practiced mitzvot in any significant way? If indeed the kingdom was swamped by idolatry during the Manasseh, Amon, and early Josiah period, we can well imagine the absence of Torah scrolls and the shock that the rediscovery of the law would give a young king who is looking to rediscover the religion of his fathers.

---

10. Radak also addresses Manasseh's repentance, as mentioned in Chronicles: If Manasseh had repented, would he not have ensured that Torah scrolls would have been written and distributed nationally? Radak's answer is that Manasseh repented so late in life that his religious reversal had little time to influence Judahite norms. Furthermore, his repentance was limited to an understanding that idolatry was forbidden, and as such, "he destroyed the idolatry when he repented, but did not set his heart to search for scrolls of the Law."

Moses' Torah Scroll

Kings talks about discovering "*the* Torah scroll," and Chronicles talks about "the book of the Torah of God, *by the hand of Moses*" (II Chr. 34:14). For this reason, many commentaries[11] see the book as an ancient Torah scroll, indeed the original Torah written by Moses himself at the end of his life (Deut. 31:26). Abarbanel writes:

> *Ḥazal* say (Sanhedrin 102b) that Manasseh would erase God's name from Torah scrolls and replace it with idolatrous names. Hence, one of the priests feared that if Moses' Torah scroll were to come into the king's hands, [Manasseh] would remove the divine names here too and replace them. And so he hid the scroll in a chamber between the walls. In Josiah's initial period, when he returned to God... the priests failed to find the scroll. But when they came to repair the house, Hilkiah found it between the walls and it was like finding a treasure; as such he said, "I have found *the* Torah scroll" .... It would not have generated such fright had it not been the selfsame Torah scroll that was penned by Moses' holy hands, directly from the Almighty.

We have identified the specific Torah scroll, but we have yet to appreciate why it generated such panic. Abarbanel boosts his interpretation with yet another detail:

> The Rabbis in the Jerusalem Talmud[12] explain that normally Moses' scroll was rolled to its beginning, but when they discovered it, they opened it at the verse: "God shall bring you, and your king which you shall set over you, to a nation which neither you nor your fathers have known" (Deut. 28:36). The king was alarmed; he saw the entire event as a miracle and a divine sign regarding the future.

The verse in question is a covenantal segment of Deuteronomy known as the *tokhaḥa*, the "rebuke," that forewarns of the paradigm in which

11. Josephus; Radak; *Daat Mikra*.
12. Y. Shekalim 6:1; Yoma 52b. The full midrash appears in Deuteronomy Rabba 27:26.

national sin and abrogation of the covenant with God will engender the land's desolation and national exile. This approach certainly fits into the narrative context, as we hear Hulda's terrible prediction:

> This is what the Lord says: I am going to bring disaster on this place and its people, according to everything written in the book the king of Judah has read. Because they have forsaken Me and burned incense to other gods and aroused My anger by all the idols their hands have made. (II Kings 22:16–17)

The King's Scroll

The Seforno (Deut. 31:26) offers a third interpretation. He suggests that the scroll found was indeed Moses's scroll, but not the five books of the Torah:

> It seems that the book found by Hilkiah was the scroll that Moses entrusted to the priests (Deut. 31:9)... containing only the "portion of the king" (Deut. 17:14–18), and in that scroll, Joshua recorded the covenant that he enacted between the nation [of Israel and God] in Shechem (see Josh. 24:26): that they should commit themselves to serve God in true devotion, in ideas and in action. When Josiah read this and realized how much they had diverged from it, he was fearful and sought God.

Seforno suggests that this was a special scroll written for the king. If we understand his comment in context, he would be referring to the scroll with selected texts that was read during the *Hak'hel* ceremony,[13] and which accompanied the king on a constant basis.[14] The passages in

---

13. Mishna Sota 7:8: "The portion read by the king: How so? At the conclusion of the first day of the festival (Sukkot) in the eighth [year], at the end of the seventh [Sabbatical] year... he reads from the beginning of 'These are the words' (Deut. 1:1) until the *Shema* (ibid., 6:4–9); and the *Shema*; and 'It will come to pass if you hear' (ibid., 11:13–21); and 'You shall surely tithe' (ibid., 14:22–29); and 'When you have finished tithing' (ibid., 26:12–15); and the portion of the king (ibid., 17:14–20); and the blessings and curses (ibid., ch. 28), until he finishes all the section."
14. The King shall "have a copy of this Teaching (*Torah*) written for him on a scroll by the levitical priests. Let it remain with him and let him read in it all his life, so that

the scroll were designed to spur the nation, "that they may hear and so learn to revere the Lord your God and to observe faithfully every word of this Teaching…to revere the Lord your God as long as they live in the land that you are about to cross the Jordan to possess" (Deut. 31:12–13). Seforno suggests that it additionally contained the text of Joshua's covenantal ceremony, held at the end of his life: "Joshua wrote all these things in the scroll of the Law of God" (Josh. 24:26).

This creative solution circumvents the issue of the absence of Torah scrolls in ancient Israel, a situation that would imply a total disruption of the tradition. It also furnishes an interesting understanding as to the king's shock upon reading the document, as it is unlikely he would have been familiar with a text from Joshua's era. Whether the content of the scroll was select texts from the Deuteronomy covenant or Joshua's covenantal speech, both are directed at the repudiation of idolatry and seem particularly suited to this historical juncture.[15]

---

he may learn to revere the Lord his God, to observe faithfully every word of this Teaching as well as these laws. Thus he will not act haughtily toward his fellows or deviate from the Instruction to the right or to the left" (Deut. 17:18–20).

15. We would be remiss in discussing Josiah's Torah scroll without at least a reference to De Wette, who in 1805 identified the "Book of the Law" discovered by Hilkiah as Deuteronomy. This theory, later adopted by Wellhausen, has become an accepted maxim in biblical academic scholarship. Essentially, it proposes that Deuteronomy was composed in the late seventh century BCE, and this "new" Mosaic history was passed off as an ancient text. The theory suggests that the legislation of a central and exclusive worship site was a new initiative, developed in Josiah's religious purge, and it constituted a radical shift from earlier Judaism which had permitted the *bamot*. Whereas Exodus allows worship "in every place where I cause My name to be remembered, [where] I will come to you and bless you" (Ex. 20:24), Deuteronomy restricts sacrifice to "the place which God will choose" (Deut. 12:5, 11, 14). Josiah's destruction of the *bamot* and other icons reflects Deuteronomy's condemnation of worship outside the Temple (ibid., 12:13–14) and the injunction, "You shall tear down their altars, smash their monuments, burn their *asherim* with fire" (ibid., 12:3).

    These observations, corroborated by significant linguistic commonalities between Deuteronomy and later prophetic books, led to the conclusion that Deuteronomy or critical sections of it – the "discovered" scroll – had in fact been composed by the priests of Josiah's period, in order to stimulate Josiah's religious reforms. [See a concise summary of the arguments in *The Jewish Study Bible*, A. Berlin and M. Z. Brettler, eds. (New York: Oxford University Press, 2004), 357–58.]

Seforno's approach is particularly attractive, as the "Book of the Covenant" becomes the centerpiece of Josiah's religious revival when it is publically read, seemingly several times – first to the elders of Jerusalem, and then to a wider audience:

> At the king's summons, all the elders of Judah and Jerusalem assembled before him. The king went up to the house of the Lord, together with all the men of Judah and all the inhabitants of Jerusalem, and the priests and prophets – all the people, young and old. And he read to them the entire text of the "covenant scroll" which had been found in the house of the Lord. The king stood by the pillar and solemnized the covenant before the Lord: that they would follow the Lord and observe His commandments, His injunctions, and His laws with all their heart and soul; that they would fulfill all the terms of this covenant

---

Needless to say, from a traditional Jewish faith perspective, the entire Pentateuch originates from Moses during the period of the Wilderness. But even modern scholars have backed off De Wette's highly speculative claim of Deuteronomy's Josianic authorship, noting that Deuteronomy does not match Josiah's reform in all its details. Josiah's father, Hezekiah, had already centralized worship in Jerusalem some one hundred years previously. Moreover, Deuteronomy does single out a particular locale for worship and a national covenantal ceremony, but that is Shechem (Deut. 27), in the north, hardly aligned with Josiah. Scholars also observe that Deuteronomy's laws reflect a rural environment that fails to reflect Josiah's era: there is no standing army, no rules of government or bureaucratic procedure, no king's court, and the laws hardly portray a nation with major urban agglomerations. As such, scholars propose a more complex, layered authorship, with its origins in an earlier period (see J. Kugel, *How to Read the Bible* [New York: The Free Press, 2007], 308–15).

One further detail worth noting regards the word *bama* and its plural, *bamot*, which are so prominent in Kings; together they appear thirty-five times. In Kings these altars reflect a nagging and unresolvable problem. However, neither the word *bama* nor the word *bamot* is invoked by Deuteronomy, not even once! If Deuteronomy were written to stimulate Josiah's reform of central worship, it seems strange that it would avoid this key term.

Entire volumes have been written on this topic, and a short footnote does little justice to such a religiously charged and textually complex debate. For more of the academic discussion challenging the Josianic origins of Deuteronomy, see *Encyclopedia Mikrait* (The Biblical Encyclopedia), vol. 2, col. 611, "Deuteronomy"; Y. M. Grintz, "The Narrative of King Josiah's Reform," in *Studies in the Book of Kings*, 351–69.

> as inscribed upon the scroll. And all the people entered into the covenant. (II Kings 23:1–3)

This public reading of the "scroll of the covenant" is a key feature of covenantal ceremonies, first at Mount Sinai itself (Ex. 24:4–8), then before Moses' death (Deut. 28:69; 29:9–28; 31:28), and later at Mount Ebal after Joshua leads Israel into the land of Canaan (Josh. 8:30–35). Each of these mass gatherings served to confirm Israel's commitment to Torah.[16] The *Hak'hel* ceremony in which the Torah is publically read by the king is similarly an opportunity, every seven years, for the nation en masse to refresh and restate its commitment to the Torah. It is appropriate that this ancient tradition serves to spearhead Josiah's religious revolution.

JOSIAH'S TRAGIC DEATH

Josiah's religious reform is dated to the eighteenth year of his reign. Only thirteen years later, he is killed in battle:

> In his days, Pharaoh Necho, king of Egypt, marched against the king of Assyria to the River Euphrates; King Josiah went to meet him, but he [Pharaoh Necho] killed him at Megiddo when he saw him. His servants conveyed his body by chariot from Megiddo to Jerusalem and they buried him in his tomb. (II Kings 23:29–30)

A single verse records Josiah's surprising and tragic death in battle. This military skirmish raises many questions. What was King Josiah looking for in his encounter with Pharaoh Necho? Why did the confrontation

16. See M. Greenberg, "The Israelite Faith in the Period of the Monarchs: Stability and Ferment," in *The History of the People of Israel, vol. 1: The Age of the Monarchies: Culture and Society*, ed. A. Malamet (Jerusalem: Am Oved, 1982), 76 [Hebrew]. He suggests that texts such as Psalm 81 were the basis for regular covenantal ceremonies convened on festive days. Psalm 81 combines the blowing of the shofar on a festival with a remembrance of the Exodus, as well as a call for covenantal loyalty, consequences for nonobservance, and the reward for following the law.

take place at Megiddo? Why did Necho kill Josiah at the moment he saw him?

Historical sources inform us that the Egyptian army was headed to battle against the Babylonian army at Carchemish, by the Euphrates.[17] The Assyrian city of Nineveh had just fallen to Babylonian forces. This defeat signaled the crumbling of Assyrian hegemony and the rise of a new regional force – Babylonia. With these tectonic shifts in the regional balance of power, Egypt, allied with Assyria, could not sit by and merely observe. Necho sought to destroy Babylonia's power before it gained full traction, thereby impeding the rise of the nascent Babylonian empire and army.

The most direct route for Necho's troops was along the coastal highway that runs through the Land of Israel. Megiddo was a fortress at the gateway to the Jezreel Valley; its access from the coast passes by way of a gorge which creates a natural bottleneck. This was an obvious strategic point from which to attack an advancing force. However, it appears that the Judahite military were no match for the Egyptian army. Chronicles records Pharaoh Necho's initial reluctance to enter into hostilities against Josiah: "What is between me and you, O King of Judah? I do not march against you this day, but against the kingdom that wars with me… refrain from interfering with me" (II Chr. 35:21). Despite this, Josiah refuses to desist. The army of Judah attacks; Necho's archers seek out the king. Once the king is killed, the battle is over.

What was Josiah's motivation in obstructing Pharaoh Necho's northward march? Speculations abound. Was Josiah interested in supporting Babylonia against Assyria?[18] Or possibly, having enjoyed a period of independence from a controlling superpower and witnessing Egypt's attempts to dominate the regional space, Josiah was concerned that he would become subject to Egyptian control. This motivated him to confront the newly crowned Pharaoh and repel his advance.[19] Tragically this was a gamble that failed.

---

17. The account in II Chr. 35 offers more detail.
18. Cogan and Tadmor, *II Kings*, 300.
19. See *Olam HaTanakh*, 203–4.

A RIGHTEOUS GENERATION?

The Talmud debates Josiah's motivation in his opposition to Pharaoh Necho. After all, Necho explicitly states his nonviolent intent. The talmudic discussion takes us to Leviticus, where the Torah promises, "If you follow My laws... no sword shall pass through the land" (26:1–6):

> Rav Judah said in the name of Rav: ...Josiah said [to himself], "Since he [Pharaoh Necho] puts his trust in his idols I will prevail over him." ... R. Shmuel b. Naḥmani said in the name of R. Yoḥanan: Why was Josiah punished? Because he failed to consult with Jeremiah.[20] On what did Josiah rely? On the divine promise contained in the words, "And no sword shall pass through your land" (Lev. 26:6). What sword? Is it the warring sword? It is already stated [in the same verse], "And I will give peace in the land" (Lev. 26:6); it must then refer to the peaceful sword. Josiah, however, did not know that his generation found but little favor [in the eyes of God]. (Taanit 22b)

This talmudic passage overlays two themes. First, Josiah perceived his reign, his era, as the realization of the divine blessings that promise peace "if you follow My laws" (Lev. 26). In other words, Josiah understood the good fortune and prosperity that characterized his period as a reward for his return to monotheism. But this pious complacency caused Josiah to make mistakes. Despite Necho's nonaggressive intent, Josiah believed that he had heavenly backing in preventing Necho from passing through the Land of Israel. From the Talmud, one senses that Josiah overestimated God's direct and immediate protection.

---

20. See M. Avioz, "Josiah's Death in the Book of Kings: A New Solution to an Old Theological Conundrum," *Ephemerides Theologicae Lovanienses* 83 (2007): 359–66. Avioz explains that the king's refusal to petition the prophet was the sin for which he lost his life. King David always consulted with God before battle, whereas King Saul did not. Jehoshaphat always consulted with God before going to war (I Kings 22:5; II Kings 3:11). Hezekiah consulted with Isaiah when confronted by war and was censured when he failed to do so. Thus when Josiah fails to appeal to the prophet, he loses the battle, and his life.

In a celebrated passage, in a speech that marked the passing of Theodore Herzl, Rav Abraham Isaac Kook advocates for a fusion of Zionism and Torah. To illustrate the Jewish need for the power and infrastructure of the modern state in partnership with the values and norms of religion, Rav Kook turns to Josiah, depicting him as a man who represented an imbalance in the system; he was religiously impassioned and devout, but his spiritual zeal overwhelmed his political decisions and ultimately brought his spiritual revolution to an end:

> Josiah elevated the spiritual aspect as no king before or after him.... To that end, he wanted Israel to have no relationship with the nations of the world. He therefore did not heed the words of Jeremiah, who advised him, in God's name, to allow the Egyptians to pass through Israel's territory.[21]

Josiah's simple faith, which fueled his determination for national spiritual isolation, cost him his life, and tragically terminated his religious revolution.

WHAT IS BEHIND THE DOOR?

But Josiah missed the mark in a second area: he misappraised the religious revolution that he had wrought. In a colorful and insightful image, the Midrash lays the blame for Josiah's demise not with Josiah personally, but rather with the wider population, who angered God:

> Josiah did not know that his entire generation worshipped idols. What did the scoffers of his generation do? They would put half of the [idolatrous] image on one door, and half on the other door. [Josiah] would send ... men to purge their homes from idolatry. They would enter but find nothing. As they left, [the idolaters] would have them close the door, so that on the inside, the idolatrous images would be reconstituted [as a single icon]. (Lamentations Rabba 1:18)

21. "The Lamentation in Jerusalem," in Bezalel Naor, *When God Becomes History: Historical Essays of Rabbi Abraham Isaac HaKohen Kook* (New York: Kodesh Press, 2016), 21–50.

This creative midrashic tale talks about homes in which idolatrous icons were painted on a double door, which was the entrance to the house. When the doors were open, they folded back against the wall, and as such the icons were hidden from view. Josiah's inspectors failed to find them, and yet the minute the supervisors left and the doors were again closed, the icon sprang back into full view of the inhabitants of the house. This imagery illustrates a deep disconnect between the king and the nation. From Josiah's vantage point the country had become overwhelmingly committed to God and His Torah, but the midrash contends that Josiah's religious revolution had failed to penetrate society. The monotheistic commitment, while adopted by public institutions, failed to seep deeper into the hearts and minds, into the living rooms, of the average citizen of Judah. This is hardly surprising; Josiah's religious revolution held sway for a mere thirteen years. It is difficult to imagine that thirteen years can uproot norms that have been entrenched for over seventy years. Josiah was out of touch with the facts on the ground; the nation was still dabbling in idolatry.

THE LOOMING SPECTER OF *ḤURBAN*

This last point should explain a certain ambivalence or even dissonance that characterizes the depiction of Josiah's period in our texts. On the one hand, no king is acclaimed quite like Josiah. But at the same time, this is a period in which we repeatedly witness predictions of *Ḥurban*:[22]

22. The prophecy of Hulda in II Kings 22:16–19 expresses a similar duality: prediction of *Ḥurban* alongside personal approval of Josiah.

Ḥazal emphasize Josiah's keen awareness of the imminent demise of the Temple when they assert that he hid away the Ark of the Covenant to ensure it would not be seized by the enemy (Yoma 53b). They draw this conclusion on the basis of the verse in II Chr. 35:3 in which Josiah instructs the priests, "Put the Holy Ark in the Temple…you no longer need to carry it back and forth on your shoulders. Now spend your time serving the Lord your God and His people Israel," and also Jer. 3:16–17: "In those days…people will no longer say, 'The Ark of the Covenant of God.' It will never enter their minds or be remembered; it will not be missed, nor will another one be made. At that time they will call Jerusalem the throne of God." Both sources might be read as implying that the Ark is being taken out of use. See also Mishna Shekalim 6:1–2; Maimonides, *Mishneh Torah*, Laws of the Temple 4:1, 2; Maccabees

> Before him there was no king like him, who turned to God with all his heart and with all his soul and with all his might, according to all the Law of Moses; nor did any like him arise after him. Still, God did not turn from the burning of His great fury, by which His anger was kindled against Judah, because of all the provocations of Manasseh. God said, "I will remove Judah from My sight, as I have removed [the northern kingdom of] Israel, and I will spurn this city that I have chosen, Jerusalem, and the house of which I said 'My name shall be there.'" (II Kings 23:25–27)

God's decree strikes us as terribly unfair. Judah has reached a point at which the nation is led by a pious king, possibly the most religious of all time. Josiah has expunged idolatry comprehensively, expending every effort to correct past wrongs. In this highly positive environment, should the sins of a past sovereign really obscure the virtues of Josiah? What about the value of repentance? How could God hold on to the sins of Manasseh while ignoring Josiah's radical religious reforms?

But this would be a misreading of the situation. Although the king was religiously impassioned, the rank and file of the nation were disconnected. Public life had changed, but inside, people's private beliefs and their personal religious commitments remained unaltered:

> Wander the streets of Jerusalem, look around and inquire, and seek in her squares whether there is but one man who does justice, who seeks truthfulness, and I will forgive her. Though they say, "As the Lord lives," they are surely swearing falsely. (Jer. 5:1–2)

As Jeremiah testifies, people used religious language, but it was empty of meaning. In this sense, Manasseh's evil period overwhelmed and eclipsed Josiah's revolution. Josiah's reforms were insufficient to eradicate the idolatry and the corruption from the minds and hearts of the people.

2:4–8, all of whom all cite the tradition of the Ark being placed in hiding. Yoma 53b also records the dissenting opinions of R. Eliezer and R. Shimon b. Yochai that the Ark was exiled to Babylonia when the Temple was destroyed.

JEREMIAH'S PERSPECTIVE: IS THERE A POINT OF NO RETURN?

Kings conveys the impression that the cultural fallout from the spiritually ruinous period of Manasseh had left the country incurable, and consequently the Temple's destruction and the national exile were inevitable and inescapable. But from a prophetic perspective, is there a point of no return at which repentance is not accepted?

I believe the situation is more complex. The prophet Jeremiah begins his mission in the thirteenth year of Josiah's reign and his tenure extends forty years, until after the national exile. Most of his prophecy reflects the foreboding of the impending national calamity: "From the north shall disaster break loose upon all the inhabitants of the land" (Jer. 1:14). The message with which he is charged is certainly a violent one – "To uproot and to smash, to destroy and overthrow" – but the possibility of repair, "to build and to plant" (Jer. 1:10), is always present. In this regard, it is important to note that notwithstanding the damage of Manasseh's era, and even after the death of Josiah,[23] the prophet Jeremiah never relinquishes the possibility that disaster may be averted; he calls for repentance until the eleventh hour. Here he speaks in God's name:

> At one moment I may decree that a nation or kingdom is to be uprooted, torn down, and destroyed. *But if that nation against which I made the decree turns back from its wickedness, then I will relent and not inflict on it the disaster I had planned*.... Now, therefore, say to the people of Judah and the inhabitants of Jerusalem... I am preparing a disaster for you and devising a plan against you. *Turn back from your evil ways,* each one of you, and mend your ways and your actions. (Jer. 18:7–11)

Kings is composed from a post-*Ḥurban* perspective. In hindsight, it assesses the collateral damage of Manasseh's reign as signaling the death knell for the kingdom of Judah. However, in real time, as events unfolded,

23. Jer. 22:1–4; 25:5; 26:2, 13; 36:3.

Jeremiah insists that no moment was too late for the kingdom to change course and save itself.[24]

Josiah stands supreme in his fervent campaign against idolatry and his enthusiastic national covenantal ceremony for which he gathers the nation at the Temple and has them pledge allegiance to the Torah and the covenant. Kings acclaims Josiah as superior to all previous and future kings. He was also known for his "justice and righteousness,"[25] yet another aspect of the Torah to which he adhered.

The structure of the biblical text underscores and intensifies the sense of unjustness surrounding Josiah's untimely demise. It lists all of Josiah's accolades, and then, surprisingly, references God's enduring anger: "*Still God did not turn from the burning of His great fury*... against Judah, because of all the provocations of Manasseh. God said, 'I will remove Judah from My sight.'" Finally, it narrates Josiah's death. The reader is left with the distinct impression that the righteous Josiah was an unfair victim, that his deep righteousness was unable to abate the fierce divine fury that had abided since Manasseh's reign.

It is for this reason that Josiah's tragic and untimely death is marked by an outpouring of national mourning,[26] unprecedented in its intensity:

> Jeremiah composed laments for Josiah, and all the singing men and the singing women spoke of Josiah in their laments as is done to this day. They were customary in Israel; and behold, they are written in the lamentations.[27] (II Chr. 35:25)

---

24. Still, it should be noted that Jeremiah is divinely proscribed from praying on the people's behalf; see Jer. 7:16; 11:14; 14:11–12, all of which indicate that he may not directly interfere with the divine decree.
25. Ibid., 22:15–16.
26. The Talmud (Megilla 3a) portrays the mourning after Josiah's death in battle as a paradigm of public grief, as it applies the verse in Zechariah 12:11, "On that day shall there be a great mourning in Jerusalem, like the mourning of Hadadrimmon in the valley of Megiddon," to the funeral of "Josiah, son of Amon, who was slain by Pharaoh Necho in the valley of Megiddon."
27. Some suggest that this refers to segments of the biblical book Lamentations. See, for example, Tosefta Taanit 2:10.

II Kings 24

Decline toward *Ḥurban*

In the aftermath of Josiah's unexpected death, events plunge downward as Kings succinctly narrates the exhausting and painful descent to national disintegration. The last four kings of Judah struggle under the crippling hegemony first of Egypt and then of Babylonia, suffering military defeat, vassalage, humiliation, deportation, siege, and torture. The sun is setting on the First Temple period and it will soon end in the conquest of Jerusalem, the exile of its people, and the Temple's destruction.

These tragic years may be represented as two parallel sequences of equal duration, the first under Egyptian domination and the second under Babylonian rule:

Name of king and source in II Kings	Duration of rule	Timeline
Jehoahaz 23:31–35	3 Months	23:31 – Jehoahaz reigns for 3 months. 23:33 – Jehoahaz is imprisoned by Pharaoh; Pharaoh taxes the kingdom of Judah. 23:34 – Pharaoh replaces Jehoahaz with his brother Eliakim, and renames him Jehoiakim. Jehoahaz is deported to Egypt.

Name of king and source in II Kings	Duration of rule	Timeline
Jehoiakim 23:36–24:6	11 Years	23:36 – Jehoiakim reigns for 11 years. 24:1 – Jehoiakim rebels against Babylonia. 24:2–4 – Military attacks on Judah, reflecting God's decree.
24:7 – Transition: Babylonia rises as the regional power		
Jehoiachin 24:8–25:7	3 Months	24:8 – Jehoiachin reigns for 3 months. 24:12 – Jehoiachin is imprisoned by Nebuchadnezzar. 24:13 – Nebuchadnezzar takes Temple and palace treasuries. 24:17 – Nebuchadnezzar replaces Jehoiachin with Mattaniah and renames him Zedekiah. 24:15 – Jehoiachin is deported to Babylonia.
Zedekiah 24:18–25:7	11 Years	24:18 – Zedekiah reigns for 11 years. 24:20 – Zedekiah rebels against Babylonia. Ch. 25 – Babylonia attacks Jerusalem; Temple is destroyed.

JEHOAHAZ

Jehoahaz[1] is crowned king by the *Am HaAretz*, the powerful aristocratic group. As Jehoahaz is not the oldest of Josiah's children, there must have been a good reason for his selection. Some speculate that he held pro-Babylonian and anti-Egyptian political views, and the ruling *Am HaAretz* faction selected him in order to continue Josiah's anti-Egyptian political orientation, the same policy that had brought about Josiah's tragic death.

1. See Jer. 22:11; I Chr. 3:15, in which he is called Shalum. It seems that Jehoahaz was a name he adopted when he ascended the throne.

Upon Pharaoh Necho's return to the region from war,[2] he enacts a series of measures that express his dominance of Judah. First he replaces King Jehoahaz with his older brother Eliakim, exiling Jehoahaz to Egypt. Jehoahaz had been on the throne for a mere three months. As an expression of his control, Necho renames Eliakim as Jehoiakim. Necho's choice evidently reflects Jehoiakim as more favorably disposed toward Egyptian rule.[3] Finally, Necho imposes a crushing tribute upon the new king.

TAXATION

Jehoiakim ascends the throne burdened with a huge, Egyptian-imposed tax tribute. How does he finance it? His direct source of income is the upper classes of society:

> Jehoiakim gave Pharaoh the silver and the gold, and he made an assessment of the land to pay the money demanded by Pharaoh. He exacted the silver and gold from the *Am HaAretz* according to the assessment, to pay Pharaoh Necho. (II Kings 23:35)

Although the landed upper classes are directly responsible for funding the national tribute, it is the lowest social stratum of society that pays the real price, as the aristocracy reduces the pay of manual laborers, insulating their own fortunes. This situation results in widespread exploitation of the poor, a societal travesty that is roundly condemned by the prophet. When the king initiates an ostentatious building project and it is the peasantry that pays the price, the prophet Jeremiah visits the sovereign with a foreboding message:

> Thus says the Lord: Go down to the palace of the king of Judah, where you shall utter this word.... Do what is just and right; res-

2. Dated by Babylonian sources to Tammuz 609 BCE.
3. *Olam HaTanakh*; *Daat Mikra*. Both commentaries also suggest the possibility that the decision may have been a product of intra-palace politics relating to the relative influence of Hamutal (Jehoahaz's mother) and Zevuda (Jehoiakim's mother).

cue from the defrauder him who is robbed; do not oppress the stranger, the fatherless, and the widow; commit no violent act and do not shed the blood of the innocent in this place.[4]

Woe to him who builds his house with unfairness and his upper chambers with injustice, who makes his fellow man work without pay, and does not give him his wages. Who thinks: I will build me a vast palace[5] with spacious upper chambers, provided with windows paneled in cedar, painted with vermilion!... Your father ate and drank and dispensed justice and equity – then all went well with him. He upheld the rights of the poor and

4. See II Kings 24:4, which records the wanton bloodshed of Jehoiakim's era, thereby linking and equating his murderous regime with that of Manasseh (ibid., 21:16). In truth, the text is highly ambiguous, and it is difficult to discern whether the bloodshed is that of Manasseh or of Jehoiakim. For an episode in which Jehoiakim hunts down and kills an innocent prophet, see Jer. 26:22–23.
5. Some see the Ramat Rachel archaeological site, dated by Yochanan Aharoni to the period of Jehoiakim, as a possible candidate for this palace. Aharoni writes:

> We did not expect a ruler of the kingdom of Judah to have built a royal palace and fort outside the borders of ancient Jerusalem, on the road between Bethlehem and Jerusalem. Above ground level, we found massive hewn stones of a type not usually used in that period, except in palaces and luxury buildings. In the stratum from the period of the destruction of the Temple, we found the handle of a pitcher that had been sealed with a Hebrew inscription: "[belonging] to Eliakim, lad of Jokhan." Albright identified the Jokhan of the inscription with Jokhinu, mentioned in Assyrian writings – none other than Jehoiakim's son Jeconiah [Jehoiachin], who ruled only three months before he was exiled to Babylonia.
>
> It is unusual in itself for a king to build a palace outside the city. It is evident from the few remains that were preserved that this was without a doubt a most magnificent palace, built with the most advanced architectural and artistic techniques of the period. In this context, it is fitting to cite the verses from Jer. 36:22 which describe how Baruch son of Neriah brought the scroll of Jeremiah's prophecy to Jehoiakim, who flung it upon the blazing brazier. It states there that "the king sat in the winter house." "Winter house" implies that he also had a summer house.... It makes sense that Jehoiakim's summer home would be located among the vineyards outside the city, next to Ramat Rachel. What a unique case in the history of biblical archaeology: The cedar window panes displayed in the Israel Museum are the very panes that Jeremiah faced as he prophesied. (Y. Aharoni, "Woe to Him Who Builds His House with Unfairness," in Luria, *Studies in Jeremiah* 2, 53–67 [Hebrew])

> needy – then all was well. That is truly heeding Me, declares the Lord. (Jer. 22:1, 3, 13–16)

Jeremiah informs the king that his rule would endure only if he desisted from the corruption that prevailed in his kingdom.

Whereas Kings renders sparse information about Jehoiakim's period, passages such as this from Jeremiah offer a window into life under Jehoiakim: huge financial pressure, the maltreatment of the poor, and political executions for enemies of the crown.[6]

NATIONAL INDIFFERENCE

Judah's affiliation with Egypt remains firm during Jehoiakim's early years, but then the geopolitical pendulum begins to swing in the opposite direction. In Jehoiakim's fourth year, 605 BCE, the Babylonian Nebuchadnezzar succeeds his father, Nabopolassar, and takes the reins of his kingdom. He immediately battles Egypt at their advance base in Carchemish and roundly defeats the Egyptian forces. He advances southward to the Mediterranean coast, capturing Ashkelon a year later. The tide has changed direction, and now Babylonia, not Egypt, is the dominant force in the region. This transition is succinctly phrased in II Kings:

> The king of Egypt did not venture out of his country again, for the king of Babylonia had seized all the land that had belonged to the king of Egypt, from the Wadi of Egypt to the River Euphrates. (24:7)

We don't know precisely at what point Judah came under Babylonian control, but notwithstanding Jeremiah's repeated warnings of exile and destruction, the people of Judah and Jerusalem remained complacent.

6. One such example would appear to be the assassination of the prophet Uriah son of Shemaiah, who prophesies against government policy and warns of the destruction of the Temple "at the start of the reign of Jehoiakim." A death sentence is pronounced against him, and although he flees to Egypt, Jehoiakim effects his extradition and he is executed in Jerusalem. Jeremiah almost meets a similar fate; see Jer. 26:20–24.

Why did they not perceive the danger? Why were they deaf to the prophet's warnings? We may point to a dual cause.

> The word which came to Jeremiah from the Lord: Stand at the gate of the house of God and there proclaim this word: … All you of Judah who enter these gates to worship God … mend your ways and your actions, and I will let you dwell in this place. Don't put your trust in illusions and say, "The Temple of God, the Temple of God, the Temple of God!" … You are relying on illusions that are of no avail. Will you steal and murder and commit adultery and swear falsely, and sacrifice to Baal, and follow other gods[7] … and then come stand before Me in this house which bears My name and say, "We are safe!" … Do you consider this house which bears My name to be a den of thieves? (Jer. 7:1–11)

Jeremiah preaches at the Temple gates. He accuses the nation of transgressing the Ten Commandments, of committing a grievous array of sins. He suggests that the Temple ritual cannot remedy or mask the corruption that characterizes Jerusalem's society. And yet the people remain dispassionate and unworried, saying, "We are safe!" Why are people unalarmed by the advancing Babylonians and the prophet's harsh predictions? Because they believe that the Temple of God is invincible, that God will never destroy His own house. This attitude became entrenched in the wake of the previous imperial invasion – that of Sennacherib of Assyria during Hezekiah's reign. Then, the towns and countryside of Judah were ravaged, but Jerusalem was miraculously spared. That powerful memory spawned a popular belief that God would never wreak ruin and destruction upon His Temple, and as a result, the people regarded any threat thereafter with nonchalance. Jeremiah looks to shake them from their apathy by reminding them of an alternative historical precedent:

7. Jeremiah's reference to murder, adultery, stealing, false oaths, and idolatry expresses the violation of the Ten Commandments.

> Just go to My place at Shiloh, where I had established My name originally, and see what I did to it because of the wickedness of My people Israel. And now, because you do all these things… I will do to the house which bears My name, on which you rely…just what I did to Shiloh. And I will cast you out of My presence as I cast out your brothers, the whole offspring of Ephraim. (7:12–15)

Shiloh was the original site of the ancient Tabernacle (the Mishkan), and yet God destroyed it due to the wickedness of Israel. God promises that the Temple will suffer the same fate if Israel continues its reprehensible way of living. The prophet's message is that the actions of the people alone will determine Jerusalem's fate. Neither the Temple nor any other factor can bestow automatic immunity.

BURNING THE WORDS OF THE PROPHET

Whereas this prophecy offers some insight into the complacency of the nation in this period, a second story displays yet another factor in the national imperviousness to God's warnings.

In Jehoiakim's fifth year, as Ashkelon is captured by the Babylonians, a fast day is called in Jerusalem.[8] Nebuchadnezzar's arrival in the region was viewed with considerable anxiety, and this day of prayer and fasting may indicate that the people were now more receptive to Jeremiah's warnings of an impending national tragedy and his call for repentance. Jeremiah has his prophecies recorded in a single scroll, prophetic messages delivered over a twenty-three-year period, and the scroll is brought to the Temple by his assistant Barukh son of Neriah. Jeremiah has been "restricted"[9] by the authorities from entering the Temple; his

---

8. See *Daat Mikra* and Cogan and Tadmor, *II Kings*, 307, who suggest that this fast day is connected to Nebuchadnezzar's conquest of Ashkelon. The fast is called in the ninth month, Kislev, and historians suggest that Ashkelon was captured and plundered in December 604 BCE.
9. Jer. 36:5. It is unlikely that Jeremiah is jailed at this point, as indicated by Rashi, as the officials recommend that Jeremiah go into hiding; see ibid., 36:19. *Daat Mikra* proposes that Jeremiah had been banned from preaching at public gatherings, and that is why he sends a messenger.

life would have been in danger had he preached publically. Received by the government secretary, a Jeremiah sympathizer,[10] the scroll is read to an assembly of government ministers, and they respond with alarm and dread.[11] The large and powerful collection of prophecies, many predating and predicting the current trouble, coupled with the apprehension and anxiety of Nebuchadnezzar's advance, give Jeremiah's words more impact. Jeremiah's predictions were beginning to materialize. The ministers decide to present the scroll to King Jehoiakim:

> It was the ninth month and the king was sitting in the winter palace, with a fire burning in front of him. Whenever Jehudi[12] read three or four columns of the scroll, [the king] cut them off with a scribe's knife and threw them into the firepot, until the entire scroll was burned in the fire. And the king and all his courtiers who heard all these words showed no fear and did not tear their clothes. Moreover, Elnathan, Delaiah, and Gemariah begged the king not to burn the scroll, but he would not listen to them. (Jer. 36:22–25)[13]

The king is absolutely impervious to the divine warnings and the messages sent by means of prophecy. This scene presents a powerful inverse image to Jehoiakim's father Josiah's discovery of the Torah scroll in II Kings 22. We might tabulate some differences in the following way:

---

10. Gemariah son of Shaphan allows Jeremiah's assistant Barukh to read the scroll to the assembled councilmen. We know that his family is sympathetic to Jeremiah, seeing that Gemariah's brother Ahikam saved Jeremiah's life (Jer. 26:24) and Shaphan, their father, was one of the ministers who took counsel with the prophetess Hulda after Josiah's discovery of the Torah scroll (II Kings 22:12, 14). In 1982, the archaeologist Yigal Shiloh discovered fifty-one clay seals in a dig in Area G of the City of David, among them a seal that named Gemariah son of Shaphan.
11. For a description of Nehama Leibowitz's emotional and political reading of this chapter, see Joy Rochwarger, "Words on Fire," in *Torah of the Mothers*, ed. O. W. Elper and S. Handelman (Jerusalem: Urim Publications, 2000), 57–81.
12. A courtier.
13. See the rabbinic reading of this episode in Moed Katan 26a.

Josiah – II Kings 22	Jehoiakim – Jeremiah 36
I have found a *scroll* of the Law *in the house of the Lord* (22:8)	Barukh read the words of Jeremiah from the *scroll, in the house of the Lord* (36:10)
Shaphan *read it in the presence of the king* (22:10)	Jehudi *read it to the king* and all the officials (36:21)
When the king *heard* the words of the Book of the Law, *he tore his clothes* (22:11)	Whevever Jehudi read... [the king] *cut them off with a knife* and threw them into the firepot... the king and all his courtiers who heard... *did not tear their clothes.* (36:23–24)

The contrast could not be more stark. Upon realizing the impending doom, Josiah tears his clothes, seeks out the prophet, and instigates a national movement of repentance. Jehoiakim cuts (K-R-A) the scroll rather than rending (K-R-A) his clothing; and Jeremiah the prophet is told to hide instead of being summoned. Whereas Josiah dispatches his officials to Hulda the prophetess, Jehoiakim forbids his courtiers even to tear their robes. God is communicating by means of His prophet, but the leadership refuses to be receptive to God's message.

RESISTING BABYLONIA

Jehoiakim was loyal to Babylonia for three years, until 601 BCE, when Egypt defeated the Babylonian forces. This was a major setback for Nebuchadnezzar, and he was forced to withdraw all the way to Babylonia. Jehoiakim, sensing Babylonia's vulnerability, renounced his vassaldom to Nebuchadnezzar (II Kings 24:1).

The following year, however, Nebuchadnezzar retaliated, directing his allies and mercenaries, "the bands of the Chaldeans and bands of the Syrians and bands of the Moabites and bands of the Ammonites, and sent them against Judah to destroy it" (24:2). Nebuchadnezzar personally returns to the region in 598 BCE, the eleventh year of Jehoiakim's reign, and besieges Jerusalem. At this point, Jehoiakim dies.[14]

14. How did Jehoiakim die? Was he killed, or did he die in the siege? There is no consensus among academic sources or in Tanakh. Whereas Kings suggests that "he slept

To summarize, Jehoiakim's ignominious reign was characterized by a deep corruption and a thorough deafness to God's word. Even a cursory reading of the book of Jeremiah demonstrates the degree to which God sounded the alarm of foreboding catastrophe to a king and nation that were unable and unwilling to conceive of the grim events to come.

JEHOIACHIN AND THE FIRST BABYLONIAN EXILE

The eighteen-year-old Jehoiachin reigned for only three months,[15] coming to power while the city was being besieged by the mighty Babylonian forces. Jerusalem hardly resisted. As we know, Jerusalem was capable of withstanding a siege for far longer than three months, and no battle or conquest is mentioned in Kings. That being the case, it is reasonable to assume that the king or his advisors made a calculated tradeoff – to surrender the king in order to save the city. This surrender and the humiliating and devastating exile that followed is dated to the eighth year of Nebuchadnezzar's reign. Since Kings hardly ever dates an event by the regnal years of a foreign ruler, this literary device merely underscores the nation's domination by the Babylonians.

Nebuchadnezzar, however, is not satisfied with the mere removal of the national figurehead and the appointment of Jehoiachin's brother Mattaniah, a ruler sympathetic to Babylonia, in his place. First, Mattaniah is renamed Zedekiah. Then Nebuchadnezzar strips the Temple of its golden vessels and empties it and the royal treasury of their wealth.

with his fathers," II Chr. 36:6–7 relates how Nebuchadnezzar deports Jehoiakim to Babylonia in chains. Rashi (II Kings 24:6), seeking to satisfy the text in both Kings and Chronicles, suggests that Jehoiakim was dragged along the ground as he was deported to Babylonia and that is how he met his death. This midrashic reading is also an attempt to accommodate Jeremiah's grim prediction that "he shall be buried with the burial of a donkey, dragged and dumped beyond the gates of Jerusalem" (Jer. 22:19), and "his corpse shall be cast out to the heat by day and the frost by night" (ibid., 36:30). The Midrash in Leviticus Rabba 19:6 offers a range of opinions, all of which suggest that during the siege, the Sanhedrin – the religious law court – willingly surrendered Jehoiakim to the enemy rather than allowing Jerusalem to be sacrificed. As can be seen, the weight of rabbinic opinion follows Chronicles.

15. Babylonian historical records chronicle the arrival of the military forces in Kislev and the surrender of Jehoiachin on 2 Adar, matching the chronology of Kings perfectly. II Chr. 36:9 records the siege at three months and ten days.

He also exiles the leaders of society. The book of Kings offers a detailed register of the deportees – the royalty, the aristocracy, the military, skilled craftsmen, and industrialists – all in all, ten thousand exiles:

> He carried away Jehoiachin to Babylonia. The king's mother, the king's wives, his officials, and the chief men of the land he took into captivity from Jerusalem to Babylonia. And the king of Babylonia brought captive to Babylonia all the men of valor... and the craftsmen and the metal workers.[16] (II Kings 24:15–16)

Among the exiles are personalities that we meet elsewhere in Tanakh:

> In the capital Shushan lived a Jew by the name of Mordecai, son of Jair son of Shimei son of Kish, a Benjaminite. Who had been exiled from Jerusalem in the group that was carried into exile along with King Jeconiah [Jehoiachin] of Judah, which had been driven into exile by King Nebuchadnezzar of Babylonia.[17] (Est. 2:5–6)

Yet another character exiled at this time is a priest – the prophet Ezekiel. The baseline of the dating system that marks his prophecy is the year of Jehoiachin's exile.[18] Ezekiel's prophetic role was to offer God's perspective to the exiles of Judah, as the tumultuous events were befalling Jerusalem.

GOOD FIGS, BAD FIGS

With the exile of Jehoiachin, Jerusalem has reached a new low point. Only "the poorest people in the land were left" (II Kings 24:14). Now, for the first time in Jewish history, we have a situation in which there are two centers of Jewish life:[19] one in exile and the other in Jerusalem. Which one shall prosper? Jeremiah's prophecy is ominous and bleak:

---

16. Possibly people responsible for the manufacture of war machinery (*Daat Mikra*).
17. Whereas the text sounds, at first glance, as if Mordecai had been exiled, it is more probable that Kish was the one who was exiled, not Mordecai.
18. See Ezek. 1:2.
19. Clearly Nebuchadnezzar wants to keep a Judahite king on the throne in Jerusalem. Why does he deport one ruler, merely to appoint another in his stead? Interestingly, Babylonian official records continue to address Jehoiachin as king, even after his exile.

> After Nebuchadnezzar king of Babylonia had taken Jeconiah, the son of Jehoiakim, king of Judah into exile from Jerusalem, together with the officials of Judah, the craftsmen, and the metal workers, and had brought them to Babylonia, God showed me this vision: behold, two baskets of figs placed before the Temple of God. One basket had very good figs, like first-ripe figs, but the other basket had very bad figs, so bad that they could not be eaten.... Then the word of God came to me: ... Like these good figs, so will I regard as good the exiles from Judah whom I have sent away from this place to the land of the Chaldeans. I will set My eyes on them for good, and I will bring them back to this land. I will build them up, and not tear them down; I will plant them, and not pluck them. I will give them a heart to know that I am the Lord, and they shall be My people and I will be their God, for they shall return to Me with their whole heart.
>
> Like the bad figs that are so bad they cannot be eaten, so will I treat Zedekiah the king of Judah, his officials, the remnant of Jerusalem who remain in this land, and those who dwell in the land of Egypt. I will make them a horror to all the kingdoms of the earth, to be a reproach, a byword, a taunt, and a curse in all the places where I shall drive them. I will send sword, famine, and pestilence upon them, until they shall be utterly destroyed from the land that I gave to them and their fathers. (Jer. 24:1–10)

Rav Yaakov Medan has suggested that the imprisonment of a reigning Judahite king in Babylonia – Jehoiachin is released after thirty-seven years! (II Kings 25:27) – was a tool to humiliate and intimidate the population of Jerusalem, as they knew that their real king was held by the Babylonians. In this same vein, King Saul fears to be taken alive as a prisoner lest the Philistines torment and torture him (II Sam. 31:4), a fate that befell Samson before him. See also Judges 1:7. One could suggest that Jehoiachin was similarly used as a psychological weapon against his people.

II Kings 25

The End

Little is recorded about the life of the last king of Judah, Zedekiah. He was Josiah's third son[1] and his original name was Mattaniah (II Kings 24:17). He was crowned and renamed under the auspices of the king of Babylonia, to whom he swore a pledge as a vassal.[2] The book of Kings furnishes no specific happening or event that transpired during the first nine years of his eleven-year rule, describing him curtly and generically: "He did that which was evil in the sight of God, according to all that Jehoiakim had done" (24:19). And in the next verse: "Indeed, Jerusalem and Judah were a cause of anger to God so that He cast them out from His presence" (24:20).

This theological assertion is stated simply and clearly: The die has already been cast against Judah and Jerusalem. The nation has infuriated God, and as such He will now distance them, "cast them out from His presence." In this regard Zedekiah is quite inconsequential. God's patience has reached its fill. The *Ḥurban* just happens to transpire on his watch. The king's name, which translates as "the righteousness of God," strikes us with no little irony, reflecting so evocatively the vindication

1. I Chr. 3:15.
2. II Chr. 36:13.

of God expressed in the lines of the book of Lamentations: "God is righteous; for I have disobeyed Him" (1:18).

When specific events are recorded of Zedekiah's life, it will be merely to explicate the fall of the kingdom. Only two milestones are worthy of mention by Kings: The first, Zedekiah's political reversal as he renounces his loyalty to Babylonia (II Kings 24:20), and the second, Zedekiah's foolish and cowardly flight from Jerusalem, which leads to his capture by the Babylonians.

TO REBEL OR NOT TO REBEL?

In contrast to the scant treatment of Zedekiah in Kings, other biblical books detail the turbulent events of this fateful period. The most difficult political dilemma with which the king had to contend was the popular aspiration to renounce Babylonian hegemony and restore independence.

One such opportunity arose in Zedekiah's fourth year of rule. During the early years of Zedekiah's reign, Nebuchadnezzar had absented himself from the region, attending to other pressing campaigns in his far-flung kingdom. But the Akkadian rebellion against Nebuchadnezzar in 595–594 BCE aroused regional hopes of overthrowing Babylonian control. Yet again, Jerusalem was the center of a southern conspiracy in which the kings of Edom, Moav, Ammon, Tyre, and Sidon convened in Jerusalem during the fourth year of Zedekiah's rule.[3] The kings were boosted by prophets who predicted the success of the rebellion and the return of the Temple vessels to Jerusalem.[4] One such prophet, Hannania ben Azzur, even promises the imminent restoration of the exiled king Jehoachin to Jerusalem.[5] Hope of independence runs high.

The opposition to these heady aspirations is the dour prophet Jeremiah, a sober counterweight to the optimism of the seditious alliance. He consistently argues in favor of submission to Babylonia and denounces the aforementioned prophets as fakes:

3. Although Jer. 27:1 states that this took place during the first year of Jehoiakim's rule, Zedekiah is explicitly mentioned in 27:3, 12, and 28:1, which strongly suggests that we are talking about Zedekiah's fourth year as king.
4. Jer. 27:9, 15–18; 28:3-4.
5. Ibid., 28:1–3.

> Do not listen to your prophets, your diviners, your dreamers, your fortune-tellers, or your sorcerers, who are saying to you, "You shall not serve the king of Babylonia," for it is a lie that they are prophesying to you.... Any nation that will bring its neck under the yoke of the king of Babylonia and serve him, I will leave on its own land, to work it and dwell there, declares God. Bring your necks under the yoke of the king of Babylonia, and serve him and his people and live.... Otherwise this city shall become a ruin. (Jer. 27:9–12, 17)

Jeremiah's consistent message is that the kingdom must submit to Babylonian rule. Independence can be salvaged if Judah remains servile to Babylonia, but rebellion is courting disaster. Jeremiah walks around Jerusalem wearing a wooden yoke in order to theatrically demonstrate his message.[6] He must contend with the violence and derision of the rival prophets, but he refuses to alter or revoke his morbid prediction. He knows that God has decreed the ascendancy of Babylonia. Even as the siege engines stand threatening Jerusalem, he insists that the people can save their lives if they surrender.[7] But no one listens. Rather, Jeremiah is perceived as the threat, cowardly weakening the national morale, or worse, seditiously siding with the enemy during a siege. He is thrown into jail.

It was certainly difficult for a king to remain passive under foreign domination, and the temptations of rebellion were too attractive. As Jeremiah had warned, disloyalty to a superpower was a hazardous enterprise, and by challenging Babylonian hegemony Zedekiah risked everything. The revolt against Babylonia never materialized in the fourth year of Zedekiah's incumbency;[8] it was only in his ninth year that the kingdom eventually rejected Babylonian rule (II Kings 24:20).[9]

---

6. Ibid., 27:2.
7. Ibid., 21:8–9; 27:12, 17; 38:2, 17.
8. We don't know quite how the revolt crumbled, but Jeremiah records how, in the fourth year of his reign, Zedekiah was summoned to appear before Nebuchadnezzar (ibid., 29:3; 51:59), which indicates that the emperor got wind of the fledgling rebellion and demanded a gesture of fealty from his vassals.
9. The Tanakh does not explain the political backdrop against which the revolt took place; it was probably linked to an alliance with Egypt. However, in the critical moments, Egypt failed to deliver effective military support. See Jer. 37:7.

Nebuchadnezzar's army arrived without delay to snuff out the revolt. The city was besieged on the tenth of the Hebrew month of Tevet, and was penetrated a year and seven months later, on the ninth of Tammuz. The true horrors of the protracted siege are depicted in *Eikha,* the book of Lamentations:

> The tongue of the nursing infant sticks
> to the roof of its mouth for thirst;
> The children beg for food,
> but no one gives to them.
> Those who once feasted on delicacies
> perish in the streets;
> ...their skin has shriveled on their bones;
> It has become as dry as wood.
> ...The hands of compassionate women
> have boiled their own children;
> They became their food
> during the destruction of the daughter of my people. (4:4–10)

From the pages of Jeremiah, King Zedekiah emerges as a weak leader, a spineless and fickle character. On the one hand he seeks Jeremiah's counsel and assistance,[10] but then, when intimidated by his own officials,[11] he submits to their demands that Jeremiah be imprisoned as a traitor.[12] When conditions turn dire, Zedekiah tries to escape Jerusalem to save his own life – at the same time abandoning his nation still entrapped within. The Babylonians apprehended him, cruelly murder his sons before his eyes, and then blind him so his final image would be the death of his children. He is taken to Babylonia and dies there.[13]

10. Ibid., 21:1–2; 37:3, 17; 38:10–27.
11. Ibid., 38:19.
12. Ibid., 38:3–5.
13. Ibid., 52:11; and see Ezek. 12:13.

THE BURNING OF THE TEMPLE

If Kings focuses neither on Zedekiah and his dilemmas nor upon the tribulations of Jeremiah, upon what does it focus? In essence, chapter 25 lists a terrible but detailed inventory of destruction and exile.

The destruction of the Temple itself is narrated in just a few short phrases. Nebuchadnezzar is not present; instead it is his henchman, Nebuzaradan, who carries out the terrible deed. Nebuzaradan bears the sobriquet *rav tabbaḥim*, probably his official government title. Literally it means "the chief cook,"[14] but the Hebrew root T-B-Ḥ can be translated either as "cook" or as "slaughter"; as such, Nebuzaradan has been seared into the Jewish memory as the "chief executioner."[15]

II Kings records the arrival of Nebuzaradan on the seventh of the Hebrew month of Av and, it seems, immediately proceeds to set the Temple and the city alight (25:7). A cross-reference in the book of Jeremiah (52:12) dates the Temple's destruction to the tenth of the month. The Talmud offers a resolution which explains the traditional commemoration of the destruction of the Temple on the ninth of Av:

> Entrance to the Temple was gained by the enemy on the seventh, and they ate and did damage therein on the seventh, on the eighth, and on the ninth. Toward the evening of the ninth they set it on fire, and it continued to burn all day on the tenth.... And this bears out the statement of R. Yoḥanan, who said: "Were I living in those days, I would have ordained the fast for the tenth of Av; for on that day the greater part of the Temple was burned." The sages of that day, however, held that the day when the calamity began should be observed as a fast day. (Taanit 29a)

---

14. This recalls Potiphar, who holds the same title; Gen. 37:36. See also Dan. 2:14. These titles may have originated with simple kitchen positions, but in time they became the titles of central government appointments, totally disconnected from any culinary context, preserving the title in name only. With regard to this, see the discussion of Sennacherib's chief henchman, Rabshakeh (the "chief butler"), in the chapter "Hezekiah Under Siege," footnote 12. See also Kiel, *Daat Mikra*; *Olam HaTanakh*.
15. This is the translation of *Targum Yonatan*. Nebuzaradan's Babylonian name, meaning "the god (Nebbo) will give seed," also rings with bitter irony.

THE ḤURBAN INVENTORY

From this point onward, chapter 25 engages in a slow and meticulous listing of the destruction and exile, as it haltingly rolls out the different facets of the national tragedy.

It begins with the burning, in descending order of importance: first the Temple, then "the king's palace, all the residences of Jerusalem, and every large house" (II Kings 25:9). It continues with the razing of the city walls (25:10). After this, Nebuzaradan begins the deportation of the residents – the "people" and the "masses" – exiling even those who had surrendered to the Babylonians, leaving only a pitiful group – "the lowly of the land" – who would maintain the agriculture (25:11–12).

Kings then turns its attention to a painstaking catalogue of the plundered Temple vessels:[16] first it lists the large bronze furnishings (25:13) and then the smaller bronze items (25:14), followed by a list of sacred gold and silver receptacles, and firepans that were used in the Temple ritual. The account lingers on the two huge decorative pillars that adorned the entrance to the inner sanctum of the Temple, lavishly detailing their fine latticework and adornments. At times this passage feels like a eulogy, the inventory and detailed language seeking to capture a hint of the lost beauty and grandeur of the nation's prime institution, now being carted as booty to Babylonia. But in the context of the book of Kings, which opens with the advent of Solomon and the detailed construction of the Temple and its vessels, one senses more than anything else the unraveling, the dismantling of that grand apparatus. The institutions of government, statehood, and religion have been thoroughly deconstructed.

The exile inventory ends with a group of city notables – the high priest, his deputy, other guards and royal officials, including the minister of defense and sixty of the *Am HaAretz* – who are deported to Nebuchadnezzar's administrative center in Riblah, Syria, and publically executed. This segment ends with the epitaph: "Judah was exiled from its land" (25:21).[17]

---

16. Jeremiah pays special attention to the exiled vessels; see, for example, Jer. 27:19–22. These also become a focal point of the Return; see Ezra 1:7; 6:5.
17. This is a direct parallel to the language of the exile of Samaria; see II Kings 17:23.

THE ASSASSINATION OF GEDALIAH[18]

The kingdom has experienced punishing humiliation, death, and destruction, yet if we imagined that the situation had reached rock bottom we would be mistaken. One further event will deal a final knockout: the assassination of Gedaliah.

After the destruction of the Temple, a depleted Jewish population remained in place. Gedaliah was appointed by the Babylonians as governor of Judah. He was an ideal candidate for the job; his father, Ahikam, had served Jehoiakim,[19] and his grandfather, Shaphan, had served Josiah,[20] and consequently he would gain the trust of the Jews. He supported cooperation with the Babylonian government: "Serve the king of Babylonia and it shall be well with you!" he said.

Gedaliah's appointment presented a return to stability for the war-torn country. In response to his appointment, Jews who had fled the country during the war now returned, repopulating their villages and farms:

> When all the Judahites who were in Moab and among the Ammonites and in Edom and in other lands heard that the king of Babylonia had left a remnant in Judah and had appointed Gedaliah the son of Ahikam, son of Shaphan, as governor over them, all the Judahites returned from all the places to which they had been driven and came to the land of Judah, to Gedaliah at Mizpah. And they gathered wine and summer fruits in great abundance. (Jer. 40:11–12)

After Gedaliah's appointment, there was a genuine possibility that despite their loss of self-government, and notwithstanding the tragedy of the destruction of the Temple, Jewish life could continue in the Land of Israel, and Jews could have set their efforts to rebuilding their lives and their national infrastructure.

---

18. The story is told in far greater detail in Jer. 40–43. For a timely reading of this story, see Uriel Simon's "The Murder of Gedaliah: An Anatomy of Self Destruction," in U. Simon, *Seek Peace and Pursue It: Topical Issues in the Light of the Bible* (Tel Aviv: Yedioth Ahronoth, 2002), 218–26 [Hebrew].
19. II Kings 22:12, 14; Jer. 26:24.
20. II Kings 22:3.

But this was not to be. Ishmael son of Nethaniah "from the royal family," and a group of royal loyalists, loathed Gedaliah's cooperation with the Babylonians and perceived it as an act of treachery, as collaboration with the enemy. They set out to assassinate Gedaliah: "They killed [Gedaliah] because the king of Babylonia had put him in charge of the land" (Jer. 41:2). They were so ardently opposed to any mode of compromise with the Babylonian forces that they justified Gedaliah's murder.

In response to Gedaliah's assassination, the common people panicked. They knew what the slaying of the Babylonian governor meant for them – soon, Babylonian troops would sweep through the country on reprisal raids to teach the civilian population a lesson of loyalty. And they decided not to wait around. The leaders of the community along with the peasantry decided to emigrate to Egypt to escape Babylonian retaliation.[21]

In the final analysis, these unscrupulous monarchists, who cruelly murdered in the name of their idealistic opposition to any cooperation or accommodation with the governing Babylonians, directly caused the flight en masse of the remaining Jewish population in Judah. As such, Gedaliah's assassination signaled the absolute death knell for the continuity of a Jewish presence in the Land of Israel. Those whom the Babylonians had failed to exile were now frightened away by the violence and political meddling of their own people.

In Jewish communities today, Gedaliah's assassination is marked by a public fast day on the third of the Hebrew month of Tishrei.[22] When we fast on Tzom Gedaliah we are mourning a terrible moment of Jewish infighting; but more significantly, we are marking the self-inflicted act by which the land became empty of Jews for the first time in seven hundred years.

REPRIEVE

> In the thirty-seventh year of the exile of Jehoiachin, king of Judah, in the twelfth month, on the twenty-seventh day of the month, Evil-merodach, king of Babylonia, in the year that he began to

21. Jer. 41:18; 43:5–7.
22. Gedaliah was killed on 1 Tishrei, but since that is the festival of Rosh HaShana, the Jewish new year, the fast is postponed.

> reign, graciously freed [lit., raised the head of] Jehoiachin, king of Judah, from prison. And he spoke kindly to him and gave him a seat above the seats of the kings who were with him in Babylonia. So Jehoiachin took off his prison garments. And every day of his life he dined regularly at the king's table, and for his allowance, a regular allowance was given him by the king, according to his daily needs, as long as he lived. (II Kings 25:27–30)

This is an enigmatic finale to Kings. Jerusalem is in ruins, its people exiled. Suddenly we read a snippet of information about the exiled king, as we jump forward thirty-seven years and hear that with the advent of a new Babylonian ruler, Jehoiachin has been released from his Babylonian incarceration. He is granted royal garb and food, and his expenses are paid by the Babylonian government; he is even granted an elevated status among other exiled kings. But why is this story included as the epilogue to the *Ḥurban*? What does it seek to convey?

Some look at this as a tale of pessimism and despair, continuing the gloom and doom of the book of Kings.[23] In this reading the king languishes in exile, any hope of a collective return to Zion an absolute impossibility. The Judahite king is absolutely dependent upon his Babylonian benefactor. *Ḥurban* in this reading is final and definitive.

Others, however, disagree, pointing to the release of the king as optimistic news.[24] Corroboration for this may be found in the language, which speaks of the restoration of Jehoiachin's "throne," and in the manner in which the king "raised the head" of Jehoiachin, a phrase which in its parallel usage in Genesis 40:13 connotes not merely freedom from incarceration but restoration to one's former position and prestige. Does the change in Jehoiachin's physical conditions and his newfound rise in status evoke some hope that better times are ahead? One phrase which strikes us – almost the final word of the book – expresses how Jehoiachin's food is bestowed "*devar yom beyomo*" (II Kings 25:30), on a daily basis.

This particular phrase appears in only one other place in Kings: at the dedication of the Temple. There Solomon says:

23. Cogan and Tadmor, *II Kings*.
24. Kiel, *Daat Mikra*.

> Let these words of mine, which I have pleaded before God, be close to the Lord God day and night, and may He maintain the cause of His servant and the cause of His people Israel, day by day – *devar yom beyomo.* (I Kings 8:59)

This, then, is a phrase of divine response to Israel's prayers. Evil-merodach's provision of Jehoiachin's daily requirements is indicative that God is in some manner engaging with His nation and acting with mercy.

If we are reflecting on Solomon, we might recall how, just a few verses earlier in that chapter, Solomon envisages a situation of exile:

> If they sin against You…and You are angry with them…so that they are carried away captive to the land of the enemy, far off or near…if they repent with all their mind and with all their heart in the land of their enemies, who carried them captive…forgive Your people who have sinned against You, and…grant them mercy before their captors that they pardon them. (I Kings 8:46–50)

Jehoiachin's reprieve offers a glimmer of hope, a sense that the tide has turned, and events may yet again shift in Israel's favor with the restoration to land, the Temple, and self-governance. Indeed, it shall be none other than Jehoiachin's grandson Zerubbabel[25] who, one generation hence, will lead the exiles back to Jerusalem and rebuild the Temple.

25. I Chr. 3:17–19; Ezra 2:1; Hag. 2:4–9.

Conclusion

After the greatest catastrophe to befall the Jewish nation – the Temple's destruction, the loss of sovereignty, and national displacement from the covenantal land to foreign soil – the need for some understanding of the historic situation was urgent. Had God rejected His nation? What would be the future of Jerusalem? Was this the end of God's city, the Temple, the Jewish people? Much like the theological questions raised in recent generations in the aftermath of the Holocaust, Jews in the post-*Ḥurban* era needed an explanation, a framework within which to understand the great calamity that had struck the Jewish people.[1]

---

1. Possibly the most audacious claim made in the wake of the national exile is brought in the book of Jeremiah. There the exiles of Judah who have settled in Egypt reject Jeremiah's words "in the name of the Lord" and tell the prophet that they fully intend to turn to idolatry! They say that when they worshipped idols:

   > ... as we used to do, we and our fathers, our kings, and our officials, in the towns of Judah and the streets of Jerusalem ... we had plenty to eat, we were well-off and suffered no misfortune. But ever since we stopped making offerings to the queen of heaven and pouring libations to her, we have lacked everything, and we have been consumed by the sword and by famine. (Jer. 44:16–18)

   In other words, the years of Manasseh were the good times, and from Josiah onward they experienced only exile and ruin. From this perspective, idolatry has given Israel success, and adherence to God has brought disaster.

Kings comes to offer a theological understanding of the *Ḥurban*. It finds answers to these questions by placing the past in a familiar covenantal paradigm. The great destruction and dislocation of the nation is framed as part of the covenantal mechanism, preordained ever since the Exodus. The fundamental theology that Israel's commitment to the covenant will bring national flourishing, whereas abrogation of the covenant will engender national ruin and eventually exile, is the principal and central theme of Kings from start to finish.

The narration of this theme begins at the historical inception of the book, when King David hands over the reins of leadership to his son Solomon. It is then that he informs his son that the stability of the monarchy would be contingent upon observance of God's laws:

> Keep the charge of the Lord your God, walking in His ways and *keeping His statutes, His commandments, His rules, and His testimonies, as it is written in the Law* of Moses, that you may prosper in all that you do and wherever you turn, that the Lord may establish His word that He spoke concerning me, saying, "If your descendants are scrupulous in their conduct, and walk before Me faithfully, with *all their heart and soul,* your line on the throne of Israel shall never end!" (I Kings 2:3–4)

God reiterated this message to Solomon not merely with regard to sovereignty but also as it relates to the Temple:

> Regarding this house you are building, *if you follow My laws and observe My rules and faithfully keep My commandments,* I will fulfill for you the promise that I gave to your father, David: I will abide among the Children of Israel, and I will never forsake My people Israel. (I Kings 6:12–13)

See also the bold and challenging words of Psalm 89, especially vv. 39–52, which accuse God of breaching His promise to David by rupturing the Davidic dynasty. These are the sorts of views with which the prophet of the age had to contend. Talmudic tradition sees Jeremiah as the author of Kings. This book then is surely his response.

God's final warning, after the Temple's dedication, states that idolatry and religious waywardness will precipitate national exile:

> If you and your descendants turn away from Me and do not *keep the commandments* [*and*] *the laws* which I have set before you, and go and serve other gods and worship them, then I will sweep Israel off the land which I gave them; I will reject the house which I have consecrated to My name; and Israel shall *become a proverb and a byword* among all peoples. And as for this house, once so exalted, everyone passing by it shall be appalled and shall hiss. *And when they ask, "Why did the Lord do thus to the land and to this house?"* they shall be told, "It is because they forsook the Lord their God *who freed them from the land of Egypt,* and they embraced other gods and worshipped them and served them; therefore, the Lord has brought all this calamity upon them." (1 Kings 9:6–9)

These are the warnings that are directed to Solomon, at the outset of the book of Kings. The terms of the covenant are clear; the penalties of its abrogation are articulated from the get-go. However, of great significance is that this covenantal paradigm is no innovation. These warnings are an echo of Deuteronomy,[2] both in theme and in intertextual phraseology. National reward and punishment as the consequence of religious observance is an understanding that is articulated by the Torah:

> But if you do not obey the Lord your God to observe faithfully *all His commandments and laws* which I enjoin upon you this day, all these curses shall come upon you and take effect.... The Lord will drive you, *and the king you have set over you,* to a nation unknown to you or your fathers.... You shall be a consternation, *a proverb, and a byword among all the peoples* to which the Lord will drive you. (Deut. 29:15, 36–37)

2. In particular see Deut. 4:25–40; 7:12–26, 19–20; 11:10–12:1; ch. 28; 29:9–28; ch.32. Kings also draws on other covenantal language and motifs, including the episode of the Golden Calf, narrated in Ex. 32–34 and the passages in Lev. 19 and 26.

> All nations will ask, "*Why did the Lord do thus to this land?* Wherefore that awful wrath?" They will be told, "Because they forsook the covenant that the Lord, God of their fathers, made with them when He freed them from the land of Egypt; they turned to the service of other gods and worshipped them, gods whom they had not experienced and whom He had not allotted to them. So the Lord was incensed at that land and brought upon it all the curses recorded in this book. The Lord uprooted them from their soil in anger, fury, and great wrath, and cast them into another land, as is still the case." (Deut. 29:23–27)

The language of Kings reflects that of Deuteronomy, emphasizing that Solomon's warnings are no more than a restatement of an ancient covenant.

Following this pattern, Kings assesses each of the kings on this very basis. When God announces Solomon's punishment, it is "because you are guilty of this – *you have not kept My covenant and the laws* which I enjoined upon you." And when we meet the greatest religious kings, such as Hezekiah and Josiah, we meet men who uphold the covenant and destroy idolatry:

> [Hezekiah] clung to the Lord;[3] he did not turn away from following Him, but kept *the commandments* that the Lord had given to Moses. (II Kings 18:6)

> [Josiah] did what was pleasing to the Lord and *he followed all the ways of his ancestor David*; he did not deviate to the right or to the left. (23:2)

In Kings, God is often patient – frequently delaying punishment[4] even up to four generations,[5] allowing for repentance. And yet there are

3. For the concept of clinging or cleaving to God (the Hebrew root D-V-K) as mandated in Deuteronomy, see Deut. 4:4; 10:20; 11:22; 13:5; 30:2.
4. Solomon, I Kings 11:12; Ahab, ibid., 21:29; Hezekiah, II Kings 20:18–19.
5. II Kings 10:30.

no surprises. The book of Kings charts a full roster of the kings who flaunted God's law and those who adhered to it. A clear accounting is made such that the evidence is undeniable that national transgression has exceeded loyalty. Exile is the direct product of Israel's breach of the covenant:

> Because the Israelites sinned against the Lord their God, *who had freed them from the land of Egypt....* *They worshipped other gods* and followed the customs of the nations.... The Lord warned Israel and Judah by every prophet [and] every seer, saying: "Turn back from your wicked ways, and observe *My commandments and My laws,* according to all the teaching that I commanded your fathers and that I transmitted to you through My servants the prophets." But they did not obey... *they spurned His laws and the covenant* that He had made with their fathers.... So the Lord spurned all the seed of Israel, and He afflicted them and delivered them into the hands of plunderers, and finally *He cast them out from His presence* [lit., face]. (17:7–18)

At the most fundamental level, Kings defends the case for the national exile. It vindicates and explains its correctness. In many ways Kings is a lengthy and detailed work of divine justification, in the spirit of Lamentations: "The Lord is in the right, for I have disobeyed Him" (Lam. 1:18). After we have read the book of Kings, the reader appreciates that Israel deserved its fate.

THE FUTURE

But what would be with the covenant from this point hence? Had God rejected His people eternally? Could the nation and Jerusalem be reunited? Ezekiel quotes the people's fears: "Our bones are dried up, and our hope is lost; we are cut off completely!" (37:11).[6] The people

6. Martin Noth claims that this perspective was shared by the author of Kings: "Clearly he saw the divine judgment which was acted out in his account of the external collapse of Israel as a nation as something final and definitive and he expressed no hope for the future, not even in the very modest and simple form of an expectation

are asking whether this the end for the Jews. One can only wonder at how confusing and challenging these questions may have seemed to the post-*Ḥurban* generation.

Some prophets offer a better future. Jeremiah proclaims that the exile will endure only seventy years;[7] Isaiah says that God had merely distanced Israel, but not divorced her.[8] We hear consolation in many other books of Tanakh, but Kings itself fails to conclude with a message of optimism and reconciliation. If Kings comes to explain why the *Ḥurban* was deserved, does it offer any hope, any reassurance that there will be a Jewish future?

Lamentations ends with a call for mercy, for a divine gesture of reprieve; its lines sound a ringing tone of desperation, a painful prayer amidst the carnage and mayhem of ruin and loss:

> You, O Lord, are enthroned forever; Your throne endures through the ages.
> Why have You forgotten us utterly, forsaken us for all time?
> Take us back, O Lord, to Yourself, and let us come back;
> Renew our days as of old!
> For truly, You have rejected us, bitterly raged against us. (5:19–22)[9]

What does Kings have to say?

PROMISES OF RETURN

I believe that although Kings fails to directly address the questions, they are answered obliquely, and with a great sense of optimism.

---

that the deported and dispersed people would be gathered together" (Martin Noth, "The Deuteronomistic History," trans. J. Doull et al., *Journal for the Study of the Old Testament Supplement* 15 [1981], 97).

7. Jer. 25:11; 29:10; and see II Chr. 36:21–22. See other passages of consolation in Jer. 31; 32:15, 37–43; 33.
8. Is. 50:1; and see the chapters of consolation from Isaiah 40–57.
9. We may speculate that so soon after the carnage and the mayhem, there was little room to express assurance of a brighter future with any certainty. Lamentations also accepts, in several verses, that Israel's misfortune was a result of its sins. See Lam. 1:5, 8, 18; 3:39–41; 5:7, 16.

First, we might say that the selfsame covenant which offers the paradigm of exile also promises the assurance of return. How so? As we have demonstrated, the covenantal theme and language of Kings finds its origin in the Torah. There we read not merely of national ruin and dispersion but of a process of reversal and national rehabilitation. There, a compassionate God refuses to rescind the covenant even after it has been shunned by Israel:

> Take care, then, not to forget the covenant that the Lord your God concluded with you, and not to make for yourselves a sculptured image in any likeness, against which the Lord your God has enjoined you. For the Lord your God is a consuming fire, an impassioned God.... The Lord will scatter you among the peoples, and only a scant few of you shall be left among the nations to which the Lord will drive you.... *But you will seek there* for the Lord your God, you will find Him, if only you seek Him with *all your heart and soul*.... For the Lord your God is a compassionate God: He will not fail you nor will He let you perish; He will not forget the covenant which He swore to your fathers. (Deut. 4:23–31)

God is "a consuming fire" when Israel sins, but in exile, when Israel seeks God "with all [their] heart and soul," God is "compassionate" and will "not forget the covenant." This is but one text among many[10] that promises a reversal of fortunes after the exile.

But a second passage, in the book of Kings itself, includes a segment that in retrospect anticipates this question.[11] King Solomon dedicates the Temple with a remarkable prayer in which he lists an array of circumstances of distress, and in each difficult situation, he affirms that God will accept the prayers that are offered to Him. The final scenario is described as follows:

---

10. See Lev. 26:40–45; Deut. 30:1–10; 32:26–43. Each of these sources, despite their differences, promise that the Jewish people will not be destroyed, and will remain attached to God, land, and history. For the question of whether redemption necessitates repentance, see Rav Yaakov Medan, "Redemption without Repentance," in *Hed Etzion*, vol. 16 (Nisan 5776) [Hebrew], also at http://en.calameo.com/read/00446742 66b75a8bbb87e.
11. See Gershon Galil, "The Message of the Book of Kings in Relation to Deuteronomy and Jeremiah," *Bibliotheca Sacra* 158 (2001): 406–14.

> When they sin against You – for there is no man who does not sin – and You are angry with them *and deliver them to the enemy, and their captors carry them off to an enemy land, near or far*; and then *they take it to heart* in the land to which they have been carried off, and they repent and make supplication to You in the land of their captors, saying: "We have sinned, we have acted perversely, we have acted wickedly," and they turn back to You *with all their heart and soul,* in the land of the enemies who have carried them off, and they pray to You in the direction of their land which You gave to their fathers, of the city which You have chosen, and of the house which I have built to Your name.... Grant them mercy in the sight of their captors that they may be merciful to them. For they are Your very own people that You freed from Egypt, from the midst of the iron furnace. May Your eyes be open to the supplication of Your servant and the supplication of Your people Israel, and may You heed them whenever they call upon You. (I Kings 8:46–53)

This remarkable passage, situated at the very moment of the dedication of the Temple during the heyday of Solomon, when any hint of exile would seem an absurd notion, reaffirms the enduring bond, even in exile, between Israel and God, and between the nation, its land, Jerusalem, and the Temple. This is Kings' way of saying that Israel will continue to be God's people, and when they seek Him "with all their heart and soul" they will be pardoned, and will once again realize the covenant between God and nation. God will not abandon His people.

In II Kings, we have encountered powerful kings, astounding prophets and disciples of prophets, priests, courtiers, foreign leaders, and mighty emperors. But the enduring message is the veracity of God's covenant to Israel, both an unbreakable relationship imbued with much divine love for Israel, and a set of rules the denial of which will lead to national ruin. Ultimately, the explanation of our historic tragedy also articulates the roadmap to our collective return.

Chronology of Kings of Judah and Israel*

David 1004–965			
Solomon 967–928			
The Kings of Judah (southern kingdom)		**The Kings of Israel (northern kingdom)**	
Rehoboam	928–911	Jeroboam	928–907
Abijah	911–908	Nadab	907–906
Asa	908–867	Baasha	906–883
Jehoshaphat	870–846	Elah	883–882
Jehoram	851–843	Zimri	882
Ahaziah	843–842	Omri	882–871
Athaliah (queen)	842–836	Ahab	873–852
Joash (Jehoash)	836–798	Ahaziah	852–851
Amaziah	798–769	Jehoram (Joram)	851–842
Azariah (Uzziah)	785–733	Jehu	842–814
Jotham	758–743	Jehoahaz	817–800
Ahaz	743–727	Jehoash (Joash)	800–784
Hezekiah	727–698	Jeroboam II	789–748
Manasseh	698–642	Zechariah	748–747
Amon	641–640	Shallum	747
Josiah	639–609	Menahem	747–737
Jehoahaz	609	Pekahiah	737–735
Jehoiakim	608–598	Pekah	735–733
Jehoiachin	597	Pekah	735–733
Zedekiah	596–586		

* Haim Tadmor, ed., *The Biblical Encyclopedia* (Jerusalem: Bialik Institute, 1962), vol. 4, cols. 301–302. All dates are Before the Common Era (BCE).

Haftarot from II Kings

Haftara	Torah Portion
4:1–37	*Vayera*
4:42–5:19	*Tazria*
7:3–20	*Metzora*
11:17–12:17	*Shabbat Shekalim*
23:1–9; 21–25	second day of Passover (outside Israel)

Index of Biblical and Rabbinic Sources

General Index

Other books in the Maggid Studies in Tanakh series:

Genesis: From Creation to Covenant
Zvi Grumet

Joshua: The Challenge of the Promised Land
Michael Hattin

Judges: The Perils of Possession (forthcoming)
Michael Hattin

I Kings: Torn in Two
Alex Israel

Isaiah (forthcoming)
Yoel Bin-Nun and Binyamin Lau

Jeremiah: The Fate of a Prophet
Binyamin Lau

Ezekiel (forthcoming)
Tova Ganzel

Jonah: The Reluctant Prophet
Erica Brown

Nahum, Habakkuk, and Zephaniah (forthcoming)
Yaakov Beasley

Haggai, Zechariah, and Malachi:
Prophecy in an Age of Uncertainty
Hayyim Angel

Ruth: From Alienation to Monarchy
Yael Ziegler

Esther: Power, Fate, and Fragility in Exile (forthcoming)
Erica Brown

Nehemiah: Statesman and Sage
Dov S. Zakheim

The fonts used in this book are from the Arno family

Maggid Books
The best of contemporary Jewish thought from
Koren Publishers Jerusalem Ltd.